A GUIDE TO JUDICIAL AND POLITICAL REVIEW OF FEDERAL AGENCIES

2nd Edition

MICHAEL E. HERZ, RICHARD MURPHY,
AND KATHRYN WATTS
EDITORS

Section of Administrative Law and Regulatory Practice
American Bar Association

ABA SECTION OF ADMINISTRATIVE LAW AND REGULATORY PRACTICE

Defending Liberty
Pursuing Justice

Cover design by ABA Publishing.

Printed in the United States of America.

19 18 17 16 15   5 4 3 2 1

Library of Congress Cataloging-in-Publication Data
A guide to judicial and political review of federal agencies, second edition / by Michael Herz, Richard Murphy, Kathryn Watts; Section of Litigation, American Bar Association.
pages cm
ISBN 978-1-63425-216-4
1. Judicial review of administrative acts—United States. 2. Administrative procedure—United States. 3. Legislative oversight—United States. I. Herz, Michael E., editor. II. Murphy, Richard W. (Law teacher), editor. III. Watts, Kathryn A., 1976- editor. IV. American Bar Association. Section of Administrative Law and Regulatory Practice, sponsoring body.
KF5425.G85 2015   342.73'066—dc23
2015019290

Discounts are available for books ordered in bulk. Special consideration is given to state bars, CLE programs, and other bar-related organizations. Inquire at Book Publishing, ABA Publishing, American Bar Association, 321 North Clark Street, Chicago, Illinois 60654.

www.ShopABA.org

CONTENTS SUMMARY

CONTENTS

PREFACE TO THE SECOND EDITION

The first edition of this volume appeared a decade ago. Our field is stable in its broad outlines but dynamic in its details, and the intervening years have required many changes and updates to the body of the text. This edition, current through 2014, reflects a raft of changes, large and small, while retaining the basic structure of the first edition.

The only part of the book that really requires no significant updating is the Preface, which we have reprinted beginning on page xiii without change. We would only incorporate by reference the discussion and, particularly, the acknowledgments set out therein, re-emphasize our gratitude to the impressive roster of scholars who made this book what it is, and particularly thank the two new authors who have come on for this edition, Emily Hammond and Glen Staszewski, who showed tremendous skill and erudition in revising and expanding the existing material.

Michael Herz, Benjamin N. Cardozo School of Law
Richard Murphy, Texas Tech School of Law
Kathryn Watts, University of Washington School of Law

PREFACE TO THE FIRST EDITION

At the beginning of the twentieth century, during an era when scholars and policymakers were fashioning the intellectual foundations of the modern administrative state, the notion of administrative independence was conceived as a bulwark to protect fledgling administrative agencies from domination by political and judicial bodies. This conception of independence was based on the notion that administrative agencies were engaged in "semi-scientific, *quasi*-judicial" work best conducted "absolutely free from the influence of politics."[1] Agency independence was not limited merely to the political dimension. In its most brash form, agency independence was often thought to encompass freedom even from judicial oversight: "Of necessity," the young legal scholar Adolf Berle preached in 1917, "a special administrative must exclude the general body—the court, the legislature, the governor and subordinate machinery—in so far as its field extends. Any other rule would mean chaos."[2]

Yet if complete administrative independence was ever an aspiration, it has never been a reality. During the zenith of the New Deal, ardent champions of administrative power such as James Landis might look forward to a "future" in which the "interesting problem . . . is the extent to which judges will withdraw, not from reviewing questions of fact, but from conclusions upon law."[3] Yet even then, as Landis acknowledged, the current law did not insulate agencies from judicial review to such a degree.[4]

The future did not bring a complete administrative independence from either judicial or political forces. Instead, it brought a codification of the right to judicial review in the 1940s,[5] the rise of "hard look review" in the 1970s and early 1980s,[6] and increasing agency supervision by the Executive Branch in the

---

1. Frank J. Goodnow, Politics and Administration 85 (1900).
2. A. A. Berle, Jr., *The Expansion of American Administrative Law*, 30 Harv. L. Rev. 430, 446-47 (1917).
3. James M. Landis, The Administrative Process 144 (1938).
4. *Id.* at 145.
5. Administrative Procedure Act, Pub. L. No. 79-404, § 10(a), 60 Stat. 237, 243 (1946), *codified at* 5 U.S.C. § 702.
6. *See* Chapter 8, section 8.01, *infra*, and Motor Vehicle Mfrs. Ass'n v. State Farm Mut. Auto Ins. Co., 463 U.S. 29, 43 (1983).

1980s and 1990s.[7] In retrospect, this history seems inevitable. Administrative agencies are expected to exercise their expertise and discretion, but they are also expected to follow the law and to be attuned to democratic forces. They have always existed somewhere between the purely political and the purely judicial realms—sufficiently independent to give range to rational, expert judgments, and yet sufficiently checked by the courts and the political branches so that they respect legal constraints and respond to the polity.

From this unique position of administrative agencies flows a central challenge of administrative law, which is to establish appropriately calibrated mechanisms for the control of administrative agencies by the political and judicial actors. In constructing these mechanisms, judges, lawmakers, and executive officials have tried to ensure that agencies remain accountable, respect legal limits, and avoid abusing their powers, but they have also tried to allow enough administrative authority and independence so that agencies can apply their expert judgment to the problems of regulation. The result is not the juggernaut of administrative power envisioned by audacious Progressives of a century ago, but a delicate balance manifested in a host of intricate statutory and doctrinal requirements regarding both judicial review and the power of the political branches to control agency activity.

This book provides a thorough overview of this law of judicial and political control of federal agencies. The primary focus is on the availability and scope of judicial review, but the concluding chapter is devoted to the control exercised by the President and the Congress. The book is a companion to two other *Guides* published by the American Bar Association's Section of Administrative Law and Regulatory Practice: *A Guide to Federal Agency Adjudication*, edited by Michael Asimow, and *A Guide to Federal Agency Rulemaking*, by Jeffrey Lubbers.

Like the adjudication volume, this book grows out of a study of the federal Administrative Procedure Act undertaken by the Section of Administrative Law and Regulatory Practice. Headed by Chief Reporter Paul Verkuil, with the editors of the present volume as Assistant Chief Reporters, the so-called "APA Project" set out to describe federal administrative law in a manner that would be both manageable and comprehensive. That undertaking was divided into six topics of administrative law: adjudication, rulemaking, the scope of judicial review, the availability of judicial review, openness in government, and government management of the administrative process. Two co-reporters took on each topic, and with the assistance of a distinguished

7. *See* Chapter 11, section 11.032, *infra*, discussing the issuance of Executive Order 12,291 in 1981 and Executive Order 12,866 in 1993.

team of associate reporters, they prepared reports summarizing the current state of the law. Most of the chapters in this volume began as those reports.

The reporters also drafted a concise statement of the law covering each of the six topics mentioned above. The Council of the ABA Section of Administrative Law and Regulatory Practice then considered, edited, and amended that draft so that the document would state consensus positions of administrative law. Finally, the Council formally approved the resulting document as a "Blackletter Statement" of federal administrative law. The *Blackletter Statement* was published in the *Administrative Law Review* in 2002.[8]

The relevant portions of the *Blackletter Statement* are set forth as an Appendix to this volume. In addition, most of the chapters reprint the specific portions of the *Blackletter Statement* that are relevant to the chapter. These portions, which are indented and in bold print, serve as executive summaries at the beginning of individual sections. The reader should be aware, then, that these portions are endorsed by the Council of the ABA Section on Administrative Law and Regulatory Practice but are not necessarily the words of the chapter author. Conversely, the portions not set forth in bold do not have the endorsement of the Section Council but are instead the views of the individual chapter author.

The views of the chapter authors are the heart of this volume. In some instances, the authors explain the consensus position found in the *Blackletter Statement*. In other instances, they elaborate on controversial points that, as a matter of necessity, were not discussed in that consensus document. And throughout all the chapters, the authors provide a level of detail that could not be included in a concise summary of law such as the *Blackletter Statement*.

The book is in three parts, of unequal length, reflecting the three topics from the APA Project that it covers. The first two chapters address the availability of judicial review of agency action, with the second chapter devoted entirely to the complicated question of standing. These are followed by eight chapters devoted to the scope of judicial review and covering issues such as deference to agency determinations of law and fact, the substantial evidence standard of review, arbitrary and capricious review, and the like. Finally, the book concludes with a chapter on the law (as opposed to the politics) of presidential and congressional control of agency action.

---

8. Section of Administrative Law & Regulatory Practice, American Bar Ass'n, *A Blackletter Statement of Federal Administrative Law*, 43 Admin. L. Rev. 17 (2002).

Many thanks are due for a project such as this. Most obviously, to the authors themselves. Biographical information on each of them follows; it is a distinguished group. Each of the authors gave generously of his or her time and expertise and produced an extraordinarily thorough and scholarly piece of work. Three of the authors were also reporters for their respective topics—Hal Bruff and Cynthia Farina (Availability of Review) and Bill Funk (Government Management)—and so deserve particular thanks. Ricky Revesz and Ernie Gellhorn were co-reporters for Scope of Review; Ricky in particular was instrumental in assembling the wonderful group of scholars who produced chapters three through nine. Paul Verkuil was Chief Reporter for the APA Project, which was the brainchild of then Section Chair Ron Cass and was shepherded along by Ron's successors: Jack Young, Ron Levin, C. Boyden Gray, Neal Eisner, and Bill Funk. Each was indispensable to its success.

Michael Herz, Benjamin N. Cardozo School of Law
John F. Duffy, George Washington University Law School

ABOUT THE EDITORS

Michael Herz (B.A., Swarthmore College; J.D., University of Chicago) is the Arthur Kaplan Professor of Law at the Cardozo School of Law, Yeshiva University, where he has also served as Vice Dean and as Co-Director of the Floersheimer Center for Constitutional Democracy. Professor Herz served as law clerk to Chief Judge Levin Campbell of the U.S. Court of Appeals for the First Circuit and Justice Byron R. White of the U.S. Supreme Court. He joined the Cardozo faculty in 1988 after three years as an attorney with the Environmental Defense Fund. Professor Herz spent a year as a Fellow at Princeton University's Program in Law and Public Affairs, is a former Chair of the ABA's Section of Administrative Law and Regulatory Practice, and serves as a public member of the Administrative Conference of the United States.

Richard Murphy (B.A., Carleton College; J.D., University of Minnesota Law School) is the AT&T Professor of Law at Texas Tech University School of Law. After graduation from law school, he clerked for Judge Stephen S. Trott of the U.S. Court of Appeals for the Ninth Circuit before returning to Minneapolis as a litigation associate at the firm of Dorsey & Whitney. He began his academic career at William Mitchell College of Law. Professor Murphy writes widely in the administrative law field and is co-author of a leading casebook. A long-time and active member of the ABA Section of Administrative Law and Regulatory Practice, he is a former member of the Council, the co-chair of the Judicial Review Committee, and a regular contributor to the live and print versions of the Section's annual *Developments* program.

Kathryn Watts (B.S., J.D., Northwestern University) is the Garvey Schubert Barer Professor of Law at the University of Washington School of Law, where she has served as Associate Dean for Research and Faculty Development and been awarded the Dean's Medal, the Norm Maleng Faculty Excellence Award, and Professor of the Year honors (twice). After graduating first in her class from Northwestern, she clerked for Judge A. Raymond Randolph of the D.C. Circuit and Justice John Paul Stevens of the U.S. Supreme Court. She then worked as an associate at Sidley Austin before becoming a Visiting Assistant Professor at Northwestern and moving to the University of Washington in 2007. She is widely published in leading journals and a past winner of the annual scholarship award from the ABA's Section of Administrative Law and Regulatory Practice. She is a member of the Section Council, the co-chair of the Judicial Review Committee, and a regular contributor to the live and print versions of the Section's annual *Developments* program.

ABOUT THE CONTRIBUTORS

Lisa Schultz Bressman (B.A., Wellesley College; J.D., University of Chicago) holds the David Daniels Allen Distinguished Chair of Law at Vanderbilt Law School, where she is also Associate Dean for Academic Affairs and from 2006 to 2010 served as co-director of Vanderbilt's Regulatory Program. She joined the Vanderbilt faculty in 1998 after working as an attorney-advisor in the Office of Legal Counsel in the U.S. Department of Justice, practicing with a Washington, D.C., law firm, and clerking for Supreme Court Justice Stephen Breyer and now-Second Circuit Judge José Cabranes. Her work focuses on statutory interpretation, administrative law, and applications of political theory to the structure of the administrative state.

Harold Bruff (B.A., Williams College; J.D., Harvard Law School) is the Nicholas Rosenbaum Professor of Law at the University of Colorado, where he was Dean of the School of Law from 1996 to 2003. He has also taught at Arizona State University, the University of Texas, and George Washington University. After graduation from law school, he enlisted as a lieutenant in the U.S. Coast Guard Reserve, serving as an assistant district legal officer. From 1979 to 1981, he served as senior attorney and advisor for the Office of Legal Counsel in the U.S. Department of Justice. He also served as consultant to the chairman of the President's Commission on the accident at Three Mile Island. Professor Bruff's scholarly interests lie in constitutional and administrative law, with a particular focus on separation of powers.

Steven P. Croley (B.A., University of Michigan; J.D., Yale Law School; Ph.D., Princeton University) is the General Counsel of the U.S. Department of Energy. From 2010 to 2014, he served in the White House; in 2012-2014 as Deputy White House Counsel. He is also a member of the Council of the Administrative Conference of the United States. He is the Harry Burns Hutchins Collegiate Professor of Law (on leave) at the University of Michigan Law School, having joined the Michigan Law faculty in 1993. From 2003 to 2006, he served as Michigan Law's Associate Dean for Academic Affairs. From 2006 to 2010, he served as a Special Assistant U.S. Attorney in the Eastern District of Michigan. He is a Member of the American Law Institute.

William Funk (B.A., Harvard University; J.D., Columbia University) is Lewis & Clark Distinguished Professor of Law at the Lewis and Clark Law School. He previously served as an assistant general counsel at the U.S. Department of Energy, principal staff member of the Legislation Subcommittee of the U.S. House of Representatives Permanent Select Committee on Intelligence, and as an attorney-advisor in the Office of Legal Counsel of the U.S. Department of Justice. Immediately after law school he clerked for Judge James Oakes of the U.S. Court of Appeals for the Second Circuit. In 2004-05, Funk was a Senior Fulbright Scholar at the University of Heidelberg. Professor Funk's scholarship is equally divided between constitutional law, environmental law, and administrative law; he is the author or co-author of leading casebooks in all three fields. He chaired the Section of Administrative Law and Regulatory Practice in 2003-2004.

Elizabeth Garrett (B.A., University of Oklahoma; J.D., University of Virginia) is the President of Cornell University and a professor of law and government. Previously, she was the Frances R. and John J. Duggan Professor of Law, Political Science, Finance and Business Economics, and Public Policy at the University of Southern California, where she also served as provost. She clerked for Judge Stephen Williams of the U.S. Court of Appeals for the D.C. Circuit and for Supreme Court Justice Thurgood Marshall. Professor Garrett served as legislative director and budget counsel for U.S. Senator David L. Boren before joining the faculty of the University of Chicago Law School in 1995. Her primary scholarly interests are the legislative process, statutory interpretation, direct democracy, the federal budget process, and administrative law.

Emily Hammond (B.S., Virginia Polytechnic Institute & State University; J.D., University of Georgia) is Professor of Law at the George Washington University Law School. She taught previously at Wake Forest School of Law and the University of Oklahoma College of Law, has served as a Hearing Examiner for the Oklahoma Water Resources Board, and is an elected member of the American Law Institute. Prior to entering academia, she clerked for the Honorable Richard W. Story of the Northern District of Georgia and practiced civil litigation. A former civil engineer who practiced in the environmental and water resources fields prior to attending law school, she focuses her scholarship on two themes: the various responses of legal institutions to scientific uncertainty and the relationship between procedural and substantive legitimacy.

Harold J. Krent (B.A., Princeton University; J.D., New York University) is Dean and Professor of Law at Chicago-Kent College of Law. After clerking for the Honorable William H. Timbers of the U.S. Court of Appeals for the Second Circuit, Dean Krent worked in the Department of Justice for the Appellate Staff of the Civil Division. He has been teaching full-time since 1987. He joined the Chicago-Kent faculty in 1994 and has served as dean since 2002. Dean Krent has consulted for the Administrative Conference of the United States, the World Bank, and the National Academy of Sciences. In addition, he has litigated numerous cases with students on behalf of indigent prisoners and has argued before the U.S. Supreme Court. His scholarship focuses on legal aspects of individuals' interaction with the government, and he is author of *Presidential Powers* (N.Y.U. Press 2005).

Ronald M. Levin (B.A., Yale University; J.D., University of Chicago) is the William R. Orthwein Distinguished Professor of Law at Washington University in St. Louis. Professor Levin is coauthor of an administrative law casebook and has written articles on a wide variety of administrative law topics. He has been centrally involved in many of the activities of the ABA's Section of Administrative Law and Regulatory Practice and was chair of the Section in 2000-2001. In addition to his activities in the ABA, Professor Levin is currently a public member of the Administrative Conference of the United States and chair of its Judicial Review Committee. He has been a consultant to the Administrative Conference and has chaired both the Section on Administrative Law and the Section on Legislation of the Association of American Law Schools.

M. Elizabeth Magill (B.A., Yale University; J.D., University of Virginia) is Dean and Richard E. Lang Professor of Law at Stanford Law School. She came to Stanford from the University of Virginia School of Law, where she served as vice dean, the Joseph Weintraub–Bank of America Distinguished Professor of Law, and the Elizabeth D. and Richard A. Merrill Professor. Before entering law school, Professor Magill was a Senior Legislative Assistant for Energy and Natural Resources for U.S. Senator Kent Conrad. Dean Magill clerked for Judge J. Harvie Wilkinson III of the U.S. Court of Appeals for the Fourth Circuit and Justice Ruth Bader Ginsburg of the Supreme Court of the United States. Her scholarship focuses on administrative law and constitutional law, particularly separation of powers theory and doctrine.

Jim Rossi (B.S., Arizona State University; J.D., University of Iowa College of Law; LL.M., Yale Law School) is Professor of Law at the Vanderbilt Law

School. He joined the academy after two years in private practice in Washington, D.C., and has also taught at Florida State, the University of North Carolina, the University of Texas, and the Chicago-Kent College of Law. Professor Rossi's books include *Energy, Economics and the Environment* (3rd edition, Foundation Press, 2010) (co-author); *Regulatory Bargaining and Public Law* (Cambridge University Press, 2005); and an edited collection of essays, *Dual Enforcement of Constitutional Norms: The New Frontier of State Constitutionalism* (Oxford University Press, 2010, with James Gardner). He has written widely on administrative law and on regulatory policy, and is one of the nation's leading experts on state administrative procedure.

Glen Staszewski (B.A., University of Wisconsin; J.D., Vanderbilt University School of Law) is Professor of Law and The A.J. Thomas Faculty Scholar at the Michigan State University College of Law, where from 2009 until 2014 he was the first Associate Dean for Research. After graduating from law school, where he served as Editor in Chief of the *Vanderbilt Law Review*, Professor Staszewski clerked for the Honorable Fortunato P. Benavides of the U.S. Court of Appeals for the Fifth Circuit. He then became a trial attorney in the Federal Programs Branch of the Civil Division of the U.S. Department of Justice before joining the MSU College of Law faculty. Professor Staszewski's scholarship focuses on issues of democratic theory and practice that arise in the making and implementation of law in the modern regulatory state.

A NOTE ON THE *BLACKLETTER STATEMENT*

As described in the preface to the first edition, this volume has its roots in the "APA Project" undertaken by the ABA Section of Administrative Law and Practice in the late 1990s. One other product of that effort was *A Blackletter Statement of Federal Administrative Law*, approved by the Section Council in 2001, published in 2002,[1] and reissued in a second edition in 2013.[2]

The relevant portions of the *Blackletter Statement* are reprinted in this volume; indeed, most are reprinted twice. The Appendix sets them out in their entirety. In addition, each chapter includes specific excerpts from the *Blackletter* interwoven with the text of the chapter. These portions are set off from the chapter text—indented and in bold print. They serve as a kind of executive summary at the beginning of the discussion of particular points. A cite to the specific portion of the *Blackletter* appears in a parenthetical at the end of each excerpt.

Two caveats are in order. First, the reader should be aware that these excerpts, though endorsed by the Council of the ABA Section of Administrative Law and Regulatory Practice, are not written by the chapter author. (By the same token, the portions *not* set out in bold do not have the endorsement of the Section Council and reflect the views of the individual chapter author.) Second, the *Blackletter* excerpts are taken verbatim from that document, but in a few instances legal developments have moved beyond the *Blackletter*'s text, which is now a few years old. That text has not been updated; however, more recent developments are flagged and discussed in the body of the chapters themselves.

1. ABA Section of Administrative Law & Regulatory Practice, A Blackletter Statement of Federal Administrative Law (2002), *reprinted in* 52 Admin. L. Rev. 17 (2002).
2. ABA Section of Administrative Law & Regulatory Practice, A Blackletter Statement of Federal Administrative Law (2d ed. 2013).

Chapter 1

AVAILABILITY OF JUDICIAL REVIEW

by Harold H. Bruff*

1.01 INTRODUCTION AND SCOPE OF CHAPTER

The law governing the availability of judicial review of administrative action in the United States is complex because it involves the interrelation of three basic legal principles. First, the Supreme Court insists that federal litigation must present a "Case" or "Controversy" within the meaning of Article III of the Constitution. Second, because all federal jurisdiction must have a statutory basis as well, litigants must identify a statutory grant of jurisdiction. Third, American administrative law is rooted in the common law, and common law principles continue to govern it, in part because courts read them into the Delphic statutory and constitutional provisions that apply.

This chapter offers brief introductions to most of the doctrines that grant and limit access to the federal courts for challenges to agency action. Topics covered include: jurisdiction and venue, sovereign immunity, causes of action

---

* Nicholas Rosenbaum Professor of Law, University of Colorado at Boulder.

to challenge agency action, timing limits (e.g., finality, exhaustion, and ripeness), and reviewability. The topic of standing is addressed in Chapter 2.

1.02 JURISDICTION AND VENUE

The Administrative Procedure Act (APA) itself does not provide jurisdiction in suits seeking review of federal administrative action, but the federal-question statute, 28 U.S.C. § 1331, generally does. General federal-question jurisdiction in district court does not apply, however, where special jurisdictional statutes such as the Hobbs Act, 28 U.S.C. § 2342, provide exclusive jurisdiction for review of specified classes of cases in the courts of appeals.

Under the generally applicable venue statute, 28 U.S.C. § 1391(e), venue is proper for a suit against an officer, an agency, or the United States "in any judicial district in which: (1) a defendant in the action resides, or (2) the cause of action arose, or (3) any real property involved in the action is situated, or (4) the plaintiff resides if no real property is involved in the action." This is a default provision that may be superseded by venue provisions in a special jurisdictional statute.

[Blackletter Statement, Part 4, § I.A.]

Challenges to federal agency actions fall within the constitutional grant of jurisdiction over federal questions; hence the initial question in a case is whether a federal statute has exercised the constitutional grant. Perhaps surprisingly, in *Califano v. Sanders,*[1] the Supreme Court held that the APA does not grant the federal courts jurisdiction to review federal administrative action. Accordingly, parties seeking such review must identify another statute conferring jurisdiction on the court in which review is sought. Generally, this jurisdictional requirement is satisfied either (1) by a specific statute granting a particular court jurisdiction to review a class of administrative actions or (2) in the absence of a specific statute, by the general federal-question statute.[2] If jurisdiction cannot be established through § 1331 or a specific statute, judicial review is likely to be unavailable. For example, in *Califano v. Sanders*, the party sought judicial review of an agency decision not to reopen a previously rejected claim for Social Security benefits. The Social Security Act barred courts from relying on § 1331 to obtain jurisdiction, and, while the Act included a specific jurisdictional grant authorizing judicial review of Social Security decisions, that grant did not extend to an agency refusal to reopen a case. Because the party could

1. 430 U.S. 99 (1977).
2. 28 U.S.C. § 1331.

not obtain jurisdiction under the Social Security Act or § 1331, the Supreme Court held that the courts had no jurisdiction to provide review. This precedent prevents parties from relying on the APA to circumvent the jurisdictional limitations that Congress has imposed in more specific statutes.

A number of cases have examined the allocation of jurisdiction between § 1331 (which confers power on the district courts) and more specific statutes (which often confer original jurisdiction on the courts of appeals). Happily, if a litigant brings suit in the wrong court, the case can be transferred to the correct one.[3] Although identifying the correct locus for review depends on interpreting the particular statute involved, the Supreme Court has favored review by the courts of appeals for reasons of judicial economy.[4] In modern times, the presence of administrative records for even informal agency actions has made appellate-style review broadly practicable. For example, in *Telecommunications Research and Action Center v. FCC*,[5] the court considered whether § 1331 conferred on the district courts jurisdiction to review a claim that the FCC had unreasonably delayed administrative action. It was undisputed that if the FCC had actually undertaken the requested administrative action, the courts of appeals rather than the district courts would have had jurisdiction to review the action pursuant to § 402(a) of the Communications Act, which granted the courts of appeals power to review "any order" of the FCC. However, because the FCC had not actually issued any order (it had just delayed taking action), jurisdiction was unclear. Nevertheless, the court of appeals held that it did have jurisdiction over the suit to compel agency action and that this jurisdiction was exclusive. The court reasoned that "where a statute commits review of agency action to the Court of Appeals, any suit seeking relief that might affect the Circuit Court's future jurisdiction is subject to the exclusive review of the Court of Appeals."[6] In subsequent cases, the D.C. Circuit has applied this reasoning to deprive district courts of jurisdiction to review challenges to administrative complaints where the administrative proceedings, once completed, would be reviewable in the courts of appeals.[7] However, district courts retain § 1331 jurisdiction over facial constitutional challenges to an agency's authorizing statute even where judicial review of the agency action authorized by the statute lies exclusively with the courts of appeals.[8]

3. 28 U.S.C. § 1631.
4. Florida Power & Light Co. v. Lorion, 470 U.S. 729, 745 (1985); Harrison v. PPG Industries, Inc., 446 U.S. 578, 593-94 (1980).
5. 750 F.2d 70 (D.C. Cir. 1984).
6. *Id.* at 78-79. *See also In re* Bluewater Network and Ocean Advocates, 234 F.3d 1305 (D.C. Cir. 2000).
7. *See* Ukiah Adventist Hosp. v. FTC, 981 F.2d 543, 549 (D.C. Cir. 1992).
8. *See* Time Warner Entertainment Co. v. FCC, 93 F.3d 957 (D.C. Cir. 1996).

Venue in a challenge to federal agency action is ordinarily proper where the plaintiff or the government defendant resides.[9] Consequently, Washington, D.C., is usually a proper venue, and some statutes make it the exclusive one.[10] A large proportion of administrative law litigation takes place in the nation's capital.

1.03 WAIVER OF SOVEREIGN IMMUNITY

> **Section 702 of the APA waives sovereign immunity of the federal government for judicial review of agency action where the plaintiff is seeking relief other than money damages. This waiver applies regardless of whether a petitioner invokes the APA's cause of action or some other cause of action. It also permits a suit seeking a financial award that does not technically constitute "money damages." A claimant seeking money damages from the federal government must invoke a waiver of sovereign immunity other than § 702.**
>
> **[Blackletter Statement, Part 4, § I.B.]**

Lawsuits challenging federal administrative action must be brought against a proper defendant. Long ago, the Supreme Court read the common-law doctrine of sovereign immunity into the Constitution, which does not mention it.[11] Hence a suit may be brought against the United States or against an officer acting within his or her official capacity only if there is a statutory waiver of the immunity. Since 1976, § 702 of the APA has waived sovereign immunity generally for suits against the United States seeking relief other than money damages. Before then, federal courts found a way to review agency action in injunctive suits through the fiction of *Ex parte Young*,[12] which held that an injunction brought against an official in his or her "personal" capacity did not encounter the bar of sovereign immunity even though the purpose and effect of the lawsuit was to bind the sovereign. Section 702's general waiver does not apply "if any other statute that grants consent to suit expressly or impliedly forbids the relief" that the plaintiff seeks.[13] Courts must therefore examine

---

9. 28 U.S.C. § 1391(e).
10. *See, e.g.*, 8 U.S.C. § 1189(c)(1) (review of designation as a foreign terrorist organization); 42 U.S.C. § 7607(b)(1) (review of regulations issued under the Clean Air Act that are national in scope).
11. Kawananakoa v. Polyblank, 205 U.S. 349, 353 (1907).
12. 209 U.S. 123 (1908).
13. 5 U.S.C. § 702.

particular statutes that plaintiffs invoke for authority to sue the government to determine whether they waive or preserve sovereign immunity.[14]

Lawsuits seeking money damages cannot employ the waiver in § 702 or the fiction of *Ex parte Young*. Various statutes authorize suits against the United States for damages; the most important are the Federal Tort Claims Act[15] and the Tucker Act.[16] These statutes have a complex case law of their own.

1.04 CAUSE OF ACTION OR DEFENSE

Many specific statutes authorize judicial review of particular types of federal agency action. An agency's enabling act may, for instance, contain a set of provisions establishing parameters for review of rules issued pursuant to that act's authority. Review pursuant to such provisions is sometimes characterized as a "special statutory proceeding." Often, the jurisdictional provisions for a special statutory review proceeding assign subject matter jurisdiction to courts of appeals (especially the D.C. Circuit).

In the absence of a special statutory review scheme, parties may seek review under APA §§ 702–704, which provide a general cause of action for parties "adversely affected or aggrieved by agency action" for which "there is no other adequate remedy in court."

Where neither a specific statute nor the APA provides a cause of action, parties may obtain review by seeking various forms of relief, including equitable relief under a federal court's general equity jurisdiction, 28 U.S.C. § 1331, declaratory relief under the Declaratory Judgment Act, 28 U.S.C. § 2201, and mandamus under 28 U.S.C. § 1361. (These forms of review, as well as review sought under the APA without authorization by a more specific statute, are sometimes described as instances of "nonstatutory review." This usage is misleading, however, because almost all of these forms of review rest on a statutory foundation.)

---

14. Match-E-Be-Nash-She-Wish Band of Pottawatomi Indians v. Patchak, 132 S. Ct. 2199, 2205 (2012).
15. 28 U.S.C. §§ 1346(b), 2671-80. When tort lawsuits are brought against officers acting within the scope of their duties, the Westfall Act immunizes them from liability and substitutes the United States as defendant, with liability governed by the FTCA. 28 U.S.C. § 2679 (b)(1), (d)(1).
16. 28 U.S.C. § 1491.

In rare circumstances, a plaintiff may sue an agency official in her personal capacity for a constitutional tort in a "*Bivens* action." See *Bivens v. Six Unknown Named Agents of Federal Bureau of Narcotics*, 403 U.S. 388 (1971). The Supreme Court has narrowly defined the availability of the *Bivens* cause of action, and it is not available where Congress has provided an adequate statutory alternative.

Rather than challenge an agency action affirmatively, under many circumstances a party may instead raise the invalidity of an agency action as a defense in a subsequent enforcement proceeding based on that agency action. The existence of a prior, adequate, and exclusive opportunity for judicial review may, however, cut off this right to raise the invalidity of the agency action as a defense in an enforcement proceeding.

[Blackletter Statement, Part 4, § I.D.]

The cause of action needed to obtain review of a federal agency action is often provided by the statute authorizing the action itself. Review pursuant to a cause of action created by an agency's enabling act is sometimes referred to as "special statutory review." Such "statutory" review provisions usually define the nature of review, for example by specifying the courts that may exercise it.

In the absence of a special statutory review authorization, litigants often invoke "nonstatutory" review, which is a misleading term because all federal jurisdiction has a statutory basis. Here the reference is to statutes that grant jurisdiction and causes of action but that do not mention specific agency actions. Thus, a litigant can invoke the general federal question jurisdiction and §§ 702-04 of the APA, which provide a cause of action against an agency action "for which there is no other adequate remedy in court." A claim for injunctive relief under a federal court's general equity jurisdiction is often joined with a request for a declaratory judgment[17] or mandamus[18] under the statutes authorizing these remedies. In addition, a party may ordinarily challenge agency action in the course of defending an enforcement action that the agency has brought.

In some circumstances a plaintiff may sue an agency official in his or her personal capacity for a constitutional tort.[19] In these cases, and where statutes

17. 28 U.S.C. § 2201.
18. 28 U.S.C. § 1361.
19. Bivens v. Six Unknown Named Agents of Federal Bureau of Narcotics, 403 U.S. 388 (1971). In Ashcroft v. Iqbal, 556 U.S. 662 (2009), the Court required allegation of "plausible" facts to support a *Bivens* claim.

authorize damages suits against officers, the defense of qualified or absolute immunity will likely be raised. These immunities have common-law origins. The Supreme Court has built categories of absolute immunity for some officials, such as the President[20] and administrative adjudicators.[21] Other officers enjoy a qualified immunity unless their conduct has violated clearly established constitutional or statutory rights.[22]

1.05 TIMING OF JUDICIAL REVIEW

Courts determine whether judicial review of administrative action is timely through a group of closely related doctrines that consider whether the issues and record are ready for judicial examination, whether early review would impair agency authority, and whether delayed review would impose unacceptable hardship on the plaintiff. Statutes, including the APA, can govern the timeliness of review.

Because administrative law's timing doctrines examine similar considerations, they can be difficult to distinguish. Fortunately, it is not always important to choose a particular label for the analysis, as long as the right questions are asked. For example, in *Ticor Title Insurance Co. v. FTC*,[23] three judges used three different timing doctrines to reach the same outcome. The discussion below will identify the emphases that characterize each doctrine. In general, when a party has forgone or proposes to forgo an available administrative process, the exhaustion doctrine applies; when the agency can initiate the next process, the problem is one of ripeness or finality.

1.051 Finality

> **Administrative law presumes that judicial review should await final agency action; interlocutory review is generally unavailable. The APA codifies this presumption at § 704, which provides, "[a]gency action made reviewable by statute and final agency action for which there is no adequate remedy in a court are subject to judicial review."**
>
> **[Blackletter Statement, Part 4, § II.A.]**

The longstanding principle that courts should review only final agency actions is codified by § 704 of the APA, which authorizes review of "final

20. Nixon v. Fitzgerald, 457 U.S. 731 (1982).
21. Butz v. Economou, 438 U.S. 478 (1978).
22. Ashcroft v. al-Kidd, 131 S. Ct. 2074, 2080 (2011).
23. 814 F.2d 731 (D.C. Cir. 1987).

agency action." There are two preconditions to a finding of finality. First, the agency action must be the "consummation" of its process, rather than a tentative or interlocutory action. Thus, in *FTC v. Standard Oil Co. of California*,[24] the Court concluded that the agency's issuance of a complaint in an APA adjudication was not final action. Hence, the company could not obtain review of the legality of the complaint until the adjudication resulted in a final order. The Court conceded that the complaint was final in the sense that it would not be reconsidered, but the Court did not wish to allow piecemeal interlocutory review of agency adjudications. There is an obvious parallel here to the reluctance of appellate courts to review interlocutory orders of trial courts, with an overlay of concern for the special attributes of administrative agencies. Preliminary actions such as these are reviewable as part of review of the final action they precede.

It is sometimes unclear when an agency's process of policy articulation has come to rest sufficiently to be final and reviewable. An instructive case is *National Automatic Laundry and Cleaning Council v. Shultz*,[25] which was a challenge to a letter from the Wage and Hour Administration stating its view that certain employees would be covered by statutory minimum wage and maximum hour requirements. The court allowed review because the action was adopted by the agency head after full internal consideration, and bore no indicia of tentativeness.[26]

In complex regulatory schemes, it may be difficult to determine the level of government at which final action occurs. For example, in two cases the Supreme Court concluded that action by administrators was not final when it was subject to review by the President.[27]

The Supreme Court has recognized an exception to the basic requirement of finality where an agency initiates action that is facially beyond its statutory jurisdiction, so that a valid final action cannot emerge. Thus, a leading case upheld review of an otherwise unreviewable action that was contrary to a specific provision in the governing statute.[28]

The second precondition to finality is that the agency action must determine private rights or obligations or otherwise carry legal consequences, as

---

24. 449 U.S. 232 (1980).
25. 443 F.2d 689 (D.C. Cir. 1971).
26. *See also* Natural Resources Defense Council v. EPA, 22 F.3d 1125, 1133 (D.C. Cir. 1994); New York Stock Exchange, Inc. v. Bloom, 562 F.2d 736, 741 (D.C. Cir. 1977).
27. Dalton v. Specter, 511 U.S. 462, 469-70 (1994); Franklin v. Massachusetts, 505 U.S. 788, 798 (1992).
28. Leedom v. Kyne, 358 U.S. 184, 190-1 (1958).

opposed to merely providing informal guidance that is not binding. Although agency interpretive rules and policy statements lack the force of law and therefore are not normally reviewable, some of them have immediate practical impact on persons subject to them. Courts have engaged in pragmatic inquiries to determine which of these agency actions should be regarded as final and binding enough for review to occur.[29]

1.052 Exhaustion of Administrative Remedies

> **An agency action may be considered "final" even though opportunities remain for seeking further review of the action within the agency itself. Nonetheless, where the *exhaustion* doctrine applies, it requires a plaintiff to seek relief from all available and adequate administrative remedies, including intra-agency appellate remedies, prior to seeking judicial review.**
>
> **[Blackletter Statement, Part 4, § II.B.]**

A general requirement that a citizen exhaust available administrative remedies before seeking judicial review antedates the APA. Because exhaustion cases involve attempts by citizens to avoid resorting to available administrative processes, the analysis tends to focus on the strength of the agency's claim for an opportunity to make a possibly dispositive resolution of the issues. The leading case is *Myers v. Bethlehem Shipbuilding Corp.*[30] The company tried to enjoin an adjudication by the National Labor Relations Board (NLRB) on the ground that the agency lacked jurisdiction because interstate commerce was not involved. The Court upheld the agency's power to find the facts upon which its own jurisdiction depended, and stressed that Congress had delegated fact-finding power to the agency rather than to federal district courts.

The Court provided a useful general discussion of the exhaustion doctrine in *McCarthy v. Madigan*.[31] The Court did not require a federal prisoner to exhaust administrative remedies before pursuing a constitutional claim for damages against prison officials because the prison grievance procedures could not provide the remedy sought in the litigation. *McCarthy* summarizes the multiple

---

29. *See, e.g.*, Pacific Gas & Electric Co. v. FPC, 506 F.2d 33, 45-49 (D.C. Cir. 1974); Appalachian Power Co. v. Environmental Protection Agency, 208 F.3d 1015, 1020-25 (D.C. Cir. 2000). *Cf.* National Mining Assoc. v. McCarthy, 758 F.3d 243, 251 (D.C. Cir. 2014) (declaring that policy statements are categorically unreviewable but that interpretive rules are sometimes reviewable).
30. 303 U.S. 41 (1938).
31. 503 U.S. 140 (1992).

factors the Court has employed in its exhaustion cases. These fall into three broad groupings. First, the Court examines the needs of the judiciary to obtain a sufficiently developed record to enable judicial review and to avoid piecemeal and possibly unnecessary litigation. Second, the Court considers the agency's need for autonomy—the opportunity to apply its expertise (or at least discretion) to the case and to correct its own mistakes. Third, the Court assesses the hardship to the plaintiff of denying review. Hardship must include something more than the ordinary cost of exhausting the administrative remedy. For example, in cases involving plaintiffs who have already forgone their administrative remedies, the Court is sensitive to the loss of criminal defenses.[32]

The Court has held that general exhaustion analysis must yield to the specific provisions of the APA. Section 704 states that agency action becomes final and hence subject to judicial review without resort to internal agency appeals unless a statute or agency rule provides otherwise (and, if a rule, unless the action is inoperative during the appeal). In *Darby v. Cisneros*,[33] the Court disapproved a longstanding judicial practice of ignoring this provision and enforced it according to its terms. A real estate developer had sought immediate judicial review of an order by HUD temporarily barring his participation in federal programs. HUD regulations provided for an administrative appeal of the order, but did not expressly make it mandatory. The Court's holding not only gave effect to a specific provision of the APA but also prevented traps for unwary litigants due to ambiguous agency procedural rules.[34] Not surprisingly, agencies often issue rules to force appeals within their internal systems.

1.053 Issue Exhaustion

> **In both APA and non-APA cases, the courts have frequently refused to consider issues that were not first raised before the agency. Courts enforce such *issue exhaustion* more stringently where the parties are expected to develop the issues in an adversarial proceeding than in circumstances in which they review the results of nonadversarial, informal hearings.**
>
> **[Blackletter Statement, Part 4, § II.B.]**

Because the essential premise of the exhaustion requirement is that agencies should have an opportunity to resolve controversies under their statutes

32. *See* McKart v. United States, 395 U.S. 185, 197 (1969).
33. 509 U.S. 137 (1993).
34. *See also* Volvo GM Heavy Truck Corp. v. Dep't of Labor, 118 F.3d 205, 209 (4th Cir. 1997).

before the courts intervene, it is natural to apply exhaustion principles to particular issues contained within a proceeding. Just as appellate courts do not consider arguments that parties failed to raise before trial courts, reviewing courts do not ordinarily consider issues parties failed to raise before agencies. This principle has more force for fully adversarial administrative hearings than for nonadversarial, informal agency hearings. Thus, in *Sims v. Apfel*,[35] the Court declined to impose an issue exhaustion requirement on Social Security disability hearings, which are inquisitorial in nature and where claimants are often unrepresented by lawyers.

Some courts have also applied the issue exhaustion doctrine to rulemaking, preventing challengers from raising issues for the first time on appeal that were not considered by the agency. This application of the doctrine is an aspect of the general focus of judicial review of rules for arbitrariness on the arguments presented to the agency during rulemaking. The underlying idea is that arbitrariness review requires an agency to give a reasoned explanation for its choice of rule, and, in general, an agency's reasoned explanation need not explain why the agency has rejected arguments that no one has brought to its attention.

1.054 Ripeness

> **To determine whether agency action is ripe for judicial review, courts balance (1) "the fitness of the issues for judicial decision" and (2) "the hardship to the parties of withholding court consideration." The Supreme Court has also advised courts to consider whether judicial intervention would unduly interfere with subsequent agency action.**
>
> **[Blackletter Statement, Part 4, § II.C.]**

Modern ripeness analysis dates from the Supreme Court's decisions in *Abbott Laboratories v. Gardner*[36] and *Toilet Goods Ass'n v. Gardner*.[37] In these companion cases, the Court considered whether two agency rules that were final were ready ("ripe") for review when no proceeding to enforce them had been brought. The Court evaluated "both the fitness of the issues for judicial decision and the hardship to the parties of withholding court consideration." In *Abbott Labs,* the Court allowed immediate review because the only issues were ones of statutory interpretation and there was hardship to the plaintiffs due to

35. 530 U.S. 103 (2000).
36. 387 U.S. 136 (1967).
37. 387 U.S. 158 (1967).

the burdens of choosing between expensive compliance with the rule or the risk of serious penalties for a violation. In *Toilet Goods*, on the other hand, the Court denied immediate review because it perceived a need for a factual record in an enforcement context and because there would be no special burdens for a company choosing to test the rule's validity.

The courts have employed the *Abbott Labs* test ever since. In a decision applying and restating the doctrine, *Ohio Forestry Ass'n, Inc. v. Sierra Club*,[38] the Court added emphasis on a consideration that would normally be part of exhaustion analysis: "whether judicial intervention would inappropriately interfere with further administrative action." The *Ohio Forestry* Court declined to allow the Sierra Club to challenge a forest management plan immediately upon its issuance. There would be later opportunities to challenge specific proposals to implement the plan, the Court said, and the club's alleged loss of the efficiencies accompanying a single challenge did not constitute hardship. Moreover, delaying review would allow the agency to refine the plan so that judicial review would be informed by an actual proposal, instead of occurring in a more abstract context.[39]

More recently, in *National Park Hospitality Association v. Department of Interior*, the Court indicated that an agency action must have "adverse effects of a strictly legal kind" to satisfy the hardship prong of *Abbot Labs.*[40] This case involved a challenge to a rule adopted by the National Park Service (NPS) declaring that concession contracts are not "contracts" within the meaning of the Contract Disputes Act (CDA). The Court concluded that, because NPS does not administer the CDA, its rule could be nothing more than a "policy statement" reflecting its views on proper application of that statute. The agency's policy statement regarding a statute it did not administer had no "strictly legal" effects and thus created no cognizable hardship.[41]

The *NPHA* Court also reiterated that hardship generally requires that agency action affect the plaintiff's "primary conduct"—*i.e.*, day-to-day activity. In *Abbott Labs,* for instance, obeying the challenged rule would have required the plaintiffs to relabel their products at great expense. NPS's declaration that concession contracts were not subject to the CDA did nothing to alter concessioners' day-to-day conduct.[42]

---

38. 523 U.S. 726, 733 (1998).
39. *See also* Reno v. Catholic Social Servs., Inc., 509 U.S. 43, 57-59 (1993); Lujan v. National Wildlife Fed'n, 497 U.S. 871, 890 (1990).
40. 538 U.S. 803 (2003).
41. *Id.* at 809.
42. *Id.* at 810.

1.055 Statutory Deadlines for Review of Agency Actions

> **Many enabling acts provide for short time limits (e.g., sixty days) for review of agency action—especially rules. In the absence of such a time limit, a six-year statute of limitations generally applies to challenges to agency action. Courts nonetheless allow post-deadline judicial review of agency rules under some circumstances. The availability of judicial review depends on whether the challenge is substantive or procedural as well as on whether the statutory time limit at issue expressly precludes untimely review.**
> **[Blackletter Statement, Part 4, § II.D.]**

Statutes authorizing review of particular agency actions often provide a time limit (e.g., 60 days) for filing a petition for judicial review in the appropriate court.[43] Where there is no specified time limit, a six-year statute of limitations generally applies to administrative appeals.[44] Because these deadlines do not begin to run until a rule is ripe for review, there is sometimes uncertainty about the start date.[45] In addition, an agency may restart a statutory time limit on judicial review by "reopening" its consideration of an earlier action in any way that appears to reexamine it.[46]

Courts do not apply all of these deadlines with absolute rigidity. In recent years, the Supreme Court has emphasized a distinction between "jurisdictional" statutory deadlines and mere "claims processing" rules subject to waiver and equitable tolling. Statutory deadlines are to be regarded as claims processing rules absent a clear statement from Congress to the contrary.[47] For example, applying this principle, the Court concluded that the 120-day limit for filing a notice of appeal with the Veterans Court is a nonjurisdictional claims processing rule.[48]

Statutory deadlines present a special challenge in rulemaking cases as courts know that affected persons are not necessarily aware of the issuance of a rule. Therefore, courts permit parties that did not timely challenge a rule to defend

---

43. *E.g.*, Federal Trade Commission Act, 15 U.S.C. § 45(c) (2000).
44. 28 U.S.C. § 2401.
45. Louisiana Envtl. Action Network v. Browner, 87 F.3d 1379, 1385 (D.C. Cir. 1996); Eagle-Picher Industries v. EPA, 759 F.2d 905 (D.C. Cir. 1985).
46. ICC v. Brotherhood of Locomotive Engineers, 482 U.S. 270, 278 (1987); Nat'l Min. Ass'n v. United States Dep't of Interior, 70 F.3d 1345, 1351 (D.C. Cir. 1995) (discussing "reopener doctrine").
47. Sebelius v. Auburn Regional Med. Ctr., 133 S. Ct. 817, 824 (2013).
48. Henderson *ex rel.* Henderson v. Shinseki, 131 S. Ct 1197, 1204-05 (2011).

an enforcement proceeding on the substantive grounds that the rule is unconstitutional or exceeds the agency's statutory authority.[49] An alternate way to raise these substantive challenges after a statutory deadline is to file a petition to revise or revoke the rule, and then to seek review of a denial of the petition.[50] This belated review is usually limited to issues considered in the denial decision and thus does not include factual or discretionary determinations underlying the original rule. Courts generally bar post-deadline procedural challenges to rules entirely.[51]

1.056 Primary Jurisdiction

> **Primary jurisdiction applies when claims properly cognizable in court contain one or more issues within the special competence of an administrative agency. In such cases, the court enables a referral to the agency, staying further proceedings so as to give the parties reasonable opportunity to seek an administrative ruling. In cases of mandatory primary jurisdiction, an agency ruling is required, and the court cannot proceed with the case until the agency has acted. In cases where an agency ruling is not required but the court might benefit from the expertise of the agency, the court may make a referral but also provide that if the agency has not ruled after a certain time the court will proceed without the agency ruling.**
>
> **[Blackletter Statement, Part 4, § II.E.]**

Primary jurisdiction is a specialized doctrine, quite similar to exhaustion, which applies when both an agency and a court have original jurisdiction over a case or an issue. In that situation, a court in which an action is brought must decide whether the agency's jurisdiction is "primary." This determination usually depends on whether the expertise or discretion that the agency is meant to exercise is implicated, and whether the uniform resolution of an issue that an agency is best situated to provide is needed. See, e.g., *United States v. Western Pacific Railroad Co.*,[52] in which the Court required the Court of Claims to defer to the primary jurisdiction of the Interstate Commerce Commission in

49. NLRB Union v. FLRA, 834 F.2d 191, 195-96 (D.C. Cir. 1987); Deering Milliken, Inc. v. OSHRC, 630 F.2d 1094, 1099 (5th Cir. 1980).
50. Auer v. Robbins, 519 U.S. 452, 459 (1997).
51. JEM Broadcasting Co., Inc. v. FCC, 22 F.3d 320, 325 (D.C. Cir. 1994); Nat'l Industrial Constructors, Inc. v. OSHRC, 583 F.2d 1048, 1053 (8th Cir. 1978).
52. 352 U.S. 59 (1956).

resolving an issue of tariff construction that required knowledge of transportation facts and policy that were within the province of the ICC.[53]

If an entire case is within an agency's primary jurisdiction, a court will dismiss it; if one or more issues are for the agency, the court can retain jurisdiction until those issues have been resolved. Judicial invocation of an agency's primary jurisdiction substantially delays resolution of a controversy and increases costs for the litigants as well. Justification for these consequences must be sought in the need for courts to receive the specialized knowledge of agencies, so that appropriate judicial deference to their views can occur.

1.06 REVIEWABILITY

Courts presume that final administrative action is reviewable. Nevertheless, Congress may, within constitutional limits, preclude or restrict judicial review. Implied limitations are drawn from the pertinent statutory scheme as a whole. In addition, some administrative actions are unreviewable because their nature or the absence of judicial standards for judging them commits them to agency discretion.

1.061 "Agency Action" as a Limit on Review under the APA

> **The APA's cause of action applies only to "agency action." Section 551(13) defines "agency action" as including "the whole or a part of an agency rule, order, license, sanction, relief, or the equivalent or denial thereof, or failure to act." Given this expansive list, the APA's definition of "agency action" rarely blocks judicial review of an agency's affirmative action or its denial of a request for action (e.g., review of a rule or a denial of a petition for rulemaking).**
>
> **[Blackletter Statement, Part 4, § III.A.]**

Judicial review under the APA applies only to "agency action," which is defined as "an agency rule, order, license, sanction, relief, or the equivalent or denial thereof, or failure to act."[54] The inclusiveness of this list means that review is ordinarily available for an agency's affirmative action or its denial of a request for a particular action (e.g., review of a rule or a denial of a petition for rulemaking).

---

53. *See also* Far East Conference v. United States, 342 U.S. 570 (1952); Texas & Pac. Ry. v. Abilene Cotton Oil Co., 204 U.S. 426 (1907).
54. 5 U.S.C. § 551(13).

Review of an agency's general "failure to act" is more problematic. Section 706(1) of the APA instructs courts to "compel agency action unlawfully withheld or unreasonably delayed." On its face, this provision seems to authorize broad judicial power to order agency action at the behest of litigants complaining of a "failure to act." Not every "failure to act" should be reviewable as "agency action," however, if only because all agencies are failing to take an infinite number of actions at any given moment. Limiting principles are therefore necessary to determine which "failure[s] to act" are subject to judicial review.

In *Norton v. Southern Utah Wilderness Alliance*, the Court responded to this problem by holding that "failure to act" is "properly understood as failure to take an *agency action*—that is, failure to take one of the [other] agency actions" listed in the APA's definition of "agency action."[55] The Court explained that this limitation permits review of "discrete" failures to act, such as failure to adopt a particular rule, but blocks "programmatic" attacks on an agency's general priorities and activities. Applying this principle, the Court rejected an environmental group's attempt to use § 706(1) to force the Bureau of Land Management (BLM) to honor a general statutory duty to ensure that the wilderness qualities of some public lands were not impaired.

A litigant might try to satisfy the requirement of discreteness by alleging that an agency has failed to take specific, affirmative action. For instance, the environmental group might have drafted a particular rule designed to protect the land in question and then sued BLM for not adopting it. This type of effort would, however, violate the principle that a court can order an agency to take an action only if it is legally required.[56] Discretionary action, by hypothesis, is not legally required. A court therefore could not order BLM to adopt a particular rule insofar as the court would, by doing so, intrude on the agency's discretion to choose among enforcement methods.

In sum, the Court has construed "failure to act" to block efforts to use the APA cause of action to obtain general judicial orders compelling agencies to discharge broad statutory duties. More particularized efforts to force agencies to take "discrete" actions will fail insofar as they require judicial intrusion on agency discretionary authority.

1.062 Statutory Preclusion or Limitation of Review

Section 701(a)(1) of the APA recognizes that Congress may by statute preclude judicial review. The Supreme Court has never decided whether the Constitution limits this preclusive power. In

55. 542 U.S. 55, 62 (2004).
56. *Id.* at 63-64.

part to avoid that question, courts will often work hard to interpret statutory language to avoid preclusive effect, requiring "clear and convincing evidence of a contrary legislative intent" to overcome the general presumption of judicial review.
[Blackletter Statement, Part 4, § III.B.]

In *Abbott Laboratories v. Gardner*,[57] the Court held that the APA embodies a "basic presumption of judicial review." This presumption serves to protect litigants seeking nonstatutory review from dismissal on grounds that Congress's failure to provide a specific statutory vehicle automatically implies its disapproval of review. The *Abbott Labs* Court required a showing of "clear and convincing evidence" for restrictions on judicial review. This presumption recognizes that both Congress and the courts ordinarily favor review of administrative action, and that nonreviewability is the exception.[58]

APA § 701(a) allows courts to review administrative action "except to the extent that—(1) statutes preclude judicial review . . . ." Only rarely has Congress explicitly barred judicial review of agency action. The best-known instances have involved the Veterans Administration. For many years Congress forbade the courts to review VA decisions of law or fact in administration of veterans' legislation. In *Johnson v. Robison*,[59] the Court read the preclusion to allow judicial consideration of constitutional claims by veterans (but not statutory ones). The Court was avoiding a lurking constitutional issue—the extent of congressional power to deny or restrict federal court jurisdiction over claims that are functionally suited to review. Ever since *Ex parte McCardle*,[60] it has been clear that Congress has broad power over federal jurisdiction. The Court has never decided whether limitations found within Article III or the Due Process Clause of the Constitution set limits to this power for administrative cases. Instead, as in *Robison*, the courts have interpreted statutes to allow judicial consideration of issues of constitutionality and statutory applicability.[61]

57. 387 U.S. 136, 140 (1967).
58. *See also* Gutierrez de Martinez v. Lamagno, 515 U.S. 417, 424 (1995); Bowen v. Michigan Academy of Family Physicians, 476 U.S. 667, 670 (1986). The history and justifications of the presumption are critically reviewed in Nicholas Bagley, *The Puzzling Presumption of Reviewability*, 127 Harv. L. Rev. 1285 (2014).
59. 415 U.S. 361 (1974).
60. 74 U.S. (7 Wall.) 506 (1868).
61. *See* Traynor v. Turnage, 485 U.S. 535, 542 (1988); Lindahl v. Office of Personnel Mgmt., 470 U.S. 768, 779 (1985). *See also* Kucana v. Holder, 558 U.S. 233, 247-49 (2010) (refusing to allow an administrative regulation to expand the scope of a statutory preclusion).

McNary v. Haitian Refugee Center, Inc.[62] provides another good example of the Court's tendency to construe statutory preclusion provisions narrowly to enable courts to review constitutional issues—as well as other legal issues that courts deem important. The statute in question barred judicial review of individual amnesty determinations except in deportation or exclusion proceedings. The *McNary* Court nonetheless allowed an alien to bring a general challenge in district court to INS procedures on due process and statutory grounds. In cases like *McNary*, the Court has allowed challenges that are collateral to particular applications of statutes that restrict review, and it has emphasized the need to protect meaningful judicial review.[63]

Congress has sometimes restricted judicial review to particular times or courts. In *Yakus v. United States*,[64] the Court upheld restrictions on time and place of review in the World War II economic controls program.[65]

Notwithstanding the Court's tendency to construe express statutory preclusion provisions narrowly, it will sometimes conclude that a statute precludes review by implication. The "clear and convincing evidence" of an intent to deny review is drawn from examination of the statutory scheme as a whole. *Morris v. Gressette*[66] held that the Attorney General's failure to object to a change in voting procedures under voting rights legislation was unreviewable because of a need for expedition. In *Block v. Community Nutrition Institute*,[67] the Court held that consumers could not obtain review of milk marketing orders because the statute created a scheme for speedy review on behalf of milk producers and handlers, which would be disrupted if consumers could mount challenges. In *Thunder Basin Coal Co. v. Reich*,[68] the Court held that the mine safety statute precluded pre-enforcement judicial review because the statute's

62. 498 U.S. 479 (1991).
63. *See* Mathews v. Eldridge, 424 U.S. 319, 330-32 (1976). After *McNary*, lower courts have struggled with the distinction. *Compare* City of Rialto v. West Coast Loading Corp., 581 F. 3d 865, 872-80 (9th Cir. 2009), *with* General Electric Co. v. Jackson, 610 F.3d 110, 125-26 (D.C. Cir. 2010).
64. 321 U.S. 414 (1944).
65. *See also* Adamo Wrecking Co. v. United States, 434 U.S. 275, 283 (1978), in which the Court held that certain restrictions on review of EPA regulations did not apply in this case, but approved in dictum the usual effect of these restrictions to deprive litigants of claims or defenses not presented within the statutory period.
66. 432 U.S. 491 (1977).
67. 467 U.S. 340 (1984).
68. 510 U.S. 200 (1994); *see also* Elgin v. Department of Treasury, 132 S. Ct. 2126, 2133-34 (2012); Shalala v. Illinois Council on Long Term Care, Inc., 529 U.S. 1, 5 (2000).

structure and legislative history evinced an intent to force challenges into a detailed statutory review scheme. But in *Sackett v. EPA*,[69] the Court would not imply a restriction against pre-enforcement review of EPA compliance orders under the Clean Water Act.

1.063 Matters Committed to Agency Discretion

> **Section 701(a)(2) of the APA recognizes that the APA's cause of action is not available "to the extent that . . . agency action is committed to agency discretion by law." This exception to the APA's general presumption of review is narrow. The Supreme Court has stated that this exception applies where statutes are written in such broad terms that there is, in effect, "no law to apply." More broadly, the Court has recognized that there are certain categories of administrative decision that are unreviewable as a matter of tradition. Functional inquiries regarding the desirability of judicial review also come into play—though not always expressly.**
>
> **[Blackletter Statement, Part 4, § III.C.]**

APA § 701(a) allows courts to review administrative action "except to the extent that—. . . (2) agency action is committed to agency discretion by law." In *Citizens to Preserve Overton Park, Inc. v. Volpe*,[70] the Court stated that this is "a very narrow exception" to the presumed reviewability of administrative action. The Court, quoting the legislative history of the APA, said that the exception is "applicable in those rare instances where 'statutes are drawn in such broad terms that in a given case there is no law to apply.'" In *Heckler v. Chaney*,[71] the Court refined this formulation by explaining that it applies "if the statute is drawn so that a court would have no meaningful standard against which to judge the agency's exercise of discretion."[72]

Chaney employed this test to hold that agency decisions declining to initiate enforcement actions are presumptively unreviewable as a category, subject to the possibility that Congress has supplied sufficient standards to guide review in a particular case. (For a case detecting such standards, see *National*

69. 132 S. Ct. 1367 (2012).
70. 401 U.S. 402, 410 (1971).
71. 470 U.S. 821, 830 (1985).
72. *See also* ICC v. Brotherhood of Locomotive Engineers, 482 U.S. 270 (1987) (agency refusals to grant reconsideration of an action not amenable to "devising an adequate standard of review").

Wildlife Federation v. EPA.[73]) The Court emphasized that refusals to enforce implicate the full range of priority-setting decisions that agencies make, and that courts are ill-suited to monitor "the many variables" involved in these decisions.[74]

Whether actions are committed to agency discretion probably depends as much on the nature of the subject matter and its amenability to review as on the particular statutory verbiage supplied by Congress. In *Lincoln v. Vigil*,[75] the Court refused to allow review of an agency's allocation of funds from a lump-sum appropriation and stressed the relation of these administrative decisions to general priority setting. And in *Webster v. Doe*,[76] the Court invoked the exception to bar APA review of decisions by the Director of Central Intelligence to dismiss employees for national security reasons. The Court's judgment that the statutory provision regarding dismissal "fairly exudes deference to the Director" was supported by the overall tenor of the CIA's organic act and the mission of the agency. The Court did, however, preserve constitutional challenges to CIA dismissals, continuing the tradition discussed above favoring judicial review of constitutional claims.

In *Massachusetts v. EPA*,[77] the Court settled a longstanding uncertainty by holding that agency denials of petitions to commence rulemaking are reviewable. In light of the similarity of these decisions to the nonenforcement decisions that *Chaney* had held unreviewable, the Court emphasized that review should be "extremely limited" and "highly deferential." In *Massachusetts*, the Court held that EPA must either begin a rulemaking to address the global warming consequences of carbon dioxide emissions from motor vehicles or explain sufficiently why it would not do so. Because the Court appeared to apply a more stringent standard than the one it was announcing, however, the decision has left lingering confusion in its wake.

---

73. 980 F.2d 765 (D.C. Cir. 1992). *See also* Cook v. FDA, 733 F.3d 1, 6-10 (D.C. Cir. 2013).
74. *See also* Ass'n of Irritated Residents v. EPA, 494 F.3d 1027, 1035 (D.C. Cir. 2007).
75. 508 U.S. 182 (1993).
76. 486 U.S. 592 (1988); *see also* Conyers v. Rossides, 558 F.3d 137, 144 (2d Cir. 2009).
77. 549 U.S. 497 (2007).

Chapter 2

STANDING

by William Funk*

2.01 OVERVIEW

The doctrine of "standing" determines whether a particular litigant is entitled to an adjudication of the particular claims asserted. These requirements are imposed by the Constitution, the courts as a matter of judicial discretion, and Congress.

[Blackletter Statement, Part 4, § IV.A.]

* Lewis and Clark Distinguished Professor of Law, Lewis and Clark Law School.

The doctrine of standing determines who may bring an action in federal court. The Constitution establishes the basic minimum requirements for standing. The Supreme Court, in addition, has as a matter of judicial discretion created additional prudential standing requirements. Finally, Congress can establish requirements for bringing particular kinds of actions. This is sometimes called statutory standing. For example, in order to bring an action under the Administrative Procedure Act, § 702 of Title 5, United States Code, requires that a person either suffer legal wrong or be adversely affected or aggrieved within the meaning of a relevant statute. This is often referred to as the requirement that a person's action be within the zone of interests of a particular statute.

2.02 CONSTITUTIONAL REQUIREMENTS

> **Article III's limitation of the judicial power to "cases" and "controversies" implies three standing requirements. First, the plaintiff must have suffered an "injury in fact"—an invasion of a legally protected interest that is (a) concrete and particularized and (b) actual or imminent, not conjectural or hypothetical. Second, there must be a causal connection between the conduct complained of and the injury—the injury has to be fairly traceable to the challenged action of the defendant, and not the result of the independent action of some third party not before the court. Third, it must be likely that the injury will be redressed by a favorable decision.**
>
> **[Blackletter Statement, Part 4, § IV.B.]**

The specifics of injury, causation, and redressability are addressed below. There are, however, some general statements about constitutional standing appropriate here. First, when there are multiple plaintiffs seeking injunctive or declaratory relief, if any one of them has standing, then courts ignore whether any of the others have standing.[1] Second, standing is to be determined as of the time at which the complaint is filed. After the filing of the complaint, changes in the facts that might have affected standing, had they occurred before the complaint, are considered under the doctrine of mootness, not standing.[2] This is important because the plaintiff has the

1. *See, e.g.*, Massachusetts v. EPA, 549 U.S. 497, 518 (2007); Rumsfeld v. Forum for Academic and Institutional Rights, Inc., 547 U.S. 47, 52, n.2 (2006); Bowsher v. Synar, 478 U.S. 714, 721 (1986).
2. *See* Friends of the Earth, Inc. v. Laidlaw Environmental Services, Inc., 528 U.S. 167, 189-192 (2000).

burden of establishing standing, but the defendant has the burden of establishing mootness. Third, one must establish standing for each form of relief sought. Thus, if a person seeks both damages and an injunction, he must establish standing as to each.[3]

Fourth, a person who appeals a judgment below must have standing to make the appeal. Ordinarily that is the case. Either the plaintiff lost and has the same elements for standing as when he brought the case, or the defendant lost and would be injured by that court decision, and reversal would redress that injury. Two recent decisions from the Supreme Court involving gay marriage that reached opposing results on standing provide a good illustration of this requirement of standing to appeal. *Perry v. Hollingsworth*[4] was the rare but not unique case in which the appellant did not have standing. In that case, persons of the same sex who wished to marry brought an action in federal court to have the California ban on same sex marriage declared unconstitutional. The attorney general of California chose not to defend the state ban, also believing it to be unconstitutional. The district court allowed the proponents of the ballot measure that was the source of the state ban to intervene to defend the ban. After the court ruled that the ban was unconstitutional, the state defendants, who had declined to defend the law in district court in the first place, refused to appeal, and appeal was brought by the intervenors. The Ninth Circuit affirmed the judgment of the district court, and the intervenors sought certiorari, which was granted. The initial question before the Court, however, was whether the intervenors even had standing to appeal the district court decision. It found that they did not, because their only injury was their ideological disagreement with the court's decision, and this generalized grievance did not qualify as a concrete and particularized injury. The Court, therefore, vacated the Ninth Circuit judgment, leaving the district court decision in place.

In contrast, in *United States v. Windsor*,[5] a person legally married to a person of the same sex sued to invalidate the federal Defense of Marriage Act. Like the California officials in *Perry*, the United States refused to defend the law, but it also maintained that it would enforce the Act. Notified that the United States would not defend the law, the House of Representatives authorized its Bipartisan Legal Advisory Group (BLAG) to intervene to defend the law. When the district court ruled against BLAG, both it and the United States appealed to the Second Circuit, and when the Second Circuit affirmed the trial court, both BLAG and the United States sought certiorari. In the

---

3. *See, e.g.*, Los Angeles v. Lyons, 461 U.S. 95, 109 (1983).
4. 133 S. Ct. 2652 (2013).
5. 133 S. Ct. 2675 (2013).

Supreme Court, the United States still refused to defend the law. The Court held that the United States had constitutional standing to appeal, because it would be injured in having to pay money to the plaintiff if she prevailed, and a court decision upholding the law would avoid this injury. The Court was mindful of the fact that the United States was not adverse on the merits with the plaintiff, but the presence of BLAG, whether or not it would have standing on its own, assured a forceful defense of the law. Thus, in *Windsor,* the United States had standing to avoid a financial injury that it had no legal or ideological objection to suffering. By contrast, in *Perry,* the proponents of the ballot measure banning gay marriage, unsupported by any official state defendants, lacked standing to avoid an ideological injury that was unconnected to any more concrete and particularized injury.

2.021 Injury

2.0211 The Constitutional Injury-in-Fact Requirement: In General

The basic Article III requirement is "injury in fact." Constitutionally cognizable injuries include not only harms to person or property and economic harm but also harm to nonmonetary intangible interests. For example, so long as it is individually experienced, harm to environmental, recreational, or aesthetic interests can support standing. The injury must be actual or imminent, not conjectural or hypothetical. Mere ideological objection to government action does not constitute a constitutionally cognizable injury.

[Blackletter Statement, Part 4, § IV.B.1.a.]

Standing issues often arise in the context of environmental litigation. The leading case of *Sierra Club v. Morton*[6] involved a challenge to the National Park Service's permit allowing the development of a large ski resort adjacent to the Sequoia National Park. The Sierra Club argued that it had standing to bring the case because there would be injury to the environment, and the Sierra Club was an environmental organization dedicated to preserving environmentally valuable areas. The Supreme Court denied standing to the Sierra Club on this basis but reiterated dictum from an earlier case[7] to the

6. 405 U.S. 727 (1972).
7. Ass'n of Data Processing Serv. Orgs., Inc. v. Camp, 397 U.S. 150, 154 (1970).

effect that injury to aesthetic, conservational, and recreational interests could satisfy the constitutional requirement for injury. Consequently, harm to the scenery, natural and historic objects, or wildlife of the park could impair a person's enjoyment of the park in a manner sufficient for standing. Moreover, the Court said the fact that environmental interests are widely shared does not make them less deserving of protection. The Court added, however, that the injury-in-fact test requires more than an injury to a cognizable interest. It requires that the party seeking review be himself among the injured.[8] Although the *type* of injury claimed by the Sierra Club could satisfy standing's injury requirement, the Sierra Club had not demonstrated that it itself (or any of its members) had suffered such an injury.

Subsequent cases have elaborated on what it means for a person to be among the injured. Organizations can be such a person if they are injured as an organization. For example, if Congress imposed a special tax on environmental organizations, the Sierra Club would suffer injury sufficient for standing. Organizations can also be an injured person if they have a member who would have standing on his own behalf, if the organization's purpose is related to the issue in the case, and if the action is not one that requires the individual member to be a named party.[9] This last requirement, for practical purposes, means that the action must be for an injunction or declaratory judgment, not for damages. For further discussion of this form of "associational standing," see § 2.03, below.

In order for the injury to be actual or imminent and not speculative, conjectural, or hypothetical, the person's use of the area to be injured must be somewhat specific. For example, in *Lujan v. National Wildlife Federation*,[10] the organization claimed standing based on the standing of individual members. These members, however, could allege only that they used lands in the vicinity of a vast tract that might be subject to mining or other resource utilization. This was not specific enough. If they had been able to allege that they actually visited and enjoyed the specific lands subject to possible mining, it would have been a different case.

In addition, the personally suffered injury must have already occurred, be currently occurring, or, if in the future, be impending rather than speculative. For example, in *Lujan v. Defenders of Wildlife*,[11] the Defenders of Wild-

---

8. *Sierra Club*, 405 U.S. at 734-735.
9. *See* Hunt v. Washington State Apple Advertising Comm'n, 432 U.S. 333 (1977).
10. 497 U.S. 871 (1990).
11. 504 U.S. 555 (1992).

life challenged a change in the Fish and Wildlife Service regulations governing required agency consultation when a federal government action might adversely affect species protected by the Endangered Species Act. The change in effect eliminated any required consultation if the federal agency action occurred abroad. The Defenders of Wildlife provided affidavits that one of its members had traveled to Sri Lanka to see endangered elephants and leopards and another had traveled to Egypt to see the endangered Nile crocodile; that the habitats of these species were at risk because of dams to be built with the help of federal funds; and that the ability of the affiants to see these creatures in the future was at risk because of the failure to consult with the Fish and Wildlife Service regarding this funding. Neither affiant had specific plans to return to Sri Lanka or Egypt in the near future, and these were the only places where their injuries could occur. Given these facts, the Court held that neither affiant could establish an injury that was certainly impending and sufficiently imminent for standing.

Similarly, in a recent decision outside the environmental law context,[12] the Court ruled that attorneys and journalists who communicated electronically with terrorists and those associated with terrorists abroad did not have standing to challenge as violative of the First, Fourth, and Fifth Amendments a provision of the Foreign Intelligence Surveillance Act (FISA) authorizing the interception of certain international communications.[13] The Court said that any injury to the plaintiffs was highly speculative, requiring a chain of assumptions including: first, that the National Security Agency (NSA) would seek to target someone the plaintiffs were communicating with; second, even if it did, that NSA would utilize its authority under FISA rather than some other authority it possesses; third, even if it did utilize the FISA provision, that the Foreign Intelligence Surveillance Court would authorize the interception; fourth, even if the court did authorize the interception, that NSA would actually acquire the targeted communication; and fifth, that even if NSA did acquire the targeted communication, that the plaintiffs would be a party to that communication. Consequently, even if there was a reasonable likelihood that their communications might be intercepted, their injury was not certainly impending.

The doctrine that mere ideological objection to government action is not injury for purposes of standing is exemplified by *Schlesinger v. Reservists Committee to Stop the War*.[14] There the plaintiffs challenged the constitutionality of

---

12. *See* Clapper v. Amnesty International USA, 133 S. Ct. 1138 (2013).
13. 50 U.S.C. § 1881a.
14. 418 U.S. 208 (1974).

members of Congress also being reserve officers in the military in violation of Article I, Section 6, Clause 2 of the Constitution, which provides that "no person holding any office under the United States shall be a member of either House during his continuance in office." The Court held that the plaintiffs lacked standing as citizens or taxpayers. The Court said that their claims implicated only the generalized interest of all citizens in constitutional governance and therefore involved merely an abstract grievance, not a concrete injury.

The Blackletter Statement asserts that "the right of a prevailing party to claim a statutory bounty satisfies the injury-in-fact requirement." This is either incorrect or something of an overstatement. No Supreme Court case has so held. Indeed, the Court has said that while a statutory bounty may create a concrete private interest, it does *not* create an injury-in-fact any more than a wager on the outcome of a lawsuit could constitute injury-in-fact to bring the lawsuit.[15] If a statute creates a statutory bounty for those who are injured by reason of a violation of that statute, then the bounty could constitute the redress necessary for standing, but the bounty would not satisfy the injury-in-fact requirement. Nevertheless, the Court has held that a person has standing to bring a *qui tam* action. In a *qui tam* action, a private person brings a lawsuit to recover money on behalf of the United States. If he prevails, he receives a percentage share of the money won on behalf of the United States. The question is why the private person has standing to bring the case inasmuch as he has suffered no injury. In a case involving a *qui tam* action under the False Claims Act,[16] the Court found that the United States had standing because it had been injured by fraud for which it could recover both treble damages and a civil penalty. The *qui tam* provision of the statute in essence effects a partial assignment of the United States' claim to the private party.[17] Historical practice had always been to allow assignees and subrogees to bring claims founded on the injury of the person from whom the assignment or subrogation came. Consequently, the Court found standing for the person bringing the *qui tam* action.

In *Massachusetts v. EPA*,[18] Massachusetts sued EPA for denying a petition for rulemaking to regulate greenhouse gas emissions from automobiles. As part of its analysis of Massachusetts' standing to bring the action, the Court emphasized that the fact that Massachusetts was suing in its sovereign capacity was "of considerable relevance."[19] The suit was at least in part based on the state's

15. Vt. Agency of Natural Res. v. U.S. *ex rel.* Stevens, 529 U.S 765, 772-73 (2000).
16. 31 U.S.C. §§ 3729(a), 3730(b)(1).
17. *Vt. Agency of Natural Res.*, 529 U.S. at 773.
18. 549 U.S. 497 (2007).
19. *Id.* at 518.

sovereign interest in its air, land, and waters. Exactly what relevance this had was not made clear in the opinion, but the obvious implication was that the rigor of the standing analysis would be lessened, because the state, by giving up some of its sovereign powers in joining the union, could not utilize some powers that it might otherwise have used to protect its sovereign interests. Suing to protect its sovereign interests is distinguished from suing in *parens patriae*, that is, on behalf of its citizens' interests. The Court has made clear that a state may not sue the federal government on the basis of *parens patriae.*[20]

2.0212 Injury from Violation of Procedural Requirements

When a challenged agency action harms an underlying substantive interest of the plaintiff, the plaintiff has standing to challenge the agency's failure to follow legally required procedures even though she cannot prove that the procedural error actually changed the substantive outcome. For example, a taxpayer whose tax liability is increased by a new regulation can challenge the adequacy of the notice of proposed rulemaking, even though it cannot be shown that adequate notice would have resulted in a more favorable regulation. However, she may be required to show that a more favorable regulation is possible. Cognizable injury cannot arise from a procedural violation without a showing that the action taken harms or endangers a concrete substantive interest of the plaintiff.

Apparently, the statutory right to attend meetings and otherwise have access to government proceedings, such as under the Government in the Sunshine Act and the Federal Advisory Committee Act, are sufficiently similar to substantive rights to be treated as such. FOIA rights and voter rights to certain information under the Federal Election Campaign Act are also substantive rights, denial of which will support standing without regard to proof of harm to a particular, underlying substantive interest.

[Blackletter Statement, Part 4, § IV.B.1.b.]

In *Lujan v. Defenders of Wildlife*,[21] the plaintiffs were unable to establish that their inability to see certain listed species presented an imminent, concrete injury, so as an alternative route to standing the Defenders argued that it

---

20. *See, e.g.*, Commonwealth of Massachusetts v. Mellon, 262 U.S. 447 (1923).
21. 504 U.S. 555 (1992).

had suffered a "procedural injury" inasmuch as the United States Agency for International Development had failed to consult with the United States Fish and Wildlife Service, as allegedly required by the Endangered Species Act. Because the Act provided that "any person" could enforce the requirements of the Act in a citizens suit, the plaintiffs argued and the court of appeals accepted that this had the effect of creating a "procedural right" in any person, the violation of which would constitute injury. The Court rejected this argument, saying that a procedural violation could not constitute a concrete injury for standing purposes but instead implicated only a "generally available grievance about government."[22]

In *Defenders*, the claimed procedural right was not one personally enjoyed by the plaintiffs; the consultation requirement in the Act did not involve the public in any way. Thus, it was not clear after *Defenders*, despite its broad language, whether a procedural violation that personally harmed someone could provide injury for standing purposes. In *Summers v. Earth Island Institute*,[23] however, the Court made clear that even the violation of a statutory requirement for public participation in an agency proceeding would not constitute injury for standing purposes to someone who wished to participate in the proceeding.

However, if a person would be injured by an agency action, then the person can challenge a procedural violation that led to that action. That is, if the law provides a procedural right in order to protect a concrete interest, an injury *to the concrete interest* provides standing for invoking the procedural right. For example, in *Earth Island Institute*, the plaintiffs wished to challenge a regulation the agency had adopted that eliminated public hearings for certain types of timber sales. The plaintiffs maintained that they would have participated in public hearings for these types of timber sales had there been any, but that alone was not a cognizable injury. If, however, they had been able to establish that a particular member enjoyed the area involved in a specific timber sale, then they could have challenged the failure to provide for a public hearing on that timber sale.

The Court's statements that procedural violations do not constitute injury for standing purposes have not distinguished procedural violations in adjudicatory proceedings from other procedural violations. However, at least two circuits have made a distinction, finding that a party to an adjudication deprived of a procedural right suffers injury for standing purposes without regard to whether the agency action resulting from the adjudication would

---

22. *See id.* at 572-73 & n.8.
23. 555 U.S. 488 (2009).

injure the party's concrete interests. The D.C. Circuit in *Electric Power Supply Ass'n v. FERC*[24] found that parties or intervenors in a FERC adjudicatory proceeding were provided a right to "fair decisionmaking" by the APA, such that a violation of the APA's prohibition on ex parte communications would constitute injury for standing purposes without having to determine whether FERC's decision would injure the concrete interests of the party or intervenor. The Ninth Circuit in *Portland Audubon Soc. v. Endangered Species Committee*[25] similarly held that an intervenor in a formal adjudication had standing to challenge a procedural violation simply because it was a participant in the proceeding. Of course, normally a party or intervenor in an adjudicatory proceeding will have a concrete interest in the outcome of the proceeding, in which case there would be no question that the person would have standing to challenge the outcome of the proceeding on procedural as well as substantive grounds.

Ordinarily, as will be discussed in more detail below, even if one can show injury, one must also show that the injury was fairly traceable to the defendant and that a favorable court decision will likely redress or avoid the injury. In the case of claimed procedural violations, however, the Court has allowed that the same requirements for redressability do not apply.[26] It would usually be impossible to show that if the agency had indeed followed the right procedures, the outcome would likely have favored the plaintiff. For example, in *Earth Island Institute* one could not say that the agency would not have approved the timber sales if only it had provided a public hearing. Rather, it suffices that it is *possible* that there could be a different outcome, more favorable to the plaintiffs, if the correct procedures were followed.[27]

The Court has recognized in certain circumstances that denial of access to documents or information can constitute injury for purposes of standing. Although the Court has never directly addressed standing in a Freedom of Information Act (FOIA)[28] case, it has in passing said that its FOIA cases "have never suggested that those requesting information under it need show more than that they sought and were denied specific agency records."[29] Presumably, the FOIA creates a right to obtain public records so that a denial of that right is an injury to a concrete interest, rather than the denial of a proce-

---

24. 391 F.3d 1255, 1262 (D.C. Cir. 2004).
25. 984 F.2d 1534, 1537 & n.4 (9th Cir. 1993).
26. *See Defenders of Wildlife*, 504 U.S. at 572 n.7.
27. *See* Massachusetts v. EPA, 549 U.S. 497, 518 (2007).
28. 5 U.S.C. § 552.
29. Public Citizen v. U.S. Dep't of Justice, 491 U.S. 440, 449 (1989).

dural right. After all, the Court has said that Congress can by statute create a legal right, the violation of which creates standing, even though there would have been no injury in the absence of the statute.[30] By extension, the Court has also said that persons seeking access to meetings and records of federal advisory committees have standing to enforce the requirements of the Federal Advisory Committee Act[31] that meetings be open and the committees' documents be available to the public.[32] Although standing has not been discussed, courts, including the Supreme Court, have routinely heard cases challenging agencies' failure to open meetings as required by the Government in the Sunshine Act. Again, presumably, the statute may be read as creating a statutory right to attend meetings of the agency, the denial of which constitutes a concrete injury for standing purposes. What is not explained is why the APA does not similarly create a statutory right to participate in agency rulemakings, the denial of which would constitute a concrete injury for standing purposes, but *Summers v. Earth Island Institute* says it does not.

2.0213 Generalized Grievances vs. Harm to Informational Rights and Other Broadly Shared Interests

A "generalized grievance" is not injury sufficient to confer standing. Thus, harm to the general interest shared by all citizens in the government conforming its conduct to law is not a judicially cognizable injury. Accordingly, a statute purporting to allow "any person" to challenge agency action cannot authorize a suit by a plaintiff without some distinct, constitutionally cognizable injury. However, a person who suffers a concrete, particularized harm does satisfy the injury requirement even though many other persons do or could suffer the same harm. Statutes can create and/or protect broadly shared interests, harm to which can constitutionally support standing. For example, individual voters can vindicate a concrete, though widely shared, right to election finance information required by statute to be made public. Similarly, an individual denied access to government information or to an agency meeting has standing to challenge the

---

30. *See, e.g.*, Warth v. Seldin, 422 U.S. 490, 514 (1975); Linda R.S. v. Richard D., 410 U.S. 614, 617 n.3 (1973).
31. 5 U.S.C. §§ 10(a), (b).
32. *Public Citizen*, 491 U.S. at 449.

denial, even though all citizens have an identical right of access. The widely shared injury, while satisfying constitutional standing requirements, may raise prudential standing concerns.
[Blackletter Statement, Part 4, § IV.B.1.c.]

The requirement for a concrete, particularized injury precludes standing for a generalized grievance, a grievance that is not particular to the individual and not concrete. For example, attempts to challenge the presence of reserve officers in Congress[33] or the failure to make public the CIA's budget[34] were dismissed for lack of standing. The claims were described as involving interests held in common by all members of the public and as having a "necessarily abstract nature."[35] Moreover, Congress's ability to create rights the violation of which creates injury for purposes of standing does not extend to statutes that in essence purport to allow any person to enforce the law. Thus, in *Lujan v. Defenders of Wildlife*,[36] notwithstanding that the Endangered Species Act provided that "any person" could sue to enforce its provisions, the Court held that only persons who would suffer concrete, particularized injuries could sue under that act.

Distinguishing "generalized grievances" from cognizable injuries that are suffered by a large number of persons is not always easy. When Public Citizen sued the Department of Justice alleging that the Justice Department's use of the ABA's Standing Committee on the Federal Judiciary for advice on potential judicial nominees violated the Federal Advisory Committee Act, the Justice Department argued that Public Citizen had suffered no concrete injury and was asserting only a general grievance.[37] The Court, however, rejected that argument. It noted that Public Citizen sought access to meetings and records of the Committee and that its requests had been refused. This was a sufficiently distinct injury to confer standing. It said: "[t]he fact that other citizens or groups of citizens might make the same complaint after unsuccessfully demanding disclosure under FACA does not lessen appellants' asserted injury."[38] Similarly, in *Federal Election Commission v. Akins*,[39] the Court upheld the ability of persons to challenge the FEC's denial of a request to list the American Israel Public Affairs Committee (AIPAC) as a "political com-

33. Schlesinger v. Reservists Committee to Stop the War, 418 U.S. 208 (1974).
34. United States v. Richardson, 418 U.S. 166 (1974).
35. *Id.* at 220.
36. 504 U.S. 555 (1992).
37. *Public Citizen*, 491 U.S. at 448-449.
38. *Id.* at 449.
39. 524 U.S. 11 (1998).

mittee" as allegedly required by the Federal Election Campaign Act. The claimed injury was the inability of the plaintiffs to obtain the information that AIPAC would have been required to supply to the FEC and that the FEC would have been required to make available to the public. The government argued that this was not a concrete, particularized injury but merely a generalized grievance of the type the Court had rejected in the past. The Court responded:

> The kind of judicial language to which the FEC points, however, invariably appears in cases where the harm at issue is not only widely shared, but is also of an abstract and indefinite nature—for example, harm to the "common concern for obedience to law." . . . Often the fact that an interest is abstract and the fact that it is widely shared go hand in hand. But their association is not invariable, and where a harm is concrete, though widely shared, the Court has found "injury in fact."[40]

Consequently, the Court concluded that "the informational injury" at issue here, directly related to voting, the most basic of political rights, is sufficiently concrete and specific that the fact that it is widely shared does not deprive Congress of constitutional power to authorize its vindication in the federal courts.[41]

There is a tension between "informational injury" as a basis for standing and the inability of a procedural violation to satisfy the injury requirement for standing. For example, in *Wilderness Society, Inc. v. Rey*,[42] an environmental group challenged a Forest Service regulation that excluded certain agency decisions from a requirement in the Forest Service Decisionmaking and Appeals Reform Act (ARA) to provide public notice of and an opportunity to comment on agency decisions. Among other things, the group claimed that its injury was the inability to obtain information about upcoming timber sales because the agency would not provide notice of the sales. The Ninth Circuit rejected that claim. It acknowledged *Akins* but distinguished it on the grounds that in *Akins* the Federal Election Campaign Act had provided an

---

40. *Id.* at 23-24.
41. *Id.* at 24-25. *See also* Massachusetts v. EPA, 549 U.S. 497, 522 (2007) (allowing challenge to failure to regulate greenhouse gases even though impacts of climate change will be widely—indeed, universally—felt, since the petitioner's injury (loss of its coastline) was particular to it).
42. 622 F.3d 1251 (9th Cir. 2010).

explicit right to sue the FEC for any violation of the Act, whereas the ARA did not. The Wilderness Society had sued under the APA. Moreover, the court noted that, were such a claim of informational injury acceptable, it would in essence overrule the Supreme Court's decision that procedural violations are not injuries for standing purposes, because most procedural violations result in some deprivation of information.[43] In *Bensman v. U.S. Forest Service*,[44] the Seventh Circuit reached the same conclusion.

This tension is most notable in National Environmental Policy Act (NEPA) cases alleging that agencies have failed to produce an environmental assessment (EA) or environmental impact statement (EIS), both of which are required to be made public. The Supreme Court, however, has told us more than once that NEPA is a procedural statute,[45] and in *Defenders of Wildlife* the Court used a NEPA example to illustrate how a procedural violation can be the basis of a lawsuit when the agency decision resulting from the defective procedure injures a concrete interest.[46] Nevertheless, a person claiming informational injury in not being able to obtain the information that would have been generated by the EA or EIS might be able to challenge an agency's failure to produce an EA or EIS without having to show any concrete injury as a result of the agency action beyond the inability to obtain the information. Indeed, the Seventh Circuit, in *Heartwood, Inc. v. U.S. Forest Service*,[47] found "compelling" the plaintiffs' claim that they suffered injury in fact in not having information from an EA that would be necessary to monitor agency activity.[48] Similarly, in *American Canoe Ass'n, Inc. v. City of Louisa Water and Sewer Comm'n,*[49] the Sixth Circuit held that environmental groups had standing to sue a publicly owned treatment works for violating its Clean Water Act permit because of the informational injury resulting from the defendant's inaccurate reporting of its discharges. The court said:

> This might be a "generalized grievance" in the sense that up to the point they request it, the plaintiffs have an interest in the information shared by every other person, but it is not an abstract grievance in the sense condemned in *Akins*: the injury alleged is not that the

43. *See id.* at 1257-60.
44. 408 F.3d 945 (7th Cir. 2005).
45. *See, e.g.*, DOT v. Public Citizen, 541 U.S. 752, 756 (2004).
46. *See Defenders of Wildlife*, 504 U.S. at 572 n.7.
47. 230 F.3d 947 (7th Cir. 2000).
48. *Id.* at 952 n.5.
49. 389 F.3d 536 (6th Cir. 2004).

> defendants are merely failing to obey the law, it is that they are disobeying the law in failing to provide information that the plaintiffs desire and allegedly need.[50]

Again, if plaintiffs need only allege informational injury to sue to enforce Clean Water Act permit requirements, there would be no need for them to show that their "concrete" interests in using the waters for fishing, boating, or swimming were affected.

While the synthesis is not perfect, the later cases—those decided after *Earth Island Institute*—seem to suggest that only if a statute specifically provides for information to be made available to the public, and if the statute provides a specific cause of action to sue to obtain that information, informational injury can be a basis for standing. The earlier cases—those decided before *Earth Island Institute*—have been more forgiving.

As indicated above, concrete, particularized injuries that are widely shared are still injuries for purposes of constitutional standing. However, the Court has indicated that as a prudential matter it might deny standing where the injury is widely shared. This "judicially self-imposed limit[] on the exercise of federal jurisdiction,"[51] is "founded in concern about the proper—and properly limited—role of the courts in a democratic society,"[52] but "unlike their constitutional counterparts, [the prudential limitations] can be modified or abrogated by Congress."[53] In cases brought under the APA, if a plaintiff satisfies the requirements of Section 702, the plaintiff will have overcome any prudential limitation.[54] For further discussion of prudential standing, see § 2.04, below.

On occasion, members of Congress, groups of Congressmen, or a house of Congress have sought to challenge statutes or executive action, asserting that they have standing by virtue of their positions.[55] Their argument has been that the statute or action caused a type of institutional injury (the diminution of legislative power), which necessarily damaged all Members and both Houses of Congress. In *Raines v. Byrd*, the Court rejected this argument when the complaint was simply that the law or action was unconstitutional or unlawful, finding that the members did not suffer individual concrete injury

50. *Id.* at 545-46.
51. Allen v. Wright, 468 U.S. 737, 751 (1984).
52. Warth v. Seldin, 422 U.S. 490, 498 (1975).
53. *See* Bennett v. Spear, 520 U.S. 154, 162 (1997).
54. *See Akins*, 524 U.S. at 19-20.
55. *See, e.g.*, Bowsher v. Synar, 478 U.S. 714 (1986); United States v. Windsor, 133 S. Ct. 2675 (2013) (BiPartisan Legal Advisory Group sought to appeal decision finding Section 3 of the Defense of Marriage Act unconstitutional).

in their capacity as Members of Congress.[56] Rather they, like other citizens, were simply upset with what they believed to be unlawful or unconstitutional action. If, however, the challenged action actually interferes with legislative prerogatives, then they may have concrete injury. For example, in *Immigration and Naturalization Service v. Chadha*,[57] the Court allowed the House and the Senate to intervene to defend the one-house veto provision under attack. In that case, declaring the one-house veto provision unconstitutional would have directly affected the powers of the House and the Senate; therefore, the Senate and the House were at risk of suffering concrete injuries.[58]

The Supreme Court has been inconsistent with respect to whether members of Congress or either house may intervene to defend the constitutionality of a statute whenever the executive branch will not. In *Chadha,* the Court categorically declared, "[w]e have long held that Congress is the proper party to defend the validity of a statute when an agency of government, as a defendant charged with enforcing the statute, agrees with plaintiffs that the statute is inapplicable or unconstitutional."[59] This broad statement, however, is subject to some doubt as to its application outside the context of *Chadha*, where the power of individual houses of Congress to take an action—the legislative veto—was subject to review. The statement is also suspect as authority because neither of the two cases on which it relied for this assertion of a broad congressional power to litigate provides *any* support for it.[60] In the first case, *Cheng Fan Kwok*, neither Congress, either house, nor any member appeared in the case as a party or *amicus*, nor did the case involve a claimed invalidity of a statute which an agency refused to defend. Instead, the Court appointed counsel as *amicus* to argue a position on the proper interpretation of a statute because the government would not defend the court of appeals decision. The second case, *Lovett*, did involve the validity of a statute that the government would not defend, but Congress appeared by counsel as an *amicus* and the Court did not hold that Congress was a proper *party*. Indeed, the Court distinguished between Congress and the parties.[61]

56. 521 U.S. 811 (1997) (members of Congress challenged the Line Item Veto Act).
57. 462 U.S. 919 (1983).
58. *See also* Coleman v. Miller, 307 U.S. 433, 438 (1939) (state legislators had standing to contest the nullification of their votes not to ratify the Child Labor Amendment).
59. *Chadha*, 462 U.S. at 940.
60. Cheng Fan Kwok v. INS, 392 U.S. 206, 210 n.9 (1968); United States v. Lovett, 328 U.S. 303 (1946).
61. *See Lovett*, 328 U.S. at 307 ("In this Court the parties and counsel for Congress have urged the same points as they did in the Court of Claims.").

Most recently, in *United States v. Windsor*,[62] the plaintiff brought an action against the United States challenging the constitutionality of the Defense of Marriage Act (DOMA). Although it technically remained a party to the case, the United States, acting through the executive branch, declined to defend the constitutionality of the statute. After receiving notice of the executive branch's position, the House of Representatives authorized its Bipartisan Legal Advisory Group (BLAG) to intervene to defend DOMA. The majority did not reach the question of whether BLAG had standing; three of the four dissenters said that BLAG did not, while Justice Alito opined that it did.[63] All that can be said for sure is that it is entirely appropriate to accept arguments made as *amici curiae* by Congress, either House, or members when there is a case that otherwise satisfies the requirements of Article III.

2.0214 Risk as Injury

The extent to which risk of harm can constitute injury for standing purposes is not clear. On the one hand, the Supreme Court has denied standing to an organization to sue on behalf of its members when it did not show that a *specific* member was threatened with an imminent concrete harm, even though it was virtually certain that *some* member would suffer a concrete harm in the foreseeable future. On the other hand, the Court found standing on behalf of organic alfalfa farmers to challenge the deregulation of genetically modified alfalfa because of the significant risk that the lack of regulation would lead to contamination of the farmers' crops. The fact that the farmers had already undertaken activities and expended funds to avoid the risk was apparently important to the Court's conclusion. In yet a third case, the Court dismissed a claim by persons challenging the constitutionality of a statute authorizing certain government electronic surveillance because it was not "certainly impending" that they would be subject to it, even though there was clearly a significant risk that they would be. The lower courts' decisions regarding risk as injury are in tension, with the D.C. Circuit holding that for increased risk to support standing there must be both (i) a substantial increase in the risk of harm and (ii) a

62. 133 S. Ct. 2675 (2013).
63. *See id.* at 2688, 2703-05, 2711-14.

substantial probability of actual harm with that increase taken into account. Other circuits have generally been more receptive to considering any significant increase in risk of physical harm as sufficient cognizable injury.

[Blackletter Statement, Part 4, § IV.B.1.d.]

If the risk of injury is so great that the injury is "imminent" or "certainly impending," then the ultimate injury would satisfy standing requirements without consideration of whether increased risk is itself injury. Contracting cancer is clearly injury, as is suffering from an automobile accident, but if EPA does not regulate as strictly as it might to prevent some pollution or the National Highway Traffic Safety Administration (NHTSA) does not regulate as strictly as it might to ensure the safety of automobiles, persons may face an increased risk of contracting cancer or suffering from an accident, but neither the cancer nor the accident would qualify as imminent or certainly impending. The question, therefore, is whether being exposed to something that increases your risk of cancer or your risk of being in an automobile accident, for example, is itself injury for purposes of standing.

At least as early as 1978, the First Circuit found standing based on risk of injury.[64] Prison inmates challenged the constitutionality of the conditions under which they were housed, in particular the fact that the prison was a fire hazard. The court rejected a challenge to the prisoners' standing, saying:

> plaintiff inmates have a personal stake in the fire-worthiness of the structure in which they are housed. Defendant Hall inaptly construes the requirement of injury as requiring proof that the inmates inevitably will suffer physical injury or death from fire before they have standing to challenge the hazardous fire conditions . . . . We find this proposition to fall far below contemporary expectations of constitutionally-mandated humane treatment. One need not wait for the conflagration before concluding that a real and present threat exists.[65]

In 1993, in *Village of Elk Grove Village v. Evans,*[66] the Seventh Circuit also found that an action that increased the risk of harm was sufficient to constitute injury. The Corps of Engineers had granted a permit to site a radio tower in a flood plain, and the town said that it incurred expenses when there was a flood and building the radio tower in the flood plain would exacerbate

---

64. Dimarzo v. Cahill, 575 F.2d 15 (1st Cir. 1978).
65. *Id.* at 18.
66. 997 F.2d 328 (7th Cir. 1993) (Posner, J.).

any flood, thereby increasing the costs to the town of dealing with the flooding. The court acknowledged that the risk was probabilistic but concluded that "even a small probability of injury is sufficient to create a case or controversy—to take a suit out of the category of the hypothetical—provided of course that the relief sought would, if granted, reduce the probability."[67] Subsequently, a number of cases in the circuits found increased risk sufficient injury for standing purposes.[68]

The courts of appeals were not unanimous, however. For example, *Shain v. Veneman*[69] was a challenge to the siting of two sewage retention ponds in a hundred-year floodplain. The plaintiffs alleged that in the event of a hundred-year flood the presence of the ponds would result in displacement of flood waters onto their property, which was adjacent to and downstream from the ponds. The court found that they did not have standing. Their claimed injury was not "imminent," because it was a matter of sheer speculation when a hundred-year flood would occur. Moreover, the court said the allegations were vague and conclusory because they did not make clear "whether the

---

67. *Id.* at 329.
68. *See* Natural Res. Def. Council, Inc. v. U.S. Food & Drug Admin., 710 F.3d 71 (2d Cir. 2013) (finding standing where a member of organization was frequently exposed to the potentially dangerous product); Baur v. Veneman, 352 F.3d 625 (2d Cir. 2003) (deciding that in the context of food and drug safety suits enhanced risk is sufficient for standing purposes if the plaintiff alleges exposure to potentially harmful products); Friends of the Earth, Inc. v. Gaston Copper Recycling, Corp., 204 F.3d 149, 160 (4th Cir. 2000) (en banc) (concluding that "[t]hreats or increased risk constitutes cognizable harm" sufficient to meet the injury-in-fact requirement); Central Delta Water Agency v. United States, 306 F.3d 938, 947-48 (9th Cir. 2002) (holding that "the possibility of future injury may be sufficient to confer standing on plaintiffs" and concluding that plaintiffs could proceed with their suit where they "raised a material question of fact . . . [as to] whether they will suffer a substantial risk of harm as a result of [the government's] policies"); Johnson v. Allsteel, Inc., 259 F.3d 885, 888 (7th Cir. 2001) (holding that the "increased risk that a plan participant faces" as a result of an ERISA plan administrator's increase in discretionary authority satisfies Article III injury-in-fact requirements); Walters v. Edgar, 163 F.3d 430, 434 (7th Cir.1998) (reasoning that "[a] probabilistic harm, if nontrivial, can support standing"); Mountain States Legal Found. v. Glickman, 92 F.3d 1228, 1234-35 (D.C. Cir. 1996) (recognizing that an incremental increase in the risk of forest fires caused by the Forest Service's action satisfied Article III standing requirements).
69. 376 F.3d 815 (8th Cir. 2004).

marginal rise in the water level will move in the direction of the plaintiffs' land, reach the property, and cause cognizable harm which would not have occurred absent the lagoons."[70] The court distinguished *Village of Elk Grove*, saying that there the flood plain was a common flood plain, not a hundred-year flood plain, which regularly imposed costs on the city. It was not clear, the court said, that the plaintiffs in *Shain* even would be alive or own the property when or if there was a flood that the ponds might affect. Despite the court's distinction, its decision was not in line with existing precedents that looked to increased risk of injury, not the likelihood that the injury would take place within a foreseen timeframe.

The D.C. Circuit in particular seemed to step back from its earlier easy acceptance of increased risk as injury. First, in a case where an environmental group had challenged EPA's regulation of ozone-depleting chemicals as being too lax, allegedly causing an increased risk to the group's members of contracting skin cancer, the court said:

> "[W]ere all purely speculative 'increased risks' deemed injurious, the entire requirement of 'actual or imminent injury' would be rendered moot, because all hypothesized, nonimminent 'injuries' could be dressed up as 'increased risk of future injury.'" We therefore generally require that petitioners demonstrate a "substantial probability" that they will be injured.[71]

The court initially characterized as "miniscule" the alleged more than ten deaths, more than 2,000 non-fatal skin cancer cases, and more than 700 cataract cases over 145 years.[72] On rehearing, however, the court decided that the figures showed that, because EPA's action allegedly created a 1 in 200,000 increased risk of contracting non-fatal skin cancer, two to four members of the environmental group could be expected to contract a non-fatal skin cancer as a result of EPA's action, and this was a sufficient increased risk to establish standing.

Two years later the D.C. Circuit denied standing to Public Citizen, which was trying to challenge a NHTSA standard for tire pressure monitoring systems as being insufficiently protective.[73] Public Citizen could not establish

---

70. *Id.* at 818.
71. Natural Res. Def. Council v. EPA, 464 F.3d 1, 6 (D.C. Cir. 2006).
72. Natural Res. Def. Council v. EPA, 440 F.3d 476, 481 (D.C. Cir. 2006), *vacated on rehearing*, 464 F.3d 1 (D.C. Cir. 2006).
73. Public Citizen, Inc. v. Nat'l Highway Traffic Safety Admin., 513 F.3d 234 (D.C. Cir. 2008).

any reliable probability as to how many of its members would be involved in automobile crashes as a result of the failure to adopt a stricter rule. In other words, notwithstanding a conceded increased risk to an organization's members, unless an organization can provide reliable estimates of the extent of the increased risk caused by a government action, it may not be able to establish standing based upon that increased risk, at least in the D.C. Circuit.

Then the Supreme Court began to be heard from. The first case addressing probabilistic injury was *Summers v. Earth Island Institute*.[74] Earlier this case was mentioned as confirming that procedural violations were not themselves injury for standing purposes. Because the environmental plaintiffs could not point to a particular forest where timber sales would be made without prior notice and comment, they could not establish that they used those forests for recreational purposes in order to establish a concrete injury from timber harvesting. Nevertheless, it was argued that because the various environmental groups that were plaintiffs had hundreds of thousands of members, and the Forest Service admitted that it would make hundreds of timber sales without providing prior notice and comment, it was virtually certain that some member of one of the organizations would use for recreational purposes one of the forests in which timber sales would occur. This argument was met with derision. Writing for the Court, Justice Scalia stated that the plaintiffs' "hitherto unheard-of-test for organizational standing"—that "there is a statistical probability that some of [its] members are threatened with concrete injury"[75]—conflicted with the Court's cases that "required plaintiffs claiming an organizational standing to identify members who have suffered the requisite harm."[76] In the context of the argument made in *Earth Island Institute*, the Court's characterization of the argument as "hitherto unheard-of" may be accurate. No one had claimed that an unknown member of an organization might happen to engage in an activity that would lead to concrete harm. However, the language the Court used could be read to apply to a number of situations in which lower courts had found increased risk—or, stated otherwise, "a statistical probability" of injury to some of the organization's members—as sufficient for standing. For example, in National Reources Defense Council (NRDC)'s challenge to EPA's regulation of ozone-depleting chemicals, it could hardly identify the members who would contract the non-fatal skin cancer, but even the D.C. Circuit had accepted standing based upon a finding that a person's increased risk of contracting the non-

74. 555 U.S. 488 (2009).
75. *Id.* at 497.
76. *Id.* at 499.

fatal skin cancer was 1 in 200,000, or that 2 to 4 members of the organization would likely do so. Of course, if the "concrete harm" was not contracting the cancer but being exposed to the increased risk, then NRDC *could* identify the members threatened with the concrete injury—i.e., all of its members—and the concrete harm would be suffered imminently.

The following year, in *Monsanto Co. v. Geertson Seed Farms*,[77] the Court unanimously found standing for organic alfalfa farmers challenging the Department of Agriculture's deregulation of genetically modified (GM) alfalfa because the deregulation would result in a "reasonable probability" that their organic alfalfa crops would be infected with the GM alfalfa. This "substantial risk" of gene flow would injure them, because they would face increased costs to test their alfalfa to ensure that it was not infected and to take measures to protect against infection.[78] Thus, a year after dissing probabilistic injury, the Court in a rare unanimous standing decision accepted standing based upon a reasonable probability or a substantial risk. Of course, *Monsanto* is distinguishable from *Earth Island Institute*. The specific farmers at risk were named plaintiffs, as opposed to the unknown members of the environmental organizations who might be at risk. Moreover, the risk to the specific plaintiffs was deemed substantial, and there was a reasonable probability that the specific plaintiffs would be harmed. Finally, the risk was substantial enough to justify the plaintiffs taking preventative and mitigating measures to avoid or minimize the risk, and the cost of those measures constituted current actual injury.

Most recently, however, a claim that seemed to be modeled after *Monsanto*'s analysis was found insufficient to establish standing. *Clapper v. Amnesty International USA*[79] involved a challenge to the constitutionality of a provision of the Foreign Intelligence Surveillance Act (FISA) that authorizes the National Security Agency to target foreigners outside the United States who might be communicating with someone in the United States. The plaintiffs included U.S. citizens in the United States who were attorneys who represented either terrorists abroad or their families and reporters who often spoke to foreigners abroad who were knowledgeable about terrorist organizations and activities. They maintained and the court of appeals found that there was a "reasonable probability" that their communications would be intercepted pursuant to the FISA provision. Moreover, because of their allegedly well-founded fear of having their communications intercepted, the plain-

77. 561 U.S. 139 (2010).
78. *Id.* at 153-54.
79. 133 S. Ct. 1138 (2013).

tiffs alleged that they suffered present injury in that they must undertake expensive measures, such as traveling abroad to communicate with their clients or sources, in lieu of using electronic means of communication.

The Court rejected plaintiffs' standing by a 5-4 vote. Justice Alito (the author of *Monsanto*) wrote for the Court. He concluded that the plaintiffs' claims of injury were not "certainly impending," because any interception pursuant to FISA would involve too many intervening steps. First, the government would have to target someone the plaintiffs communicated with. Second, NSA would have to use the FISA provision as authority, although there allegedly were other authorities that might be used instead. Third, even if NSA did use the FISA provision, it would have to obtain approval from the Foreign Intelligence Surveillance Court, which might be denied. Fourth, even if the surveillance was authorized by the court, NSA would have to successfully intercept the communications sought. Fifth, even if NSA successfully intercepted the communications sought, they might not involve the plaintiffs' communications. Finally, the Court dismissed the claimed current injury of having to take costly measures to avoid being intercepted, saying plaintiffs "cannot manufacture standing merely by inflicting harm on themselves based on their fears of hypothetical future harm that is not certainly impending."[80] The Court distinguished *Monsanto* on the grounds that in that case there was factual evidence that GM alfalfa was being planted "in all the major alfalfa seed production areas" and that "bees that pollinate alfalfa have a range of at least two to ten miles and the alfalfa seed farms were concentrated in an area well within the bees' pollination range."[81] In *Clapper*, however, the plaintiffs presented "no concrete evidence to substantiate their fears, but instead rest[ed] on mere conjecture about possible governmental actions."[82]

The *Clapper* opinion acknowledged that the Court has not always invoked a requirement that the claimed injury be "certainly impending." The Court said:

> Our cases do not uniformly require plaintiffs to demonstrate that it is literally certain that the harms they identify will come about. In some instances, we have found standing based on a "substantial risk" that the harm will occur, which may prompt plaintiffs to reasonably incur costs to mitigate or avoid that harm. But to the extent that the "substantial risk" standard is relevant and is distinct from the "clearly impending" requirement, respondents fall short of even that stan-

---

80. *Id.* at 1151.
81. *Id.* at 1153-1154.
82. *Id.* at 1154.

> dard, in light of the attenuated chain of inferences necessary to find harm here. In addition, plaintiffs bear the burden of pleading and proving concrete facts showing that the defendant's actual action has caused the substantial risk of harm. Plaintiffs cannot rely on speculation about "the unfettered choices made by independent actors not before the court."[83]

One might reasonably question whether the likelihood of bees spreading GM alfalfa pollen to organic alfalfa farms was any greater than the likelihood of NSA intercepting the plaintiffs' communications with known terrorists and their families. Two factors distinguish *Clapper* from the more common risk case. First, as suggested by the preceding block quotation, normally there are not a series of independent actors whose choices are unknown. More like the bees in *Monsanto*, the risks are scientifically predictable (within a greater or lesser range perhaps) as a result of clearly impending action—in *Monsanto* the deregulation of GM alfalfa and in EPA or NHTSA cases, for example, an agency regulation that predictably will cause a risk of disease or injury. Second, in *Clapper* the Court emphasized that its "standing inquiry has been especially rigorous when reaching the merits of the dispute would force us to decide whether an action taken by one of the other two branches of the Federal Government was unconstitutional,"[84] and that it has "often found a lack of standing in cases in which the Judiciary has been requested to review actions of the political branches in the fields of intelligence gathering and foreign affairs."[85] While it is predictable that the government will cite *Clapper*'s "certainly impending" requirement in future cases, the noted distinctions may well defeat a rigorous application of this requirement.

While not strictly a "risk" case, *Friends of the Earth, Inc. v. Laidlaw Environmental Services, Inc.*[86] is often cited in discussion of such cases. In *Laidlaw*, persons living near a river sued Laidlaw under the Clean Water Act's citizen suit provision, seeking an injunction against its continued discharge of mercury in violation of its Clean Water Act permit. Because there was no evidence of harm to the environment from Laidlaw's discharges, Laidlaw argued that the plaintiffs lacked standing. The Court, however, said that the plaintiffs had a "reasonable fear" of using the river for recreational purposes in light of the defendant's continuous and pervasive illegal discharges of pollutants into the river. Neither the Supreme Court nor lower

83. *Id.* at 1150 n.5.
84. *Id.* at 1147.
85. *Id.*
86. 528 U.S. 167 (2000).

courts subsequently have quantified or provided any test for when a fear is reasonable. Nevertheless, for the fear to be reasonable it would seem that the risk must be significant to some degree. Accordingly, some cases that might be litigated on the basis of risk to the plaintiffs may instead be litigated on the basis of the reasonable fear suffered by the plaintiffs.[87]

2.0215 Taxpayer Standing

In general, a taxpayer does not suffer cognizable injury because the federal government spends money in a manner objectionable to the taxpayer. The one limited exception involves federal appropriations for religious purposes. Although the doctrinal basis for this exception has been undermined over the years, the foundational decision has continuously been distinguished rather than overruled.

[Blackletter Statement, Part 4, § IV.B.1.e.]

In 1923, in *Frothingham v. Mellon,*[88] the Supreme Court held that a federal taxpayer does not have standing to challenge a federal statute because it results in the unconstitutional expenditure of tax dollars. With one exception, the rule that a taxpayer does not suffer a cognizable injury from the unlawful or unconstitutional use or expenditure of federal funds continues today. The one exception was carved out in *Flast v. Cohen*[89] at the height of the Warren Court's activism. In *Flast,* taxpayers sued to enjoin the expenditure of federal funds for use in religious schools to teach reading, arithmetic, and other subjects and for the purchase of textbooks for use in those schools. Chief Justice Earl Warren, writing for the Court, said that the question of standing "does not, by its own force, raise separation of powers problems related to improper judicial interference in areas committed to other branches of the Federal Government."[90] Instead, it "is related only to whether the dispute sought to be adjudicated will be presented in an adversary context and in a form historically viewed as capable of judicial resolution."[91] The Court, therefore, found no absolute bar to taxpayer standing, but it required that the federal taxpayer must have "the personal stake and interest that impart the necessary concrete adverseness to

---

87. *See, e.g.*, Friends of the Earth, Inc. v. Gaston Copper Recycling Corp., 204 F.3d 149 (4th Cir. 2000).
88. 262 U.S. 447 (1923).
89. 392 U.S. 83 (1968).
90. *Id.* at 95.
91. *Id.* at 101.

such litigation."[92] In the case of an Establishment Clause challenge to federal spending, the Court said that requirement was satisfied because the taxpayer was challenging action under the Taxing and Spending Clause, and the challenge was based upon a specific constitutional limitation.

Subsequent cases, however, have not followed *Flast*'s analysis; indeed, they have expressly rejected it, concluding that standing is essentially a question of separation of powers.[93] The spending of dollars from the Treasury does not create concrete injury to a taxpayer; after all, expenditures and tax receipts generally have little relation to one another. Moreover, a favorable court decision would not change the taxpayer's taxes. To date, the Court has not overruled *Flast*, despite calls from some justices to do so,[94] but it has limited it to its specific facts—taxpayer Establishment Clause challenges to federal expenditures authorized by legislation.[95]

The Court in earlier cases accepted that if a taxpayer could show an actual, good-faith out-of-pocket connection between the taxes he paid and the government expenditure, then he could meet the requirements for standing.[96] The Court has found such injuries only with respect to certain municipal expenditures.[97]

---

92. *Id.*
93. *See, e.g.*, Clapper v. Amnesty International USA, 133 S. Ct. 1138, 1146-47 (2013).
94. *See, e.g.*, Arizona Christian School Tuition Org. v. Winn, 131 S. Ct. 1436, 1450 (2011) (Scalia, J., concurring).
95. *See* Hein v. Freedom From Religion Foundation, Inc., 551 U.S. 587 (2007) (finding no standing for taxpayers to bring Establishment Clause challenge against federal agency's use of federal money from general appropriations to fund conferences to promote President's "faith-based initiatives"); Valley Forge Christian College v. Americans United for Separation of Church and State, Inc., 454 U.S. 464 (1982) (finding no standing for taxpayers to challenge on Establishment Clause grounds the federal donation of land pursuant to Property Clause to a religious institution). The Court has extended the general bar on taxpayer standing to apply to state taxpayers as well. *See* Arizona Christian School Tuition Org. v. Winn, 131 S. Ct. 1436 (2011) (finding no standing for taxpayers to bring Establishment Clause challenge against Arizona law granting dollar-for-dollar tax credit to persons who donate to school tuition organizations that provide scholarships to students attending private schools, many of which are religious); DaimlerChrysler Corp. v. Cuno, 547 U.S. 332 (2006) (finding no standing for state taxpayers to challenge Ohio franchise tax credit).
96. *See* Doremus v. Board of Ed. of Borough of Hawthorne, 342 U.S. 429, 434-435 (1952). *See also* Massachusetts v. Mellon, 262 U.S. 447, 486-487 (1923).
97. *See* Crampton v. Zabriskie, 101 U.S. 601 (1879).

2.022 Causation and Redressability

The constitutional requirements of *causation* and *redressability*—often together referred to as "nexus"—ensure that there is at least a reasonable probability that the plaintiff's injury was caused by the defendant and will be remedied by the relief requested from the court.

Although stated as distinct requirements, causation and redressability are typically analysed in tandem because it is rare that one exists without the other. However, if the court's remedial options are limited by statute or other law, the injury may indeed be traceable to the defendant's action, but not redressable by the available remedies. For example, a plaintiff who has suffered an environmental injury caused by the defendant will be denied standing on redressability grounds where the wrongdoing had ceased before the suit was filed, the plaintiff cannot demonstrate a reasonable likelihood that it will recur, and the only statutory remedies are prospective injunctive relief and civil penalties payable to the government.

Analysis of causation and redressability tends to be very fact specific, and in general there is no ready formula for predicting when a court will conclude that the causal chain has become too uncertain or attenuated. Cases attempting to challenge either favorable tax treatment of a third party or decisions not to prosecute appear to follow a pattern of dismissal on the basis of an absence of either causation or redressability.

Whether causation and redressability exist can be highly dependent upon how the injury is defined. For example, if the harm to a plaintiff challenging an affirmative-action program is defined as not obtaining the relevant position or contract, the plaintiff will rarely have standing, since almost never would a particular disappointed applicant be able to show it would have obtained the benefit but for the challenged program. However, the Court instead defines the injury in such cases as a lack of opportunity to compete for the desired outcome according to permissible criteria, a definition that eliminates problems of causation or redressability.

A similar definitional issue is posed by the suggestion, advanced by some judges, that complaints by regulatory beneficiaries categorically present difficult causation and redressability

problems not faced by regulated entities. For example, it has been argued that consumers who can satisfy the particularized injury requirement and wish to challenge an agency's failure to adopt more rigorous fuel economy standards for automobiles must also show that if a more demanding rule were adopted, manufacturers would change their designs rather than pay noncompliance penalties. Because the standard for redressability is only that the favorable court decision would "likely" redress (or avoid) the injury, the plaintiff should have to show only that it is likely that the manufacturer will comply with the law.

Complaints about procedural violations provide another example. If the injury is defined as the actual agency decision, the plaintiff will normally not satisfy standard nexus requirements, since it will be possible, even likely, that the agency could have reached, and on remand will reach, the same outcome even following proper procedures. The Court, however, has made clear that when the alleged violation is procedural, the normal standards for redressability do not apply. It suffices if the procedures exist to protect a concrete interest of the plaintiff and a favorable outcome on the merits will be possible if the correct procedures are followed.

Redressability issues can also arise under citizen suit provisions that provide only injunctive relief and payment of civil penalties to the government when the complained-of action has ceased after filing of the action, making an injunction inappropriate. While arguably, paying civil penalties to the government does not redress the injury to the citizen plaintiff, the Court has said that such penalties deter future violations and therefore satisfy the redressability requirement.

[Blackletter Statement, Part 4, § IV.B.2.]

Causation and redressability are the two additional constitutional requirements for standing in addition to injury. The canonical requirement for "causation" is a showing that the injury is "fairly traceable" to the actions of the defendant.[98] For "redressability" it is a showing that the plaintiff's injury is "likely," not "merely speculative," to be redressed or avoided by a favorable

98. *See, e.g.*, *Clapper*, 133 S. Ct. at 1147.

court ruling.[99] The burden is on the plaintiff initially to allege, and ultimately to provide evidence of, the facts necessary to meet these requirements.

Causation and redressability are usually different sides of the same coin. If the defendant's actions will cause injury, then usually an injunction not to engage in the action will redress (avoid) that injury. Indeed, the failure to satisfy the causation requirement will almost invariably mean there would be a failure to satisfy the redressability requirement. For example, in *Eastern Kentucky Welfare Rights Org. v. Simon* (*EKWRO*),[100] a welfare rights organization sued the Internal Revenue Service for granting tax-exempt status to hospitals that refused to treat poor patients without charge. The Court found that the group failed to show either that the injury (its members' inability to obtain free treatment at a particular hospital) was fairly traceable to the hospital's tax treatment or that a favorable court decision would likely redress the injury, because the hospital might well choose to pay the tax and not treat indigents for free rather than avoid the tax and have to treat them for free. Sometimes courts find a lack of causation when they equally could find a lack of redressability and vice versa.

As indicated in the *Blackletter Statement*, what is characterized as the injury can be critical. For example, challenges to affirmative action programs are usually brought by someone who did not qualify for affirmative action and who did not get a contract, a job, or admission to a university. If the claimed injury is the failure to get the contract, job, or admission, it would normally be very difficult to show that it was the affirmative action program that was the cause of the injury or that setting aside the affirmative action program would result in the plaintiff getting the contract, job, or admission. These plaintiffs have standing, however, because the Court has characterized the injury as being denied the ability to compete on an equal basis.[101] *That* injury is caused by the challenged program and would be redressed by its elimination.

The Court has said on several occasions that it is more difficult for persons to show causation and redressability when their injury is the direct result of actions taken by someone not before the court.[102] This is often the case when the claim is that an agency has not regulated or not regulated sufficiently, and

---

99. *See, e.g.*, Sprint Communications Co. v. APCC Services, Inc., 554 U.S. 269, 273 (2008).

100. 426 U.S. 26 (1976).

101. *See, e.g.*, Gratz v. Bollinger, 539 U.S 244, 262 (2003); Northeastern Florida Chapter of Associated General Contractors of America v. City of Jacksonville, Fla., 508 U.S. 656 (1993).

the claim is brought by a person who would benefit by that government regulation. The *EKWRO* case mentioned above is a good example. There the claimed injury was the inability of poor people to receive free treatment from a particular hospital, but it was the IRS whose action (or inaction) the plaintiffs were challenging. It was not clear that the hospital's failure to treat poor people for free was fairly traceable to the IRS's non-enforcement of its requirements for charitable hospitals. Moreover, there was no evidence that the hospital, if faced with the need to treat indigents for free in order to retain its tax exemption, would in fact choose to treat the indigents rather than forgo its tax exemption. Similarly, in *Warth v. Seldin*,[103] the Court found that plaintiffs had failed to show causation when they claimed that a town's zoning laws effectively excluded poor and minority persons from living in the town, but they failed to show that their "inability to locate suitable housing in the town reasonably [could] be said to have resulted, in any concretely demonstrable way, from the town's alleged constitutional and statutory infractions."[104] Earlier, under the consideration of procedural violations and injury, it was noted that the Court has said that when the claimed violation is procedural, a plaintiff does not need to meet "all the normal standards for redressability and immediacy."[105] In *Defenders of Wildlife*, the Court gave this example:

> [O]ne living adjacent to the site for proposed construction of a federally licensed dam has standing to challenge the licensing agency's failure to prepare an environmental impact statement, even though he cannot establish with any certainty that the statement will cause the license to be withheld or altered, and even though the dam will not be completed for many years.[106]

---

102. *See, e.g.*, Lujan v. Defenders of Wildlife, 504 U.S. 555, 562 (1992); Warth v. Seldin, 422 U.S. 490, 505 (1975).
103. 422 U.S. 490 (1975).
104. *Id.* at 504.
105. *Defenders of Wildlife*, 504 U.S. at 572 n.7.
106. *Id.* The Court says nothing here about causation, although it would be no less difficult or impossible to show that the concrete injury—the flooding of the plaintiff's land—was fairly traceable to the failure to prepare an environmental impact statement (EIS) than it would to show that a court decision requiring the agency to prepare an EIS would be likely to avoid the injury. However, the concrete injury would be fairly traceable to the government action of licensing the dam, which would be unlawful action because of the failure to prepare the EIS. That is, in assessing causation, one asks not whether the procedural violation causes the injury but whether the challenged conduct causes the injury. Here the challenged conduct is the licensing of the dam, even though the violation is the failure to prepare the EIS.

The Court has not identified what standards substitute for the "normal standards," other than that a favorable court decision ordering the required procedures *could* result in an outcome that would redress (or avoid) the concrete injury.

Most citizen suit provisions in environmental laws do not provide for damages; they provide for injunctive relief and civil penalties to be paid to the United States. If the unlawful polluting action has ceased before the complaint is filed, an injunction would not lie, and civil penalties paid to the United States would not redress any past injury suffered by the plaintiff, such as not being able to use a polluted river for recreation.[107] However, if the unlawful polluting continues after the complaint is filed, then, even if injunctive relief is not appropriate but the case is not moot, perhaps because after the complaint was filed the defendant voluntarily ceased the offending activity, civil penalties paid to the United States have been held to provide redressability. The theory explained in *Friends of the Earth, Inc. v. Laidlaw Environmental Services*[108] was "that the penalties would redress [the plaintiffs'] injuries by abating current violations and preventing future ones."[109]

The requirement that a favorable court decision redress the plaintiff's injury, either through future avoidance of the injury or compensation for its past effects, does not require *total* redress. All that is required is that the injury be alleviated in some way. For example, in *Massachusetts v. EPA*,[110] a favorable court decision might require EPA to restrict carbon dioxide pollution from new automobiles but its effect on sea rise, the injury suffered by Massachusetts, would be minimal, although positive. Nevertheless, this was enough redress to provide standing.[111] This principle had been accepted law in the lower courts prior to *Massachusetts v. EPA*.[112]

2.03 ASSOCIATIONAL STANDING

An association has standing in its own right if it satisfies the above constitutional tests. In addition, an association has standing to sue on behalf of its members when (a) one or more identi-

---

107. *See* Steel Co. v. Citizens for a Better Environment, 523 U.S. 83, 103-09 (1998).
108. 528 U.S. 167, 185-88 (2000).
109. *Id.* at 187.
110. 549 U.S. 497 (2007).
111. *Id.* at 526.
112. *See, e.g.*, Public Interest Research Group of New Jersey, Inc. v. Powell Duffryn Terminals Inc., 913 F.2d 64 (3d Cir. 1990).

fied members would have standing to sue in their own right; (b) the interests it seeks to protect are germane to the organization's purpose; and (c) neither the claim asserted nor the relief requested requires the participation of individual members in the lawsuit. The second of these criteria is construed very leniently. The third effectively limits associations suing on behalf of their members to declaratory or injunctive relief, because if the redress required the payment of monetary damages, the persons to whom the damages would be paid would have to be parties themselves.

[Blackletter Statement, Part 4, § IV.C.]

An association, like any other legal entity, may sue to protect its interests if it satisfies the requirements for standing.[113] An association may also sue as a representative of its members if it meets a three-part test for standing.[114] This is called variously "associational standing," "organizational standing," or "representational standing." First, the association must have a member who would have standing on his own behalf; in cases brought by associations this is what courts focus on. Second, "the interests it seeks to protect" must be "germane to the organization's purpose."[115] Problems in meeting this requirement are few and far between, as invariably a lawsuit an organization wishes to take the time and resources to bring relates to its interests. There are apparently no federal cases denying standing for failure to meet this requirement. Third, "neither the claim asserted nor the relief requested [can] require[] the participation of individual members in the lawsuit."[116] As a practical matter this means that the action must be for declaratory or injunctive relief, because the effect of an injunction or declaratory judgment will redress (or avoid) the injury suffered by the organization's members without their being named plaintiffs. An action for damages, on the other hand, if successful, would result in the damages going to the named plaintiff—the organization—not to the members who actually suffered the injury. Consequently, damages paid to the organization would not redress the members' injury.

---

113. *See* Warth v. Seldin, 422 U.S. 490, 511 (1975); Nat'l Ass'n for Advancement of Colored People v. Button, 371 U.S. 415 (1963).

114. *See* Hunt v. Washington State Apple Advertising Comm'n, 432 U.S. 333, 343 (1977).

115. *Id.*

116. *Id.*

2.04 PRUDENTIAL STANDING REQUIREMENTS

Three judicially self-imposed "prudential" restrictions further limit standing beyond the constitutional minima. Congress may, by statute, override prudential restrictions on standing.

First, parties cannot raise claims or defenses that rest on a third party's legal rights (the *jus tertii* limitation). The *jus tertii* prohibition plays an important role in constitutional litigation but has not been very significant in limiting review of agency action under the APA or specific organic statutes. A litigant attempting to challenge government action on grounds that it violates the constitutional rights of a third party may be prohibited from doing so unless (1) the litigant has suffered an injury in fact; (2) the litigant and the third party stand in some close relationship; and (3) "some hindrance" impedes the third party's ability to assert her own rights.

Second, the plaintiff's interests must be within the "zone of interests" regulated or protected by the constitutional or statutory provision relied upon. In challenges to agency action, this requirement is subsumed under the APA requirements discussed in § IV.E.

Finally, the Court has sometimes stated that "generalized grievances" are precluded by prudential standing requirements. However, other cases have distinguished between "generalized grievances," which are not injuries for Article III purposes, and "widely shared" injuries, which satisfy Article III's standing requirement, but which perhaps should be left to the political process to rectify. Whenever Congress has created a cause of action that allowed persons suffering generalized grievances to sue, the Court has always held that the limitation was constitutional rather than prudential.

[Blackletter Statement, Part 4, § IV.D.]

Prudential standing, like other areas of the law created as a matter of judicial discretion, is not cabined by any statutory or constitutional text and consequently is subject to some fluctuation. Moreover, the word "standing" in the term, as in "statutory standing" discussed in § 2.05, has resulted in some confusion with Article III standing principles. In two recent cases, the Court has questioned the analytical underpinnings of prudential standing as a matter of judicial discretion. In *Lexmark International, Inc. v. Static Control*

Components, Inc.,[117] Justice Scalia wrote for a unanimous Court and discussed prudential standing at length. He introduced his discussion by saying that the concept of prudential standing is in tension with "our recent reaffirmation of the principle that 'a federal court's obligation to hear and decide' cases within its jurisdiction is virtually unflagging."[118] He nevertheless acknowledged that the Court had "adverted to a 'prudential' branch of standing" that encompassed "three broad principles: '"the general prohibition on a litigant's raising another person's legal rights, the rule barring adjudication of generalized grievances more appropriately addressed in the representative branches, and the requirement that a plaintiff's complaint fall within the zone of interests protected by the law invoked."'"[119] As to the last of these, which was claimed by the defendants in the case, he wrote:

> Although we admittedly have placed that test under the "prudential" rubric in the past, it does not belong there. . . . Whether a plaintiff comes within "the 'zone of interests'" is an issue that requires us to determine, using traditional tools of statutory interpretation, whether a legislatively conferred cause of action encompasses a particular plaintiff's claim.[120]

In a footnote, concededly dictum, Justice Scalia also disposed of prudential standing as related to generalized grievances, noting that recent cases have held that cases raising generalized grievances—suits "'claiming only harm to [the plaintiff's] and every citizen's interest in proper application of the Constitution and laws, and seeking relief that no more directly and tangibly benefits him than it does the public at large'"[121]—do not satisfy the Article III requirements for standing; prudence has nothing to do with it.[122] As for *jus tertii*, he noted that the Court had sometimes framed the issue as whether the plaintiff had a statutory cause of action and sometimes as a prudential question. Because the *Lexmark* case did not raise any third-party is-

117. 134 S. Ct. 1377, 1386-88 (2014).
118. *Id.* at 1386 (quoting Sprint Communications, Inc. v. Jacobs, 134 S. Ct. 584, 591 (2013) (quoting Colorado River Water Conservation Dist. v. United States, 424 U.S. 800, 817 (1976))).
119. *Id.*
120. *Id.* at 1387
121. Lujan v. Defenders of Wildlife, 504 U.S. 555, 573-574 (1992).
122. *See Lexmark*, 134 S. Ct. at 1387 n.3 (citing Lance v. Coffman, 549 U.S. 437, 439 (2007) (per curiam); DaimlerChrysler Corp. v. Cuno, 547 U.S. 332, 344-46 (2006); *Defenders of Wildlife*, 504 U.S. at 573-74).

sue, "consideration of that doctrine's proper place in the standing firmament can await another day."[123]

The above suggests that the doctrine of prudential standing is in flux. What follows is an iteration of the current law on the subject.

2.041 Jus Tertii

The Supreme Court has long maintained the presumption that as a matter of judicial discretion courts should not entertain suits by persons invoking the rights of another person.[124] In *Singleton v. Wulff*,[125] the Court explained:

> The reasons are two. First, the courts should not adjudicate such rights unnecessarily, and it may be that in fact the holders of those rights either do not wish to assert them, or will be able to enjoy them regardless of whether the in-court litigant is successful or not. Second, third parties themselves usually will be the best proponents of their own rights.[126]

As an initial matter, this issue almost never arises in the context of judicial review of agency action under the APA or a specific statute, because that review has been specifically authorized by statute, and the *jus tertii* limitation as a prudential limitation on the courts' jurisdiction can be overcome by legislative authorization. The issue in these cases is whether the person is within the zone of interests of the particular statute. Nevertheless, even in cases not authorized by statute, the Court has almost always found an exception to overcome the *jus tertii* limitation, such that the rule seems to be honored largely in the breach.[127]

The Supreme Court has enunciated a three-part test for overcoming the *jus tertii* limitation: (1) the litigant must have suffered an injury (or one must be imminent); (2) the litigant and the third party must stand in some close

---

123. *Id.*

124. *See, e.g.*, Barrows v. Jackson, 346 U.S. 249, 255 (1953).

125. 428 U.S. 106 (1976).

126. *Id.* at 113-14.

127. *See* Note, *Standing to Assert Constitutional* Jus Tertii, 88 HARV. L. REV. 423 (1973). While this Note is fairly old, its analysis is still valid. Still, in *Kowalski v. Tesmer*, 543 U.S. 125 (2004), the Court did dismiss claims on the basis of the *jus tertii* rule, and in *Miller v. Albright*, 523 U.S. 420, 445 (1998), two justices concurred in the judgment against the plaintiff on the basis of the *jus tertii* rule.

relationship; and (3) "some hindrance" must impede the third party's ability to assert her own rights.[128] The first requirement, injury to the litigant, is an element of Article III standing and therefore must be present in any case. However, the Court has not always specified or required the other two requirements, on occasion finding an exception to the prudential bar on third-party standing even though one or more of these requirements was not considered (or met in fact).[129]

The second requirement, that the litigant and the third party stand in some close relationship, is often present. In several cases, the doctor-patient relationship was deemed close enough for the doctor to assert the rights of the patient,[130] and in at least two cases, an attorney-client relationship was deemed close enough.[131] Indeed, in a substantial number of cases the idea of a "close relationship" has been strained to the breaking point or ignored altogether. Justice Thomas listed several instances in a concurrence calling for a reassessment of the Court's third-party standing doctrine:

> We have held, for instance, that beer vendors have standing to raise the rights of their prospective young male customers, see *Craig v. Boren*, 429 U.S. 190, 192-197 (1976); that criminal defendants have standing to raise the rights of jurors excluded from service, see *Powers v. Ohio*, 499 U.S. 400, 410-416 (1991); that sellers of mail-order contraceptives have standing to assert the rights of potential customers, see *Carey v. Population Services Int'l*, 431 U.S. 678, 682-684 (1977); that distributors of contraceptives to unmarried persons have standing to litigate the rights of the potential recipients, *Eisenstadt v. Baird*, 405 U.S. 438, 443-446 (1972); and that white sellers of land

---

128. Powers v. Ohio, 499 U.S. 400, 410-11 (1991). There are two separate areas of *jus tertii* law not addressed by the *Powers v. Ohio* test but which have their own distinct tests—the overbreadth doctrine under the First Amendment Freedom of Speech Clause and the inability of third parties to raise the Fourth Amendment claims of others in order to suppress evidence allegedly unlawfully seized. These two areas are beyond the scope of this chapter.
129. *See, e.g.*, Craig v. Boren, 429 U.S. 190, 194-96 (1976) (not discussing or considering any closeness of relationship between a vendor of beer and underage males wishing to purchase beer).
130. *See, e.g.,* Singleton v. Wulff, 428 U.S. 106 (1976).
131. *See* Caplin & Drysdale, Chartered v. United States, 491 U.S. 617 (1989); Dep't of Labor v. Triplett, 494 U.S. 715 (1990).

have standing to litigate the constitutional rights of potential black purchasers, see *Barrows v. Jackson*, 346 U.S. 249, 254-258 (1953).[132]

On the other hand, in *Kowalski v. Tesmer*,[133] the Court held that attorneys did not have a close enough relationship to prospective indigent clients to challenge a state law denying the appointment of appellate counsel following plea-based convictions.[134] The Court distinguished the cases finding attorney-client relationships sufficiently close on the ground that those cases involved an attorney with an *existing* client, not unknown, *possible* prospective clients.[135] This strict application of this requirement is unique, as Justice Thomas's list indicates.[136]

The third requirement is that "some hindrance" impedes the third party's ability to assert her own rights. In *Powers*, in which a criminal defendant challenged the exclusion of African-Americans from his jury by peremptory challenges, it was said that an individual juror so excluded would have a difficult time making a case and would have little incentive to bring a case.[137] Similarly, in *Singleton v. Wulff*, the Court said that a doctor could invoke a woman's right to obtain an abortion because "there are several obstacles" to a woman trying to assert her own rights.[138] One was a desire to protect her own privacy, and the other was the imminent mootness of the claim, but the Court acknowledged that both of these obstacles could be overcome.[139] In many, if not most, cases this requirement has simply been ignored or stretched in order to find an exception. For example, in *Craig v. Boren*, the Court ignored any requirement that there be some hindrance to men between the ages of 18 and 21 challenging the law restricting them but not similarly aged women

---

132. *Kowalski*, 543 U.S. at 134-35 (Thomas, J., concurring).
133. 543 U.S. 125 (2004).
134. *Id.* at 132.
135. *Id.*
136. The Court's uniquely strict application of both the "close relationship" and third-party hindrance requirements, *see* text accompanying note 142, *infra* (quoting the Court's treatment of the hindrance requirement), is probably explained by the fact that the lower court had found the indigent criminal defendants to be barred by Younger v. Harris, 401 U.S. 37 (1971), abstention, and the idea that the attorneys could make an end-run around this abstention doctrine by claiming third-party standing did not appeal to the Court.
137. *Powers*, 499 U.S. at 414-15.
138. *Singleton*, 428 U.S. at 117.
139. *Id.*

from buying 3.2% beer.[140] On the other hand, in *Kowalski v. Tesmer*,[141] the Court held that indigent criminal defendants did not suffer a hindrance in challenging a state law denying appointment of appellate counsel in plea-based convictions. "While we agree that an attorney would be valuable to a criminal defendant challenging the constitutionality of the scheme, we do not think that the lack of an attorney here is the type of hindrance necessary to allow another to assert the indigent defendants' rights."[142]

Although the Court often invokes one or more of the above requirements in passing on whether an exception to the *jus tertii* doctrine should apply, the Court seems more to be looking at the particular facts and circumstances in the case to answer two questions—whether the plaintiff's success would directly further the interests of the third party and whether the plaintiff will be at least as good an advocate for the right as the third party would be. The former question sometimes may be answered by a "close relationship" between the plaintiff and the third party, but as suggested by the number of cases where the exception was made but there was no "close relationship," the real issue is not the closeness of the relationship but the identity of interests, such that the plaintiff's success will equally redound to the benefit of the third party. Similarly, the latter question sometimes might be answered in the affirmative because of a hindrance to the third party bringing suit on her own behalf, but again the real issue is not the existence of a hindrance *per se* but the at least equal ability of the plaintiff to advocate for the third party's right.

2.042 The Zone-of-Interests Test

It is said that a second prudential limitation is that a person cannot invoke a statutory or constitutional right if he is not within the "zone of interests" regulated or protected by that right. Although the Court has on occasion made such a reference,[143] more recently it has affirmatively rejected the classification of the zone-of-interests test as a prudential limitation.[144] Instead, the zone-of-interests test simply requires a court "to determine, using traditional tools of statutory interpretation, whether a legislatively conferred cause of action encompasses a particular plaintiff's claim."[145] That requirement is discussed in § 2.05 below.

---

140. *Craig*, 429 U.S. at 194-97.
141. *Kowalski*, 543 U.S. at 131-33.
142. *Id.* at 132.
143. *See, e.g.*, Elk Grove Unified School Dist. v. Newdow, 542 U.S. 1, 12 (2004).
144. *See* Lexmark Int'l, Inc. v. Static Control Components, Inc., 134 S. Ct. 1377, 1387 (2014).
145. *Id.*

2.043 Generalized Grievances

Similarly, on occasion the Court has been unclear as to whether "generalized grievances" were precluded by Article III or by prudential limitations.[146] Again, however, the Court recently has been explicit that "generalized grievances" are not injuries for Article III standing purposes; "[t]hey are barred for constitutional reasons, not 'prudential' ones."[147]

2.044 Additional Judge-made Requirements: Ripeness and Adversity

Although the Blackletter Statement and the Court in *Lexmark* only refer to prudential standing based on the above three principles, there are at least two other principles that can be included in this group—one of longstanding and one recently re-articulated. The longstanding "prudential standing" principle is the requirement that a case be "ripe" for review.[148] In *Susan B. Anthony List v. Driehaus*,[149] the claim was that the case was not "ripe" for adjudication. Justice Thomas wrote for again a unanimous Court and reiterated that:

> To the extent respondents would have us deem petitioners' claims nonjusticiable "on grounds that are 'prudential,' rather than constitutional," "[t]hat request is in some tension with our recent reaffirmation of the principle that 'a federal court's obligation to hear and decide' cases within its jurisdiction 'is virtually unflagging.'"[150]

Because the case satisfied the established test for ripeness—fitness of the case for judicial decision and hardship to the parties by delaying review[151]—he concluded that "we need not resolve the continuing vitality of the prudential ripeness doctrine in this case."[152]

---

146. *See, e.g.*, Warth v. Seldin, 422 U.S. 490, 499 (1975).
147. *See Lexmark*, 134 S. Ct. at 1387 n.3.
148. It might be said that ripeness should not go to standing, because standing is about who may bring a case, while ripeness is about when a case may be brought. There is some merit to this argument, but that aspect of Article III standing that asks whether an injury is imminent is about timing, and ripeness, once Article III concerns are met, is clearly a "prudential" justiciability doctrine.
149. 134 S. Ct. 2334 (2014).
150. *Id.* at 2347 (quoting *Lexmark*, 134 S. Ct. at 1386 (quoting *Sprint Communications*, 134 S. Ct. at 591)).
151. *See, e.g.*, Abbott Laboratories v. Gardner, 387 U.S. 136 (1967).
152. *Susan B. Anthony List*, 134 S. Ct. at 2347.

The re-articulated prudential standing principle, which counsels dismissal in the absence of genuinely adverse parties, was recently addressed by Justice Kennedy, writing for a bare majority of the Court in *United States v. Windsor*.[153] Having found that the government had Article III standing to seek review of the court of appeals decision against it, notwithstanding the government's agreement with that court's decision, Justice Kennedy addressed whether as a matter of prudential standing the appeal should be dismissed for a lack of adverse parties.[154] He concluded that it should not for two reasons: first, the *amicus* presence of the Bipartisan Legal Advisory Group assured that there would be vigorous adversarial argument against the government and respondent; second, practical concerns resulting from the consequences of dismissing the case on prudential grounds weighed in favor of hearing the case.[155] Nevertheless, it cannot be denied that this discussion of prudential standing is in tension with the language and thrust of *Lexmark* and *Susan B. Anthony List*, inasmuch as Justice Kennedy introduced his discussion of prudential standing by referring to "'countervailing considerations [that] may outweigh the concerns underlying the usual reluctance to exert judicial power.'"[156] That is, he refers to "'a usual reluctance to exert judicial power,'" even when Article III concerns are met, whereas in both *Lexmark* and *Susan B. Anthony List* the unanimous Court refers to "a federal court's obligation to hear and decide cases within its jurisdiction '[being] virtually unflagging.'"[157] It should be noted that the four "liberals" who joined Justice Kennedy's opinion (Justices Breyer, Ginsburg, Sotomayor, and Kagan) are not usually known to agree with the idea that there is "a usual reluctance to exert judicial power."

2.05 STATUTORY STANDING

The general statutory standing requirement for review of agency action under the APA is codified in § 702, which provides that

153. 133 S. Ct. 2675 (2013). This particular form of prudential standing limitation was not unheard of before *Windsor;* in *Immigration and Naturalization Service v. Chadha*, a somewhat similar situation arose, and the Court stated, apparently in dictum, that "there may be prudential, as opposed to Art. III, concerns about sanctioning the adjudication of this case in the absence of any participant supporting the validity of the statute." 462 U.S. 919, 940 (1983).
154. 133 S. Ct. at 2687. Some would have thought, as did three of the dissenters, that the lack of adverse parties was an Article III consideration, not a prudential consideration.
155. *Id.* at 2687-88.
156. *Id.* at 2687 (quoting Warth v. Seldin, 422 U.S. 490, 500-501 (1975)).
157. *Lexmark*, 134 S. Ct. at 1386; *Susan B. Anthony List*, 134 S. Ct. at 2347.

"[a] person suffering legal wrong because of agency action, or adversely affected or aggrieved by agency action within the meaning of a relevant statute, is entitled to judicial review thereof." Although this language significantly broadened pre-APA availability of review to challenge agency action, it does not confer standing to the limits of what is constitutionally possible. In addition to showing that she has suffered a constitutionally cognizable injury caused by the agency's action, the plaintiff relying upon § 702 must show that her injury is "arguably within the zone of interests to be protected or regulated by the statute . . . in question."

Individual regulatory statutes may contain their own statutory standing provisions. Statutory language authorizing challenge by "any person aggrieved" has traditionally been interpreted to confer standing to the full extent of Article III, without regard to such prudential limitations as the zone-of-interests requirement. Citizen-suit provisions (e.g., those conferring standing on "any person" without further requirements) are usually given the same interpretation. Other kinds of statutory standing provisions are typically construed to incorporate the zone-of-interests test and other prudential requirements absent evidence of a different legislative intent.

[Blackletter Statement, Part 4, § IV.E.}

The term "statutory standing" has been used by the Court to address when a statute provides a right to sue. Most recently, however, the Court has said that this usage is misleading. The Court seems to have based this observation on the premise that characterizing a requirement in terms of "standing" suggests that it is a prerequisite for subject-matter jurisdiction—as is true for constitutional standing. This connection does not hold for what has been called "statutory standing" because "the absence of a valid (as opposed to arguable) cause of action does not implicate subject-matter jurisdiction, i.e., the court's statutory or constitutional power to adjudicate the case."[158] In other words, the only question presented by "statutory standing" is whether a statute provides the plaintiff with a cause of action.

The APA creates a cause of action in section 702 for persons suffering legal wrong or adversely affected or aggrieved within the meaning of a relevant statute. Persons who are subject to government regulation invariably

158. *Lexmark*, 134 S. Ct. at 1387 n.4 (quoting Verizon Md. Inc. v. Public Serv. Comm'n of Md., 535 U.S. 635, 642–643 (2002)).

satisfy the "suffering legal wrong" requirement, as the government regulation interferes with their liberty or property. The terms "adversely affected or aggrieved" come into play with respect to regulatory beneficiaries and persons who may be harmed by government regulation or support of another person, for example, companies harmed by government subsidization of their competitors. The phrase "adversely affected or aggrieved" has been interpreted by the Court as synonymous with being injured for purposes of standing.[159] Consequently, anyone satisfying the Article III standing requirements will have been "adversely affected or aggrieved."

Section 702 further requires, however, that the person seeking judicial review be adversely affected or aggrieved "within the meaning of a relevant statute." To determine whether this additional condition has been satisfied, the Court has applied a "zone of interests" test.[160] If the plaintiff is a person whom the statute was intended to protect, then it is clear that the person can challenge agency action under that statute that adversely affects him,[161] but the Supreme Court has extended the coverage of the zone of interests much more broadly. It has said that the "essential inquiry is whether Congress 'intended for [a particular] class [of plaintiffs] to be relied upon to challenge agency disregard of the law.'"[162] That is, even if Congress enacted a statute without intending to protect a particular class of plaintiffs, a member of that class will fall within the zone of interests protected by the statute as long as Congress intended this class to enforce the statute's provisions. In applying this test, the Court has not insisted that there be any legislative history to support a finding of such intent. Rather, the Court seems to intuit whether Congress would have wished a class of plaintiffs to be able to challenge the agency action in light of the policies underlying the act in question. Or stated another way, "if there is reason to believe that a party's interest in statutory enforcement will advance, rather than hinder, the operation of a statute, the court can reasonably assume that Congress intended to permit the suit."[163]

---

159. *See, e.g.*, Trafficante v. Metropolitan Life Ins. Co., 409 U.S. 205, 209 (1972) (interpreting "person aggrieved" as reaching the limits of Article III); Sierra Club v. Morton, 405 U.S. 727 (1972) ("adversely affected" the equivalent of injury for purposes of Article III standing).

160. *See, e.g.*, Barlow v. Collins, 397 U.S. 159, 164-65 (1970).

161. *See, e.g.*, *id.*

162. Clarke v. Securities Indus. Ass'n, 479 U.S. 388, 399 (1987) (quoting Block v. Cmty. Nutrition Inst., 467 U.S. 340, 347 (1984)).

163. Honeywell International, Inc. v. EPA, 374 F.3d 1363, 1370 (D.C. Cir. 2004), *opinion on another point withdrawn in part on reconsideration*, 393 F.3d 1315 (D.C. Cir. 2005).

For example, in *Clarke v. Securities Industry Ass'n*,[164] an association of securities brokers and dealers brought an action to challenge Treasury's approval of applications of two banks to open discount brokerage subsidiaries as violating the National Bank Act. The association's claim was that the Act's ban on national banks engaging in branch banking precluded the establishment of brokerage offices other than at a bank's principal place of business. The purpose of the anti-branch banking provision, as reflected in the Act's general purposes, was to keep national banks from gaining a monopoly control over credit and money through unlimited branching. Because the securities brokers and dealers would compete with these new bank-owned discount brokerage subsidiaries, the Court said they had an interest that had a "plausible relationship" to the policies of the act, to limit the branching activities of national banks.[165] "'Congress [has] arguably legislated against the competition that [respondent seeks] to challenge' by limiting the extent to which banks can engage in the discount brokerage business and hence limiting the competitive impact on nonbank discount brokerage houses."[166] This approach has been used in a number of cases where companies were found within the zone of interests of statutes intended to restrict their competitors, even though those statutes were not enacted to protect the interests of the companies.[167]

The Court has stressed that a person should be found to be within the zone of interests if the person is "arguably within the zone of interests"[168] and has stated more than once that the test "is not meant to be especially demanding,"[169] excluding only those whose interests are "so marginally related to or inconsistent with the purposes implicit in the statute that it cannot reasonably be assumed that Congress intended to permit the suit."[170] Consequently, the Court

---

164. 479 U.S. 388 (1987).
165. *Id.* at 403.
166. *Id.* (quoting Investment Company Institute v. Camp, 401 U.S. 617, 620 (1971)).
167. *See* Ass'n of Data Processing Service Orgs., Inc. v. Camp, 397 U.S. 150, 156 (1970); Arnold Tours, Inc. v. Camp, 400 U.S. 45, 46 (1970); Investment Co. Inst. v. Camp, 401 U.S. 617, 620 (1971); Clarke v. Securities Indus. Ass'n, 479 U.S. 388, 394-403 (1987); Nat'l Credit Union Admin. v. First Nat'l Bank & Trust Co., 522 U.S. 479, 487-500 (1998).
168. *See, e.g.*, Bennett v. Spear, 520 U.S. 154, 175 (1997); *Nat'l Credit Union Admin.*, 522 U.S. at 488.
169. Match-E-Be-Nash-She-Wish Band of Pottawatomi Indians v. Patchak, 132 S. Ct. 2199, 2210 (2012); *Clarke*, 479 U.S. at 399.
170. *Id.*

has rarely found persons not to be within the zone of interests for purposes of section 702.[171]

The D.C. Circuit has seemingly carved out an exception to this general tendency with regard to suits by companies complaining that their competitors are not regulated strictly enough under various environmental laws.[172] As the court explained in *Honeywell International Inc. v. E.P.A*,[173] these cases involve a type of challenge that has the potential for frustrating rather than furthering the operation of the statute because resolving them would require the court to assess the right level of regulatory strictness, or second-guess the agency's exercise of judgment.[174] By contrast, in the Supreme Court's competition cases, and in some of the D.C. Circuit's competition cases, the suit only required a court to say yes or no to the statutory authority of the agency, thus avoiding manipulation of agency discretion.

An issue that has divided the courts of appeal and about which the Supreme Court has issued conflicting opinions is whether the zone-of-interests test is jurisdictional and therefore cannot be waived by the defendant and can be raised by the court *sua sponte*.[175] In *Lexmark International, Inc. v. Static Control Components*,[176] the Court added dictum that appears to resolve the issue. After explaining that the zone-of-interests test speaks to whether a plaintiff has a cause of action, the Court noted the general principle that "the absence of a valid (as opposed to arguable) cause of action does not implicate subject matter jurisdiction."[177] Thus, at least where it is "arguable" that a plaintiff seeks to protect interests that are "arguably within the zone of interests," this test appears to be non-jurisdictional.

---

171. One case is Air Courier Conference of Am. v. Am. Postal Workers Union, AFL-CIO, 498 U.S. 517 (1991), in which the Court found that the postal workers union was not within the zone of interests of the law prohibiting private carriage of mail, where the Postal Service was allowing certain private carriage of mail, despite the accepted adverse effects on the union's membership from reducing the use of the Postal Service for carrying mail.
172. *See* Association of Battery Recyclers, Inc. v. EPA, 716 F.3d 667 (D.C. Cir. 2013); Cement Kiln Recycling Coal. v. EPA, 255 F.3d 855 (D.C. Cir.2001); Hazardous Waste Treatment Council, Inc. v. EPA, 861 F.2d 277, 282-86 (D.C. Cir. 1988) (per curiam).
173. 374 F.3d 1363, 1370-71 (D.C. Cir. 2004), *opinion on another point withdrawn in part on reconsideration*, 393 F.3d 1315 (D.C. Cir. 2005).
174. *See* Scheduled Airlines Traffic Offices v. Dep't of Defense, 87 F.3d 1356, 1360-61 (D.C. Cir.1996).
175. *See Ass'n of Battery Recyclers, Inc.*, 716 F.3d at 674 (Silberman, J., concurring) (discussing state of the law).
176. 134 S.Ct. 1377 (2014).
177. *Id.* at 1386 n.4 (citations omitted).

Chapter 3

JUDICIAL REVIEW OF STATUTORY ISSUES UNDER THE *CHEVRON* DOCTRINE

by Emily Hammond, Elizabeth Garrett, and M. Elizabeth Magill*

* Emily Hammond is Professor of Law, The George Washington University Law School; Elizabeth Garrett is President of Cornell University; and M. Elizabeth Magill is Dean and Richard E. Lang Professor of Law, Stanford Law School.

The authors thank research assistant Sam B. Guthrie, J.D., University of Virginia School of Law (2014).

3.01 INTRODUCTION

> **The court will set aside an agency action if it finds that the action exceeds the authority granted, or violates limitations imposed, by a federal statute.**
>
> **APA § 706(2)(C)**

Agencies must operate within the confines of statutory limitations. This bedrock principle places fidelity to statutes at the core of administrative legitimacy, and is embodied in the Administrative Procedure Act (APA). In particular, § 706(2)(C) provides that reviewing courts are to "hold unlawful and set aside agency action . . . found to be . . . in excess of statutory jurisdiction, authority, or limitations, or short of statutory right."[1] As a result, agencies' actions are frequently challenged on the ground that their actions are inconsistent with a relevant statute.

Outside of the administrative law context, courts vigorously guard their authority to "say what the law is."[2] That is, they typically interpret statutes *de novo*. Under longstanding administrative law principles, however, courts often afford some deference to agencies' interpretations of their statutory mandates. The modern embodiment of this deference is found in *Chevron, U.S.A., Inc. v. Natural Resources Defense Council*,[3] which has become the most-cited and most-discussed decision in administrative law.

Under *Chevron*, when agencies act with the force of law in interpreting

---

1. 5 U.S.C. § 706(2)(C).
2. Marbury v. Madison, 5 U.S. (1 Cranch) 137, 177 (1803).
3. 467 U.S. 837 (1984). For symposium treatment of *Chevron* at thirty, see generally 83 FORDHAM L. REV. (forthcoming 2014).

their statutory mandates, judicial review follows a two-step process.[4] At "step one," courts ask whether Congress expressly addressed the matter. If so, the analysis ends and Congress's choice prevails.[5] If not, the court proceeds to "step two," in which it upholds the agency's construction if the agency has adopted a permissible interpretation of the statute.[6] This chapter is devoted to the meaning and application of the *Chevron* decision. This part addresses rationales for the *Chevron* approach and conceptual understandings of what a *Chevron* analysis should entail. Part 3.02 addresses step one of *Chevron*, and Part 3.03 addresses step two.

3.011 The *Chevron* Decision

Prior to *Chevron*, courts often afforded some level of deference to agencies' interpretations of their statutory mandates,[7] but there was no systematic method for doing so. Generally, there is consensus in the literature that the *Chevron* Court did not mean to depart substantially from previously accepted principles of judicial review of administrative agencies. [8] Indeed, Justice John

---

4. Chapter 4, *infra*, discusses when *Chevron* does and does not apply. An empirical study of Supreme Court decisions between 1983 and 2005 in which agency interpretation of a statute was at issue reported that the Court applied *Chevron* in only 8.3% of those opinions. William N. Eskridge, Jr. & Lauren E. Baer, *The Continuum of Deference: Supreme Court Treatment of Agency Statutory Interpretations from* Chevron *to* Hamdan, 96 GEO. L.J. 1083, 1090 (2008). Other issues of *Chevron*'s applicability are sometimes referred to as presenting a "step zero," involving, for example, a determination whether the agency has acted with the force of law, United States v. Mead Corp., 533 U.S. 218 (2001). *See* Cass R. Sunstein, Chevron*'s Step Zero*, 92 VA. L. REV. 187 (2006) (describing step zero).
5. *Chevron*, 467 U.S. at 842-43.
6. *Id.* at 843.
7. *See id.* at 844 n.14 (collecting sources).
8. *See, e.g.*, Jack M. Beermann, *End the Failed* Chevron *Experiment Now: How* Chevron *Has Failed and Why It Can and Should Be Overruled*, 42 CONN. L. REV. 779, 782 (2010); Gary Lawson & Stephen Kam, *Making Law Out of Nothing At All: The Origins of the* Chevron *Doctrine*, 65 ADMIN. L. REV. 1, 33 (2013) ("As far as statutory interpretation doctrine was concerned, all of the parties and Justices seemed to view the *Chevron* case as an application of well-settled law."); Peter L. Strauss, *"Deference" Is Too Confusing—Let's Call Them* "Chevron *Space" and* "Skidmore *Weight*," 112 COLUM. L. REV. 1143, 1161 (2012) (noting "the Court was . . . unaware of the turmoil its unanimous decision in *Chevron* would stir up").

Paul Stevens—the author of *Chevron*—has noted that he did not think the *Chevron* case did anything more than simply follow "really pretty well-settled law."[9] But the case's two-step process and broad language mandating deference in the face of ambiguous statutory language quickly became a doctrine, and it generated significant attention, criticism, and ongoing debate about its justifications. Part of *Chevron*'s allure and durability can be attributed to its apparently straightforward methodology—though that appearance is misleading.

In *Chevron*, the petitioners challenged Environmental Protection Agency (EPA) regulations promulgated under the Clean Air Act (CAA). Those regulations interpreted the term "stationary source" in the CAA to include not just a single emissions point but an entire facility.[10] Under this "bubble" policy, a plant could install or modify a single piece of equipment without triggering certain stringent requirements, provided the change did not increase the plant's total emissions given offsetting reductions elsewhere at the facility.[11] The Court upheld the agency's interpretation, setting forth as it did so the now-familiar two-step test:

> First, always, is the question whether Congress has directly spoken to the precise question at issue. If the intent of Congress is clear, that is the end of the matter; for the court, as well as the agency, must give effect to the unambiguously expressed intent of Congress. If, however, the court determines Congress has not directly addressed the precise question at issue, the court does not simply impose its own construction on the statute, as would be necessary in the absence of an administrative interpretation. Rather, if the statute is silent or ambiguous with respect to the specific issue, the question for the court is whether the agency's answer is based on a permissible construction of the statute.[12]

According to *Chevron*'s reasoning, if a statute does not resolve the question, Congress has implicitly delegated that question to the agency.[13] In that setting, a court "may not substitute its own construction of a statutory provision for a reasonable interpretation made by the administrator of an agency."[14]

---

9. John Paul Stevens & Linda Greenhouse, *A Conversation with Justice Stevens*, 30 Yale L. & Pol'y Rev. 303, 315 (2012).
10. 467 U.S. at 840.
11. *Id.*
12. *Id.* at 842-43 (footnotes omitted).
13. *Id.* at 844-45.
14. *Id.* at 844.

Thus, the *Chevron* Court defined the reviewing court's role to be less extensive than not only the traditional one of saying what the law is, but also the role apparently envisioned in the APA, which provides that "the reviewing court shall decide all relevant questions of law, [and] interpret . . . statutory provisions."[15] Instead, *Chevron* instructed that in the context of regulatory statutes, silence or ambiguity triggers judicial deference to reasonable agency interpretations of the statute.[16] Thus, *Chevron* has significant institutional implications, shaping the relationship among the branches of government and serving as a kind of "counter-*Marbury* for the administrative state."[17]

There is no single widely accepted rationale for *Chevron*. In addition to characterizing statutory ambiguities as implicit delegations by Congress, the Court justified deference on two additional grounds: agency expertise[18] and the superior democratic accountability of agencies as compared to courts.[19] As commentators have gained familiarity with the doctrine, they have developed a variety of theories supporting deference, including: (1) the doctrine embodies a constitutional norm that counsels judicial deference as a matter of Article III values;[20] (2) deference is rooted in matters of comparative institu-

15. 5 U.S.C. § 706.

16. *See* Thomas W. Merrill & Kristin E. Hickman, Chevron*'s Domain*, 89 Geo. L.J. 833, 833-34 (2001) (explaining that by expanding the zone of mandatory deference, *Chevron* "effected a fundamental transformation in the relationship between courts and agencies").

17. *See* Cass R. Sunstein, *Law and Administration After* Chevron, 90 Colum. L. Rev. 2071, 2074 (1990) ("This principle [of deference to reasonable agency interpretations] is quite jarring to those who recall the suggestion, found in *Marbury v. Madison* . . . , that it is for judges, and no one else, to 'say what the law is.'") (quoting *Marbury v. Madison*, 5 U.S. (1 Cranch) 137, 177 (1803)); *see also* Cynthia R. Farina, *Statutory Interpretation and the Balance of Power in the Administrative State*, 89 Colum. L. Rev. 452 (1989) (discussing separation-of-powers implications of *Chevron*); Jonathan T. Molot, *The Judicial Perspective in the Administrative State: Reconciling Modern Doctrines of Deference with the Judiciary's Structural Role*, 53 Stan. L. Rev. 1 (2000) (arguing that *Chevron* is inconsistent with the Founders' view of the appropriate judicial role in statutory interpretation).

18. 467 U.S. at 844-45.

19. *Id.* at 865-66; *see also* FDA v. Brown & Williamson Tobacco Corp., 529 U.S. 120, 132 (2000). In more recent cases, the Court has described *Chevron* as based on a congressional directive rather than a judge-made rule. *See, e.g.*, United States v. Mead Corp., 533 U.S. 218 (2001).

20. Mark Seidenfeld, Chevron*'s Foundation*, 86 Notre Dame L. Rev. 273 (2011) (Article III values).

tional competence as between courts and agencies; (3) by delegating to agencies authority to act with the force of law, Congress has allocated interpretive authority between institutions;[21] and/or (4) agencies possess superior democratic accountability relative to courts.[22]

Just as there is there is no general consensus as to *Chevron*'s proper justification, so there is no general consensus as to how *Chevron* should operate. Although the case continues to be the most-cited in administrative law, courts and scholars have yet to agree on answers even to such basic questions as what analysis is properly undertaken in each step. For these reasons, as well as its apparent malleability,[23] it can be difficult to predict how a particular court will approach a *Chevron* analysis. Most of these issues are taken up in Parts 3.02 and 3.03 below. First, however, one particular conceptual debate—the question whether *Chevron* is more properly understood as having only one step—is detailed below.

3.012 Just One Step?

Some commentators and even, on occasion, the Supreme Court have expressed the view that *Chevron* is comprised of only one step.[24] The judi-

---

21. John F. Duffy, *Administrative Common Law in Judicial Review*, 77 Tex. L. Rev. 113, 199-203 (1998) (delegation); E. Donald Elliott, Chevron *Matters: How the* Chevron *Doctrine Redefined the Roles of Congress, Courts and Agencies in Environmental Law*, 16 Vill. Envtl. L.J 1, 14 (2005) (contending it is an "executive function for an agency, acting under presidential supervision, to answer statutory questions left open by Congress."); Elizabeth Garrett, *Legislating* Chevron, 101 Mich. L. Rev. 2637 (2003) (discussing institutional aspects of *Chevron* and the importance of congressional delegation); Merrill & Hickman, *supra* note 16, at 878 (allocations of authority).
22. John F. Manning, *Constitutional Structure and Judicial Deference to Agency Interpretations of Agency Rules*, 96 Colum. L. Rev. 612, 617 (1996) (grounding *Chevron* in presumed congressional preference that politically accountable agencies make policy rather than reviewing courts).
23. Thomas J. Miles & Cass R. Sunstein, *Do Judges Make Regulatory Policy? An Empirical Investigation of* Chevron, 73 U. Chi. L. Rev. 823, 832-34 (2006) (presenting results of study revealing that conservative Justices were more likely to validate conservative agency interpretations, while liberal Justices were more likely to validate liberal agency interpretations).
24. The practice was documented early in the post-*Chevron* years. Orin S. Kerr, *Shedding Light on* Chevron*: An Empirical Study of the* Chevron *Doctrine in the U.S. Courts of Appeals*, 15 Yale J. on Reg. 1, 30 (1998) (observing that 28% of courts of appeals decisions in 1995-96 "condensed the two-step test into a single question of whether the interpretation was 'reasonable'").

cial approach typically follows the formulation of Justice Scalia's majority opinion in *Entergy Corp. v. Riverkeeper*: "[The agency's] view governs if it is a reasonable interpretation of the statute—not necessarily the only possible interpretation, nor even the interpretation deemed *most* reasonable by the courts."[25] As further explained, if the law is clear, "any agency interpretation contradicting what Congress has said would be unreasonable."[26] In *Entergy Corp.*, the Court's approach blurred the traditional two steps: it reviewed the statutory text, other sections in the same statute, and the statutory structure, before offering an analysis that demonstrated why the agency's approach was reasonable.[27]

Courts of appeals have begun to explicitly follow this approach. In *Northern Natural Gas Co. v. Federal Energy Regulatory Commission*, the D.C. Circuit stated that it would review Federal Energy Regulatory Commission's statutory interpretation "for reasonableness under the familiar standard of *Chevron*, which as specified in *Entergy Corp. v. Riverkeeper*, means (within its domain) that a 'reasonable agency interpretation prevails.'"[28] By this method, the court concluded that "[t]he Commission's interpretation is fully consistent with the obvious meaning of the statute."[29] The Ninth Circuit made a similar pronouncement in *Gila River Indian Community v. United States*: "We defer to the agency's interpretation as long as it is a reasonable one. The Supreme Court has clarified that where an agency interpretation is reasonable, courts may invoke *Chevron* step two at the outset to uphold the agency decision."[30]

On the other hand, the Supreme Court and the lower courts continue to follow the two-step formulation in the majority of cases.[31] In *City of Arlington v. FCC*, for example, Justice Scalia's majority opinion clearly ref-

---

25. 556 U.S. 208, 218 (2009).
26. *Id.* at 218 n.4.
27. *Id.* at 218-26; *see also* Cuomo v. Clearing House Ass'n, 557 U.S. 519 (2009) (not expressly emphasizing one-step approach, but analytically demonstrating that method).
28. 700 F.3d 11, 14 (D.C. Cir. 2012) (citations omitted).
29. *Id.*
30. Gila River Indian Cmty. v. United States, 697 F.3d 886, 895 (9th Cir. 2012) (citing *Entergy Corp.*, 556 U.S. at 218) (citations omitted).
31. *See, e.g.*, Astrue v. Capato *ex rel.* B.N.C., 132 S. Ct. 2021 (2012); Mayo Found. for Med. Educ. & Research v. United States, 131 S. Ct. 704, 705 (2011); White Stallion Energy Ctr., LLC v. E.P.A., 748 F.3d 1222, 1234 (D.C. Cir. 2014).

erenced *Chevron*'s two steps.[32] This formulation was of interest because Justice Scalia has argued that *Chevron* is best understood as consisting of only one step. For example, in *United States v. Home Concrete & Supply, LLC*, Justice Scalia's concurring opinion emphasized that "'Step 1' has never been an essential part of *Chevron* analysis. Whether a particular statute is ambiguous makes no difference if the interpretation adopted by the agency is clearly reasonable—and it would be a waste of time to conduct that inquiry."[33]

Although these inconsistencies in *Chevron*'s verbal formulation can seem confusing, a close look at what the courts are doing sheds light on the appropriate analytical method. Moreover, this analysis can be used to understand another of *Chevron*'s analytical puzzles: how to conduct the step-two analysis. Consider the approach in *Holder v. Martinez Guitierrez*, in which Justice Kagan's opinion for a unanimous Court stated that the agency's position "prevails if it is a reasonable construction of the statute, whether or not it is the only possible interpretation or even the one a court might think best."[34] The Court then considered the agency's interpretation in light of the statutory text, definitions, history, and context.[35] *Holder* thus follows an approach similar to that of *Entergy Corp.* It compares the agency's interpretation to the statutory language, asking whether the interpretation is foreclosed by the statute and relying on "traditional tools" of statutory construction to do so. As discussed in more detail below,[36] this approach revitalizes *Chevron*'s direction to consider the "precise question," and uses the challenged interpretation itself to define what that question is. Thus, although the test is formulated differently, the analysis is consistent with step one.

Next, both *Holder* and *Entergy* examined the reasonableness of the agency's interpretation. This approach considers whether the agency reasonably chose an interpretation from the spectrum of options available to it under the statute.[37] As numerous scholars have noted—and as recently endorsed by the Supreme Court—this analysis is best viewed as an application of the arbitrary-and-capricious standard.[38] Moreover, it is consistent with a

---

32. 133 S. Ct. 1863, 1868 (2013).
33. 132 S. Ct. 1836, 1846 n.1 (2012) (citation omitted).
34. 132 S. Ct. 2011, 2017 (2012) (citations omitted).
35. *Id.* at 2017-19.
36. *See infra* Part 3.021.
37. *See* Gary Lawson, *Reconceptualizing* Chevron *and Discretion: A Comment on Levin and Rubin*, 72 Chi.-Kent L. Rev. 1377, 1378-79 (1997).
38. *See infra* Part 3.032.

robust approach to step two, which is described in more detail below.[39]

Scholars have heavily influenced the one-step debate; two of the leading viewpoints further clarify the *Chevron* analysis. First, Matthew Stephenson and Adrian Vermeule have reasoned that if an agency's construction is contrary to the clear statutory language, then, *a fortiori*, it is not permissible.[40] As they further explain, *Chevron*'s departure from the view that only courts say what the law is—to one that shares judicial authority for statutory interpretation with agencies—means that "interpretation is an exercise in identifying the statute's range of reasonable interpretations, a range that opens up a 'policy space' within which agencies may make reasoned choices."[41] They frame the one-step approach to *Chevron* as an inquiry into interpretive reasonableness, which is context-specific and eliminates what they view as unnecessary bickering over what sources should be consulted in step two as opposed to step one.[42] Finally, they suggest that the inquiry into reasoned decisionmaking is no different from a traditional hard-look, *State Farm* analysis, and ought to be conducted independently, if necessary, only after the statutory permissibility issue is resolved.[43]

By contrast, Kenneth Bamberger and Peter Strauss argue that the step-one inquiry ought to encompass the matter of statutory permissibility, while step two ought to encompass reasonableness.[44] Their primary objections are aimed at ensuring analytical clarity. First, they argue that if courts themselves are not clear whether their holdings emanate from a conclusion that statutory language is clear, then the preclusive effects of their reasoning under *National Cable &*

---

39. *See* Kenneth A. Bamberger & Peter L. Strauss, Chevron*'s Two Steps*, 95 Va. L. Rev. 611, 611 (2009) (asserting that *Chevron* "prescribes two analytic inquiries . . . . [Q]uestions of implementation assigned to independent judicial judgment (Step One) from questions regarding which the courts' role is limited to oversight of agency decisionmaking (Step Two)") (footnote omitted). As discussed *infra* Part 3.032, the step-two analysis may also be understood as a variation of hard look review under the arbitrary-and-capricious standard.
40. Matthew C. Stephenson & Adrian Vermeule, Chevron *Has Only One Step*, 95 Va. L. Rev. 597, 599 (2009).
41. *Id.* at 602 (footnote omitted).
42. *Id.* at 607-08.
43. *Id.* at 604.
44. Bamberger & Strauss, *supra* note 39, at 624-25.

Telecommunications Ass'n v. Brand X are difficult to discern.[45] Second, they argue that although step two is properly viewed as an arbitrary-and-capricious analysis, the particular context presented by *Chevron* cases means that step two is not the same as a hard-look, *State Farm* approach.[46]

It seems unlikely that the courts will definitively resolve this debate anytime soon. After all, as anyone practicing administrative law knows, most issues in this field depend for their resolution on highly context-specific analyses. However, in an attempt to achieve clarity for purposes of this chapter, *Chevron*'s first and second steps are considered distinctly here, albeit with abundant recognition that the boundaries between the steps are blurry. If a court departs from the two-step framework, it should be very clear whether its holding is based on the scope of interpretive authority permitted the agency (traditionally a step-one determination), or the agency's interpretation within that scope (traditionally a step-two determination). Clarity in this regard is necessary for *Brand X* purposes and advisable for ensuring that the judicial role is appropriately exercised.[47]

3.02 STEP ONE OF *CHEVRON V. NATURAL RESOURCES DEFENSE COUNCIL*

> **Under step one of the *Chevron* test, the reviewing court determines whether the statutory meaning with respect to the precise issue before it is "clear" (and thus, not "ambiguous").**
> **[Blackletter Statement, Part 3, § II.B.]**

According to the *Chevron* decision, the first task for reviewing courts is to determine "whether Congress has directly spoken to the precise question

---

45. *Id.* at 616 (citing Nat'l Cable & Telecomms. Ass'n v. Brand X Internet Servs., 545 U.S. 967, 982–83 (2005)). As set forth in Chapter 4, the *Brand X* decision holds that only judicial determinations that statutes are clear (at the traditional first step) have preclusive effect sufficient to block an agency from claiming *Chevron* deference for an alternative statutory construction.
46. *Id.* at 625.
47. For a principled one-step analysis, see *Global Crossing Telecomms v. Metrophones Telecomms., Inc.*, 550 U.S. 45 (2007). *See also* Stephenson & Vermeule, *supra* note 40, at 605 (calling *Global Crossing* "[a] model opinion" for its one-step analysis). For an analysis that does not attend to the *Brand X* problem, see *Edelman v. Lynchburg Coll.*, 535 U.S. 106, 114 (2002) (declining to consider whether *Chevron* even applied to agency interpretation of a term in light of the Court's view that the agency interpretation was reasonable).

at issue."[48] The opinion does not dictate a particular method of statutory interpretation for the step-one inquiry. In a footnote, however, it states: "The judiciary is the final authority on issues of statutory construction and must reject administrative constructions which are contrary to clear congressional intent. If a court, *employing traditional tools of statutory construction*, ascertains that Congress had an intention on the precise question at issue, that intention is the law and must be given effect."[49]

Several approaches to step one have emerged, which differ in the precision with which the statute is scrutinized and the scope of materials reviewed to conduct this inquiry.[50] This part explores the "precise question" issue before turning to matters involving the scope of materials courts consult to determine whether Congress has "directly spoken."

3.021 Framing the Precise Question at Issue

The key passage and footnote from *Chevron* that articulate the method of statutory interpretation refer four times to congressional intent on the "precise" or "specific" issue confronting the court.[51] Nevertheless, this aspect of the *Chevron* test is seldom explicitly discussed in opinions interpreting regulatory statutes.[52] And because Congress rarely speaks so directly, particularly in settings that lead to litigation, strict application of this language would result in a majority of courts reaching step two.[53] To understand why, consider that the emphasis on the precise question requires comparing the statutory language to the agency's interpretation. If a court discerns a general desire, for example, to promote health or safety, it cannot infer from that general purpose a clear meaning on a narrower question when the statutory

---

48. 467 U.S. at 842.
49. *Id.* at 843 n.9 (emphasis added) (citations omitted).
50. *See* Beermann, *supra* note 8, at 817 (listing various versions); Seidenfeld, *supra* note 22, at 303 ("The level of judicial activism inherent in step one represents a sliding scale.").
51. *See* 467 U.S. at 842-43 & n.9.
52. *But see, e.g.*, Mayo Found. for Med. Educ. & Research v. United States, 131 S. Ct. 704, 711 (2011) (summarily noting that statute does not define term "student" or "attend to precise question whether medical residents are subject to FICA"). *But see* Gonzalez v. Reno, 212 F.3d 1338, 1348 (11th Cir. 2000) (finding that Congress had spoken to the question of what aliens could apply for asylum but finding silence on the precise question of what procedures must be followed to apply or what information should be included in an application).
53. *See* Beermann, *supra* note 8, at 817 (making this point).

language relevant to the precise and specific question is ambiguous. Instead, it should defer to an agency interpretation that is consistent with the statutory language and the general purpose animating the legislation.

In *Chevron*, for example, the Court concluded that the 1977 Clean Air Act Amendments reflected the general congressional intent to pursue certain environmental objectives while allowing reasonable economic growth. But the Court could not find in the text or legislative history any "actual intent" of Congress on the precise issue of whether the bubble concept was compatible with the term "stationary source."[54] Indeed, the Court noted with respect to the legislative history that "[t]he general remarks [of relevant lawmakers] 'were obviously not made with this narrow issue in mind and they cannot be said to demonstrate a Congressional desire.'"[55] Thus, it is not acceptable at step one for a court to ascertain a general meaning of statutory terms that could support several more precise understandings and then to select among those specific alternatives. In such a case, courts must defer to the agency's selection, as long as the interpretation it chooses is permissible.[56]

A rigorous focus on articulating the legal issue can help to clarify the appropriate judicial treatment of steps one *and* two. As Ronald Levin has argued, step one's precise-question inquiry ought to be "whether Congress has clearly ruled out an option the agency has chosen, or a premise on which the agency has sought to act."[57] This approach would avoid cases where courts, at step two, reject a particular understanding of admittedly ambiguous statutory language as inconsistent with clear congressional intent. It would clarify the *Chevron* test and the scope of the court's role if judges would reframe the precise question and explicitly cast such analyses as step one inquiries.

3.022 Methods of Determining Congressional Intent

As described above, *Chevron* instructs courts to rely on "traditional tools of statutory construction" at step one. The scope of what "traditional tools"

54. 467 U.S. at 861.
55. 467 U.S. at 862 (quoting Jewell Ridge Coal Corp. v. Mine Workers, 325 U.S. 161, 168-69 (1945)).
56. *See also* Yellow Transp., Inc. v. Michigan, 537 U.S. 36 (2002) (overturning state court's reasonable construction of statute where agency had adopted different permissible reading).
57. Ronald A. Levin, *The Anatomy of* Chevron*: Step Two Reconsidered*, 72 Chi.-Kent. L. Rev. 1253, 1283 (1997).

entail, however, is a matter of debate.[58] Most courts agree that such resources as statutory text, content and structure, canons of construction, and legislative history are appropriate,[59] but a distinct minority attempts to find a plain meaning primarily from the statute's text.[60] Depending on which sources a reviewing court consults, it may be more or less likely to reach step two.[61] The debate about the proper approach mirrors a larger discussion about statutory interpretation generally. This section thus begins by introducing the debate from a *Chevron*-specific context before turning to the particular resources courts consult at step one.

3.0221 Approaches to Statutory Interpretation

The step-one debate over statutory interpretation largely concerns two competing methodologies: some form of intentionalism versus textualism. Intentionalism has long been the dominant interpretive approach of the courts. For example, *Chevron* itself explicitly viewed the objective of interpretation at step one as determining the intent of Congress—an inquiry that may turn to legislative history to illuminate statutory meaning and congressional intent.[62] Although the Court began with the statutory language, it also considered committee reports and statements by key legislators on the floor of Congress.[63] Only after canvassing the legislative history and still finding no clear congressional intent did the Court conclude that the statute was ambiguous.[64]

---

58. A detailed examination of various approaches to statutory construction is beyond the scope of this chapter. For descriptions and a collection of sources relevant to textualism, intentionalism, and purposivism, see Lisa Shultz Bressman, Chevron*'s Mistake*, 58 DUKE L.J. 549, 551-52 (2009).
59. *See, e.g.*, Dole v. United Steelworkers of Am., Inc., 494 U.S. 26, 35 (1990).
60. *See, e.g.*, MCI v. AT&T, 512 U.S. 218, 225-27 (1994).
61. *See* Antonin Scalia, *Judicial Deference to Administrative Interpretations of Law*, 1989 DUKE L.J. 511, 521 (1989) ("One who finds more often (as I do) that the meaning of a statute is apparent from its text and from its relationship with other laws, thereby finds less often that the triggering requirement for *Chevron* deference exists.") (emphasis omitted).
62. *See* Stephen Breyer, *On the Uses of Legislative History in Interpreting Statutes*, 65 S. CAL. L. REV. 845 (1992) (discussing the appropriate use of legislative history by courts to provide context and suggest meanings considered by Congress); Peter Strauss, *The Courts and the Congress: Should Judges Disdain Political History?*, 98 COLUM. L. REV. 242 (1998) (same).
63. *See Chevron,* 467 U.S. at 851-53.
64. *Id.* at 851-53; *see also* Babbitt v. Sweet Home Chapter of Cmtys. for a Great Oregon, 515 U.S. 687, 708 (1995).

But a different method—textualism—is used by a significant minority of judges, in large part through the advocacy of Justice Scalia.[65] Textualists are not particularly concerned with discovering congressional intent, at least inasmuch as it differs from the directives found in the statutory language itself. Rather, they argue that legislative history is unreliable and often strategically used by legislators to influence courts. They further contend that using legislative materials violates the bicameralism and presentment requirements in the Constitution by elevating non-statutory materials to the level of law.[66] Thus, textualists do not use history at step one, not because they think it is more appropriately used by agencies at step two, but because they think it off-limits for courts, period.

An especially stark example of the competing views is provided by the majority and dissenting opinions in *Zuni Public School District No. 89 v. Department of Education*.[67] At issue was the Department of Education's construction of a statute involving how to calculate the disparity between per-pupil expenditures among local school districts within a state. In making the determination, the agency was to "disregard" school districts with "per-pupil expenditures . . . above the 95th percentile or below the 5th percentile of such expenditures."[68] For 30 years, the agency made this calculation by ranking districts by per-pupil expenditures, and then calculating the percentiles based on the total number of students in attendance. A school district challenged this approach, contending the percentiles should be calculated based purely on expenditures.[69]

The Court split 5-4 on the issue of how to apply *Chevron* step one. Justice Breyer's majority opinion began by noting that although the district's strongest argument rested on the statutory text, there were numerous reasons to reject the district's reading of that text.[70] First, the Court noted that the lan-

---

65. *See* ANTONIN SCALIA, A MATTER OF INTERPRETATION: FEDERAL COURTS AND THE LAW 23-47 (1997).

66. *See* Adrian Vermeule, *Interpretive Choice*, 75 N.Y.U. L. REV. 74 (2000) (arguing that legislative history should not be used by courts because judges are not competent to separate strategic or inaccurate materials from materials that reflect genuine intent); *see also* John Manning, *Textualism as a Nondelegation Doctrine*, 97 COLUM. L. REV. 673 (1997) (making the constitutional argument).

67. 550 U.S. 81 (2007).

68. *Id.* at 86.

69. As applied to the school district, the agency's approach meant that the district was not able to obtain certain funding from the state. *Id.* at 88.

70. *Id.* at 89-90.

guage was technical and specialized, suggesting Congress's intent that the agency should fill any gaps.[71] Second, the Court explained that the legislative history revealed not only that the agency had provided the statutory language, but also that Congress had acquiesced in the agency's interpretation.[72] Finally, the Court considered various dictionary definitions, and the wording of other more precise statutes, and ultimately concluded the language was ambiguous.[73]

In a scathing opinion by Justice Scalia, the dissenters strongly criticized the majority for "policy-driven interpretation."[74] After detailing why the text of the statute pointed to a different outcome, the dissent took aim at the use of legislative history in statutory interpretation. "The only thing we know for certain both Houses of Congress . . . agreed upon is the text."[75] Reliance on legislative history threatened to import judicial policy preferences into the analysis.[76] The dissent further argued that the rule of law is threatened when the ordinary meaning of statutory text is laid aside in preference for fictional legislative intent.[77]

The *Zuni* example should not be read to overstate the debate.[78] Most judges do rely on legislative history—a fact that has been documented.[79] However, the influence of textualism has had an additional effect on the *Chevron* doctrine's application. Perhaps in order to ensure the votes of textualist justices in close cases, the Supreme Court sometimes evaluates step one in a manner more closely resembling textualism.[80] For example, in *K Mart Corp.*

---

71. *Id.* at 90.
72. *Id.* at 90-91.
73. *Id.* at 93-100.
74. *Id.* at 109 (Scalia, J., dissenting).
75. *Id.* at 116.
76. *Id.* at 117.
77. *Id.* at 119, 122.
78. For other examples, compare Justice Stevens's majority opinion in *Babbitt v. Sweet Home Chapter of Cmtys. for a Great Oregon*, 515 U.S. 687 (1995), with Justice Scalia's dissent in the case; or the opinions by Justice Scalia for the Court and Justice Stevens in dissent in *City of Chicago v. Environmental Def. Fund*, 511 U.S. 328 (1994).
79. *See* Eskridge & Baer, *supra* note 4, at 1136.
80. *See, e.g.*, Nat'l R.R. Passenger Corp. v. Boston & Maine Corp., 503 U.S. 407, 417-18 (1992) (eliminating reference to congressional intent in framing step-one standard); Bankers Life & Casualty Co. v. United States, 142 F.3d 973, 982-83 (7th Cir. 1998) (characterizing *Boston & Maine Corp.* as a stage in the Supreme Court's "ongoing development" of *Chevron*, "especially regarding the scope of the initial inquiry into statutory meaning"); *see also*

v. Cartier, Inc.,[81] both Justice Kennedy (writing for the Court) and Justice Brennan (concurring in relevant part) applied the *Chevron* test, but the majority articulated the test in a way much more compatible with a textualist approach and with few references to legislative intent or legislative history. The majority described the step-one process as "ascertaining the plain meaning of the statute,"[82] stating that deference is due if the agency interpretation of ambiguous language is "not in conflict with the plain language of the statute."[83] By contrast, Justice Brennan's concurrence was replete with references to the intent of Congress. Unlike the majority, he did not limit his search for intent to the language and structure of the statute but also relied on extensive discussion of the legislative materials and drafting history.[84]

The important lesson here is that *Chevron* opinions can be expected to vary in the scope of materials they consider at step one. This is partly a result of judges' views of statutory interpretation, but may be influenced by other factors. The next sections present the various materials judges may consult at step one; these sections are roughly arranged from least to most controversial.

3.0222 Sources of Statutory Meaning

Courts consult a wide variety of sources to determine statutory meaning at step one. These include (a) the statutory text, definitions, and context; (b) dictionary definitions; (c) textual canons of construction; (d) legislative purpose; (e) legislative history; (f) agency interpretations; and (g) normative canons of construction. Each is presented below.

3.02221 Statutory Text, Definitions, and Context

Statutory language is the primary source of meaning for courts. Indeed, one of the least controversial canons of construction is that, absent evidence

---

Thomas W. Merrill, *Textualism and the Future of the* Chevron *Doctrine*, 72 Wash. U. L.Q. 351 (1994) (discussing changes in *Chevron* as a result of the rise of textualism).

81. 486 U.S. 281 (1988).

82. *Id.* at 291.

83. *Id.* at 292.

84. *See, e.g., id.* at 303-05; *see also* Mayo Found. for Med. Educ. & Research v. United States, 131 S. Ct. 704, 711 (2011) (holding statute was ambiguous and proceeding to step two after very summary approach to step one, focusing primarily on the statutory text and other sections of same statute).

of some special usage, statutory terms should be understood according to their ordinary meaning.[85] In *Chevron*, for example, the Court worked to determine the "common English usage" of the text at issue;[86] this approach is typically the starting point for step one.[87]

Courts also pay particular attention to definitions in statutes, especially when terms are used in ways that differ from their ordinary meaning. In *Astrue v. Capato ex rel. BNC*, for example, the Court consulted various statutory definitions of the word "child" in determining whether the Social Security Administration had properly determined that the Social Security Act's survivor benefits did not extend to posthumously-born children.[88] Further, even where a particular term is not defined in the section of the statute at issue, courts may consult definitions in other parts of the statute for illumination.[89]

At *Chevron* step one, judicial interpreters also consider aspects of the larger statutory framework to provide meaning to particular statutory provisions. First, judges will consult the statutory provisions in proximity to the term at issue.[90] Next, courts will frequently consult the entire statutory scheme

---

85. *See* WILLIAM N. ESKRIDGE, JR., PHILIP P. FRICKEY, & ELIZABETH GARRETT, LEGISLATION AND STATUTORY INTERPRETATION 259-61 (2d ed. 2006).
86. *Chevron, U.S.A., Inc. v. Natural Res. Def. Council, Inc.*, 467 U.S. 837, 860 (1984); *see also* HUD v. Rucker, 535 U.S. 125, 129 (2002) (using plain meaning approach to interpret "any" as having an expansive meaning in a federal law requiring that public housing leases include a clause terminating the lease for "any drug-related criminal activity" on or off premises by a tenant, member of the household, or guest).
87. *E.g.*, Roberts v. Sea-Land Servs., Inc., 132 S. Ct. 1350, 1356 (2012) (emphasizing that starting point is ordinary meaning); FCC v. AT&T Inc., 131 S. Ct 1177, 1182 (2011) (considering ordinary meaning). Courts also rely on conventions related to grammar. *See, e.g.*, Barnhart v. Walton, 535 U.S. 212, 217-18 (2002) (using grammar rules concerning modifiers at step one but finding the language remained ambiguous); Nat'l Credit Union Admin v. First Nat'l Bank & Trust Co., 522 U.S. 479, 500, 502 (1998) (referring to conventions such as use of plural rather than singular nouns and participles rather than prepositions).
88. 132 S. Ct. 2021, 2027-28 (2012); *see also* Gustafson v. Alloyd Co., Inc., 513 U.S. 561, 573-75 (1995) (consulting statutory definition of "prospectus").
89. *E.g.*, *Chevron*, 467 U.S. at 859-62.
90. *See, e.g.*, Astrue v. Capato ex rel. B.N.C., 132 S. Ct. at 2032 (considering text, surrounding provisions, and dictionary for meaning of "child"); Northeast Md. Waste Disposal Auth. v. EPA, 358 F.3d 936, 944-45 (D.C. Cir. 2004) (considering how four sentences in Clean Air Act should be read together).

or context, including sections of the statute passed at different times. They will try to adopt a meaning that makes the most sense of the statute as a whole and promotes coherence.[91] Less frequently, judges also consider related statutes in order to formulate a meaning of the relevant terms "with a view to their place in the overall statutory scheme."[92]

3.02222 Dictionary Definitions

Courts frequently rely on dictionary definitions as evidence of ordinary usage of words found in regulatory statutes, absent an indication that Congress used the words in some specialized sense. While the use of dictionaries is a generally accepted practice, the matter of selecting which dictionary to use is a matter of debate.[93] For example, the opinions in *MCI Telecommunications Corp. v. AT&T*[94] include arguments about the relative merits of *Webster's Third New International Dictionary* (a descriptive dictionary that Justice Scalia argues promotes colloquial and erroneous usage as correct usage) and those of *Webster's Second* (a prescriptive dictionary favored by the textualist Justice).

Often a court discovers that there are alternative dictionary definitions for crucial words. In some cases, the existence of alternative dictionary definitions, "each making some sense under the statute," leads the court to conclude that the statute is ambiguous or incomplete.[95] In other cases, the court will conclude that only one definition is sensible and thus resolve step one by asking whether the agency interpretation meets that particular definition. The Court took the latter approach in *MCI Telecommunications*, in an opinion authored by Justice Scalia.[96] There, the Court considered the meaning of the

---

91. *See, e.g., Gustafson*, 513 U.S. at 568-73; Visiting Nurses Ass'n of Sw. Ind. v. Shalala, 213 F.3d 352 (7th Cir. 2000).
92. FDA v. Brown & Williamson Tobacco Corp., 529 U.S. 120, 133 (2000) (quoting Davis v. Mich. Dep't of Treasury, 489 U.S. 803, 809 (1989)); *see also* Zuni Pub. Sch. Dist. No. 89 v. Dep't of Educ., 550 U.S. 81, 98 (2007) (noting term at issue was defined more precisely in other statutes); Indep. Ins. Agents of Am., Inc. v. Hawke, 211 F.3d 638, 643 (D.C. Cir. 2000) (considering subsequent statutes in interpreting the term "incidental powers" in the National Bank Act).
93. *See* Ellen Aprill, *The Law of the Word: Dictionary Shopping in the Supreme Court*, 30 Ariz. St. L.J. 275 (1998); Note, *Looking It Up: Dictionaries and Statutory Interpretation*, 107 Harv. L. Rev. 1437 (1994).
94. 512 U.S. 218 (1994).
95. *See* Nat'l R.R. Passenger Corp. v. Boston & Maine Corp., 503 U.S. 407, 418 (1992).
96. *MCI Telecommunications*, 512 U.S. 218.

word “modify.” With one exception, the definitions in several dictionaries included a connotation of “changing moderately or in incremental fashion.”[97] Only one definition among many, contained in *Webster’s Third*, defined “modify” also to mean “to make a basic or important change in.”[98] Justice Scalia concluded that this outlier definition was based either on intentional distortions of the word or on careless or ignorant misuse.[99] He refused to find an ambiguity triggering deference because of “a meaning set forth in a single dictionary . . . which not only *supplements* the meaning contained in all other dictionaries, but *contradicts* one of the meanings in virtually all other dictionaries. Indeed, contradicts one of the alternative meanings contained in the out-of-step dictionary itself.”[100] Having concluded that Congress intended “modify” to mean only incremental change, the Court next inquired whether the agency’s interpretation was within that meaning, and answered the question in the negative.[101]

3.02223 Textual Canons of Construction

Courts have long used a set of rules of interpretation as a guide to statutory meaning; these rules are referred to as the canons of statutory construction. It is helpful to distinguish between the types of canons that courts may apply. *Textual* canons, discussed in this section, are linguistic guides that may be applied to the statutory language itself. *Normative* canons, by contrast, advance certain policy values or normative principles. The latter are more controversial and are discussed below. The canons have been criticized as insufficiently determinate and susceptible to strategic manipulation by judges seeking their preferred policy outcomes.[102] This assessment exaggerates the malleability of the canons. While canons cannot give definite answers in all cases, some canons are generally employed by judges in a relatively principled manner and can shed real light on statutory meaning. These widely accepted canons of construction operate as default rules to guide not only judicial interpretation but also legislative drafting.

---

97. *Id.* at 225.
98. *Id.* at 225-26.
99. *Id.* at 228.
100. *Id.* at 227.
101. *Id.* at 229-32.
102. *See, e.g.*, Karl N. Llewellyn, *Remarks on the Theory of Appellate Decision and the Rules or Canons About How Statutes Are to Be Construed*, 3 Vand. L. Rev. 395 (1950).

The question for the *Chevron* analysis is which canons are considered as traditional tools of statutory construction suitable for judicial use at step one. One difficulty is that canons are employed to clarify and narrow meaning, so their use necessarily implies some amount of ambiguity or lack of clarity in the statutory text. To put it differently, canons usually do not come into play if the language is self-evidently clear, incapable of more than one meaning.[103] Of course, recourse to dictionary definitions, statutory structure, and legislative purpose, uncontroversial as part of the step-one inquiry, occurs because the statutory text, standing alone, is not entirely pellucid. Thus, even though use of the canons signals some ambiguity in the statutory text, the current judicial practice of using most of the canons to discern statutory meaning at step one is consistent with other interpretive practices.

Many textual canons are guides to what a particular statutory provision would typically mean to an ordinary speaker of the language. They reflect shared linguistic conventions and understandings, and are often used by courts at step one. In addition, there is a group of textual canons aimed more at describing the linguistic conventions of legislative drafters than those of ordinary people. Like the ordinary language canon, these other textual canons are widely used at step one.[104] Note, however, that courts are careful to emphasize that the canons may not be used where they conflict with other indicators of statutory meaning.[105]

Examples of these canons are the rule against surplusage;[106] the related

---

103. *See* Thomas W. Merrill, *Judicial Deference to Executive Precedent*, 101 YALE L.J. 969, 988 (1992) (primarily in the context of normative canons, observing that "one would expect that if a court could interpret a statute only by invoking a canon, it would be forced to acknowledge that the issue is one to which Congress has not clearly spoken").

104. *See, e.g.,* Indep. Ins. Agents of Am., Inc. v. Hawke, 211 F.3d 638, 644-45 (D.C. Cir. 2000) (explaining when textual canons are appropriately used at step one).

105. *E.g.*, Assn' of Private Sector Colls. and Univs., 681 F.3d 427, 444 (D.C. Cir. 2012).

106. *E.g.*, Nat'l Ass'n of Home Builders v. Defenders of Wildlife, 551 U.S. 644, 669 (2007); Nat'l Credit Union Admin. v. First Nat'l Bank & Trust Co., 522 U.S. 479, 501 (1998); *see also* Freeman v. Quicken Loans, 132 S. Ct. 2034, 2040-43 (2012) (declining to determine whether *Chevron* applied to agency policy statement in light of conclusion, reached in part using canon against surplusage, that statute was unambiguous).

canons of *noscitur a sociis*[107] and *ejusdem generis*;[108] the canon of *expressio unius est exclusio alterius*;[109] the canon that different statutory sections are to be interpreted so as to be consistent with one another;[110] the canon that words in a statute must be read in the context of the overall statutory scheme;[111] and the related canons that Congress is not presumed to do a futile thing and that each statutory provision should be given effect.[112]

3.02224 Legislative Purpose

Courts routinely consider statutory purpose in their search for unambiguous statutory meaning. Although policy arguments relevant in choosing

---

107. *Compare, e.g.*, Babbitt v. Sweet Home Chapter of Cmtys. for a Great Or., 515 U.S. 687, 702 (1995) (concluding court of appeals had erred in applying *noscitur a sociis*), *with id.* at 720-21 (Scalia, J., dissenting) (arguing the canon should have applied); *see also* Freeman v. Quicken Loans, Inc., 132 S. Ct. 2034, 2042 (2012) (declining to consider *Chevron*'s applicability in light of conclusion that statute was unambiguous, and relying in part on *noscitur a sociis*).
108. *E.g.*, Christopher v. SmithKline Beecham Corp., 132 S. Ct. 2156, 2171 (2012) (relying on *ejusdem generis* to determine meaning of statute after determining that agency was entitled to neither *Auer* nor *Skidmore* deference.).
109. *See, e.g.*, Christensen v. Harris Cnty, 529 U.S. 576, 583 (2000); *Indep. Ins. Agents of Am., Inc. v. Hawke,* 211 F.3d 638, 644-45 (D.C. Cir. 2000) (rejecting agency's interpretation at step one based on the tandem canons "of avoiding surplusage and *expressio unius*"); *see also* Chevron v. Echazabal, 536 U.S. 73, 80 (2002) (using canon in interpreting a provision of the American with Disabilities Act). Although the Court determined that the canon could not be applied to the text it was interpreting, its analysis implicitly accepts the use of this canon at step one. *See also id.* at 87 (considering surplusage canon at step one but finding it inapplicable).
110. *See, e.g.*, United Transp. Union-Ill. Legislative Bd. v. Surface Transp. Bd., 169 F.3d 474, 480 (7th Cir. 1999). *But see* Envtl. Def. v. Duke Energy Corp., 549 U.S. 561, 574 (2007) ("A given term in the same statute may take on distinct characters from association with distinct statutory objects calling for different implementation strategies.").
111. Nat'l Ass'n of Home Builders v. Defenders of Wildlife, 551 U.S. 644, 666 (2007); *see also* Friends of the Everglades v. S. Fla. Water Mgmt. Dist., 570 F.3d 1210, 1222-27 (11th Cir. 2009) (evaluating meaning of statutory term, context in which term is used, and broader context of statute as a whole, with some discussion of statutory purpose).
112. *See, e.g.*, Halverson v. Slater, 206 F.3d 1205, 1207 (D.C. Cir. 2000).

among competing meanings for ambiguous statutory language are more properly within the province of the agency in its step-two role,[113] the general purpose of Congress in enacting a certain regulatory framework may provide compelling evidence of legislative intent with respect to particular provisions and provide evidence of the range of meanings permissible under the statute. For example, in interpreting provisions of the Telecommunications Act of 1996, Justice Breyer considered both the legislative history and the statutory purpose to "illuminate [the Act's] language."[114] Interpreting statutory language with the larger legislative purpose in mind may provide some guidance at step one, although purpose is often framed at such a level of generality that it cannot satisfactorily clarify ambiguous language.

3.02225 Legislative History

As described above, whether legislative history is an acceptable source of meaning is a matter of some debate. Some of the major *Chevron* decisions, many written by Justice Scalia, pointedly ignore legislative history.[115] Yet overall the use of legislative history at step one is alive and well.[116]

For an example of where legislative history, among other things, trumped the apparent clear language of the statute, consider *FDA v. Brown & Williamson Tobacco Corp.*[117] There, the Supreme Court held that the term "drug" in the Food, Drug, and Cosmetic Act did not extend to nicotine; thus the FDA lacked jurisdiction to issue regulations aimed at reducing tobacco consumption among minors. In addition to the overall context of the statute, the Court exhaustively documented the regulatory and statutory backdrop over a thirty-five year period, complete with detailed discussions of legislative history.[118] *Brown & Williamson* is an important reminder of the weight such history can carry in statutory interpretation.[119]

---

113. *See, e.g., Chevron*, 467 U.S. at 864-66.
114. AT&T Corp. v. Iowa Utils. Bd., 525 U.S. 366, 412 (1999) (Breyer, J., concurring in part and dissenting in part); *see also* Presley v. Etowah Cnty. Comm'n, 502 U.S. 491, 508-09 (1992) (rejecting agency's interpretation on the basis of structure and purpose arguments); CSX Transp. v. United States, 867 F.2d 1439, 1443 (D.C. Cir. 1989) (considering structure and purpose of the Staggers Rail Act at step one).
115. Eskridge & Baer, *supra* note 4, at 1135.
116. *Id.*
117. 529 U.S. 120 (2000).
118. *See id.* at 143-59.
119. Note that the dissent also relied on legislative history. *See id.* at 164-66 (Breyer, J., dissenting).

3.02226 Agency Interpretations

Courts also may consult agency interpretations at step one as a relevant tool of statutory construction.[120] The Supreme Court in *Solid Waste Agency of Northern Cook County v. United States Army Corps of Engineers*, for example, looked to the agency's relatively contemporaneous interpretation of a statute to discern legislative intent.[121] Courts have long considered agency interpretations of statutory language to be persuasive evidence of statutory meaning for various institutional reasons.[122] Agency staff often play a major role in drafting legislation; agencies are responsible for the initial application of the statute; and agencies' day-to-day interactions with particular statutes make it likely that they will have a relatively sophisticated view of how a statute fits into a coherent regulatory scheme.[123]

Two conceptual difficulties may arise when courts consider agencies' interpretations at step one. First, agencies' interpretations often rely on legislative history, which relates to the discussion in Part 3.0221 above. For most judges, considering legislative history is not problematic, and is even more persuasive viewed from the lens of agencies, which are sophisticated and regular users of legislative history. Textualists, however, would deny courts access to legislative history at step one regardless of the means by which it is

---

120. In addition, a typical judicial opinion will often set forth both parties' arguments in the context of fully developing the court's analysis. Thus, it is not unusual to find a *Chevron* step one discussion describing the agency's interpretation and arguments. A court's mere description of an agency's arguments, however, should be distinguished from a court's giving such arguments weight because they are made by the agency. *See, e.g.*, Astrue v. Capato *ex rel.* B.N.C., 132 S. Ct. 2021, 2030–31 (2012) (citing agency's and petitioner's briefs with respect to analysis of statutory text).
121. 531 U.S. at 167-68.
122. *See, e.g.*, Norwegian Nitrogen Prods. Co. v. United States, 288 U.S. 294, 315 (1933) (pre-*Chevron* decision giving weight to "contemporaneous construction of a statute by the [people] charged with the responsibility of setting its machinery in motion, of making the parts work efficiently and smoothly while they are yet untried and new"); *see also* United States v. American Trucking Associations, 310 U.S. 534, 549 (1940) (citing *Norwegian Nitrogen* and also noting that more weight should be accorded to the agency's view of legislative intent when the agency helped draft the statutory language).
123. *See* Peter L. Strauss, *When the Judge is Not the Primary Official with Responsibility to Read: Agency Interpretation and the Problem of Legislative History*, 66 CHI.-KENT L. REV. 321, 329, 334 (1990).

presented. Using textualist techniques, it is possible that a court may find an unambiguous statutory meaning at step one that an agency has discarded as inconsistent with legislative history.

Second, it is important to note that the mere consideration of agency interpretations at step one is distinct from the deference given to reasonable agency interpretations at step two. At step one, courts simply look to agencies for assistance in discerning statutory meaning, acknowledging agencies' role in the lawmaking process but cognizant of the danger that agencies may have incentives to mischaracterize legislative intent.[124] In contrast, at step two, courts consider whether the agencies made a reasoned choice among permissible interpretations. But in practice, the lines between these steps are often blurred. This is particularly true in recent decisions in which courts themselves have departed from a strict two-step analysis.[125]

3.02227 Normative Canons

As mentioned above, normative canons do not mirror widespread linguistic conventions; instead, these canons reflect and advance certain policy values. With some exceptions discussed below, courts use these canons at step one to help them determine the extent to which statutory meaning is clear. In some cases, the canons appear to be used as part of the step-two inquiry, although these cases usually involve the "belatedly discovered clear meaning" analysis that Ronald Levin argues closely resembles a court's task at step one.[126] In other words, although the court finds that the statutory language is ambiguous, it holds that a particular canon of construction rules out the agency's interpretation because it is inconsistent with the statute as interpreted with the guidance of the canon.[127]

---

124. For discussion of the relevance of agency interpretations under *Skidmore*, *see* Chapter Five, *infra*.

125. For an example of blurring generally, see *Zuni Pub. School Dist. No. 89 v. Dep't of Educ.*, 550 U.S. 81, 91 (2007) (at step one, calling agency's interpretation reasonable in light of statutory purpose). For an only-one-step example, see *Holder v. Martinez Gutierrez*, 132 S. Ct. 2011, 2021 (2012) (stating agency's "experience implementing the INA, that statutory text, administrative practice, and regulatory policy" pointed to the reasonableness of the agency's construction).

126. *See* Levin, *supra* note 57, at 1283.

127. *See, e.g.*, Qualcomm Inc. v. FCC, 181 F.3d 1370 (D.C. Cir. 1999) (holding that under the canon of constitutional doubt, agency interpretation of an ambiguous statute that raised a serious constitutional question with regard to retroactive application was not entitled to deference when a reasonable and clearly

While not attempting to provide an exhaustive list of normative canons, this section provides an overview of three of the most common varieties for *Chevron* purposes: canons relating to the democratic process; canons protecting underenforced constitutional norms; and canons protecting important social policies, including regulatory norms.

3.02228 Canons Relating to the Democratic Process

Occasionally courts rely on canons that link congressional activity to presumptions about Congress's intent. These canons are most frequently found at step one, though they also appear at step two.[128] For example, the reenactment doctrine provides that when "Congress reenacts statutory language that has been given a consistent judicial construction, [courts] often adhere to that construction in interpreting the reenacted statutory language."[129]

It is not always clear which canons belong in this category. Consider the canon that riders to appropriations bills should be narrowly construed. Some have classified this as a textual rule that reflects legislative understandings.[130] Perhaps that is right; after all, both houses have adopted internal rules designed to limit the scope of appropriations riders. But those enacting a rider in a particular instance might not have intended a narrow construction, in which case this canon would more properly be categorized, and justified, as a normative canon related to failures in the legislative process.

---

constitutional alternative was available); *see also* Edward J. DeBartolo Corp. v. Fla. Gulf Coast Bldg. & Constr. Trades Council, 485 U.S. 568 (1988) (declining to defer to an interpretation by the NLRB when the construction posed a serious question of validity under the First Amendment and other reasonable interpretations of the language were possible, but apparently deciding the case at step one).

128. *E.g.*, Barnhart v. Walton, 535 U.S. 212, 226-27 (2002) (Scalia, J., concurring) (acknowledging reenactment doctrine at step two).

129. Cent. Bank of Denver, N.A. v. First Interstate Bank of Denver, N.A., 511 U.S. 164, 185 (1994) (discussing doctrine in non-*Chevron* case); *see* FDA v. Brown & Williamson Tobacco Co., Inc., 529 U.S. 120, 143-59 (2000) (reasoning Congress had ratified FDA's long-held position that it lacked jurisdiction to regulate tobacco); Kristen E. Hickman, *The Need for* Mead: *Rejecting Tax Exceptionalism in Judicial Deference*, 90 MINN. L. REV. 1537, 1582 (2006) (noting potential inconsistency of doctrine with *Chevron*'s stance of agency flexibility, but suggesting doctrine is similar to other considerations of legislative history).

130. *See, e.g.*, Sunstein, *supra* note 17, at 2107.

Applying these canons may serve important goals. If courts declined to apply such canons at step one and allowed agencies to use discretion in deciding whether to rely on them, the incentivizing effects of these canons (to adopt policies consistent with these normative principles) would be reduced. Moreover, if these substantive canons are designed to minimize possible bad consequences of a flawed legislative process, they serve purposes additional to the primary judicial goal of assessing statutory meaning.

3.02229 Canons Protecting Underenforced Constitutional Norms

A second set of substantive canons protects underenforced constitutional norms—that is, constitutional principles that courts do not protect by the more aggressive means of invalidating statutes, and that Congress is apt to slight when legislating.[131] Take, for example, the nondelegation doctrine. The Supreme Court has invalidated federal statutes as violations of the nondelegation doctrine only twice in U.S. history.[132] But the concept remains vibrant because it supports canons of statutory construction that require narrow interpretations of broad statutory language, limiting Congress's ability to make open-ended delegations to agencies.[133]

Similarly, the canon that statutory language will be interpreted so that it does not raise serious constitutional doubts protects separation-of-powers values, preserves judicial legitimacy, and provides a practical means of promoting judicial efficiency.[134] The canon that legislation is presumed to have

---

131. An exhaustive list of such canons is beyond the scope of this Chapter. For a full typology and analytical treatment, see Dan T. Coenen, *A Constitution of Collaboration: Protecting Fundamental Values with Second-Look Rules of Interbranch Dialogue*, 42 WM. & MARY L. REV. 1575 (2001). For consideration of these norms in the administrative law context, see Kenneth A. Bamberger, *Normative Canons in the Review of Administrative Policymaking*, 118 YALE L.J. 64 (2008); for their extension to dialogue between courts and agencies, see Emily Hammond Meazell, *Deference and Dialogue in Administrative Law*, 111 COLUM. L. REV. 1722, 1777-78 (2011).
132. A.L.A. Schechter Poultry Corp. v. United States, 295 U.S. 495 (1935); Panama Refining Co. v. Ryan, 293 U.S. 388 (1935).
133. *See* Indus. Union Dep't v. Am. Petrol. Inst., 448 U.S. 607, 646 (1980) (plurality decision) (favoring construction of statute that avoided nondelegation concerns); *see* Cass R. Sunstein, *Nondelegation Canons*, 67 U. CHI. L. REV. 315 (2000).
134. *See* Solid Waste Agency of N. Cook Cnty. v. Army Corps. of Eng'rs, 531 U.S. 159, 172 (2001) ("Where an administrative interpretation of a statute in-

only prospective effect absent a specific indication to the contrary protects an aspect of due process that courts tend not to protect aggressively in the civil context.[135] Other canons relate to federalism, such as the rule that ambiguous federal statutes will not be interpreted to preempt state law,[136] or the rule that ambiguous language will not be interpreted to intrude on areas of traditional state authority or important state governmental functions.[137]

The use of these canons is not without controversy, even outside the administrative law context.[138] Nevertheless, courts frequently rely on such rules. An issue particular to the *Chevron* context relates to which institution—courts or agencies—ought to have primacy in applying such canons. As Kenneth Bamberger explains, the majority approach is to use such canons to resolve textual ambiguity and find statutory meaning clear even if an agency interpretation would otherwise be entitled to evaluation in step two.[139] The Court explained this approach in *I.N.S. v. St. Cyr* in applying the presumption against retroactive legislation:

> We only defer . . . to agency interpretations of statutes that, applying the normal "tools of statutory construction," are ambiguous. Because a statute that is ambiguous with respect to retroactive application is

---

vokes the outer limits of Congress' power, we expect a clear indication that Congress intended that result."); Emily Hammond Meazell, *Scientific Avoidance: Toward More Principled Judicial Review of Legislative Science*, 84 IND. L.J. 239, 262 (2009) (listing rationales and collecting sources).

135. *See, e.g.,* Bowen v. Georgetown Univ. Hosp., 488 U.S. 204, 208 (1988).

136. *See* Nat'l Ass'n of Regulatory Utility Comm'rs v. FCC, 880 F.2d 422 (D.C. Cir. 1989).

137. *See* Gregory v. Ashcroft, 501 U.S. 452 (1991); *see also Solid Waste Agency*, 531 U.S. at 172-173 (requiring a clear statement at step one in order to find congressional intent to "permit[] federal encroachment upon a traditional state power" and refusing to consider *Chevron* deference in this context).

138. *See* Meazell, *supra* note 131, at 1724 n.3 (collecting sources); *see also* William N. Eskridge, Jr. & Philip P. Frickey, *Quasi-Constitutional Law: Clear Statement Rules as Constitutional Lawmaking*, 45 VAND. L. REV. 593 (1992) (explaining and critiquing clear statement rules).

139. Bamberger, *supra* note 131, at 77-80; *see, e.g., Edward J. DeBartolo Corp.*, 485 U.S. at 575; Univ. of Great Falls v. NLRB, 278 F.3d 1335, 1340 (D.C. Cir. 2002) (holding that "the constitutional avoidance canon of statutory interpretation trumps *Chevron* deference"). *But see* Merrill & Hickman, *supra* note 16, at 914-15 (arguing that canon should trump *Chevron* only when the interpretation that is rejected would have been unconstitutional, not when the choice merely avoids deciding the constitutional issue).

> construed under our precedent to be unambiguously prospective, there is, for *Chevron* purposes, no ambiguity in such a statute for an agency to resolve.[140]

In other words, many substantive canons that establish an unambiguous meaning are in fact triggered by the presence of ambiguity. If the canon against retroactive legislation requires clear language or specific legislative history to overcome its presumption and no clear congressional indication can be discovered, then the application of the canon leads to a finding that Congress did not intend the law to have retroactive effect. These cases demonstrate that the use of these canons at step one may increase the number of cases decided by the Court at this stage.[141]

The minority approach, however, argues that agencies are better positioned to consider the constitutional implications of their interpretations, making consideration of the normative canons better suited for step two.[142] In practice, one can find many examples of both.

3.022210 Canons Protecting Social Policies, Including Regulatory Norms

A third set of normative canons protects important social policies and values, including regulatory norms. These include the rules that exemptions to tax laws should be construed narrowly; remedial statutes should be construed broadly; and laws should be interpreted to favor Native Americans.[143] Like the other canons, there is significant variation in judicial practice with regard to their application at step one.[144] On the one hand, the proper use of

---

140. INS v. St. Cyr, 533 U.S. 289, 320 n.45 (2001) (citations omitted).

141. For a similar analysis, see Holland v. Pardee Coal Co., 269 F.3d 424 (4th Cir. 2001).

142. *See* Bamberger, *supra* note 131, at 81-84.

143. For a discussion of such canons, see generally *id.*

144. *Compare, e.g.*, Ramah Navajo Chapter v. Lujan, 112 F.3d 1455, 1462 (10th Cir. 1997) (canon favoring Native Americans in interpretation trumps *Chevron* deference), *with* Haynes v. United States, 891 F.2d 235, 239 (9th Cir. 1989) (deferring to agency interpretation that competes with the canon), *and* Ariz. Pub. Serv. Co. v. EPA, 211 F.3d 1280, 1294 (D.C. Cir. 2000) ("In light of the . . . canon of statutory interpretation calling for statutes to be interpreted favorably towards Native American nations, we cannot condemn as unreasonable the EPA's interpretation of 'reservations.'"). *See also* Philip P. Frickey, *A Common Law for Our Age of Colonialism: The Judicial Divestiture of Indian Tribal Authority over Nonmembers*, 109 YALE L.J. 1, 18-27 (1999) (discussing the uneven application of the canon generally and rationales justifying it).

these canons is often intertwined with the sort of policy decisions for which agencies are better suited than courts. Some courts therefore do not apply them at step one, a practice that allows agencies to decide how best to protect these policies and values within the framework of the regulatory statute.[145] On the other hand, if courts view these canons as relatively settled default rules that provide an interpretive scheme against which Congress legislates, they may be comfortable using them at step one.[146]

In sum, the judicial practice with respect to normative canons is inconsistent, and courts often fail to explain their choices regarding whether to deploy them at step one or at step two. This inconsistency stems from larger debates about both the canons' and *Chevron*'s justifications.[147]

3.03 STEP TWO OF *CHEVRON V. NATURAL RESOURCES DEFENSE COUNCIL*

3.031 *Chevron*'s Second Step

> **If the statutory meaning on the precise issue before the court is not clear, or if the statute is silent on that issue, the court is required to defer to the agency's interpretation of the statute if that interpretation is "reasonable" or "permissible" ("step two" of *Chevron*).**
>
> **[Blackletter Statement, Part 3, § II.B.]**

As described in the previous sections, *Chevron* directs that an administrative agency's construction of the statute it administers should be considered

---

145. *See* Mich. Citizens for an Indep. Press v. Thornburgh, 868 F.2d 1285, 1292-93 (D.C. Cir. 1989) ("*Chevron* implicitly precludes courts picking and choosing among various canons of statutory construction to reject reasonable *agency* interpretations of ambiguous statutes."); Public Citizen v. Young, 831 F.2d 1108, 1113-18 (D.C. Cir. 1987) (although court concluded particular statutory language was clear, it hinted that in matters of statutory ambiguity, agencies could properly consider the canon *de minimis non curat lex* to avoid costly regulation when risks are minimal).

146. *See, e.g.*, King v. St. Vincent's Hosp., 502 U.S. 215, 220-21 n.9 (1991) (in non-*Chevron* case, presuming that Congress legislates with understanding of interpretive principles like canon that statues conferring veterans' benefits should be construed in favor of beneficiaries).

147. Readers seeking more detail are referred to the extensive analysis provided by Bamberger, *supra* note 131.

under a two-part test.[148] The court first must determine whether the statute resolves the question. If a court determines that Congress has not addressed the question at issue,

> the court does not simply impose its own construction on the statute, as would be necessary in the absence of an administrative interpretation. Rather, if the statute is silent or ambiguous with respect to the specific issue, the question for the court is whether the agency's answer is based on a permissible construction of the statute.[149]

3.032 The Step-Two Inquiry: Equating Reasonableness with Arbitrary-and-Capricious Review

Once a court reaches the second step of *Chevron*, it must defer to an agency's "reasonable"[150] or "permissible"[151] construction of the statute. Thus, a reviewing court must affirm an agency's interpretation even if it is not the best interpretation or the interpretation that the court would have selected in the first instance.[152] Agencies, moreover, are free to change their interpretations of ambiguous statutes; the fact of a change by itself does not mean that the new interpretation is unreasonable.[153] And even if a court has previously interpreted a term in a statute an agency is charged with administering, the agency may later depart from the court's interpretation, provided the prior judicial decision did not hold that its construction followed from the unambiguous terms of the statute.[154]

---

148. An empirical study of courts of appeals decisions in 1995 and 1996 observed that agencies prevailed at step two 89% of the time. Kerr, *supra* note 24, at 31. The overall win rate for agencies (accounting for steps one and two) was 73%. *Id.* A more recent study of Supreme Court opinions from 1983 to 2005 did not consider agency win rates at each step but observed an overall *Chevron* win rate for agencies of 76.2%. Eskridge & Baer, *supra* note 4, at 1122.
149. *Chevron*, 487 U.S. at 843 (footnotes omitted).
150. *Id.* at 845.
151. *Id.* at 843.
152. *Id.* at 843 n.11; *see* Household Credit Servs., Inc. v. Pfennig, 541 U.S. 232, 244 (2004) (stating that court of appeals had erred by "substituting [its] own interstitial lawmaking for that of the [agency]" (internal quotations omitted)).
153. Mayo Found. for Med. Educ. & Research v. United States, 131 S. Ct. 704, 712 (2011); Nat'l Cable & Telecomms. Ass'n v. Brand X Internet Servs., 545 U.S. 967, 981-82 (2005); *Chevron*, 467 U.S. at 863-64; Nat'l Mining Ass'n v. Kempthorne, 512 F.3d 702, 710 n.5 (D.C. Cir. 2008).
154. *Brand X*, 545 U.S. at 982-83.

Defining precisely what constitutes a permissible construction of a statute, or what materials a court will consider in making that determination, is no simple enterprise. One reason for this difficulty is that there are two schools of thought regarding the analysis that should be undertaken at step two.

The first approach is for reviewing courts to conduct thorough step-one analyses but only perfunctory step-two analyses.[155] Consequently, these opinions lack self-conscious explanations of what courts should examine at step two. In *Astrue v. Capato ex rel. B.N.C.*, for example, the Supreme Court engaged in a detailed step-one analysis but, at step two, did little more than refer to that analysis in concluding the construction was permissible.[156] This approach to step two provides support to the contention, discussed above at Part 3.012, that *Chevron* has only one step.

By contrast, a growing consensus holds that the step-two analysis should entail arbitrary-and-capricious review.[157] On this view, at step one, a court determines whether Congress has clearly foreclosed an agency's statutory construction; at step two, the court checks whether the agency has itself offered an explanation for its choice that satisfies the requirement of reasoned decisionmaking associated with arbitrariness review of policy choices. The

---

155. *See, e.g.*, Astrue v. Capato *ex rel.* B.N.C., 132 S. Ct. 2021, 2033-34 (2012) (in opinion in which steps one and two were not clearly delineated, Court conclusorily stated that the agency's reading was entitled to deference after considering statutory term, statutory context, and legislative purpose); Friends of the Everglades v. S. Fla. Water Mgmt. Dist., 570 F.3d 1210, 1227-28 (11th Cir. 2009) (after conducting step-one analysis and opining that the statutory text could bear either party's proffered meaning, court upheld agency's construction "because [it] is one of the two readings we have found is reasonable"; no distinct step-two analysis). For an explanation of this development, see Beermann, *supra* note 8, at 810-15.

156. 132 S. Ct. 2021, 2033-34 (2012).

157. *See* 5 U.S.C. § 706(2)(A) (providing that courts shall hold unlawful agency actions that are "arbitrary, capricious, an abuse of discretion, or otherwise not in accordance with law"). For seminal arguments in favor of this approach, see Levin, *supra* note 57; Mark Seidenfeld, *A Syncopated* Chevron*: Emphasizing Reasoned Decisionmaking in Reviewing Agency Interpretations of Statutes*, 73 TEX. L. REV. 83 (1994). For a more recent essay collecting sources in support of a consensus, see Bamberger & Strauss, *supra* note 39, at 621 & n.39. Numerous courts equate the standards in passing. *See, e.g.*, Nat'l Mining Ass'n v. Kempthorne, 512 F.3d 702, 710 n.4 (D.C. Cir. 2008) (noting overlap between two standards and concluding that because agency interpretation was reasonable under step two, it also survived an arbitrary-and-capricious challenge).

Supreme Court recently made the connection explicit in *Judalang v. Holder*.[158] There, the Court applied arbitrary-and-capricious review to the Board of Immigration Appeals' decision concerning a deportable alien's eligibility for discretionary relief. The government had argued that the applicable test was instead *Chevron*'s step two, but even while rejecting that approach, the Court noted: "Were we to do so, our analysis would be the same, because under *Chevron* step two, we ask whether the agency interpretation is 'arbitrary or capricious in substance.'"[159]

Even so, the scope of what courts will consider under this more rigorous approach varies. For example, courts that do not consider the broader tools of statutory construction at step one, such as canons of construction and legislative history, may apply these tools instead at step two. But opinions that have already considered such materials at step one can appear awkward when they also look to these materials at step two because the analyses appear duplicative. Such materials may include all the conventional statutory sources: the terms or sections of the text of the statute, the overall structure of the statute, the legislative history, and the court's understanding of the purpose of the statute.[160] The range of statutory materials thus varies, and the comprehensiveness of the examination varies as well.[161]

---

158. 132 S. Ct. 476, 483 n.7 (2011).

159. *Id.* (internal citation omitted). The Court explained that the arbitrary-and-capricious standard was more apt because the agency decision did not involve an interpretation of statutory language. *Id.*

160. *See, e.g.*, Your Home Visiting Nurse Servs., Inc. v. Shalala, 525 U.S. 449, 452-57 (1999) (examining the statutory purpose of one provision and consistency with other provisions of the relevant statute); Smiley v. Citibank (S.D.), N.A., 517 U.S. 735, 745 (1996) (examining judicial, common usage, and legal dictionary definitions of a key term at the time of passage of the relevant act); Babbitt v. Sweet Home Chapter of Cmtys. for a Great Oregon, 515 U.S. 687, 697-708 (1995) (examining dictionary definition of key term, statutory purposes and structure, and legislative history); NationsBank of N.C., N.A. v. Variable Annuity Life Ins. Co., 513 U.S. 251, 259-61 (1995) (examining the terms of the act); Rust v. Sullivan, 500 U.S. 173, 184-85, 188-90 (1991) (examining language of the statute, legislative history, congressional intent); Republican Nat'l Comm. v. FEC, 76 F.3d 400, 406 (D.C. Cir. 1996) (examining the statute, legislative history, purpose of the statute); Strickland v. Maine Dep't Human Servs., 48 F.3d 12, 21 (1st Cir. 1995) (examining purpose of the statute).

161. Compare the abbreviated discussion in *Smiley*, 517 U.S. at 745, and *NationsBank*, 513 U.S. at 259-61, with the more comprehensive discussion in *Sweet Home*, 515 U.S. at 697-708.

This method is best improved by being clear about the inquiries at each of the two steps. As described above in Part 3.021, when courts ask at step one whether Congress has "spoken to the precise question at issue,"[162] they compare the statute *to the interpretation that the agency has proffered.* With the agency's interpretation of the statute in mind, the court looks to the statute to determine whether the statute is ambiguous enough to permit the agency's interpretation. In other words, at step one the court asks whether the statute *forecloses*—through its clarity—the agency's interpretation.[163] *Chevron* itself followed this approach to step one. There, at step one, the Court did not ask generally whether "stationary source" was ambiguous, but rather whether the meaning of those terms permitted the agency's bubble policy.[164]

Clarifying how step one actually operates reveals why approaches to step two that focus on statutory meaning seem so awkward. When, at step one, a court compares the agency's interpretation to the statute and determines that the statute does *not* preclude the agency's approach, the court has already decided that the agency's interpretation is within the range of permissible interpretations permitted by the statute. That is, the court has answered the very question that, on the statutory understanding of step two, a look to the statutory materials at the second step might provide. In that context, another

---

162. Chevron, U.S.A., Inc. v. Natural Res. Def. Council, Inc., 467 U.S. 837, 842 (1984).

163. *See, e.g.*, Household Credit Servs., Inc. v. Pfennig, 541 U.S. 232, 240-42 (2004) (considering whether the Truth in Lending Act precludes the agency's view that the term "finance charge" in the statute does not include over-limit fees); Atlantic Mutual Ins. Co. v. Comm'r of Internal Revenue, 523 U.S. 382, 389 (1998) (considering whether the meaning of a key term precludes the agency's view); *Smiley*, 517 U.S. at 739 (noting that "it would be difficult indeed to contend that the word 'interest' in the National Bank Act is unambiguous with regard to the point at issue here"—that is, whether "interest" includes late-fees charged on credit cards, as the agency maintains); *Babbitt*, 515 U.S. at 703 (statute does not unambiguously preclude agency's approach); Consumer Fed'n of Am. v. Dept. of Health and Human Servs., 83 F.3d 1497, 1503 (D.C. Cir. 1996) (rejecting, at step one, challenger's argument that the terms of the statute prevent the agency's approach and concluding that the statute permits the agency's approach); Nat'l Recycling Coalition, Inc. v. Browner, 984 F.2d 1243, 1250 (D.C. Cir. 1993) (holding at step one that "the statutory language does not clearly preclude the [EPA's] interpretation").

164. *See Chevron*, 467 U.S. at 845 (describing its conclusion at step one as being that "Congress did not have a specific intention on the applicability of the bubble concept in these cases").

look at statutory materials—to determine whether the agency's interpretation is within the acceptable range of interpretations—is superfluous and hence bound to be unwieldy and ill-defined.

Nevertheless, such materials may be relevant at step two. Accepting the view that step two is a specialized application of arbitrary-and-capricious analysis, it makes sense that an agency might refer to statutory materials to explain why it chose the particular interpretation it did from the range of permissible options. The important point is that step two places a court in its oversight role, evaluating the agency's rationale for its consideration of relevant factors and reasoning in support of the interpretation adopted. If a statutory term is susceptible of more than one interpretation, therefore, this approach requires the agency to explain how it selected the interpretation it did. Because the *Chevron* context is concerned with interpretations of statutes, the best view is that "relevant factors" ought to include the agency's own statutory analysis.[165] Indeed, it is entirely consistent with the hard-look doctrine's general application—which varies with the circumstances[166]—to conceive of *Chevron* step two simply as a specialized variant within this larger context.

3.033 Other Step-Two Principles

While it is difficult to draw overarching principles from step-two cases, a few guideposts have developed. For example, to qualify for deference at step two, an agency must act with appreciation of its own discretion to interpret the ambiguous term. In *Negusie v. Holder*, the Supreme Court considered the Board of Immigration Appeals' (BIA) determination that the so-called "persecutor bar" in the Refugee Act of 1980 disqualifies an alien from being withheld from removal even if the persecution was coerced.[167] First, the Court considered each party's arguments as to the statutory text, concluding that its

---

165. *See* Bamberger & Strauss, *supra* note 39, at 622.

166. *See* Beermann, *supra* note 8, at 807 n.108 (noting that the Supreme Court has tailored the arbitrary-and-capricious test according to the context); Emily Hammond Meazell, *Super Deference, the Science Obsession, and Judicial Review as Translation of Agency Science*, 109 MICH. L. REV. 733 (2011) (describing variability and collecting sources); Seidenfeld, *supra* note 20, at 310-11 (noting importance of context); *cf.* Bamberger & Strauss, *supra* note 39, at 625 (noting that for step two, "the focus may be on interpretive method, as opposed to the fact-intensive judgments at issue in *State Farm*").

167. 555 U.S. 511 (2009).

silence on the point was not conclusive.[168] Next, the Court evaluated whether a prior Supreme Court decision was controlling; it distinguished the earlier case as relating to a different statutory scheme enacted for different purposes.[169] The BIA had considered itself bound by the earlier decision and thus, had not yet exercised its discretion.[170] As a result, the Court remanded the matter to the agency for additional consideration.[171] This treatment is consistent with the idea that step two is a form of arbitrariness review—an agency cannot make a choice based on reasoned decisionmaking where it does not understand that it has a choice to make. It also reflects the basic proposition that an agency can be upheld only on the basis of the rationale it articulated in making its decision.[172]

Courts are also mindful of agency interpretations that appear to ignore or misunderstand important statutory provisions. In the first case in which an agency lost at step two before the Supreme Court, *AT&T Corp. v. Iowa Utilities Board*,[173] this was one of the agency's failings. The Supreme Court invalidated an aspect of a Federal Communication Commission's (FCC) order implementing the 1996 Telecommunications Act. At issue was the FCC's determination that incumbent local exchange carriers be required to make available a minimum of seven of their network elements to requesting carriers. The objection by the incumbent carriers was that, in compiling the list of network elements incumbents had to make available, the FCC had failed to take account of the statute's requirements that the elements be made available only if access was "necessary" and lack of access to such elements would "impair" an entrant's ability to provide local service. The Supreme Court agreed. Although the portion of the Court's opinion invalidating this aspect of the FCC order does not cite *Chevron*, it adopts a step-two approach insofar as it frames its analysis in terms of whether the agency had given adequate consideration to its choice—*i.e.*, whether it had engaged in reasoned decisionmaking.[174] The Court concluded that the agency had not done so

---

168. *Id.* at 517—18.
169. *Id.* at 520.
170. *Id.* at 523.
171. *Id.* at 523-24.
172. This point is elaborated in chapter 9, *infra*,
173. 525 U.S. 366 (1999).
174. *Id.* at 386–92. For commentary characterizing *Iowa Utilities Board* Court as a step two decision, see *id.* at 397–401 (Souter, J., dissenting from this portion of the Court's opinion); Lisa Schultz Bressman, Schechter Poultry *at the Millennium: A Delegation Doctrine for the Administrative State*, 109 YALE L.J. 1399, 1399–1400 (2000); Michael Herz, *Judicial Review*, *in* DEVELOP-

given that its action was premised on a statutory construction that was "not in accord with the ordinary and fair meaning" of the statutory terms,[175] read the "necessary and impair" provision out of the statute,[176] and was based on a misunderstanding of another provision of the statute. Courts will also consider whether an agency has sufficiently explained an interpretive choice that appears to contradict the statute's language.[177] And as discussed above, courts have also considered such issues as whether an agency has reasonably considered normative canons of construction[178] and legislative history.

MENTS IN ADMINISTRATIVE LAW AND REGULATORY PRACTICE 1998–1999, at 52–54 (Jeffrey S. Lubbers ed. 2000) (describing *Iowa Utilities* as a step-two case, but noting how under the Court's approach steps one and two "collapse into one another").

175. *Iowa Utilities Bd.*, 525 U.S. at 389–90.

176. *Id.* at 390.

177. Hill v. Norton, 275 F.3d 98, 99 (D.C. Cir. 2001).

178. Bamberger, *supra* note 131; *supra* Part 3.02227.

Chapter 4

THE APPLICABILITY OF THE *CHEVRON* DOCTRINE—"*CHEVRON* STEP ZERO"

by Steven Croley and Richard Murphy*

4.01 INTRODUCTION

In *Chevron U.S.A. Inc. v. Natural Resources Defense Council*,[1] the Supreme Court provided a two-step formulation for judicial consideration of an administrative agency's interpretation of a regulatory statute that it administers. According to *Chevron*'s now-boilerplate language:

---

* Steven Croley is Harry Burns Hutchins Collegiate Professor of Law, University of Michigan Law School (on leave) and Richard Murphy is AT&T Professor of Law, Texas Tech University School of Law.

1. 467 U.S. 837 (1984).

> First, always, is the question whether Congress has directly spoken to the precise question at issue. If the intent of Congress is clear, . . . the court, as well as the agency, must give effect to the unambiguously expressed intent of Congress. If, however, the court determines Congress has not directly addressed the precise question at issue, the court does not simply impose its own construction on the statute, as would be necessary in the absence of an administrative interpretation. Rather, if the statute is silent or ambiguous . . . the question for the court is whether the agency's answer is based on a permissible construction of the statute.[2]

Ever since the Court announced this framework, courts and commentators have analyzed and debated the meaning and implications of *Chevron* deference. Whatever its nuances, plainly this doctrine contemplates a less active role for the judiciary in interpreting regulatory statutes, at least relative to other kinds of statutes. In this vein, *Chevron* has famously been characterized as "a counter-*Marbury* for the administrative state."[3]

Whether the *Chevron* doctrine applies to an agency's statutory construction is therefore an issue of considerable importance. Nonetheless, *Chevron* left unanswered important questions concerning the scope of its application.[4] In that case, the Supreme Court extended deference to a statutory construction that the EPA adopted via notice and comment of a phrase in the Clean Air Act. These circumstances made for a very strong case for deference. Agencies, however, interpret statutes through a wide variety of other means—e.g., through formal adjudication, pursuant to interpretive rules or policy statements, through informal adjudication, during the course of litigation, and so on. This variety raises questions about which sorts of agency statutory constructions deserve *Chevron*'s strong deference and which do not. The problem of determining whether *Chevron* applies has come to be called *Chevron*'s "step zero."

This chapter begins by explaining the *Mead*[5] and *Barnhart*[6] frameworks that the Supreme Court has established for resolving the step-zero question.

---

2. *Id.* at 842-43 (footnotes omitted).
3. Cass R. Sunstein, *Law and Administration after* Chevron, 90 Colum. L. Rev. 2071, 2075 (1990).
4. *See especially* Thomas W. Merrill & Kristin E. Hickman, Chevron*'s Domain*, 89 Geo. L.J. 833, 858 (2001) (identifying and analyzing numerous questions regarding the scope of the *Chevron* doctrine's applicability).
5. United States v. Mead Corp., 533 U.S. 218 (2001).
6. Barnhart v. Walton, 535 U.S. 212 (2002).

Oversimplifying somewhat for purposes of this introduction, these frameworks together establish that, where an agency adopts a construction of statutory language that it is specially charged with administering:

- if the agency used notice-and-comment, formal adjudication, or similarly "formal" and extensive means to adopt the statutory construction, it merits *Chevron* deference;
- if the agency used less extensive means, then *Chevron*'s applicability depends on a multi-factor inquiry.

After discussing these two general frameworks, the chapter turns to refinements and applications of step zero in specific settings.

4.02 TWO MAJOR SUPREME COURT CASES ON *CHEVRON*'S SCOPE

Starting from a *Marbury*-style presumption that courts are in charge of determining legal meaning, *Chevron*'s deference to agency statutory constructions demands some sort of justification. In *Chevron* itself, the Court relied on a mix of justifications. It observed that, insofar as statutory construction implicates policymaking, agencies have greater expertise and political legitimacy to make the relevant choices.[7] It also styled *Chevron* deference as a function of implicit congressional delegation. Courts should defer to an agency's reasonable construction of a statute that the agency administers because that is what Congress wants[8]—even though it generally does not say so. Along these lines, in its 2006 opinion in *Long Island Care at Home, Ltd. v. Coke,* the Court reiterated that, to determine *Chevron*'s applicability, "the ultimate question is whether Congress would have intended, and expected, courts to treat an agency's rule, regulation, application of a statute, or other agency action as within, or outside, its delegation to the agency of [statutory] 'gap-filling' authority."[9]

This approach leaves the problem of identifying those circumstances in which Congress expects courts to extend *Chevron* deference to agencies. As detailed below, the Court has devised two quite different approaches. Neither, it seems fair to say, involves inquiry into "actual" congressional intent.

---

7. Chevron, U.S.A., Inc. v. Natural Res. Def. Council, 467 U.S. 837, 865-66 (1984).
8. *Id.* at 843.
9. 551 U.S. 158, 173-74 (2007).

Rather, the Court has identified factors that, in its view, justify the stance that a reviewing court should affirm an agency's reasonable choice among plausible statutory constructions rather than attempt to devise and impose a better one. The Court has then projected its views onto the screen of congressional intent.[10]

The first of these approaches, the *Mead*[11] framework, indulges the plausible premise that Congress would expect statutory constructions promulgated via relatively involved and transparent procedures—notably including notice-and-comment rulemaking and formal adjudication—to warrant *Chevron*'s deferential treatment. Where an agency has produced its statutory construction by one of these means, it is generally a straightforward matter to determine with little analysis that *Chevron* applies.

Agency statutory constructions produced through less extensive and participatory procedures, such as interpretive rules and policy statements promulgated without notice and comment, cannot make the same easy, straightforward claim to *Chevron* deference under *Mead*. *Chevron* deference may, however, be available under the *Barnhart*[12] framework. This approach instructs courts to extend *Chevron* deference based on consideration of factors such as agency expertise, the complexity of the statute at issue, the importance of the question, etc. *Barnhart*, in essence, instructs courts to apply *Chevron* where agency comparative advantages in interpretation—and the limited benefits of imposing a novel judicial construction—justify this deferential treatment. Notably absent from *Barnhart,* although it cites *Mead,* is any express reliance on the latter's theme of congressional intent and implicit delegation. However, later cases discussing the reach of *Chevron*, such as *Long Island Care at Home* noted above, do emphasize that *Chevron* hinges on congressional intent. One can square this circle, albeit with some strain, by characterizing *Barnhart* as requiring application of *Chevron* where it is reasonable to do so, and presuming that Congress, naturally, wants what is reasonable.

---

10. *Cf.* Mark Seidenfeld, Chevron*'s Foundation,* 86 Notre Dame L. Rev. 273, 281 (2011) (observing that the Court's frameworks for step zero "are much less confusing if they are seen as relying on the court determining not what Congress intended, but rather on factors that would make it reasonable for Congress to have intended that agencies enjoy interpretive primacy").
11. United States v. Mead Corp., 533 U.S. 218 (2001).
12. Barnhart v. Walton, 535 U.S. 212 (2002).

4.021 The *Mead* Framework and Its Safe Harbors

The Supreme Court issued its most important statement on *Chevron*'s applicability in *United States v. Mead Corp.*[13] This case arose out of a dispute over a Customs Service tariff classification. The Customs Service had reclassified Mead Corp.'s "day planner" as a "bound" "diary" under the codified Harmonized Tariff Schedule of the United States, thereby subjecting it to an import tax. This reclassification took the form of a "ruling letter." Customs issues thousands of these letters per year from dozens of offices across the country, without notice and comment, to determine the tariffs applicable on specific goods. They bind their recipients and Customs officials until they are modified or revoked. Third parties were advised that they could cite ruling letters as persuasive authority but should not rely on them as they could be changed without notice to the broader public.

The Supreme Court rejected Customs' contention that *Chevron* deference applied to its ruling letter. Summarizing principles for determining the scope of *Chevron,* the Court declared:

> We hold that administrative implementation of a particular statutory provision qualifies for *Chevron* deference when it appears [a] that Congress delegated authority to the agency generally to make rules carrying the force of law, and [b] that the agency interpretation claiming deference was promulgated in the exercise of that authority. Delegation of such authority may be shown in a variety of ways, as by an agency's power to engage in [a] adjudication or [b] notice-and-comment rulemaking, or by [c] some other indication of a comparable congressional intent.[14]

Practically speaking, this approach creates a safe harbor for *Chevron* deference for an agency's interpretation of a statute that it is specially charged with administering as long as the agency used notice and comment, formal adjudication, or similarly extensive procedures to develop the interpretation. The Court justified this approach in terms of likely congressional intent,

---

13. 533 U.S. 218 (2001). *Mead* superseded the Court's effort to specify the scope of *Chevron* in an opinion issued just the year before, Christensen v. Harris Cnty., 529 U.S. 576 (2000) (holding that an opinion letter, "like interpretations contained in policy statements, agency manuals, and enforcement guidelines, all of which lack the force of law," did not warrant *Chevron* deference).
14. *Mead Corp.*, 533 U.S. at 226-27.

explaining: "It is fair to assume generally that Congress contemplates administrative action with the effect of law when it provides for a relatively formal administrative procedure tending to foster the fairness and deliberation that should underlie a pronouncement of such force."[15] Along these same lines, the Court noted that most of its own cases applying *Chevron* deference "have reviewed the fruits of notice-and-comment rulemaking or formal adjudication."[16] The Court also conceded, however, that *Chevron* can apply outside of these safe harbors—so long as Congress has given "some other indication" of its intent that *Chevron* should apply.[17] The Court did not spell out the nature of these "other" indications, leaving them for further case-law development.

Applying its new framework, the Court concluded that *Chevron* deference did not extend to Customs' ruling letters.[18] With regard to the delegation prong, the Court observed that the congressional grant of power to issue binding classifications applicable to specific transactions "did not bespeak the legislative type of activity that would naturally bind more than the parties to the ruling."[19] Just as the concept of "law" presumes general applicability, an agency's statutory construction cannot carry the "force of law" in the *Chevron* sense without some expectation of general applicability—which the delegation to issue ruling letters did not contemplate. With regard to the second prong, the Court concluded that Customs had not, in any event, meant to imbue the ruling letter with the force of law: Customs did not use notice and comment to create them, specifically advised third parties against relying on them, and "churned out" 10,000 to 15,000 ruling letters per year from 46 offices. The sheer volume of ruling letters alone rendered the claim that the letters might carry the force of law "self-refuting."[20]

15. *Id.* at 230. The Court's use of the term "formal" to specify procedures that can earn *Chevron* deference was understandable but somewhat unfortunate given the preexisting vernacular of administrative law. It has long been common to describe notice-and-comment rulemaking as a type of "informal" rulemaking. For the purposes of *Mead*, however, this type of rulemaking is "formal" enough to warrant *Chevron* deference.
16. *Id.* at 229-30.
17. *Id.* at 231. *Mead* thus rejected the Court's suggestion a year earlier in *Christensen*, 529 U.S. at 587, that rules adopted without notice and comment in opinion letters, policy statements, manuals, etc. must be categorically excluded from *Chevron* deference.
18. *Mead Corp.*, 533 U.S. at 234.
19. *Id.* at 232.
20. *Id.*

The Court declined, however, to hold that Customs' ruling letter merited no deference at all. Although *Chevron*'s strong deference did not apply, *Skidmore* deference did. A court applying *Skidmore* should adopt the statutory construction it deems most persuasive, but only after careful consideration of the agency's construction. The weight of the agency's construction in a given case "will depend upon the thoroughness evident in its consideration, the validity of its reasoning, its consistency with earlier and later pronouncements, and all those factors which give it power to persuade, if lacking power to control."[21] The Court, accordingly, remanded the case to the Court of Appeals for the Federal Circuit, instructing it to consider the Customs ruling under *Skidmore*.[22]

In sum, *Mead* declares that *Chevron* applies where: (a) Congress has granted an agency power to imbue a statutory construction with the "force of law" and (b) the agency used this power. Statutory constructions produced via relatively extensive and participatory procedures, such as notice-and-comment rulemaking or formal adjudication, will generally satisfy both prongs of the *Mead* framework. (Contexts where these procedures do *not* earn *Chevron* deference are discussed in §§ 4.031 and 4.032 below.) Outside these safe harbors, *Chevron* may or may not apply. The Court gave little specific guidance in *Mead* to make this determination other than to direct reviewing courts' attention to congressional intent.

4.022 *Barnhart*'s Multi-factor Inquiry

Just a year after *Mead,* the Court issued an opinion shedding light on *Chevron*'s applicability outside of the *Mead* safe harbors in *Barnhart v. Walton.*[23] This case revolved around the meaning of the term "disability" for determining eligibility for Social Security benefits. The Social Security Agency had issued its interpretation in an opinion letter as early as 1957. Decades later and perhaps in response to the litigation itself, the agency embedded its interpretation in a rule issued via notice and comment, thus clearly earning *Chevron* deference under *Mead.*

Writing for eight justices, Justice Breyer took the opportunity to explain that *Chevron* would have applied even without the protection of the notice-and-comment rulemaking. He explained:

---

21. Skidmore v. Swift & Co., 323 U.S. 134, 140 (1944). *See generally* Chapter 5, *infra.*
22. *Mead Corp.,* 533 U.S. at 238-39. On remand, the Court of Appeals again concluded that the agency had misread the statute. Mead Corp. v. United States, 282 F.3d 1342 (Fed. Cir. 2002).
23. 535 U.S. 212 (2002).

> [T]he Agency's interpretation is one of long standing. . . . In this case, the interstitial nature of the legal question, the related expertise of the Agency, the importance of the question to administration of the statute, the complexity of that administration, and the careful consideration the Agency has given the question over a long period of time all indicate that *Chevron* provides the appropriate legal lens through which to view the legality of the Agency interpretation here at issue.[24]

This multi-factor, rule-of-reason approach to determining *Chevron*'s scope is obviously in some tension with *Mead*'s more formal, two-pronged inquiry, and it puts even more strain on the Court's insistence that *Chevron* deference is a function of congressional intent. In essence, *Barnhart* advises a court, when reviewing an agency's statutory construction produced by informal means, to assess any relevant factors suggesting that better results will be achieved by affirming the agency's reasonable statutory construction rather than by imposing the court's own independent judgment. An agency's pertinent expertise and careful consideration of a problem, for instance, weigh in favor of trusting its statutory construction. Where an agency lacks pertinent expertise or gives a sloppy explanation for its statutory construction, more aggressive judicial review is in order. Examples of judicial applications of *Barnhart* are explored in § 4.033 below.

Like other multi-factor tests, the *Barnhart* framework is vulnerable to the charge that it is indeterminate and thus costly to apply. Courts sometimes limit this cost by declaring that they need not resolve the step-zero issue of *Chevron*'s applicability because an agency's statutory construction is sufficiently strong that it should prevail regardless of whether it has earned *Chevron*'s thumb on the interpretive scale.[25] Commentators have named this practice "*Chevron* avoidance."[26]

---

24. *Id.* at 221-22.

25. *See, e.g.*, Durr v. Shinseki, 638 F.3d 1342, 1348 (11th Cir. 2011) (declining to decide whether *Chevron* or *Skidmore* deference applies to Veterans Administration personnel handbooks); Cervantes v. Holder, 597 F.3d 229, 233 n.5 (4th Cir. 2010) (declining to determine whether *Chevron* or *Skidmore* deference applies to nonprecedential decisions by a single member of the Board of Immigration Appeals).

26. Adrian Vermeule, *Our Schmittian Administrative Law*, 122 HARV. L. REV. 1095, 1127-29 (2009) (describing cases of *Chevron* avoidance); Lisa Schultz Bressman, *How* Mead *Has Muddled Judicial Review of Agency Action*, 58 VAND. L. REV. 1443, 1464-69 (2005) (discussing *Chevron* avoidance).

4.03 REFINEMENTS AND APPLICATIONS OF STEP ZERO

4.031 Notice-and-Comment Rulemaking

> ***Chevron* principles apply to an agency's interpretation of a statute the agency administers where that interpretation is embodied in a rule that has the force of law.**
> **[Blackletter Statement, Part 3, § II.C(1)(a).]**

Mead's recognition that notice-and-comment rulemaking nearly guarantees *Chevron* deference was consistent with prior judicial applications of that doctrine, as well as its underlying logic. As mentioned above, *Chevron* itself involved a notice-and-comment rulemaking by the EPA, pursuant to which the EPA interpreted the term "source" in the Clean Air Act Amendments of 1977. Subsequently, application of *Chevron* deference to substantive rules promulgated via notice and comment became common and unproblematic.[27] This comes as no great shock. Substantive rulemaking most clearly entails agency exercise of policy judgment, under authority delegated by Congress. Also, where notice and comment is used, substantive rulemaking entails a relatively open and deliberative process. As the *Chevron* Court emphasized, it is in such circumstances where considerations of agency expertise and political accountability counsel most strongly in favor of deference.[28]

Mead's promise of *Chevron* deference for statutory constructions vetted through notice-and-comment rulemaking is not absolute, however. Recall that under the first prong of *Mead*, *Chevron* deference requires that Congress "delegated authority to the agency generally to make rules carrying the force of law." Where an agency acts beyond the scope of its delegated authority to imbue statutory constructions with the force of law, *Chevron* does not apply. For example, *Chevron* would not apply were EPA, for some reason, to include a gloss on the Occupational Safety and Health Act in a rule that EPA promulgated via notice and comment. This type of distinction was dispositive in *Gonzales v. Oregon,* in which the Attorney General claimed *Chevron* deference for a rule interpreting "legitimate medical purpose" as used by the

---

27. *See, e.g.*, AT&T Corp. v. Iowa Utilities Bd., 525 U.S. 366 (1999); Smiley v. Citibank, N.A., 517 U.S. 735 (1996). *See also* Robert A. Anthony, *Which Agency Interpretations Should Bind Citizens and the Courts?*, 7 YALE J. ON REG. 1, 44 (1990).
28. *Chevron*, 467 U.S. at 843-44, 865-66.

Controlled Substances Act (CSA) to exclude assisted suicide.[29] The Attorney General has rulemaking authority under the CSA, but shares it with the Secretary of Health and Human Services. Among other reasons for denying *Chevron* deference, the Court concluded that the Attorney General's authority under the CSA did not extend to making medical judgments. (For further discussion of *Chevron*'s applicability where multiple agencies implement a statute, see § 4.034, below.)

In theory, it is also possible for a statutory construction vetted through notice-and-comment rulemaking to fail to win *Chevron* deference at the second prong of *Mead,* which checks whether the agency invoked its delegated power. For example, an agency might, for whatever reason, use notice and comment without intending to imbue a rule with the force of law. The Supreme Court's opinion in *Long Island Care at Home, Ltd. v. Coke* indicates that this sort of attack is generally unpromising.[30] In this case, the Department of Labor had promulgated a regulation using notice and comment but inserted it into a section of the Code of Federal Regulations labeled "Interpretations." The Second Circuit relied on this point and related evidence to conclude that the rule did not merit *Chevron* deference. The Supreme Court reversed. It explained that the real touchstone of *Chevron*'s applicability is congressional intent. Courts should assume Congress intended for *Chevron* deference to apply to an agency's reasonable statutory interpretation, falling within its statutory authority, where the rule "sets forth important individual rights and duties, where the agency focuses fully and directly upon the issue, [and] where the agency uses full notice-and-comment procedures to promulgate a rule."[31] The Department of Labor's regulation satisfied all of these conditions, and thus *Chevron* applied, even though the agency had, after a fashion, identified the regulation as interpretive in nature, thus implying it lacked the force of law.

4.032 Formal Adjudication

> ***Chevron* principles apply to an agency's interpretation of a statute the agency administers where the interpretation was developed in the course of formal adjudication, except where the adjudicating agency's lawmaking power is limited by virtue of a "split-enforcement" statutory scheme, in which lawmaking au-**

29. 546 U.S. 243 (2006).
30. 551 U.S. 158 (2007).
31. *Id.* at 173.

thority over the same subject has been vested in an enforcing agency.

[Blackletter Statement, Part 3, § II.C(1)(b).]

Well before *Mead,* the Supreme Court made clear that *Chevron* deference is not confined to interpretations occasioned by agency rulemaking, but extends also to agency interpretations made in connection with formal adjudications, including enforcement actions.[32] *INS v. Aguirre-Aguirre*, which involved an individual deportation determination, is illustrative. There, the Court of Appeals had set aside a determination by the Board of Immigration Appeals (BIA) on the ground that the BIA incorrectly interpreted the statutory phrase "serious nonpolitical crime." The Supreme Court reversed, explaining that the BIA should be accorded *Chevron* deference when it gives ambiguous statutory terms "'concrete meaning through a process of case-by-case adjudication.'"[33]

Consistent with *Mead,* the rule that formal adjudication triggers *Chevron* deference is subject to a catch. *Chevron* only applies to the extent that Congress has granted an agency the power to imbue a statutory construction with the force of law. This requirement is generally not problematic for those agencies that enjoy both adjudicatory and rulemaking power. Congress sometimes, however, establishes split-enforcement schemes that allocate enforcement and policymaking powers to one agency but adjudicatory power to another. One example is the Federal Mine Safety and Health Review Commission, an adjudicating agency whose counterpart, the Mine Safety and Health Administration, also within the Department of Labor, has been assigned the task of policymaking. Similarly, the Occupational Safety and Health Administration sets policy through regulations, while the Occupational Safety and Health Review Commission adjudicates alleged violations of those regulations. This split-enforcement scheme raised the problem of determining which agency should have authority to resolve ambiguities in regulations—the agency that promulgated them (OSHA) or the agency applying them (OSHRC). In *Martin v. OSHRC*,[34] the Court held that reviewing courts should extend *Auer*

---

32. *See, e.g.*, INS v. Aguirre-Aguirre, 526 U.S. 415, 425 (1999) (Board of Immigration Appeals order); National R.R. Passenger Corp. v. ICC, 503 U.S. 407, 418-19 (1992) (ICC order); DeBartolo Corp. v. Florida Gulf Coast Bldg. & Constr. Trades Council, 485 U.S. 568 (1988) (NLRB order); INS v. Cardoza-Fonseca, 480 U.S. 421, 446 (1987) (INS hearing).
33. *Aguirre-Aguirre*, 526 U.S. at 425 (quoting *Cardoza-Fonseca*, 480 U.S. at 448-49).
34. 499 U.S. 144 (1991).

deference, which requires deference to an agency's reasonable construction of its own regulations, to the promulgator, OSHA, because Congress had assigned policymaking duties to it, not OSHRC.[35] Along these same lines, lower courts have held that they owe *Chevron* deference to the policymaking agency, not the adjudicator, in split-enforcement schemes where the two agencies adopt conflicting interpretations of a statute they jointly administer.[36] In the absence of a conflicting interpretation by the policymaker, however, some courts have held that an adjudicating agency's statutory construction can still merit *Chevron* deference.[37]

4.033 "Informal" Proceedings

> ***Chevron* principles apply to an agency's interpretation of a statute the agency administers where the interpretation was developed in the course of informal agency action if the agency's conferred authority and other statutory circumstances demonstrate that "Congress would expect the agency to be able to speak with the force of law" in taking such action; or the interstitial nature of the legal question, the related expertise of the agency, the importance of the question to administration of the statute, the complexity of that administration, and the careful consideration the agency has given the question over a long period of time indicate that *Chevron* deference is appropriate.**
>
> **[Blackletter Statement, Part 3, §§ II.C(1)(c), (d).]**

---

35. *Id.* at 152-53. *Auer* deference applies to an agency's construction of its own regulations, whereas *Chevron* deference applies to an agency's construction of a statute it administers.
36. For cases extending *Chevron* deference to the policymaker rather than the adjudicator, see, e.g., Pattison Sand Co., LLC v. Federal Mine Safety and Health Rev. Comm'n, 688 F.3d 507, 512-13 (8th Cir. 2012); Sec'y of Labor v. Excel Mining, LLC, 334 F.3d 1, 5-6 (D.C. Cir. 2003); Joy Technologies, Inc. v. Sec'y of Labor, 99 F.3d 991, 995 (10th Cir. 1996). For cases extending more limited *Skidmore* deference to the policymaking agency, see, e.g., Vulcan Const. Materials, L.P. v. Federal Mine Safety and Health Rev. Comm'n, 700 F.3d 297, 312 (7th Cir. 2012); North Fork Coal Corp. v. Federal Mine Safety and Health Rev. Comm'n, 691 F.3d 735, 742 (6th Cir. 2012).
37. Pendley v. Federal Mine Safety & Health Rev. Comm'n, 601 F.3d 417, 423 (6th Cir. 2010); Olson v. Federal Mine Safety & Health Rev. Comm'n, 381 F.3d 1007, 1011 (10th Cir. 2004).

Chevron principles do not apply to agency interpretations that are embodied in policy statements, manuals, enforcement guidelines, interpretive rules, and other such documents unless the agency's conferred authority and other statutory circumstances demonstrate that "Congress would expect the agency to be able to speak with the force of law" in taking such action.
[Blackletter Statement, Part 3, § II.C(2)(e).]

Ever since *Chevron* was decided, courts have shown periodic reluctance to apply its form of deference to agency statutory constructions developed without extensive procedures akin to notice and comment or formal adjudication. Such agency statutory constructions often appear in the guise of agency guidelines, manuals, opinion letters, and so on. Sometimes courts have extended *Chevron* deference to such agency interpretations, sometimes they have not.

Just a year before issuing its *Mead* decision, the Court addressed this problem in *Christensen v. Harris County*.[38] In this case Justice Thomas, writing for a five-justice majority, rejected application of *Chevron* deference to an opinion letter issued by the Department of Labor's Wage and Hour Division. Justice Thomas first noted that the interpretation at issue had not been "arrived at after, for example, a formal adjudication or notice-and-comment rulemaking."[39] He then broadly declared that "[i]nterpretations such as those in opinion letters—like interpretations contained in policy statements, agency manuals, and enforcement guidelines, all of which lack the force of law—do not warrant *Chevron*-style deference."[40]

Mead backtracked on any suggestion in *Christensen* that extensive agency procedures are *required* for *Chevron* deference, but its treatment of this issue was notably vague. As noted above, the Court conceded that Congress can use "some other indication" than a grant of authority to engage in notice-and-comment rulemaking or relatively formal adjudication to signal that it expects an agency's statutory construction to merit *Chevron* deference.[41] The

---

38. 529 U.S. 576 (2000).
39. *Id.* at 587.
40. *Id.*
41. United States v. Mead Corp., 533 U.S. 218, 227 (2001). To some extent, the Court was forced to make this concession as it recently had extended *Chevron* deference to a statutory interpretation embedded in a letter issued to a private party by a Senior Deputy Comptroller of the Currency. *Id.* at 231 (citing *NationsBank of N.C., N.A. v. Variable Annuity Life Ins. Co.*, 513 U.S. 251 (1995)).

Court did not, however, specify what these other indications might be. *Mead* thus provided little additional guidance regarding when *Chevron* might, for instance, appropriately apply to a policy statement issued without notice and comment or to the results of an informal adjudication.

Still, the Court's treatment of the Customs ruling letter at issue in that case did identify one important factor that courts have since used to determine that an agency statutory construction does *not* warrant *Chevron* deference. Recall that Customs produced over ten thousand such ruling letters per year and expressly warned third parties not to rely on them. Law is supposed to be generally applicable. As Customs had not committed to general application of the ruling letter it had issued to Mead Corp., it followed that Customs had not imbued this letter with *Chevron*'s "force of law."[42] Following this logic, courts have found that an agency's failure to commit to general application of a statutory construction precludes *Chevron* deference.[43]

In *Barnhart v. Walton,*[44] the Supreme Court squarely addressed the problem of determining the applicability of *Chevron* to statutory constructions developed informally, but it did so in a way that compounded rather than eliminated indeterminacy. As discussed above in § 4.022, *Barnhart* instructs courts to apply a multi-factor inquiry to determine if *Chevron* applies to agency statutory constructions. Relevant factors include: "the interstitial nature of the legal question, the related expertise of the Agency, the importance of the question to administration of the statute, the complexity of that administration, and the careful consideration the Agency has given the question over a long period of time."[45] The Court's list of factors include many that suggest that an agency has a comparative advantage over the courts in choosing the "best" statutory construction—e.g., "related expertise" and "careful consideration . . . over a long period of time." Other factors suggest that imposing a judicial construction may have limited value—e.g., an "interstitial" legal question, by hypothesis, has limited reach. In essence, a court should apply *Chevron* where, after consideration of any such factors as may seem relevant, it determines that it is better to trust an agency's reasoned and reasonable statutory construction than to impose its own.

---

42. United States v. Mead Corp., 533 U.S. 218, 232 (2001).

43. *See* Price v. Stevedoring Servs. of Am., Inc., 697 F.3d 820, 826-28 (9th Cir. 2012) (en banc). For a decision using generality to justify *Chevron* deference for informally developed statutory constructions, see Schneider v. Feinberg, 345 F.3d 135, 143 (2d Cir. 2003).

44. 535 U.S. 212 (2002).

45. *Id.* at 222.

A litigant is likely to be able to find useful (if not dispositive) applications of the *Barnhart* factors given that this case, as of this writing, has been cited in judicial opinions nearly 1,000 times.[46] This section will close with two examples from this vast sea—one deploying the *Barnhart* factors to justify applying *Chevron*, and the other refusing to do so.

In *Managed Pharmacy Care v. Sebelius,* the plaintiffs challenged a decision by the Secretary of Health and Human Services to approve two State Plan Amendments (SPAs) submitted by California that would reduce reimbursement rates under Medicaid for various medical services and equipment.[47] Among many other complex requirements, § 30(A) of the relevant statutory provision mandated that a state Medicaid plan must provide "methods and procedures" sufficient

> to assure that payments are consistent with efficiency, economy, and quality of care and are sufficient to enlist enough providers so that care and services are available under the plan at least to the extent that such care and services are available to the general population in the geographic area.[48]

The plaintiffs contended that California's SPAs were inconsistent with § 30(A) because the state had failed to submit cost studies in support of most of its proposed reductions; the agency read § 30(A) not to require such studies.

The Ninth Circuit began its analysis by applying the *Brand X* doctrine (discussed below in § 4.037) to conclude that its precedent interpreting § 30(A) to require consideration of costs was not binding in the instant case. It then explained that *Chevron* deference was owed to the Secretary's construction of § 30(A) even though SPA approval did not involve extensive procedures such as notice and comment or formal adjudication. The Court observed that interested providers had, in fact, "offered extensive input" to the

---

46. *See, e.g.*, Fournier v. Sebelius, 718 F.3d 1110 (9th Cir. 2013) (applying *Barnhart* factors to conclude that *Chevron* deference applied to Secretary's interpretation of "dental exclusion" for Medicare coverage), *cert. denied,* 134 S. Ct. 1501 (2014); Hagans v. Comm'r of Soc. Sec., 694 F.3d 287 (3rd Cir. 2012) (discussing *Christensen, Mead,* and *Barnhart*; concluding that *Chevron* deference did not apply to "Acquiescence Ruling" by the Social Security Administration), *cert. denied,* 134 S. Ct. 1274 (2014); Mylan Labs., Inc. v. Thompson, 389 F.3d 1272, 1280 (D.C. Cir. 2004) (extending *Chevron* deference to FDA letter due to "complexity of the statutory regime. . . , the FDA's expertise [and] the careful craft of the scheme it devised").
47. 716 F.3d 1235 (9th Cir. 2013), *cert. denied,* 134 S. Ct. 900 (2014).
48. 42 U.S.C. § 1396a(a)(30)(A) (hereinafter "§ 30(A)").

Secretary's delegate, the Center for Medicare and Medicaid Services (CMS), as it determined whether to approve the SPAs. The court added that, although the use of a statutorily authorized and extensive process such as notice and comment is "clear evidence" that Congress expects an agency's legal construction to carry the force of law, "it is not the only evidence of such congressional intent." In the absence of such procedures, courts determining whether to apply *Chevron* should also consider, inter alia, the *Barnhart* factors.

Application of the *Barnhart* factors in *Managed Pharmacy Care* led the Ninth Circuit firmly to the conclusion that *Chevron* should apply to the Secretary's statutory construction. It seems fair to say that a dominant theme of the court's discussion was respect for the immensity and difficulty of the Secretary's project in implementing Medicaid, "a colossal undertaking." The court observed that the statutory terms at issue, which included "sufficient," "efficiency," and "economy," were "amorphous" and defining them implicated agency expertise.[49] Administering Medicaid was "nothing if not complex."[50] The executive branch had "been giving careful consideration to the ins and outs of the program since its inception, and the agency is the expert in all things Medicaid."[51] Moreover, "Congress explicitly granted the Secretary authority to determine whether a State's Medicaid plan complies with federal law."[52] Given this much, the court eagerly extended *Chevron* deference to the agency.

Fox v. Clinton, by contrast, provides a good illustration of a court's adamant refusal to apply *Chevron* to a poorly explained statutory construction issued with little if any visible procedure.[53] Dr. Fox, a Jewish-American by birth, appealed the Department of State's denial of his request for a Certificate of Loss of Nationality (CLN) confirming that he had given up his American nationality either due to his naturalization by Israel or by his swearing of an oath of allegiance to it. The agency's final denial of this request took the form of a letter issued by an official with the Bureau of Consular Affairs. The court noted that *Chevron* deference could apply in the absence of extensive procedures, and it discussed several cases in which a court, after applying the *Barnhart* factors, had extended *Chevron* deference to an agency decision "clearly intended to have general applicability and the force of law."[54] The

49. *Id.* at 1247-48.
50. *Id.* at 1248.
51. *Id.*
52. *Id.* at 1249.
53. 684 F.3d 67 (D.C. Cir. 2012).
54. *Id.* at 77-78.

agency letter most emphatically did not deserve this treatment, however, as "the Department offered little more than uncited, conclusory assertions of law in a short, informal document that does not purport to set policy for future CLN determinations."[55]

4.034 Statutes that Apply to Multiple Agencies

> ***Chevron*** **principles do not apply to agency interpretations of statutes that apply to many agencies and are specially administered by none, such as the APA, FOIA, or the National Environmental Policy Act (although *Chevron* may apply to interpretations of statutes administered by two or a few agencies).**
>
> **[Blackletter Statement, Part 3, § II.C(2)(a).]**

Many foundational statutes apply to multiple agencies, including, for example, the Administrative Procedure Act itself, as well as the Freedom of Information Act (FOIA), the Federal Advisory Committee Act, and the National Environmental Policy Act. Courts do not extend *Chevron* deference to constructions of these generally applicable statutes by agencies that are not specially charged with administering them.[56] An agency that does play a special role in implementing a generally applicable statute may, however, earn deference for its statutory construction. For example, Congress has charged the Office of Management and Budget (OMB) with promulgating guidelines for implementing FOIA and the Privacy Act, and courts have held that these guidelines are entitled to *Chevron* deference.[57]

Where two or a few agencies jointly administer a statute (such as the Longshore and Harbor Worker's Compensation Act), and especially where more than one agency is authorized to issue regulations under a single act (such as the

---

55. *Id.* at 78.
56. *See, e.g.*, Metro. Stevedore Co. v. Rambo, 521 U.S. 121, 137 n.9 (1997) (APA); Collins v. Nat'l Transp. Safety Bd., 351 F.3d 1246, 1253 (D.C. Cir. 2003) ("For generic statutes like the APA, FOIA, and FACA, the broadly sprawling applicability undermines any basis for deference, and courts must therefore review interpretative questions de novo."); Al-Fayed v. CIA, 254 F.3d 300, 307 (D.C. Cir. 2001) (FOIA); DuBois v. USDA, 102 F.3d 1273, 1285 n.15 (1st Cir. 1996) (NEPA); Benavides v. U.S. Bureau of Prisons, 995 F.2d 269, 272 n.2 (D.C. Cir. 1993) (Privacy Act).
57. Envtl. Protection Information Ctr. v. U.S. Forest Serv., 432 F.3d 945, 947 (9th Cir. 2005) (FOIA); Maydak v. United States, 363 F.3d 512 (D.C. Cir. 2004) (Privacy Act).

Americans with Disabilities Act), the issue of which agency, if any, is owed deference can be complicated. The Supreme Court has acknowledged the difficulty but not explained how to resolve it.[58] If one agency has exclusive responsibility for enforcing particular portions of the act in question, *Chevron* will apply if the agency is acting within the scope of its delegated authority but not otherwise.[59] By contrast, where multiple agencies have "specialized enforcement responsibilities but their authority potentially overlaps," de novo review may be necessary to prevent regulatory inconsistency.[60] Also emphasizing the importance of consistency, at least one lower court has ruled that where agencies that jointly administer a statute coordinate and agree on the interpretation of the statutory term, *Chevron* deference is appropriate.[61]

4.035 Interpretations of Criminal Statutes by the Prosecuting Agency

> ***Chevron* principles do not apply to agency interpretations of criminal statutes where the agency's power with respect to the statute consists solely of the power to prosecute offenses in court. [Blackletter Statement, Part 3, § II.C(2)(b).]**

58. *See* Bragdon v. Abbott, 524 U.S. 624, 642 (1998); Long v. Soc. Sec. Admin., 635 F.3d 526, 534 (Fed. Cir. 2011) (noting "courts have addressed but left unresolved the issue of whether *Chevron* deference is appropriate where multiple agencies are responsible for administering a statute"). *See generally* Russell L. Weaver, *Deference to Regulatory Interpretations: Inter-Agency Conflicts*, 43 Ala. L. Rev. 35 (1991).
59. Gonzales v. Oregon, 546 U.S. 243, 258 (2006) (rejecting Attorney General's claim to *Chevron* deference for interpretation of "legitimate medical purpose" in the Controlled Substances Act; although the Attorney General possesses rulemaking authority under the Act, this authority does not extend to making medical judgments); Collins v. Nat'l Transp. Safety Bd., 351 F.3d 1246, 1253 (D.C. Cir. 2003) (observing that "for statutes where expert enforcement agencies have mutually exclusive authority over separate sets of regulated persons, ... concerns [regarding inconsistency] don't work against application of *Chevron* deference").
60. *Collins*, 351 F.3d at 1253. *See also* DeNaples v. Office of Comptroller of Currency, 706 F.3d 481, 487 (D.C. Cir. 2013) (distinguishing between "generic statutes like the APA, FOIA, and FACA, statutes ...under which agencies have specialized—but potentially overlapping—authority, and statutes where expert enforcement agencies have mutually exclusive authority over separate sets of regulated persons") (citation and quotation marks omitted).
61. *See* Individual Reference Servs. Group v. FTC, 145 F. Supp. 2d 6, 23-24 (D.D.C. 2001) (citing National Treasury Employees Union v. MSPB, 743 F.2d 895, 916-17 (D.C. Cir. 1984)).

Chevron applies to regulatory agencies' interpretations of regulatory statutes. Accordingly, courts have refused to show *Chevron* deference to the Justice Department's interpretations of the criminal provisions of the U.S. Code. Indeed, *Chevron*'s inapplicability in this context was established in the years immediately following the *Chevron* decision.[62] Courts have provided several explanations for why *Chevron* deference does not apply to prosecutors. First, courts, not adversarial prosecutors, are the proper administrators of federal criminal statutes.[63] Second, the rule of law and due process require that criminal law be clear, which in turn implies there is not room for interpretive flexibility commonly associated with deference to administrative agencies' interpretations of statutes.[64] Third, prosecutorial entities such as the Justice Department would have too many incentives to interpret criminal statutes expansively,[65] although whether that general tendency distinguishes prosecutorial agencies from regulatory agencies is not so obvious. At any rate, for all of these reasons courts have "never thought that the interpretation of those charged with prosecuting criminal statutes is entitled to deference."[66]

---

62. *See, e.g.*, United States v. McGoff, 831 F.2d 1071, 1077 (D.C. Cir. 1987) ("We are, in short, far outside *Chevron* territory here.").

63. *See* Crandon v. United States, 494 U.S. 152, 177 (1990) (Scalia, J., concurring). *See also* George v. Junior Achievement of Cent. Indiana, Inc., 694 F.3d 812, 816 (7th Cir. 2012) (noting that *Chevron* is inapplicable where the "Secretary has no delegated rulemaking or adjudicative authority" and acts solely as "a prosecutor, bringing suits asking for judicial enforcement"); Michel v. I.N.S., 206 F.3d 253, 262 (2d Cir. 2000) ("[C]ourts owe no deference to an agency's interpretations of state or federal criminal laws, because the agency is not charged with the administration of such laws."); United States v. W. Elec. Co., 900 F.2d 283, 297 (D.C. Cir. 1990) (observing that "agencies' legal views are deferred to only when they make a determination (either quasi-legislative or quasi-judicial) that has independent legal significance—as opposed to when they act in a prosecutorial role").

64. *See McGoff*, 831 F.2d at 1077. *But see* Sash v. Zenk, 439 F.3d 61, 67 n.6 (2d Cir. 2006) (Sotomayor, J.) (extending *Chevron* deference to Bureau of Prisons' interpretation of statute governing good-time credits; holding that "where an agency gives clear notice of the meaning of a statute by regulation, and where it is reasonable to charge defendants with notice of the agency's interpretation, *Chevron* deference will apply prior to the rule of lenity"); Elliot Greenfield, *A Lenity Exception to* Chevron *Deference,* 58 BAYLOR L. REV. 1, 38-46 (2006) (assessing judicial approaches to the interaction of *Chevron* and the rule of lenity).

65. *See Crandon*, 494 U.S. at 177-78 (Scalia, J., concurring).

66. *Id.*

On the other hand, courts have extended *Chevron* deference to a regulatory agency's interpretation of its enabling act even though that act criminalizes certain behavior.[67] Similarly, when a statute makes violation of an agency regulation a crime—as do most of the environmental laws, for example—and the regulation itself receives *Chevron* deference, the result is in essence *Chevron* deference with regard to a criminal statute, just not to the prosecuting agency.[68]

4.036 Interpretations Representing Merely an Agency's Litigation Posture

> ***Chevron* principles do not apply to agency interpretations that represent merely the agency's litigating posture developed after the agency's decision.**
>
> **[Blackletter Statement, Part 3, § II.C(2)(d).]**

Courts have been especially unwilling to extend *Chevron* deference where an agency's interpretation is adopted or asserted solely in the course of litigation. Where an agency offers an interpretation for the first time in a legal brief or, worse, during oral argument, that interpretation will not enjoy *Chevron* deference.

Bowen v. Georgetown University[69] captures Supreme Court sentiment here. In *Bowen*, the Court refused to extend *Chevron* deference to HHS's interpretation of a provision of the Medicare Act on the ground that the offered interpretation was merely a litigating position "wholly unsupported by regulations, rulings, or administrative practice."[70] The Court explained: "[W]e have declined to give deference to an agency counsel's interpretation of a statute where the agency itself has articulated no position on the question, on the ground that 'Congress has delegated to the administrative official and not

67. Babbitt v. Sweet Home Chapter of Cmtys. for a Great Or., 515 U.S. 687, 704 n.18 (1995) (deferring to the Secretary's interpretation of "take" under the Endangered Species Act); Alliance for Cannabis Therapeutics v. DEA, 930 F.2d 936, 939 (D.C. Cir. 1991) (extending *Chevron* deference to formal order by the Drug Enforcement Agency classifying marijuana under the Controlled Substances Act).
68. *See, e.g.*, United States v. O'Hagan, 521 U.S. 642 (1997) (deferring to SEC's interpretation of "fraudulent" in the context of a criminal prosecution).
69. 488 U.S. 204 (1988).
70. 488 U.S. at 212.

to appellate counsel the responsibility for elaborating and enforcing statutory commands.'"[71]

On the other hand, an interpretation developed through a notice-and-comment rulemaking will enjoy *Chevron* deference even if the rulemaking itself was prompted by litigation. The Supreme Court made this clear in *Smiley v. Citibank*:[72]

> Nor does it matter that the regulation was prompted by litigation, including this very suit. . . . [W]e have before us . . . a full-dress regulation, issued by the Comptroller . . . and adopted pursuant to the notice-and-comment procedures of the [APA] designed to assure deliberation. . . . That it was litigation which disclosed the need for the regulation is irrelevant.[73]

The crucial question, in other words, is whether an interpretation was developed purely to support a litigating position, especially by agency counsel not charged with administering the statute in question,[74] or instead represents a genuine and procedurally sufficient effort at agency policymaking. Post-hoc rationalizations by agency counsel in the course of litigation are not

---

71. *Id.* (quoting Investment Co. Inst. v. Camp, 401 U.S. 617, 628 (1971)). *See also* Miller v. Clinton, 687 F.3d 1332, 1340 (D.C. Cir. 2012) ("We do not, for example, defer to post hoc interpretations contained in agency briefs.") (collecting authority).
72. 517 U.S. 735 (1996).
73. *Id.* at 741. *See also* Barnhart v. Walton, 535 U.S. 212, 221 (2002) (rejecting argument that interpretation embedded in rule issued after notice and comment should be disregarded because it had been adopted recently and "perhaps in response to this litigation"); United Seniors Ass'n, Inc. v. Shalala, 182 F.3d 965, 970 (D.C. Cir. 1999) (interpretation promulgated as a rule 10 days after oral arguments still warranted *Chevron* deference where agency had previously expressed similar interpretation in the course of congressional testimony).
74. *Compare* Sidwell v. Express Container Servs., Inc., 71 F.3d 1134, 1142 & n.13 (4th Cir. 1995) (citing *Bowen* and refusing to defer to agency interpretation because legal arguments made in support of agency's interpretation extended beyond any supported by the memorandum itself), *with* Appalachian Regional Healthcare, Inc. v. Shalala, 131 F.3d 1050, 1054 (D.C. Cir. 1997) (deferring and noting that agency counsel's fuller articulation of interpretation contained in agency's "terse" adjudication decision does not render interpretation merely a litigating position).

entitled to *Chevron* deference.[75] This point holds with all the more force to agency interpretations that change during the course of litigation or that constitute litigation-inspired departures from previous agency interpretations.[76]

4.037 *Chevron*'s Relation to Stare Decisis

> ***Chevron* principles do not apply to agency interpretations that contradict the interpretation of a statute given in a controlling judicial decision if that court's opinion indicates that its interpretation follows from the unambiguous terms of the statute and thus leaves no room for agency discretion.**
>
> **[Blackletter Statement, Part 3, § II.C(2)(c).]**

Suppose that a court determines that an agency statutory interpretation does not qualify for *Chevron* deference—perhaps because it was developed without sufficiently extensive and transparent procedures. Following the Court's instructions in *Mead,* the reviewing court applies *Skidmore* deference and concludes that, although the agency statutory interpretation is at least reasonable, it is not the best available, and rejects it. The agency, however, is not yet done. It adopts the rejected interpretation again, but this time uses notice-and-comment rulemaking. The new regulation is challenged in court in another round of proceedings. Do principles of stare decisis require that the new regulation be set aside? Or do principles of *Chevron* deference trump the earlier court decision?

The law on this point was muddled until the Supreme Court's decision in *National Cable & Telecommunications Association v. Brand X Internet Services.*[77] In that case, petitioners sought review of the FCC's determination that broadband Internet access provided by cable companies amounted to an "information service" rather than a "telecommunications service." The Ninth Circuit vacated in part, relying on circuit precedent holding that cable modem service is a "telecommunications service."[78] The Supreme Court reversed:

---

75. *See also* Parker v. Office of Personnel Mgmt., 974 F.2d 164, 166 (1992) (refusing to extend *Chevron* deference to "unsubstantiated affidavit" of agency official interpreting statute) (citing *Bowen*).

76. *See* Fla. Manufactured Housing Ass'n, Inc. v. Cisneros, 53 F.3d 1565, 1574 (11th Cir. 1995).

77. 545 U.S. 967 (2005).

78. *See* Brand X Internet Servs. v. FCC, 345 F.3d 1120 (9th Cir. 2003) (concluding that it was bound by AT&T v. City of Portland, 216 F.3d 871 (9th Cir. 2000); relying on Neal v. United States, 516 U.S. 284, 294-95 (1996) (declaring that "[o]nce we have determined a statute's meaning, we adhere to our

> A court's prior judicial construction of a statute trumps an agency construction otherwise entitled to *Chevron* deference only if the prior court decision holds that its construction follows from the unambiguous terms of the statute and thus leaves no room for agency discretion.[79]

In other words, for the judicial precedent to trump, it must indicate that, had the court in the earlier proceedings applied *Chevron* deference to the agency construction, the court would have rejected it at step one as "unambiguously foreclose[d]."[80] If the precedent does not exclude the possibility that the agency's construction might fall within the range of reasonable choices, then that construction can lay claim to *Chevron* deference notwithstanding the precedent. This conclusion avoids the awkward result of making the availability of *Chevron* deference depend on timing.

Justice Scalia wrote a tart dissent in which he charged the majority with "yet another breathtaking novelty: judicial decisions subject to reversal by Executive officers."[81] The majority responded that this critique was misplaced

---

ruling under the doctrine of stare decisis, and we assess an agency's later interpretation of the statute against that settled law")).

79. *Brand X*, 545 U.S. at 982. The Court applied this principle to a lower court precedent. Whether it would apply this same principle to its own precedents is not absolutely clear. Justice Stevens concurred subject to the caveat that the majority's approach "would not necessarily be applicable to a decision by this Court that would presumably remove any pre-existing ambiguity." *Id.* at 1003 (Steven, J., concurring). A few years later, Justice Breyer, writing for a four-justice plurality, applied the *Brand X* framework to a Supreme Court precedent in *United States v. Home Concrete & Supply LLC,* 132 S. Ct. 1836 (2012). Justice Kennedy authored a four-justice dissent declining to reach the issue of *Brand X*'s applicability to Supreme Court precedents but adding that the issue had not yet been resolved. *Id.* at 1851-52 (Kennedy, J., dissenting). Justice Scalia rejects the *Brand X* framework altogether. *Brand X,* 545 U.S. at 1015 (Scalia, J., dissenting).

80. *Brand X*, 545 U.S. at 982-83. For examples of application of this principle by lower courts, see, e.g., Managed Pharmacy Care v. Sebelius, 716 F.3d 1235 (9th Cir. 2013) (holding that precedent that did not hold that it "represented the *only* reasonable interpretation" of a statute did not block application in later litigation of *Chevron* deference to agency's later interpretation), *cert. denied,* 134 S. Ct. 900 (2014); Metropolitan Hosp. v. U.S. Dept. of Health and Human Services, 712 F.3d 248, 255-59 (6th Cir. 2013) (explaining "that *Brand X* gives stare decisis effect to a prior judicial construction of a statute only when made as a *Chevron* step-one holding" and discussing implications).

81. *Brand X*, 545 U.S. at 1015 (Scalia, J., dissenting).

because, under *Chevron,* "a court's opinion as to the best reading of an ambiguous statute an agency is charged with administering is not authoritative."[82] The Court's approach in *Brand X* does not enable precedents to be reversed by an agency "any more than a federal court's interpretation of a State's law can be said to have been 'reversed' by a state court that adopts a conflicting (yet authoritative) interpretation of state law."[83]

Subsequently, in *United States v. Home Concrete & Supply, LLC*, a plurality of the Court clarified that determining whether a judicial precedent forecloses later invocation of *Chevron* does not depend on whether the statute at issue is "ambiguous" in some abstract, linguistic sense.[84] This case turned on interpretation of a provision of the tax code that extended the time for the Government to assess a deficiency from three to six years under some circumstances. The Court had interpreted the same operative language in 1958 in *Colony v. Commissioner of Internal Revenue.*[85] In that opinion, the Court had noted that the language at issue was not "unambiguous." Many decades later in *Home Concrete,* the government tried to use this concession in tandem with *Brand X* to trump the *Colony* Court's construction.[86]

Writing for four justices, Justice Breyer explained that the government's argument missed the underlying point of *Brand X,* which is that "it is for agencies, not courts, to fill statutory gaps."[87] The fact that the *Colony* Court, writing long before *Chevron,* had described the statutory language at issue as "ambiguous" did not necessarily mean that there was a gap to fill. *Chevron* instructs courts to use the full panoply of "traditional tools of statutory construction" when determining if Congress had an intent with regard to a particular issue. Consistent with this instruction, the *Colony* Court had held that the taxpayer's textual argument was "better," that the legislative history foreclosed the Commissioner's preferred interpretation, and that this interpretation, if followed, would "create a patent incongruity in the tax law."[88] Given this analysis, the *Colony* Court, notwithstanding its concession of linguistic ambiguity, had determined that Congress had a controlling intent. As there was no statutory gap to fill, there was no space for *Chevron* to trump stare decisis.

---

82. *Id.* at 983.
83. *Id.* at 983-84.
84. 132 S. Ct. 1836 (2012) (plurality opinion).
85. 357 U.S. 28 (1958).
86. 132 S. Ct. at 1843 (plurality opinion).
87. *Id.* (quoting *Brand X,* 545 U.S. at 982).
88. *Id.* at 1844.

4.038 *Chevron* and Interpretations of Agency Jurisdiction

> **Although in general courts have extended *Chevron* deference to agencies' interpretations of the boundaries of their own statutory jurisdiction, *Chevron* principles have uncertain application to an agency interpretation that significantly expands the agency's previously recognized jurisdiction.**
>
> **[Blackletter Statement, Part 3, § II.C(3).][89]**

Until recently, the applicability of *Chevron* to an agency's statutory interpretation bearing on its "jurisdiction," or the scope of its power, was controversial.[90] Many shared an intuition against deference in this setting, fearing that agencies might abuse their *Chevron* authority to build empires and self-aggrandize. One main counter to this argument is that, in the agency context, the difference between jurisdictional and nonjurisdictional agency statutory constructions is illusory. In *City of Arlington v. FCC*, Justice Scalia authored the majority opinion emphatically adopting this latter view, proclaiming "judges should not waste their time in the mental acrobatics needed to decide whether an agency's interpretation of a statutory provision is 'jurisdictional' or 'nonjurisdictional.'"[91]

Justice Scalia suggested that efforts to distinguish agency statutory constructions according to whether they are "jurisdictional" might have roots in

---

89. As this subsection explains, this passage from the *Blackletter Statement* has been superseded by the Supreme Court's recent opinion in City of Arlington v. FCC, 133 S. Ct. 1863 (2013), which held that *Chevron*'s applicability does not depend on whether an agency's statutory construction is "jurisdictional."
90. *See, e.g.*, Miss. Power & Light Co. v. Miss., 487 U.S. 354, 381-82 (1988) (Scalia, J., concurring) (contending that "there is no discernible line between an agency's exceeding its authority [*i.e.*, "jurisdiction"] and an agency's exceeding authorized application of its authority"). *Cf. id.* at 386-87 (Brennan, J., dissenting) (contending that "[a]gencies do not 'administer' statutes confining the scope of their jurisdiction, and such statutes are not 'entrusted' to agencies"). *See also* Ernest Gellhorn & Paul Verkuil, *Controlling* Chevron-*Based Delegation*, 20 Cardozo L. Rev. 989 (1999) (contending *Chevron* deference should not extend to jurisdictional issues). *But see* Quincy M. Crawford, Chevron *Deference to Agency Interpretations that Delimit the Scope of the Agency's Jurisdiction*, 61 U. Chi. L. Rev. 957 (1994) (contending that *Chevron* should apply to agency jurisdictional determinations).
91. 133 S. Ct. 1863, 1870 (2013).

a mistaken analogy to the judicial system. For the courts, he explained, the distinction between jurisdictional and nonjurisdictional is meaningful: "Whether the court decided *correctly* is a question that has different consequences from the question whether it had the power to decide *at all*." Thus "a jurisdictionally proper but substantively incorrect judicial decision is not ultra vires."

This distinction does not apply to agencies. It does not matter whether an agency action is characterized as marking an improper assertion of power or an improper application of an accepted power. In either event, if the charge is substantively correct, the agency action is ultra vires. The real question is therefore "always, simply, *whether the agency has stayed within the bounds of its statutory authority*."[92] As such, "there is no principled basis for carving out some arbitrary subset of such claims as 'jurisdictional.'"[93] After insisting on this point, Justice Scalia toured through precedents to establish that the Court had consistently applied *Chevron* regardless of the "jurisdictional" label.

Chief Justice Roberts authored a vigorous dissent, joined by Justices Kennedy and Alito. He contended that use of the term "jurisdiction" in this context caused needless confusion. Properly understood, the real question revolved around allocating power to determine whether Congress intended an agency to enjoy *Chevron* authority to construe a given statutory provision with the force of law.[94] He insisted that *Chevron* should not apply to this threshold issue of *Chevron*'s applicability.[95]

To some extent, the majority and the dissent may have been talking past each other in *City of Arlington*. It is not clear that they had in mind the same definition of "jurisdictional questions." One definition would be that such questions concern determining the persons, places, or activities over which an agency has authority. Thus, questions such as whether a wetland is "water of the United States," or whether a tobacco cigarette is a "drug" or "drug delivery device," or, for that matter, whether an entire facility can be a "source" under the Clean Air Act are all "jurisdictional" in this sense. The cases surveyed by Justice Scalia as examples of the Court deferring to jurisdictional interpretations are generally of this sort. In contrast, the Chief

92. *Id.* at 1868 (emphasis in original).
93. *Id.* at 1869.
94. *Id.* at 1879-80 (Roberts, C.J., dissenting).
95. *Id.* at 1880 (Roberts, C.J., dissenting) ("But before a court may grant such deference, it must on its own decide whether Congress—the branch vested with lawmaking authority under the Constitution—has in fact delegated to the agency lawmaking power over the ambiguity at issue.").

Justice has in mind not agency determinations regarding which persons, places, or activities they can regulate but rather agency determinations as to whether they possess the primary interpretive authority contemplated by *Chevron* deference. He insists that courts, not agencies, must determine which questions of statutory construction fall within an agency's *Chevron* power to resolve with the force of law. In fact, Justice Scalia might actually agree with the proposition.[96]

96. For an argument along these lines, see Michael Herz, *Deference Running Riot: Separating Interpretation and Lawmaking Under* Chevron, 6 ADMIN. L.J. AM. U. 187 (1992). Herz argues that, on the one hand, "[w]hatever it is that *Chevron* requires, it requires it equally with regard to substantive and jurisdictional questions." *Id.* at 218. But, "[o]n the other hand, *Chevron* does not require a court to accept an agency's view of the scope of its delegated *authority*, jurisdictional or substantive. By definition, Congress *cannot* have left this determination to the agency." *Id.* at 219.

Chapter 5

JUDICIAL REVIEW OF STATUTORY ISSUES OUTSIDE OF *CHEVRON*

by Michael Herz*

5.01 INTRODUCTION

The foregoing chapters have explored when courts owe "*Chevron* deference" to agency interpretations and what that means. But suppose *Chevron* does *not* apply; how should a court approach a statutory issue then? In the absence of a relevant agency interpretation, the question is the general one of how judges should interpret statutes. That's a topic for another book. This chapter addresses the narrower problem of how a court treats an agency's interpretation of a statute when *Chevron* does not apply.

5.02 *SKIDMORE v. SWIFT & CO.*

Even in situations in which *Chevron* principles do not apply, . . . courts ordinarily will give some deference or weight to an

* Arthur Kaplan Professor of Law, Benjamin N. Cardozo School of Law, Yeshiva University. Thanks to Ron Levin and Kevin Stack for comments and corrections on an earlier draft.

agency's interpretation of a statute that it administers. In these circumstances, as the Supreme Court ruled in *Skidmore v. Swift & Co.*, 323 U.S. 134 (1944), the agency's view can have "power to persuade," as distinguished from "power to control."
[Blackletter Statement, Part 3, § II.D.]

The idea that agency interpretations of statutes should influence courts long predates *Chevron*. Historically, judicial practice was inconsistent, varying between something close to a rubber-stamp of agency interpretations and independent judicial interpretation with barely a nod toward the agency's views.[1] Anticipating later caselaw, commentators' efforts to bring coherence to this area of law tended to focus on whether Congress could be said to have decided the issue itself or assigned it to the agency to decide.[2] While the ultimate determination of statutory meaning remained with the court,[3] the statute itself might delegate the underlying policy question to the agency, particularly in instances where the agency itself has the task of applying the law to particular factual settings.[4]

Much of this caselaw has been supplanted by *Chevron* and its progeny, but not all. Of the "granddaddy" cases, the most significant is *Skidmore v. Swift & Co.*[5] Privately employed firefighters sued their employer under the Fair Labor Standards Act. They argued that time spent on call in the firehouse was working time, for which they were owed overtime pay. The employer responded, in Justice Jackson's pithy phrase, that while on call the firefighters were "waiting

---

1. *See* RICHARD J. PIERCE, JR. ET AL., ADMINISTRATIVE LAW AND PROCESS 397-98 (5th ed. 2009); Stephen Breyer, *Judicial Review of Questions of Law and Policy*, 38 ADMIN. L. REV. 363, 365-67 (1986).
2. *See, e.g.*, Breyer, *supra* note 1, at 368-72; Ronald M. Levin, *Scope-of-Review Doctrine Restated: An Administrative Law Section Report*, 38 ADMIN. L. REV. 239, 247-48 (1986).
3. *See, e.g.*, SEC v. Sloan, 436 U.S. 103, 119 (1978) (noting that agency interpretation merits "great weight" but must yield before contrary statutory meaning); Volkswagenwerk v. FMC, 390 U.S. 261, 272 (1968) ("The construction put on a statute by the agency charged with administering it is entitled to deference by the courts, and ordinarily that construction will be affirmed if it has a 'reasonable basis in law.' But the courts are the final authorities on issues of statutory construction . . . .") (citations omitted).
4. *See, e.g.*, NLRB v. Hearst Publ'ns, Inc., 322 U.S. 111, 132 (1944) (accepting NLRB's conclusion that newspaper sellers are "employees" within the meaning of the statute).
5. 323 U.S. 134 (1944).

to be engaged" rather than "engaged to wait."[6] The lower courts ruled for the employer, concluding that waiting was, by definition, not working time; the Supreme Court reversed and remanded. It found that the courts below should have taken into account the Interpretive Bulletins issued by the Wage and Hour Administrator, which eschewed the categorical approach they had taken.

The essential and much-quoted portion of the opinion reads:

> [T]he rulings, interpretations and opinions of the Administrator under this Act, while not controlling upon the courts by reason of their authority, do constitute a body of experience and informed judgment to which courts and litigants may properly resort for guidance. The weight of such a judgment in a particular case will depend upon the thoroughness evident in its consideration, the validity of its reasoning, its consistency with earlier and later pronouncements, and all those factors which give it power to persuade, if lacking power to control.[7]

The judicial approach articulated in *Skidmore* has three notable characteristics. First, the agency interpretation matters but does not bind the courts. It provides "guidance" and has "weight," but it does not "control." A court is thus freer to disagree with the agency than it is in *Chevron* step two. Second, this sort of deference lies on a sliding scale. The weight of a particular agency interpretation depends on the circumstances. Third, in *Skidmore* itself it seemed that this approach was linked to the nature of the lawsuit—in particular, to the fact that the agency was not a party. Congress had not given the Wage and Hour Administrator authority to regulate with the force of law or to adjudicate individual violations. *Skidmore v. Swift & Co.* was private litigation. The court was necessarily the fact-finder, the law-applier, and, accordingly, the gap-filler. This setting requires independent judicial judgment in a way that direct review of the agency's exercise of delegated authority might not.[8]

---

6. *Id.* at 137 ("Facts may show that the employee was engaged to wait, or they may show that he waited to be engaged. His compensation may cover both waiting and task, or only performance of the task itself.").
7. *Id.* at 140. Notably, Justice Jackson cited no authority for these propositions. This is not because none existed, but rather because these ideas were well-settled. Although *Skidmore* gets all the cites in our day, that is because it has become the iconic representative of a large body of case law, not because it was novel or "simply [Jackson's] remarkable invention." Peter Strauss, *In Search of* Skidmore, FORDHAM L. REV. (forthcoming), *available at* http://ssrn.com/abstract=2287343.
8. *See generally* Ronald M. Levin, *Identifying Questions of Law in Administrative Law*, 74 GEO. L.J. 1, 56-58 (1985).

Despite some initial uncertainty,[9] *Skidmore* survives *Chevron*. For example, *Equal Employment Opportunity Commission v. Arabian American Oil Company* ("*Aramco*")[10] concerned whether Title VII of the Civil Rights Act of 1964, prohibiting discrimination in employment, covers foreign activities of U.S. companies. An EEOC interpretive guideline concluded that the Act does apply abroad. The Court disagreed, but cited *Skidmore* and observed that the agency's view, though not binding, carried some weight.[11]

Aramco, like *Skidmore* itself, was a suit between two private parties. In *United States v. Mead Corp.*,[12] however, the Court made clear that *Skidmore* also applies on direct review of agency action. The U.S. Customs Service had classified Mead's "day planner" as a "diary," thereby subjecting it to a tariff. It did so in a "ruling letter." Dozens of Customs Service offices issue thousands of ruling letters every year, without notice and comment. Mead sought judicial review of the classification, and the Court of Appeals for the Federal Circuit set aside the ruling as inconsistent with the statute. The Supreme Court reversed. After concluding that *Chevron* did not apply,[13] it held that a reviewing court *should* afford the interpretation *Skidmore* deference and remanded to allow the Court of Appeals to do so.[14]

---

9. *See, e.g.*, EEOC v. Arabian Am. Oil Co., 499 U.S. 244, 259 (1991) (Scalia, J., concurring) (arguing that *Chevron* completely supplanted *Skidmore*); Mead Corp. v. United States, 185 F.3d 1304, 1306-08 (Fed. Cir. 1999) (holding that statutory interpretations that did not merit *Chevron* deference are reviewed de novo), *rev'd*, 533 U.S. 218 (2000).
10. 499 U.S. 244 (1991).
11. *Id.* at 257-58. *See also* Christensen v. Harris Cnty., 529 U.S. 576, 587-88 (2000) (granting *Skidmore* but not *Chevron* deference to an interpretation of the Fair Labor Standards Act that was contained in an opinion letter written by the Acting Administrator of the Wage & Hour Division); Bragdon v. Abbott, 524 U.S. 624, 641-42 (1998) (not deciding whether *Chevron* applied to the regulations in question because "it is enough to observe that the well-reasoned views of the agencies implementing a statute" merit *Skidmore* deference).
12. 533 U.S. 218 (2000). *Mead* is discussed at greater length in Chapter Four, *supra*.
13. *Id.* at 227-34.
14. *Id.* at 234-38. On remand, the Federal Circuit cited *Skidmore* and purported to place some weight on the agency's interpretation, but again found that the agency had misread the statute. Mead Corp. v. United States, 283 F.3d 1342, 1346-50 (Fed. Cir. 2002).

Mead reinvigorated the *Skidmore* doctrine.[15] In numerous decisions since, the federal courts have invoked *Skidmore* and stated that agency interpretations to which *Chevron* does not apply still merit respect under *Skidmore*. In doing so, they have made no distinction whatever between private litigation and suits to which the agency is a party. *Skidmore* deference is due, then, whenever an agency has expressed views about the meaning of a statute it administers and *Chevron* is inapplicable. Similarly, *Skidmore* also applies when the ordinary *Chevron*-like rules of strong deference to an agency's interpretation of its own regulations are inapplicable.[16] Just how *much* respect *Skidmore* affords these interpretations is both variable and disputed, and is the subject of the next section.

5.03 THE NATURE OF *SKIDMORE* DEFERENCE

> **In determining whether and to what extent an agency interpretation deserves *Skidmore* deference, courts are guided by such factors as the thoroughness evident in its consideration, the validity of its reasoning, and its consistency with earlier and later pronouncements.**
>
> **In various circumstances, the rigor of a court's scrutiny when it applies *Skidmore* sometimes appears to resemble *Chevron* deference, but at other times it appears significantly more intrusive. No clear pattern emerges from the cases.**
>
> **[Blackletter Statement, Part 3, § II.D.]**

---

15. The rise and fall and rise of *Skidmore* is recounted in detail in Kristin E. Hickman & Matthew D. Krueger, *In Search of the Modern* Skidmore *Standard*, 107 COLUM. L. REV. 1235, 1239-50 (2007).
16. As fully discussed in Part III of Chapter 6, *infra*, the longstanding principle has been that courts give particular deference to an agency's interpretation of its own regulations. *See, e.g.*, Auer v. Robbins, 519 U.S. 452 (1997). In recent years, the Supreme Court has carved out limited circumstances where that general approach does not apply. In those cases, the agency's interpretation of its own regulation does receive *Skidmore* deference. *See, e.g.*, Christopher v. Smithkline Beecham Corp., 132 S. Ct. 2156, 2169 (2012). *See also* Independent Training & Apprenticeship Program v. Calif. Dept. of Industrial Relations, 730 F.3d 1024 (9th Cir. 2013) (rejecting *Auer* deference because of notice concerns but applying *Skidmore* and *upholding* the agency's interpretation).

5.031 The "Quality" of *Skidmore* Deference

It is common to view "*Skidmore* deference" and "*Chevron* deference" as different in degree, the first being "weak" and second "strong." This is misleading; the two are different in kind.[17]

Under *Skidmore* an agency interpretation influences but does not bind; it is a relevant factor, but only one of many inputs, along with text, purpose, history, and so on. The agency's view has "weight"; by definition, then, it can be "outweighed" by other indications of statutory meaning. The agency interpretation never supplants or obviates the need to examine other indicia of statutory meaning.

Under *Chevron* step two, in contrast, courts are not deciding what the statute means.[18] The premise is that the statute has no clear meaning (though it sets some boundaries). Because the agency is engaged in an essentially legislative task, assigned to it by Congress in light of its superior accountability and expertise, the Court must accept the agency's decision as long as it is not foreclosed by the statute and it meets standards of reasoned decisionmaking. Under *Skidmore*, the court independently interprets the statute; the agency's interpretation is one factor among many that will affect its conclusion.[19] Under *Chevron*, the agency is the decisionmaker; under *Skidmore,* the court is. Under *Chevron*, courts "defer" in the sense of acceding to or accepting, as in deferring to someone else's authority. Under *Skidmore*, courts "defer" in the sense of giving weight to, taking seriously, respecting. The distinction is captured in Peter Strauss's suggestion that the term "deference" be abandoned altogether in favor of "*Skidmore* weight" and "*Chevron* space."[20]

---

17. A very helpful general discussion is Peter L. Strauss, *"Deference" is Too Confusing— Let's Call Them "*Chevron *Space" and "*Skidmore *Weight"*, 112 Colum. L. Rev. 1143 (2012).
18. Views as to what courts *are* doing within step two are divided. *See* Chapter Three, § II.B.2, *supra*; Appendix, *Scope of Review*, Part II.B, *infra.*
19. *See* Estate of Landers v. Leavitt, 545 F.3d 98, 105 (2d Cir. 2008); Russell L. Weaver, *The Emperor Has No Clothes:* Christensen, Mead *and Dual Deference Standards*, 54 Admin. L. Rev. 173, 178 (2002); Robert A. Anthony, *Which Agency Interpretations Should Bind Citizens and the Courts?,* 7 Yale J. on Reg. 1, 13 (1990) (noting that under *Skidmore* final decisionmaking power "remains with the court").
20. Strauss, *supra* note 17, at 1145 ("'*Chevron* space' denotes the area within which an administrative agency has been statutorily empowered to act in a manner that creates legal obligations or constraints . . . . '*Skidmore* weight' addresses the possibility that an agency's view on a given statutory question may in itself warrant respect by judges who themselves have ultimate interpretive authority."). In an earlier formulation of the same idea, Professor Strauss

For example, in *Alaska Department of Environmental Conservation*, Justice Ginsburg observed that in *Chevron* the Court had "accorded *dispositive effect* to EPA's interpretation of an ambiguous [statutory] provision" whereas the interpretation here "does not qualify for the dispositive force described in *Chevron*."[21] Instead, it merely "warrant[ed] respect."[22] The Court *agreed* with the agency, but it did not *defer* in the strong sense.[23] In other recent cases, the Court has cited *Skidmore* but ultimately rejected the agency interpretation—not because it was unreasonable, but because it was wrong.[24] Exactly how much weight or respect the Court *in fact* accorded the agency interpretation in each of these cases is undeterminable. It is often hard to tell whether *Skidmore* is doing any work. Judicial opinions sometimes cite *Skidmore* and acknowledge that some deference is due, but otherwise proceed without any additional reference to or apparent influence by *Skidmore*.[25]

If the quantity of deference is hard to pin down, the quality is clear enough. In these cases the Court took its task to be to make (1) a *judicial*

---

spoke of "weight" in the *Skidmore* setting and "obedience" in the *Chevron* setting. Peter L. Strauss, Administrative Justice in the United States 371 & n.104 (2d ed. 2002). *See also* Michael Herz, *Deference Running Riot: Separating Interpretation and Lawmaking under* Chevron, 6 Admin. L.J. Am. U. 187 (1992).

21. Alaska Dep't of Env. Cons. v. EPA, 540 U.S. 461, 487 (2004) (emphasis added).
22. *Id.* (quoting Washington State Dep't of Social & Health Servs. v. Guardianship Estate of Keffeler, 537 U.S. 371, 385 (2003)). These quotations from *Alaska DEC* are selective; Justice Ginsburg's wording is not always so precise. *See infra* notes 48-49 and accompanying text.
23. Similar Supreme Court decisions upholding agency interpretations under *Skidmore* are Kasten v. Saint-Gobain Performance Plastics Corp., 131 S. Ct. 1325 (2011); Federal Express Corp. v. Holowecki, 552 U.S. 389 (2008); Wash. State Dep't of Soc. and Health Servs. v. Estate of Keffeler, 537 U.S. 371 (2003).
24. *See, e.g.*, Christopher v. SmithKline Beecham Corp., 132 S. Ct. 2156, 2169 (2012) (rejecting agency's interpretation of its own regulation); Wyeth v. Levine, 555 U.S. 555, 576-81 (2009); Gonzales v. Oregon, 546 U.S. 243, 269 (2006); Christensen v. Harris Cnty., 529 U.S. 576, 587 (2000).
25. *See, e.g.*, Annachamy v. Holder, 686 F.3d 729, 732 (9th Cir. 2012) (agreeing with the agency); Lopez v. Terrell, 654 F.3d 176, 183-87 (2d Cir. 2011) (same); Pub. Citizen, Inc. v. U.S. Dep't of Health and Human Servs., 332 F.3d 654, 661, 664 (D.C. Cir. 2003) (disagreeing with the agency). *See also* Breyer, *supra* note 1, at 379 ("[O]ne can find many cases in which the opinion suggests the court believed the agency's legal interpretation was correct and added citations to 'deference' cases to bolster the argument.").

determination (2) of the meaning of *the statute* (3) to which the agency interpretation was *relevant* but *not controlling*.

One final point concerns *Skidmore* and stare decisis. As discussed in the previous chapter, a judicial determination that an agency interpretation is reasonable under step two of *Chevron* leaves the agency free to change its views notwithstanding the judicial ruling.[26] This is because the court has not determined the meaning of the statute; it has only determined that the statute leaves the agency room to do what it did. In a *Skidmore* case, in contrast, the court determines, by its own lights, the correct meaning of the statute. Under principles of stare decisis and legislative supremacy, in general that reading binds both future courts and the agency.[27]

The plot thickens, however, if a later, conflicting agency interpretation is reviewed under *Chevron*. Recall that *Chevron* deference is based on the premise that Congress has delegated to an agency the authority to choose among reasonable constructions of a statute it administers. Courts retain, however, the ultimate authority to determine scope of this discretion. Consistent with this allocation of authority, an agency cannot use its *Chevron* authority to adopt a statutory construction inconsistent with a judicial precedent insofar as that precedent makes plain that the agency's preferred construction is unreasonable. In other words, if the judicial precedent indicates that the agency's statutory construction should lose at step one of *Chevron*, then the judicial precedent should control. Insofar, however, as a judicial precedent chooses among reasonable statutory constructions within a zone of ambiguity, that precedent trenches on the agency's authority recognized by *Chevron*'s step two. Accordingly, the Court in *Brand X* advised that under *Chevron*, "a court's opinion as to the best reading of an ambiguous statute an agency is charged with administering is not authoritative." Therefore, an "agency's decision to construe that statute differently from a court does not say that the court's holding was legally wrong."[28] It

26. Nat'l Cable & Telecomms. Ass'n v. Brand X Internet Servs., 545 U.S. 967, 982-86 (2005).
27. *See, e.g.*, Neal v. United States, 516 U.S. 284, 294-96 (1996) (adhering to Court's own prior interpretation of statute notwithstanding agency's subsequent, conflicting regulation). Richard Murphy has argued, however, that agencies should retain the same interpretive flexibility under *Skidmore* as under *Chevron*. Richard W. Murphy, *A "New" Counter-*Marbury*: Reconciling* Skidmore *Deference and Agency Interpretive Freedom*, 56 ADMIN. L. REV. 1, 37-50 (2004).
28. *Brand X*, 545 U.S. at 983 (emphasis added). *See also* Edelman v. Lynchburg Coll., 535 U.S. 106, 114 & n.8 (2002) (implying that the agency might be free in the future to alter an interpretation that the Court had upheld under *Skidmore*).

follows that an agency's *Chevron*-eligible statutory construction can trump a court's earlier *Skidmore* construction provided the court's opinion does not make clear that the question belongs in step one.[29]

5.032 But See . . .

The foregoing account is both descriptively accurate and, in my view, normatively appealing. However, it is not unanimously held. Two prominent experts in particular would reject it: Antonin Scalia and Stephen Breyer. They reject it in quite different ways however. To oversimplify, the Scalia position is that there is only *Chevron*; the Breyer position is that there is only *Skidmore*.

For Justice Scalia, *Skidmore* is an anachronism; there are no *Skidmore* cases and no such thing as *Skidmore* deference.[30] On this account, *Chevron* completely displaced *Skidmore*. Indeed, he would reject the whole idea of deference as "weight" as opposed to "obedience." "[T]he rule of *Skidmore* deference is an empty truism and a trifling statement of the obvious."[31] "In my view this [*i.e. Skidmore* deference] doctrine (if it can be called that) is incoherent, both linguistically and practically. To defer is to subordinate one's own judgment to another's."[32] Accordingly, *Chevron* applies any time there is an "authoritative" agency interpretation.

---

29. For example, in *United States v. Home Concrete & Supply, LLC*, the Court held that a statutory construction it had adopted in 1958 trumped a Treasury Regulation even though the earlier decision had conceded that the language at issue was not "unambiguous." 132 S. Ct. 1836, 1843 (2012) (discussing Colony, Inc. v. Commissioner of Internal Revenue, 357 U.S. 28 (1958)). The Court explained that *Chevron* instructs courts to deploy all the "traditional tools of statutory construction" to determine if Congress has itself addressed an issue or instead left a statutory gap for an agency to fill. Although it had, writing decades before *Chevron,* conceded linguistic ambiguity, the *Colony* Court had adopted its construction based on the "better side of the textual argument," legislative history, and avoidance of a "patent incongruity in the tax law." As such, read in context, the *Colony* Court opinion made "clear" that Congress had not left a statutory gap for the agency to fill. *Id.* at 1844.
30. Smith v. City of Jackson, Miss., 544 U.S. 228, 243-47 (2005) (Scalia, J., concurring); U.S. v. Mead Corp., 533 U.S. 218, 250-59 (2001) (Scalia, J., dissenting).
31. *Id.* at 250.
32. Kasten v. Saint-Gobain Performance Plastics Corp., 131 S. Ct. 1325, 1340 n.6 (2011) (Scalia, J., dissenting).

The Breyer position is less straightforward and not propounded with the same force and explicitness. Justice Breyer has never actually said that "there is only *Skidmore*," and he might object to the characterization. Indeed, he has written opinions that rely exclusively on *Chevron*[33] or distinguish it from *Skidmore*.[34] Nonetheless, in numerous opinions Justice Breyer has indicated a lack of interest in the fine points of the *Chevron* doctrine or in subtle distinctions between *Skidmore* and *Chevron*.[35] He insists that courts take agency interpretations seriously, virtually always taking a multi-factored, case-by-case approach. Under this approach there seems little or no qualitative difference between *Chevron* and *Skidmore*; they are at most different points on a continuum.[36]

---

33. *See, e.g.*, Barber v. Thomas, 560 U.S. 474, 487, 489 (2010); Coeur Alaska, Inc. v. Southeast Alaska Conservation Council, 557 U.S. 261, 292-93 (2009) (Breyer, J., concurring); Entergy Corp. v. Riverkeeper, Inc., 556 U.S. 208, 234-35 (2009) (Breyer, J., concurring in part and dissenting in part).
34. *See, e.g.*, City of Arlington v. FCC, 133 S. Ct. 1863, 1876 (2013) (Breyer, J., concurring).
35. *See, e.g.*, Mutual Pharmaceutical Co., Inc. v. Bartlett, 133 S. Ct. 2466, 2481 (2013) (Breyer, J., dissenting) (citing both *Chevron* and *Skidmore*, and their progeny, articulating multiple factors, and ultimately arguing against deference in the particular instance); Wos v. E.M.A. ex rel. Johnson, 133 S. Ct. 1391, 1403-04 (2013) (Breyer, J., concurring) (noting that while "this case does not fall directly into a case-defined category" of deference, such as *Chevron* or *Skidmore*, the agency's views still merit attention – "I cannot measure the degree of deference with the precision of a mariner measuring a degree of latitude. But it is still worth noting that the agency's determination has played some role in my own decision."); Long Island Care at Home v. Coke, 551 U.S. 158, 172-73 (2007); Meyer v. Holley, 537 U.S. 280, 287-88 (2003) (noting that "we ordinarily defer to an administering agency's reasonable interpretation of a statute" and citing both, and only, *Chevron* and *Skidmore*, without elaboration or distinction); Barnhart v. Walton, 535 U.S. 212, 215 (2002).
36. *See* Kasten v. Saint-Gobain Performance Plastics Corp., 131 S. Ct. 1325, 1335 (2011); *id.* at 1340 & n.5 (Scalia, J., dissenting); Bruesewitz v. Wyeth LLC, 131 S. Ct. 1068, 1086 (2011) (Breyer, J., concurring); Christensen v. Harris Cnty., 529 U.S. 576, 596 (2000) (Breyer, J., dissenting); Breyer, *supra* note 1, at 379-81 (1986) (arguing for loose reading of *Chevron* incorporating pre-*Chevron* considerations); Hickman & Krueger, *supra* note 15, at 1248; Cass R. Sunstein, Chevron *Step Zero*, 92 VA. L. REV. 187, 198-202 (2006).

5.033 The "Quantity" of *Skidmore* Deference and the Sliding Scale

Quantifying *Skidmore* deference is a challenge. One can pile up a lot of synonyms without accumulating much understanding. Agency interpretations "are 'entitled to respect,'"[37] or "respectful consideration,"[38] or "some weight"[39]—though probably not "considerable weight."[40] Such deference has been described as something "less than *Chevron* but more than acknowledgment that the agency's position is more convincing than its adversaries'."[41] or a "non-trivial boost."[42] Agency interpretations provide "guidance"[43] and constitute "persuasive authority"[44]; they have, to go back to the source, the "power to persuade if lacking the power to control."[45]

Moreover, the Supreme Court's vocabulary and practice have varied. For example, in *Christensen* and *Gonzales* the majority interpreted the statute for itself, citing *Skidmore* but seeming quite unmoved by the agency's views.[46] In contrast, in *Alaska DEC* the Court made *Skidmore* deference sound a lot like *Chevron* deference,[47] for which it was fairly taken to task by the dissenters.[48] A similar variation can be seen in the courts of appeals.[49]

---

37. Christensen v. Harris Cnty., 529 U.S. 516, 587 (2000) (quoting Skidmore v. Swift & Co., 323 U.S. 134, 140 (1944)).
38. Air Brake Sys. v. Mineta, 357 F.3d 632, 643 (6th Cir. 2004).
39. Martin v. Occupational Safety and Health Review Comm'n, 499 U.S. 144, 157 (1991).
40. Chevron, U.S.A., Inc. v. Natural Res. Def. Council, Inc., 467 U.S. 837, 844 (1984).
41. Collins v. Nat'l Transp. Safety Bd., 351 F.3d 1246, 1254 (D.C. Cir. 2003) (citations omitted).
42. *Id.*
43. Yates v. Hendon, 541 U.S. 1, 18 (2004) (quoting Skidmore v. Swift & Co., 323 U.S. 134, 140 (1944)).
44. Reich v. S. New Eng. Telecomms. Corp., 121 F.3d 58, 65 (2d Cir. 1997).
45. *Skidmore*, 323 U.S. at 140.
46. Christensen v. Harris Cnty., 529 U.S. 516, 582-87 (2000).
47. Alaska Dep't of Env. Cons. v. EPA, 540 U.S. 461, 485 (2004) ("the Agency has rationally construed the Act's text and [its] construction warrants our respect and approbation"); *id.* at 488 (concluding that agency interpretation is not "impermissible"); *id.* at 493 (describing EPA's interpretation as "rational" and "surely permissible").
48. *Id.* at 517 (Kennedy, J., dissenting) (objecting that "the majority ends up giving EPA the very *Chevron* deference—and more—it says should be denied" in an opinion that "is chock full of *Chevron*-like language").
49. Hickman and Krueger, *supra* note 15, at 1259-91.

This *variation* does not necessarily indicate *inconsistency*. Some variation is built in to the doctrine, which calls for a sliding scale under which the level of deference varies with the circumstances. Thus, there are in theory infinite gradations of *Skidmore* deference.[50]

Drawing on the canonical language in Justice Jackson's opinion,[51] courts have long identified particular factors that enhance or undermine the agency interpretation.

Consistency. Skidmore observes that the deference due an agency's interpretation hinges in part on "its consistency with earlier and later pronouncements" and countless opinions have echoed this statement.[52] Indeed, if there is a single most important *Skidmore* factor, it is the agency's consistency over time.

Exactly the opposite rule applies under *Chevron*[53]—a decision that itself afforded "*Chevron* deference" to an agency flip-flop.[54] This difference in

---

50. Commentators have noted that the result is variation and confusion and offered proposals to simplify the doctrine. *See id.* at 1293-97 (suggesting that courts should assess the *Skidmore* factors to determine whether to give an agency either strong, intermediate, or little deference); Amy Wildermuth, *Solving the Puzzle of Mead and Christensen: What Would Justice Stevens Do?*, 74 FORDHAM L. REV.1877, 1910-12 (2006) (arguing that *Skidmore* should be more of a yes/no inquiry and that *if* it applies it should be a simple thumb on the scale or tie-breaker when competing interpretations are in equipoise).
51. *See supra* note 7 and accompanying text.
52. *See, e.g.,* Kasten v. Saint-Gobain Performance Plastics Corp., 131 S. Ct. 1325, 1335 (2011); Fed. Express Corp. v. Holowecki, 552 U.S. 389, 399 (2008) (noting that "the relevant interpretive statement ... has been binding on EEOC staff for at least five years"); *Alaska DEC*, 540 U.S. at 488, 495 (stressing the deference due EPA's "longstanding, consistently maintained interpretation"); Barnhart v. Walton, 535 U.S. 212, 220 (2002) (noting that the Court will "normally accord particular deference to an agency interpretation of 'longstanding' duration") (quoting North Haven Bd. of Ed. v. Bell, 456 U.S. 512, 522 n.12 (1982)); In re Daley, 717 F.3d 506, 509 (6th Cir. 2013) ("[E]ven th[e] modest influence [due under *Skidmore*] is unavailing when the agency's position is a moving target."); Tablada v. Thomas, 533 F.3d 800, 808 (9th Cir. 2008); McGraw v. Barnhart, 450 F.3d 493, 501 (10th Cir. 2006); Barnett v. Weinberger, 818 F.2d 953, 960-61 (D.C. Cir. 1987).
53. Nat'l Cable & Telecomms. Ass'n v. Brand X Internet Servs., 545 U.S. 967, 981-82 (2005).
54. *Chevron*, 467 U.S. at 857-58.

approach reflects the basic distinction between the two types of deference. Agency inconsistency undermines deference if there is a right answer, since at least one of the agency positions must be wrong. But *Chevron*'s premise is that there is no right answer.

Contemporaneousness. An interpretation adopted around the time that the statute itself was enacted will carry greater weight than one developed later.[55] This is particularly true if the agency itself was involved in drafting the statutory language.[56]

(Implicit) Congressional Approval. Deference is enhanced by perceived congressional endorsement. Indeed, this is one reason longstanding consistent interpretations have particular weight; Congress's failure to override the agency suggests that it concurs in the interpretation, which is thus "correct."[57] This inference of approval becomes stronger if Congress revisits the statute and does not change the relevant provision. However, courts are wary of placing too much weight even on reenactment.[58] While the Supreme Court has stated that "Congress is presumed to be aware of an administrative or judicial interpretation when it re-enacts a statute without change,"[59] the argument for deference will fare much better if it can be shown that Congress was *actually* aware of the interpretation it is supposed to have implicitly endorsed.[60]

---

55. *See, e.g.,* EEOC v. Arabian Am. Oil Co., 499 U.S. 244, 257 (1991); Udall v. Tallman, 380 U.S. 1, 16 (1965).
56. *See, e.g.,* Shapiro v. United States, 335 U.S. 1, 12 n.13 (1948).
57. *See, e.g.,* Bob Jones Univ. v. United States, 461 U.S. 574, 599 (1983) (remarking that since Congress had corrected misconstructions of statutes by agencies in the past, its failure to modify Internal Revenue Service (IRS) rulings of which it was definitely aware "leave[s] no doubt that the IRS reached the correct conclusion"); SEC v. Sloan, 436 U.S. 103, 120-21 (1978); Zemel v. Rusk, 381 U.S. 1, 11 (1965); David R. Woodward & Ronald M. Levin, *In Defense of Deference: Judicial Review of Agency Action*, 31 Admin. L. Rev. 329, 334 (1979).
58. *See, e.g.,* OfficeMax, Inc. v. United States, 428 F.3d 583, 595-96 (6th Cir. 2005).
59. Merrill Lynch, Pierce, Fenner & Smith, Inc. v. Curran, 456 U.S. 353, 382 n.66 (1982) (internal quotations omitted).
60. *See, e.g.,* Solid Waste Agency of N. Cook Cnty. v. United States Army Corps of Eng'rs, 531 U.S. 159, 169 (2001) ("Although we have recognized congressional acquiescence to administrative interpretations of a statute in some situations, we have done so with extreme care."); Public Citizen, Inc. v. U.S. Dep't of Health & Human Servs., 332 F.3d 654, 668-69 (D.C. Cir. 2003) (stressing the absence of any evidence of congressional familiarity with the administrative interpretation).

Agency Expertise. In *Skidmore* itself, Justice Jackson emphasized that in the pursuit of his duties the Administrator had "accumulated a considerable experience in the problems of ascertaining working time in employments . . . and a knowledge of the customs prevailing in reference to their solution," and he noted the "specialized experience and broader investigations and information" available to the agency.[61] Courts consistently give, or purport to give, greater deference when the agency interpretation lies in a particularly tricky, arcane, or technical area, whether the complexity be statutory or factual.[62]

The converse is also true. An agency interpretation that rests entirely on the standard materials of judicial interpretation—statutory text, legislative

---

61. Skidmore v. Swift & Co., 323 U.S. 134-138-39 (1944). There is some tension between this basis for enhanced deference and the proposition that contemporaneous interpretations are especially weighty, since by definition the contemporaneous interpretation precedes the accumulation of experience under the particular statute. *Cf.* Ronald M. Levin, *Mead and the Prospective Exercise of Discretion*, 54 ADMIN. L. REV. 771, 783 n.54 (2002) (pointing to similar tension between cases affording deference on the basis of agency experience and those affording deference on the basis of the need for flexibility in handling new problems as to which the agency has no experience).
62. *See, e.g.*, Fed. Express Corp. v. Holowecki, 552 U.S. 389, 403 (2006) (noting that the issue was "a matter for the [EEOC] to decide in light of its experience and expertise"); *Alaska DEC*, 540 U.S. at 492 (referring to EPA as "the expert federal agency charged with enforcing the Act"); Aluminum Co. of Am. v. Cent. Lincoln People's Util. Dist., 467 U.S. 380, 390 (1984); E.I du Pont de Nemours & Co. v. Train, 430 U.S. 112, 134 & 135 n.25 (1977); Christensen v. Harris Cnty., 529 U.S. 576, 597 (2000) (Breyer, J., dissenting) ("[A]n agency's views, particularly in a rather technical case such as this one, 'meri[t] our respect."); Sai Kwan Wong v. Doer, 571 F.3d 247, 260 (2d Cir. 2009) ("[I]n cases such as those involving Medicare or Medicaid, in which CMS, 'a highly expert agency, administers a large complex regulatory scheme in cooperation with many other institutional actors, the various possible standards for deference'—namely, *Chevron* and *Skidmore*—'begin to converge.'") (citations omitted); Pronsolino v. Nastri, 291 F.3d 1123, 1133 (9th Cir. 2002) (noting that deference was appropriate because the case involved "an intricate statutory scheme addressing technically complex environmental issues" and "a complicated, science-driven statute").

history, judicial precedent—will not be especially weighty, for here the agency has no particular comparative advantage over a court.[63]

Congressional Direction to Defer. Some older *Skidmore* cases stated that greater weight is given to an agency interpretation that rests on a specific statutory authorization.[64] This factor would now seem to be obsolete. If the "statutory authorization" is the authority to make rules with the force of law, that does not simply give the interpretation particular weight under *Skidmore*; it moves us into *Chevron* territory.[65] Accordingly, since *Mead* very few courts have invoked this idea.

---

63. *See, e.g.*, Gonzales v. Oregon, 546 U.S. 243, 269 (2006) ("The deference here is tempered by the Attorney General's lack of expertise in this area and the apparent absence of any consultation with anyone outside the Department of Justice who might aid in a reasoned judgment."); Malacara v. Garber, 353 F.3d 393, 401 (5th Cir. 2003); *cf.* SEC v. Chenery Corp., 332 U.S. 194, 209 (1947) (upholding agency interpretation resting on expertise that it had previously rejected when it rested on interpretation of case law).
64. *See, e.g.*, Herweg v. Ray, 455 U.S. 265, 274-75 (1982) (deferring to interpretation that had "legislative effect"); *see generally* Thomas W. Merrill, *Judicial Deference to Executive Precedent*, 101 YALE L.J. 969, 973 (1992).
65. For example, in *General Electric Co. v. Gilbert*, 429 U.S. 125 (1976), the Court stated that an interpretive rule not promulgated pursuant to express statutory authority should be accorded less weight than "administrative regulations which Congress has declared shall have the force of law, or to regulations which under the enabling statute may themselves supply the basis for imposition of liability." *Id.* at 141 (citations omitted). After *Mead*, the latter type of regulations would not receive especially strong *Skidmore* deference; they would be covered by *Chevron*. Indeed, the language of these opinions resonates perfectly with *Chevron*. *See, e.g.*, Heckler v. Campbell, 461 U.S. 458. 466 ("Where, as here, the statute expressly entrusts the Secretary with the responsibility for implementing a provision by regulation, our review is limited to determining whether the regulations promulgated exceeded the Secretary's statutory authority and whether they are arbitrary and capricious."); *Herweg*, 455 U.S. at 274-75 (deferring to interpretation with "legislative effect"); Batterton v. Francis, 432 U.S. 416, 424-26 & nn.8-9 (1977) (distinguishing delegated "legislative power" from nondelegated "interpretative power" and according great deference to agency interpretations using former). On the other hand, if the agency has not exercised its delegated authority to write rules with the force of law, then (a) *Chevron* is inapplicable and (b) the unutilized authority has no bearing on the strength of deference under *Skidmore*. A recent example is McMaster v. United States, 731 F.3d 881 (9th Cir. 2013).

Deliberation and Procedural Formality. Skidmore states the "thoroughness evident in [the agency's] consideration" will affect the weight of its interpretation. This idea recurs in later cases[66] and rests on the common-sense view that thorough consideration increases the chances of a correct conclusion.

A related but distinct idea is that deference should vary with the extensiveness of the procedures followed by the agency. Courts and commentators alike assume that the level of deference varies with the formality, openness, and comprehensiveness of the agency proceedings.[67] *Mead* gives an indirect boost to this idea by linking (though not equating) notice-and-comment rulemaking with *Chevron* deference. Unsurprisingly, then, courts often state that greater deference is due an interpretation that emerges from a full, open process such as notice-and-comment rulemaking.[68]

Finally, some courts have emphasized that an interpretation merits greater weight if it is "not merely ad hoc but . . . is applicable to all cases."[69] The intuition here is that if an interpretation is more legislative in nature—applicable across the board rather than articulated only to resolve or apply in a

---

66. *See* Christensen v. Harris Cnty., 529 U.S. 576, 595 (2000) (Stevens, J., dissenting) (arguing that agency's view "merits our respect" because it was "thoroughly considered"); Arobelidze v. Holder, 653 F.3d 513, 520-21 (7th Cir. 2011) (noting, in rejecting agency interpretation, that its "consideration was far from thorough"); Doe v. Leavitt, 552 F.3d 75, 81 (1st Cir. 2009).
67. *See, e.g.*, Mutual Pharmaceutical Co. v. Bartlett, 133 S. Ct. 2466, 2481 (2013) (Breyer, J., dissenting) (declining to defer to FDA regarding preemption where agency had held no hearings, received no public input, and only expressed its views in briefs filed in litigation); Kevin W. Saunders, *Interpretative Rules with Legislative Effect: An Analysis and a Proposal for Public Participation*, 1986 Duke L.J. 346, 371-82.
68. *See, e.g.*, Christopher v. SmithKline Beecham Corp., 132 S. Ct. 2156, 2169 (2012); Wyeth v. Levine, 555 U.S. 555, 576-81 (2009) (finding that agency's view "does not merit deference" because, among other things, it was adopted without notice and comment); Reno v. Koray, 515 U.S. 50, 61 (1995) (internal agency guideline that is not "subject to the rigors of the [APA], including public notice and comment," is entitled only to "some deference") (internal quotation marks omitted); Doe v. Leavitt, 552 F.3d 75, 81-82 (1st Cir. 2009); Structural Indus. v. United States, 356 F.3d 1366, 1370 (Fed. Cir. 2004); Rubie's Costume Co. v. United States, 337 F.3d 1350, 1356 (Fed. Cir. 2003).
69. Chauffer's Training School, Inc. v. Spellings, 478 F.3d 117, 129 (2d Cir. 2007). *Accord* Doe v. Leavitt, 552 F.3d 75, 81 (1st Cir. 2009); Estate of Landers v. Leavitt, 545 F.3d 98, 110 (2d Cir. 2008).

specific instance—it is likely to reflect a more thorough, careful, and well-reasoned agency process.

The Persuasiveness of the Agency's Reasoning. With dismaying frequency, courts assert that the persuasiveness or validity of the agency's reasoning is one of the factors affecting the weight to be given the agency's views.[70] This proposition is either a truism or incoherent. Undeniably, a powerfully reasoned agency view is more likely to be upheld than a poorly reasoned one. Courts reward "reasoned decisionmaking." However, to accept an interpretation because it is "persuasive" is not to *defer* but rather to *agree*.[71]

The Supreme Court has done much to sow this confusion. For example, the *Mead* opinion explicitly lists "the persuasiveness of the agency's position" as one of the *Skidmore* factors.[72] However, this is not what *Skidmore* actually says. On Jackson's formulation, the *Skidmore* factors are the things that give the agency's interpretation "the power to persuade"; to say that the agency's "persuasiveness" is one of the things that give it "the power to persuade" is tautological. The ultimate question is whether the court is persuaded.

Similarly, in a problematic but much-quoted formulation, the *Christensen* majority opinion stated that agency interpretations are "'entitled to respect' . . ., but only to the extent that those interpretations have the 'power to persuade.'"[73] This is self-contradictory. *Everything*, including the arguments

---

70. *See e.g.*, Power v. Barnhart, 292 F.3d 781, 786 (D.C. Cir. 2002) ("Under *Skidmore*, we grant an agency's interpretation only so much deference as its persuasiveness warrants."); Catskill Mountains Chapter of Trout Unlimited, Inc. v. City of New York, 273 F.3d 481, 491 (2d Cir. 2001) ("[T]he agency position should be followed to the extent persuasive."); Reich v. Interstate Brands Corp., 57 F.3d 574, 577 (7th Cir. 1995) ("[W]e give the Secretary's bulletins the respect their reasoning earns them.").
71. As one casebook nicely puts it: "We would not say that a court persuaded by the excellent brief of a private litigant to decide in its favor is deferring to the litigant's lawyers." PETER L. STRAUSS ET AL., GELLHORN & BYSE'S ADMINISTRATIVE LAW: CASES AND COMMENTS 975 (11th ed. 2011).
72. U.S. v. Mead Corp., 533 U.S. 218, 228 (2001). *See also* Vance v. Ball State University, 133 S. Ct. 2434, 2443 n.4 (2013) ("To [defer to the EEOC] would be proper only if the EEOC Guidance has the power to persuade . . . . [W]e do not find the EEOC Guidance persuasive.").
73. Christensen v. Harris Cnty., 529 U.S. 576, 587 (2000). *See also* Gonzales, 546 U.S. at 256 (observing that "under *Skidmore*, we follow an agency's rule only to the extent it is persuasive," and "we do not find the Attorney General's opinion persuasive"); Public Citizen, 332 F.3d at 662-71 (concluding that *Skidmore* deference was due, but rejecting agency's view as "unpersuasive"

of the lawyers in the case, is entitled to respect "to the extent [it has] the power to persuade." Under this approach, if the court agrees with the agency it will label the interpretation persuasive and "defer" to it, whereas if it disagrees, it will label the interpretation "unpersuasive" and ignore it.[74] For example, consider this sentence from a court of appeals opinion: "[T]he Director is not entitled to *Skidmore* respect . . . because his position . . . is simply unpersuasive, notwithstanding its inclusion in the agency's manual and the Director's consistent application of [this interpretation] for some time."[75] This is not deference; the court is reaching an independent conclusion. On this approach, *Skidmore* means nothing more than "we will defer to the agency if we believe the agency is right."[76] If that's what it means, it means nothing at all, and *Skidmore* deference is a fiction.

The problem arises in part because "persuasive" has two meanings. It is sometimes used to mean "tending to persuade" (e.g., "he's a persuasive advocate, but in the end I did not agree") and sometimes to mean "successful in persuading" (e.g., "I found her persuasive so I voted for her proposal"). On the former meaning, someone can be persuasive but still leave her listeners "unpersuaded"; on the latter, someone is persuasive only if she persuades her listeners. In the *Skidmore* setting, "persuasive" should mean "tending to per-

---

because statutory text, history, and purpose were all against it); *see also id.* at 670 n.25 (invoking views of the Department's Inspector General "not because they legally command our deference, but because we find them logically persuasive.").

74. *See* Jim Rossi, *Respecting Deference: Conceptualizing* Skidmore *Within the Architecture of* Chevron, 42 WM. & MARY L. REV. 1105, 1131-34 (2001). *See also* Catskill Mountains Chapter of Trout Unlimited, Inc. v. City of New York, 273 F.3d 481, 491 (2d Cir. 2001).

75. Price v. Stevedoring Servs. of America, Inc., 697 F.3d 820, 832-33 (9th Cir. 2012). *See also id.* at 833 ("[T]he Board's explanations as to the contested issues here are not persuasive and would thus not be entitled to deference in any event.").

76. *See* David J. Barron & Elena Kagan, Chevron*'s Nondelegation Doctrine*, 2001 SUP. CT. REV. 201, 227 n.98 (wondering aloud whether "*Skidmore* deference amounts to something more than a court saying 'we will defer to the agency if we believe the agency is right'"); *see also* Panel, *Agency Preemption: Speak Softly, But Carry a Big Stick?*, 11 CHAP. L. REV. 363, 382 (2008) (comments of Ronald A. Cass) ("[T]hat's why the notion of *Skidmore* deference is a wonderful concept for courts, which means that they do what the agency says when they would've done it without the agency doing it anyway.").

suade," not "convincing."[77] The *Skidmore* factors are circumstances that make the agency's interpretation more or less "persuasive"; the interpretation's "persuasiveness" is not itself a *Skidmore* factor.

5.034 No Deference at All?

Are there settings in which neither *Skidmore* nor *Chevron* applies? One could imagine a *Skidmore* counterpart to the *Chevron* caselaw about "step zero." An interpretation might merit *Skidmore* deference only if made by a particular agency, or in a particular format, or by someone at a certain level, or after a certain process, or pursuant to a clear congressional mandate. Some cases do suggest that *Skidmore* deference will only apply to an interpretation that is "authoritative,"[78] and several Courts of Appeals have held that *Skidmore*, like *Chevron*, deference does not apply to positions articulated only in the course of litigation.[79] However, the majority position is that any agency interpretation counts—although in light of the circumstances of its issuance it may not count for much. To analogize to the law of evidence, factors such as source, format, process, and so on go to "weight" rather than "admissibility."

Nonetheless, it is not uncommon for a court essentially to ignore an agency interpretation, reaching an independent judgment about the meaning

---

77. *See* Kasten v. Saint-Gobain Performance Plastics Corp., 131 S. Ct. 1325, 1340 n.6 (2011) (Scalia, J., dissenting) ("If one has been persuaded by another, so that one's judgment accords with the other's, there is no room for deferral—only for agreement.").
78. *See, e.g.*, Air Brake Sys. v. Mineta, 357 F.3d 632, 643 (6th Cir. 2004) ("Under *Skidmore* . . . federal courts give respectful consideration to authoritative interpretations that lack the force of law . . . ."); S. Utah Wilderness Alliance v. Dabney, 222 F.3d 819, 828-29 (10th Cir. 2000) (refusing any sort of deference to agency interpretation set out in Draft Policies that had not been finalized).
79. Alaska v. Federal Subsistence Board, 544 F.3d 1089, 1095 (9th Cir 2008); In re UAL Corp., 468 F.3d 444, 450-51 (7th Cir. 2006); S. Utah Wilderness Alliance, 222 F.3d at 827-28. The caselaw regarding *Skidmore* deference for litigating positions is canvassed in Bradley George Hubbard, Comment, *Deference to Agency Statutory Interpretations First Advanced in Litigation? The* Chevron *Two-Step and the* Skidmore *Shuffle*, 80 U. Chi. L. Rev. 447 (2013) (concluding that agency litigating positions, whether as party or amicus, do merit *Skidmore* deference). For the argument that no deference at all should be given under *Skidmore* if the decision is not carefully reasoned and does not involve the application of agency expertise, see Wildermuth, *supra* note 48, at 1910-11.

of the statute. Among Supreme Court decisions, *Christensen* and *Gonzales* are leading examples, but they are not alone.[80] The Court has also sometimes essentially ignored the agency's interpretation even when agreeing with it.[81] An empirical study of *Skidmore* in the federal courts of appeals found that in the 106 decisions reviewed, courts took this "independent judgment" approach in twenty, the sliding scale approach in seventy-nine, and an indeterminate approach in seven.[82]

How best to understand these decisions?

Some "independent judgment" cases are probably sliding-scale cases, but ones in which the *Skidmore* factors so undermine the interpretation as to deprive it of any weight at all. Imagine an interpretation that contradicted a longstanding agency view, and was recent, novel, inexpert, unexplained, and about a basic, nontechnical legal issue. Add all that up, and there is no deference left.[83]

Second, sometimes courts accord the agency interpretation some weight, but simply disagree with the agency's position. Some agency interpretations are wrong. If a court concludes that the statute just does not say what the agency thinks it says, then the court can be unpersuaded, and refuse to "defer" in the strong sense, while still giving some (minimal) "weight" to the

---

80. *See also* Vance v. Ball State University, 133 S. Ct. 2434, 2443 n.4 (2013).
81. *See, e.g.*, Sandifer v. United States Steel Corp., 134 S. Ct. 870, 876 n.5 (2014) (noting that the government had expressly not urged the Court to defer to the relevant agency's vacillating interpretation of the relevant statutory term); Raymond B. Yates, M.D., P.C. Profit Sharing Plan v. Hendon, 541 U.S. 1 (2004); Clackamas Gastroenterology Assocs. v. Wells, 538 U.S. 440 (2003).
82. Hickman and Krueger, *supra* note 15, at 1271.
83. *See, e.g.*, Wyeth v. Levine, 555 U.S. 555, 576-81 (2009) (finding that agency's view "does not merit deference" because it was adopted without notice and comment, ran counter to statutory purposes, and reversed a long-held position); Fayus Enters. v. BNSF Ry. Co., 602 F.3d 444, 447 (D.C. Cir.) (stating that the court owes no deference to a passing and conclusory dictum in a Surface Transportation Board opinion); Structural Indus., Inc. v. United States, 356 F.3d 1366, 1370-71 (Fed. Cir. 2004) (holding that customs determination "should not enjoy deference under *Skidmore*" because it was adopted without notice-and-comment procedures, did not reflect a consistent position, and turned on particularized factual questions); Hall v. U.S. Envtl. Prot. Agency, *273 F.3d 1146, 1155-56 (9th Cir. 2001) (acknowledging need to give interpretation appropriate weight under Skidmore but concluding that because it was almost wholly unexplained as well as inconsistent with prior agency positions it was due essentially no weight at all*).

rejected interpretation.[84] The distinction between giving no weight and almost no weight to a rejected interpretation is largely academic. Note that if a court determines that the agency interpretation is just inescapably incorrect, it can just stop there; regardless of how the *Skidmore* factors cut, they cannot add up to enough to overcome the court's understanding of the statute. This is perhaps the best way to understand recent Supreme Court decisions in which the majority seems to give the back of its hand to *Skidmore*.[85]

Third, and related, an agency interpretation might receive no deference because it stands as an unadorned and unexplained conclusion, unsupported by *any* explanation.[86] It is rare for an agency to offer an interpretation as such—e.g., an interpretive rule or policy statement explaining statutory meaning—without any explanation. But sometimes an agency decision rests on an unarticulated interpretation. For example, the Copyright Office's decision to register a copyright includes an implicit determination that the item is copyrightable. Sitting by designation as a district judge, Judge Easterbrook has stated that that interpretation does not receive *Skidmore* deference because it is not accompanied by any explanation.[87]

---

84. *See, e.g.*, Barber v. Thomas, 560 U.S. 474, 503 (2010) (Kennedy, J., dissenting) ("[D]eference is not owed to an agency view, however consistently held, that from the start has been premised on legal error."); United States v. Casasola, 670 F.3d 1023, 1030 (9th Cir. 2012) (concluding that agency interpretations in question "are not worthy of any deference, because they conflict with the words and obvious meaning of the statute.").
85. Recent examples of the Supreme Court rejecting an interpretation as just wrong (or "unpersuasive") without marching through the factors include: University of Texas Southwestern Medical Center v. Nassar, 133 S. Ct. 2517, 2533-34 (2013); Wos v. E.M.A. ex rel. Johnson, 133 S. Ct. 1391, 1402 (2013); and Christopher v. SmithKline Beecham Corp. 132 S. Ct. 2156, 2169-70 (2012).
86. Handron v. Secretary Dep't of Health and Human Servs., 677 F.3d 144, 151 (3d Cir. 2012) (holding that agency interpretation "is entitled to no deference under *Skidmore*" where "that interpretation was not explained"); Lawson v. FMR, LLC, 670 F.3d 61, 82 (1st Cir. 2012) (finding that OSHA regulations "are not entitled to *Skidmore* deference for several reasons," including the fact that the "notice of final rulemaking here contains no reasoning to support OSHA's construction").
87. Pivot Paint Int'l, Inc. v. Charlene Prods., Inc., 170 F. Supp. 2d 828, 831 (N.D. Ill. 2001).

Finally, deference is only due to statements that actually count as an interpretation of the statute. An agency statement must actually purport to interpret a statute and not express views on some other matter.[88]

5.04 THE INTERACTION OF *SKIDMORE* AND *CHEVRON*

While *Skidmore* and *Chevron* are both alive and well, their precise interaction is unclear. *Mead* and its progeny treat the two as entirely distinct; either *Skidmore* applies or *Chevron* does, and never the twain shall meet. However, there may still be some overlap.

5.041 *Skidmore* Within *Chevron*

In determining whether *Chevron* applies at all ("step zero"), and in examining the statute to see if Congress spoke to the matter in question ("step one"), a court is performing the traditional judicial task of looking for a legislative determination. If none can be found, the court has two choices. It can make something up, in light of statutory purposes and its own sense of sound policy, or it can accept the agency's "interpretation" (which, by definition, is itself made up). *Chevron* insists that the court do the latter, acknowledging that the statute does not provide an answer, and, except in extreme cases, accepting the agency's policymaking. "[T]he whole point of *Chevron* is to leave the discretion provided by the ambiguities of a statute with the implementing agency."[89]

Under *Skidmore*, in contrast, the ultimate decision remains with the court and rests, at least in theory, on the statute itself. The "*Skidmore* factors" are indicia that the agency has correctly read the statute. They are irrelevant to *Chevron* deference because in step two there is no single correct reading; the agency is making a discretionary policy decision within statutory boundaries rather than "interpreting" the statute.

A *Chevron* step-one case, then, is essentially the same as a *Skidmore* case. They are both settings in which the court itself is determining the

---

88. Carter v. Welles-Bowen Realty, Inc., 736 F.3d 722, 727-28 (6th Cir. 2013) (refusing to defer, and finding *Skidmore* simply inapplicable, to an agency policy statement that "does not present its multifactor test as the agency's interpretation of the Act but only as guidelines that the agency intends to consider").

89. Nat'l Cable & Telecomms. Ass'n v. Brand X Internet Servs., 545 U.S. 967, 981 (2005) (quoting Smiley v. Citibank (South Dakota), N.A., 517 U.S. 735, 742 (1996).

meaning of the statute and there is a relevant agency interpretation in the background. On this understanding, *Skidmore* applies within step one. Indeed, the *Chevron* opinion directs courts to apply the "traditional tools of statutory construction" in step one,[90] and consideration of agency views is emphatically such a tool.

This is not the mainstream judicial view. To my knowledge, no court has expressly stated that *Skidmore* applies within step one; some courts have expressly rejected any sort of deference within step one.[91] Nonetheless, the *Skidmore* factors "seem to keep popping up as considerations that courts recite while applying *Chevron* step one,"[92] suggesting that something along these lines may be happening. And there is significant academic support for the proposition that *Skidmore* applies within step one. [93]

Alternatively, there is some support for the idea that *Skidmore* applies within step two. Professor Rossi supports this approach, arguing that *Skidmore* should create a test of "reasonableness with bite" under step two.[94] And courts do sometimes seem to be operating under *Skidmore* when ostensibly considering the reasonableness of an agency interpretation under step two.[95]

---

90. *See* Chevron, U.S.A., v. Natural Res. Def. Council, Inc., 467 U.S. 837, 843 n.9 (1984).

91. *See, e.g.,* Mylan Pharms., Inc. v. U.S. Food and Drug Admin., 454 F.3d 270, 275 (4th Cir. 2006) ("At the first step a court focuses purely on statutory construction without according any weight to the agency's position . . . .").

92. Levin, *supra* note 59, at 782 n.50. Levin cites Babbitt v. Sweet Home Chapter of Cmtys. for a Great Or., 515 U.S. 687, 703-04 (1995) (deferring to agency in light of its expertise); Pension Benefit Guar. Corp. v. LTV Corp., 496 U.S. 633, 651-52 (1990) (same); Good Samaritan Hosp. v. Shalala, 508 U.S. 402, 417 (1993) (stating that inconsistency militates against deference); and Pauley v. Bethenergy Mines, Inc., 501 U.S. 680, 698 (1991) (same).

93. William N. Eskridge, *Expanding* Chevron*'s Domain: A Comparative Institutional Analysis of the Relative Competence of Courts and Agencies to Interpret Statutes*, 2013 WISC. L. REV. 411, 449-50; Herz, *supra* note 20, at 208-09; Michael Herz, *Purposivism and Institutional Competence in Statutory Interpretation*, 2009 MICH. ST. L. REV. 89, 120; Glen Staszewski, *Statutory Interpretation as Contestatory Democracy*, 55 WM. & MARY L. REV. 221, 264 n.208 (2013); Strauss, *supra* note 17, at 1165; Strauss, *supra* note 7, at 8.

94. Rossi, *supra* note 72, at 1137-46.

95. *See, e.g.*, Zuni Pub. Sch. Dist. No. 89 v. Dep't of Educ., 550 U.S. 81 (2007).

5.042 Must Courts Choose Between *Skidmore* and *Chevron*?

> **When faced with uncertainty as to whether its review should be governed by *Chevron* or *Skidmore*, a court will sometimes declare that it does not need to choose, because it would uphold, or would reject, the agency's interpretation under either standard. [Blackletter Statement, Part 3, § II.D.]**

If a court finds statutory meaning clear, or clear enough, it will be unnecessary to choose between *Chevron* and *Skidmore*. As long as the court is reading the statute itself, giving some weight to the agency interpretation, the analysis and the outcome will be the same under either regime; the two "standards basically converge."[96]

The question then arises whether the official level of deference—*Skidmore* versus *Chevron*, and degrees within *Skidmore*—even matters to the outcome. It frequently will not, for three reasons.

First, take the doctrine at face value. Where the statute is clear enough to allow the court to resolve the case in step one of *Chevron*, then the court would uphold or set aside the agency view, as the case may be, under either *Skidmore* or *Chevron*.[97] Similarly, any agency interpretation that is so unrea-

---

96. Levin, *supra* note 59, at 780.

97. *See, e.g.,* Fed. Express Corp. v. Holowecki, 552 U.S. 389, 399 (2008); Gen. Dynamics Land Systs., Inc. v. Cline, 540 U.S. 581, 600 (2004) ("[W]e neither defer nor settle on any degree of deference because the Commission is clearly wrong."); Edelman v. Lynchburg College, 535 U.S. 106, 113-14, 118 (2002) (noting that because the agency interpretation was "unassailable" and the one that the Court would reach if it were "starting from scratch," it did not have to choose between *Skidmore* and *Chevron*); Encarnacion ex rel. George v. Astrue, 568 F.3d 72, 79 (2d Cir. 2009); Feemster v. BSA Ltd. P'ship, 548 F.3d 1063, 1068 (D.C. Cir. 2008) (noting that the agency interpretation would fail under either *Chevron* or *Skidmore*); Padash v. INS, 358 F.3d 1161, 1168 & n.6 (9th Cir. 2004) (rejecting agency interpretation within step one of *Chevron* because statute was not ambiguous, but noting that even if some deference were due it would be only *Skidmore* deference and would not suffice to override the court's own understanding of the statute); Navarro v. Pfizer Corp., 261 F.3d 90, 103 & n.7 (1st Cir. 2001) (applying *Skidmore* but rejecting the agency's interpretation of its regulation and noting that "even if *Chevron* applied, we still would not defer to the EEOC interpretive guidance because the regulation in question is not ambiguous"); North Fork Coal Corp. v. Federal Mine Safety & Health Review Comm'n, 691 F.3d 735, 745 (6th Cir. 2012) (Sutton, J., dissenting) ("The proper standard of review—whether under *Skidmore* or *Chevron*—makes no difference, as the relevant language of the statute defeats the Secretary's argument either way.").

sonable that it fails *Chevron* step two will also fail *Skidmore* a fortiori. Finally, where an agency interpretation seems "persuasive" under *Skidmore*, it is, again a fortiori, "reasonable" under *Chevron*.[98] So, the difference between treating the agency view as presumptively binding rather than merely persuasive will matter only in one category of cases: those in which the court, were it to decide the issue for itself, would disagree with the agency, but the statutory issue is sufficiently unclear to move it from step one to step two. In these circumstances, the court would uphold the agency interpretation under *Chevron* but set it aside under *Skidmore*. Such cases surely exist, but they are likely to be few and far between.[99]

Second, it is not clear that we can or should take the doctrine at face value. Deference rules do not reliably constrain judges. Experience with *Chevron* has shown that judges have not simply folded their tents and ceded the field to agencies. One judge's ambiguity is another's clarity, one's reasonableness another's arbitrariness. It is more common than one might have hoped to find judges, or justices, agreeing that a statute is clear but disagreeing as to what it clearly means. It is even more common to find one concluding that the statute is clear and deciding the case under step one and another finding it unclear and

---

98. *See, e.g.,* Taproot Administrative Servs., Inc. v. Commissioner, 679 F.3d 1109, 1115 n. 14 (9th Cir. 2012); Bonneville Int'l Corp. v. Peters, 347 F.3d 485, 490 (3d Cir. 2003) ("Because we find that the Copyright Office's interpretation is persuasive even under the less demanding standard of *Skidmore* deference, we need not go on to parse out whether *Chevron* deference should, in fact, be accorded the Copyright Office's regulation here."); FEC v. National Rifle Ass'n, 254 F.3d 173, 186-87 (D.C. Cir. 2001) (upholding under *Chevron* step two an agency interpretation that seemed altogether persuasive applying *Skidmore*); Gen. Dynamics Land Systs., Inc. v. Cline, 540 U.S. 581, 605-06 (2004) (Thomas, J., dissenting) (concluding that "because the EEOC's interpretation is consistent with the best reading of the statute," it was unnecessary to decide whether *Chevron* applied).

99. Bill Funk reviewed the first 25 or so cases decided by the Courts of Appeals immediately after *Mead* in which the court chose one or the other standard of deference. In only one of these did the court state that the choice between *Skidmore* and *Chevron* actually made a difference to the outcome. William Funk, Presentation to the ABA Section of Administrative Law and Regulatory Practice (Washington, DC, Nov. 2001). That single case was *Matz v. Household International Tax Reduction Inv. Plan*, 265 F.3d 572 (7th Cir. 2001), in which the court first upheld an IRS interpretation under *Chevron* and then, on remand after *Mead* came down, set aside the interpretation under *Skidmore*. It may be noteworthy that this case, like *Skidmore* itself, was a private lawsuit rather than the judicial review of agency action.

moving on to step two. The highly subtle, multi-factored distinctions of *Skidmore*, with not just two but infinite gradations, would be even more difficult than *Chevron* for any judge but Hercules to apply in a consistent and finely calibrated manner. Judges could not apply such subtly different standards of review even if they tried, and they may not always try.[100]

Third, this point is a general one that recurs with regard to all verbal formulations of different standards of review.[101] Several empirical studies have concluded that the official standard of review has remarkably little effect on actual outcomes; courts generally uphold agencies two-thirds to three-quarters of the time regardless of the articulated standard of review.[102] Moreover, recall the disagreement between Justices Breyer and Scalia discussed above. Justice Scalia is the Court's most strident defender of *Chevron*, which, everyone knows, dictates strong deference. Justice Breyer is the Court's greatest *Chevron* skeptic and *Skidmore* enthusiast. Yet of all the current Justices, it is Scalia who most often votes to reject agency interpretations and Breyer who most often votes to uphold them.[103]

5.05 CONCLUSION

Skidmore is alive and well. When *Chevron* does not apply but an agency has expressed a view as to the meaning of a statute it administers, courts must give weight to the agency's view. In contrast to "deference" under *Chevron*'s

---

100. For a general assault on the manipulability of sliding scale deference, including citations to similar assessments, see Eric R. Womak, *Into the Third Era of Administrative Law: An Empirical Study of the Supreme Court's Retreat from* Chevron *Principles in* United States v. Mead, 107 DICK. L. REV. 289, 294-95 & nn. 29-36 (2002).

101. *See* Adrian Vermeule, Mead *in the Trenches*, 71 GEO. WASH. L. REV. 347, 357 (2003) (suggesting that "adding an extra tier of deference is, in a pragmatic sense, simply not feasible, given the cognitive constraints under which real-world adjudication occurs"); United States v. McKinney, 919 F.2d 405, 423 (7th Cir. 1990) (Posner, J., concurring).

102. Citations to and an overview of these studies can be found in Richard J. Pierce, *What Do the Studies of Judicial Review of Agency Actions Mean?*, 63 ADMIN. L. REV. 77 (2011).

103. In *Chevron* cases decided between 1989 and 2005, Justice Breyer voted to uphold the agency 82% of the time, more than any other justice. Justice Scalia voted with the agency 52% of the time, less than any other justice. Cass R. Sunstein & Thomas J. Miles, *Depoliticizing Administrative Law*, 58 DUKE L.J. 2193, 2206-07 (2009).

step two, when *Skidmore* applies the agency view does not bind the court. Instead, the court must reach its own determination of what the statute means. But in exercising that function, it cannot ignore the agency's views. Just how much weight those views carry will depend on the circumstances. While at the end of the day *Skidmore* poses no obstacle to a court that simply disagrees with the agency's interpretation, it does teach that courts should be influenced by the agency's views.

Chapter 6

JUDICIAL REVIEW OF NONSTATUTORY LEGAL ISSUES

by Harold J. Krent*

6.01 INTRODUCTION

A court reviewing agency action under the Administrative Procedure Act "shall decide all relevant questions of law [and] interpret constitutional and statutory provisions,"[1] compel agency action "unlawfully withheld,"[2] and set aside agency action that is "not in accordance with law," violates the Constitution, or occurred "without observance of procedure required by law."[3] Thus, the legal questions a court must decide are hardly limited to the interpretation of statutes. This chapter addresses how courts handle nonstatutory legal issues. In most instances, courts determine legal requirements independently, without any deference—*Chevron*, *Skidmore*, or otherwise—to the agency's views. However, courts have traditionally deferred to an agency's reading of its own regulations. Why and to what extent they should do so is explored below.

---

* Dean and Professor of Law, IIT Chicago-Kent College of Law.

1. 5 U.S.C. § 706.
2. *Id.* § 706(1).
3. *Id.* § 706(2)(A), (B), (D).

6.02 GROUNDS ON WHICH A COURT WILL SET ASIDE AGENCY ACTION

The court will set aside an agency action if it finds that the action exceeds the authority granted, or violates limitations imposed, by

1. **the Constitution;**
2. **an agency rule having the force of law (as opposed to, for example, internal operating procedures);**
3. **federal common law, in the rare cases in which it applies;**
4. **any other source of law that is binding upon the agency, including a consent decree or other judicial order, international law, and (to the extent applicable and enforceable by their terms) executive orders.**

Except as [described in § 6.03,] below, in resolving legal issues arising under the foregoing sources of law, courts have no established tradition of deference to any agency, although they occasionally give some weight to the agency's views.

[Blackletter Statement, Part 3, §§ III.A, III.B.]

6.021 The Constitution

The authority of the federal courts to keep federal agencies within constitutional limits is unquestioned. As long as review is not precluded, courts must assess whether agency actions comply with constitutional commands. Courts consider constitutional challenges to the very existence of agencies[4] as well as to the permissibility of individual agency actions.[5]

Particularly when exercising an adjudicative function, agencies themselves may consider a wide range of constitutional issues. In reviewing these determinations, courts afford no deference to the agencies' construction of the constitutional principle at stake.[6]

6.022 Agency Rules with the Force of Law

Agency rules having the force and effect of law are as binding on agencies as the Constitution and statutes. Accordingly, courts may review

4. *See, e.g.*, Morrison v. Olson, 487 U.S. 654 (1988) (upholding constitutionality of Office of Independent Counsel).
5. *See, e.g.*, Marshall v. Barlow's, Inc., 436 U.S. 307 (1978) (addressing constitutionality of agency search).
6. *Cf.* United States v. Nixon, 418 U.S. 683, 703-05 (1974).

agency action for conformance with previously promulgated rules,[7] including rules of procedure.[8]

The Third Circuit's decision in *Furnari v. Warden*[9] is instructive. There, an inmate challenged a parole commission's decision denying him a *de novo* hearing that he claimed was necessary in light of newly offered exculpatory evidence. The court found that the agency's own rules required it to provide a new statement of reasons for denying parole given the new evidence; its failure to do so required granting habeas relief (in the form, presumably, of a new parole hearing).[10]

Cases such as *Furnari* do not readily suggest when a rule or regulation should be considered binding. Certainly, all rules issued through formal or notice-and-comment rulemaking bind the agencies, but so do rules reached through a less formal process when they invite reliance from regulated entities and the public.[11] Although line-drawing problems arise, courts are more likely to find a rule enforceable when its wording is mandatory and/or appears to bind the agency and when the rule is relevant to private ordering. Agency regulations more akin to internal operating procedures bind the agency as a matter of politics but not law. Private parties cannot sue the agency directly for failure to comply with rules or policy statements lacking the force of law.[12] Unlike the situation in *Furnari*, such rules will be enforced at the discretion of the agency.

---

7. Ballard v. Commisisoner, 544 U.S. 40, 59 (2005) (governmental entities are "obliged to follow [their] own Rules"); United States ex rel. Accardi v. Shaughnessy, 347 U.S. 260, 265-67 (1954); Arizona Grocery Co. v. Atchison, Topeka & Santa Fe Ry., 284 U.S. 370, 390 (1932).
8. Vitarelli v. Seaton, 359 U.S. 535, 539-40 (1959).
9. 218 F.3d 250 (3d Cir. 2000).
10. *Id.* at 255. *See also* Schroeder v. West, 212 F.3d 1265, 1270 (Fed. Cir. 2000); Moret v. Karn, 746 F.2d 989, 992 (3d Cir. 1984).
11. *Cf.* United States v. Caceres, 440 U.S. 741 (1979) (declining to exclude evidence obtained in violation of IRS procedural rule because the rule did not invite reliance from targets of investigation); *see also* American Farm Lines v. Black Ball Freight Service, 397 U.S. 532, 537 (1970).
12. *See, e.g.*, Schweiker v. Hansen, 450 U.S. 785, 788-89 (1981) (holding that Social Security Administration's Claims Manual lacked the force of law and was not judicially enforceable); Haitian Refugee Center v. Baker, 953 F.2d 1498, 1508 (11th Cir. 1992); Romeiro de Silva v. Smith, 773 F.2d 1021 (9th Cir. 1985); Pasquini v. Morris, 700 F.2d 658, 662-62 (11th Cir. 1983). *Cf.* In re Surface Mining Regulation Litig., 627 F.2d 1346, 1357 (D.C. Cir. 1980) (stating that an agency directive implementing President's Executive Order was to be treated as a discretionary rule).

This is not to suggest that agency internal operating procedures, general statements of agency policy, or requirements set out in staff manuals have no impact. When published, agencies can rely on such rules,[13] and if agencies depart from their terms, they must explain why they are changing the rules of the game midstream. Thus, even though internal operating procedures and staff manuals may not be directly enforceable, aggrieved litigants may argue successfully that the agency acted arbitrarily by failing to comply with previously articulated policies. The theory of such relief is not reversal for legal error, but reversal because of an abuse of discretion—the "action is, without legitimate reason and adequate explanation, inconsistent with prior agency policies or procedures."[14]

Irrespective of whether an agency rule has the force of law, disputes often arise over the meaning of regulations. Like statutes, regulations can be, and often are, ambiguous. Courts must then decide how much weight to afford the agency's interpretation of the regulation. (No deference will be afforded if the meaning of the regulation is plain.) The level of deference afforded to an agency's interpretation of its own regulation is discussed below.[15]

6.023 Federal Common Law

Federal courts rarely invoke federal common law as a basis for constraining agencies. On occasion, however, courts have relied squarely on their own lawmaking authority to invalidate administrative decisions. One recurrent example involves res judicata and collateral estoppel.[16] In general these preclusion doctrines apply to administrative adjudications just as they do to judi-

---

13. 5 U.S.C. § 552(a)(1).
14. A Blackletter Statement of Federal Administrative Law, Scope of Review § V.F (reprinted in Appendix); Chapter Eight, § II.F, *infra*. *See* American Petroleum Inst. v. EPA, 684 F.3d 1342 (D.C. Cir. 2012) (considering argument that agency had departed from its own guidelines, though concluding that it had not). Some internal rules are merely precatory, and courts rarely will find that agencies acted arbitrarily merely by failing to follow such rules.
15. *See* § III, *infra*.
16. Tait v. Western Md. Ry., 289 U.S. 620 (1933); Clark-Cowlitz Joint Operating Agency v. FERC, 775 F.2d 366, 373-76 (D.C. Cir. 1985) (holding that agency's interpretation of statute was barred by res judicata and collateral estoppel), *on rehrg.*, 826 F.2d 1074 (D.C. Cir. 1987) (holding agency's interpretation not precluded).

cial decisions.[17] Accordingly, where a party has had a full and fair opportunity to litigate a particular claim or issue of fact or law before an agency tribunal it will, barring unusual circumstances, be unable to relitigate before another agency or a court. And that restriction in turn operates as a constraint on agency authority.

For instance, consider the First Circuit's decision in *Bath Iron Works Corp. v. Director, OWCP*.[18] There, an employee injured on the job initially obtained benefits through state workers' compensation proceedings. He received an award of 25 percent disability due to a serious knee injury and, when the disability worsened over time, successfully applied for an increase to a 50 percent award. Thereafter, the employee sought a further award from the employer under the federal Longshore and Harbor Workers Compensation Act.[19] The Department of Labor's Benefits Review Board granted him full disability, rejecting the employer's argument that the extent of the disability had been conclusively litigated in the state proceeding and could not now be revisited. The First Circuit, however, reversed the agency's determination. Noting that "the tendency is plainly in favor of applying collateral estoppel in administrative contexts,"[20] it held that the state agency's prior determination precluded consideration of this issue by the Board. In doing so, the court imposed a federal common law requirement on the agency.

Preclusion doctrines do not apply to the federal government and its components with quite the force that they apply to private parties. Most importantly, offensive non-mutual collateral estoppel cannot be invoked against the federal government—an agency is free to relitigate an issue on which it previously lost if it does so in a separate matter against a different party.[21] But in a matter involving *the same party*, an agency is bound by its, or a court's, prior adjudicative determination, assuming the standard requirements of collateral estoppel have been satisfied.[22]

---

17. Restatement (Second) of Judgments § 83 (1982).
18. 125 F.3d 18 (1st Cir. 1997).
19. 33 U.S.C. §§ 901 et seq.
20. *Bath Iron Works*, 125 F.3d at 21.
21. United States v. Mendoza, 464 U.S. 154 (1984).
22. United States v. Stauffer Chemical Co., 464 U.S. 165 (1984) (holding that EPA could not relitigate in a different circuit an issue already litigated against the same party in another case involving virtually identical facts); PTO v. FLRA, 672 F.3d 1095, 1096-97 (D.C. Cir. 2012) (holding FLRA collaterally estopped by its own prior conclusion regarding legality of a term in a collective bargaining agreement).

6.024 Other Sources of Binding Law

This is a catchall category that covers all sources of law other than those mentioned above. Courts may independently construe—and redress violations of—any relevant legal constraint on agency action. For instance, agencies are bound by, and courts will enforce, the terms of a valid consent decree.[23] In addition, and of growing importance, agencies must follow the law of nations as well as domestic law.[24]

Executive orders issued by the President constitute a final source of constraint on agencies. A presidential executive order, by definition, channels the conduct of agency officials. A failure to conform to such orders, however, generally cannot be second-guessed in court. First, most executive orders expressly state that they are not enforceable[25] and courts uniformly respect such limitations.[26] Second, even absent such explicit language, courts have held that executive orders resting on the President's inherent authority to manage the executive branch do not provide an enforceable limit on the

---

23. United States v. Armour & Co., 402 U.S. 673, 681-83 (1971); *see generally* "Authority of the United States to Enter Settlements Limiting the Future Exercise of Executive Branch Discretion," Memorandum from Acting Assistant Attorney General Randolph D. Moss to Associate Attorney General Raymond C. Fisher (June 15, 1999), *available at* http://www.justice.gov/olc/consent_decrees2.htm. Judicial enforcement of consent decrees against agencies has not been uncontroversial. For an extended attack on the appropriateness and constitutionality of the practice, see Michael T. Morley, *Consent of the Governed or Consent of the Government? The Problems with Consent Decrees in Government-Defendant Cases*, 16 U. PA. J. CONST. L. 637 (2014).
24. *Cf.* Weinberger v. Rossi, 456 U.S. 25 (1982) (construing regulation narrowly to avoid conflict with the law of nations).
25. The following language is typical:

    > This order is intended only to improve the internal management of the executive branch and is not intended to, nor does it create any right, benefit, or trust responsibility, substantive or procedural, enforceable at law or equity by a party against the United States, its agencies, its officers, or any person. This order shall not be construed to create any right to judicial review involving the compliance or noncompliance of the United States, its agencies, its officers, or any other person with this order.

    E.O. 12,989, § 6-609; *see also* E.O. 12,866, § 10.
26. *See, e.g.*, Chen v. Carroll, 48 F.3d 1331, 1338-40 (4th Cir. 1995); State of Michigan v. Thomas, 805 F.2d 176, 187 (6th Cir. 1986).

agency's powers.[27] Although courts typically do not enforce executive orders, an agency head may face political repercussions for not following them.[28]

However, courts will enforce an executive order if the order "has a specific foundation in congressional action."[29] Accordingly, when an executive order directly implements and is authorized by a statute, judicial enforcement may be obtainable.[30]

6.03 DEFERENCE TO AN AGENCY'S INTERPRETATION OF ITS OWN REGULATION

Pursuant to what is sometimes called *"Auer"* or *"Seminole Rock"* deference, a court must accept an agency's interpretation of its own regulation unless the agency's interpretation is "plainly erroneous or inconsistent with the regulation." *Auer v. Robbins*, 519 U.S. 452, 461 (1997) (quoting *Bowles v. Seminole Rock & Sand Co.*, 325 U.S. 410, 414 (1945)). The Supreme Court has

---

27. *See, e.g.*, Zhang v. Slattery, 55 F.3d 732, 748 (2d Cir. 1995).
28. *See id.* ("For whatever reasons, the Attorney General did not adhere to this order and the Bush Administration did not follow up on it. However, it is not the role of the federal courts to administer the executive branch."); In re Surface Mining Regulation Litig., 627 F.2d 1346, 1357 (D.C. Cir. 1980); Indep. Meat Packers Ass'n v. Butz, 526 F.2d 228, 234 (8th Cir. 1975).
29. *Surface Mining Regulation Litig.*, 627 F.2d at 1357. It is not clear whether the theory of these decisions is that such orders create a private right of action themselves or merely create legal requirements that can be enforced under the APA. At least one court has seemed to suggest that the two amount to the same thing: only an Executive Order that creates a private right of action is enforceable under the APA. Dong v. Slattery, 84 F.3d 82, 86 (2d Cir. 1996).
30. *See, e.g.*, City of Albuquerque v. U.S. Dep't of the Interior, 379 F.3d 901, 905-06, 913-14 (10th Cir. 2004) (considering a claim that agency violated Executive Order in choosing office space); City of Carmel-By-The-Sea v. U.S. Dep't of Transportation, 123 F.3d 1142 (9th Cir. 1997); Sierra Club v. Peterson, 705 F.2d 1475 (9th Cir. 1983); Legal Aid Soc'y of Alameda County v. Brennan, 608 F.2d 1319 (9th Cir. 1979); Chambers v. United States, 451 F.2d 1045, 1050, 1053 (Ct. Cl. 1971) (awarding backpay for the government's violation of an executive order regarding nondiscriminatory employment practices); Wildlands CPR, Inc. v. U.S. Forest Service, 872 F. Supp. 2d 1064 (D. Mont. 2012) (finding that EOs governing use of off-road vehicles on public lands had force and effect of law and were intended to create a private right of action, but that the agency had complied with the orders' requirements).

applied *Auer* deference to agency interpretations, as in litigation briefs, that are not the outgrowth of any formal process within the agency as long as it appears that the interpretation reflects the agency's fair and considered judgment. A lesser degree of deference is sometimes considered appropriate where Congress has not delegated lawmaking authority to the agency or where an agency seeks deference for an interpretation of a regulation that merely parrots the language of the statute.

[Blackletter Statement, Part 3, § III.C.]

Although courts have no reason to defer to an agency's construction of another agency's regulation,[31] they generally will uphold an agency's plausible construction of its own regulation.[32] Indeed, traditionally the deference courts afford agencies' interpretations of their own regulations is at least as strong, and arguably stronger, than that given interpretations of statutory terms under *Chevron*.

The seminal case is *Bowles v. Seminole Rock & Sand Co.*[33] In considering a dispute over a regulation issued by the Office of Price Administration, the Court concluded that the Secretary's own interpretation of the contested words "highest price" should control:

> Since this [case] involves an interpretation of an administrative regulation a court must necessarily look to the administrative construction of the regulation if the meaning of the words used is in doubt. . . . [T]he ultimate criterion is the administrative interpretation, which becomes of controlling weight unless it is plainly erroneous or inconsistent with the regulation.[34]

The Court has often invoked *Seminole Rock* and reiterated its "plainly erroneous or inconsistent" standard.[35]

Deferring to an agency's interpretation of its own ambiguous regulations has several possible rationales. In part, *Chevron* principles apply with equal

---

31. *See* Nat'l Treasury Employees Union v. FLRA, 848 F.2d 1273, 1275 (D.C. Cir. 1988).
32. *See, e.g.*, Martin v. OSHRC, 499 U.S. 144, 150-51 (1991) (describing basic justifications for judicial deference to an agency's interpretation of its own regulation).
33. 325 U.S. 410 (1945).
34. *Id.* at 413-14.
35. *See, e.g.*, Thomas Jefferson Univ. v. Shalala, 512 U.S. 504, 512 (1994) (collecting examples).

force in this setting. If Congress has delegated power to the agency to fill in legislative gaps, then courts should defer to any reasonable interpretations that the agency forwards of its own gap-filling regulations. It is more legitimate for an agency than a court to undertake that function: "the power authoritatively to interpret its own regulations is a component of the agency's delegated lawmaking powers."[36] The agency has more expertise and is more politically accountable than courts. Moreover, agencies arguably should have the flexibility to adjust interpretations of regulations as social needs evolve. Congress has entrusted agencies with the power to make law through regulations and to define what those regulations mean. In addition, on intentionalist premises, the agency, as the author of the regulation, might be thought to best understand its meaning. Finally, even if an interpretation seems a stretch, because the agency could rewrite the regulation to adopt that interpretation explicitly, a court might see little point in rejecting the interpretation.

Exactly how *Seminole Rock* deference compares to *Chevron* deference is difficult to say with great confidence. The usual judicial formulations of *Seminole Rock* deference sound (even) more deferential than *Chevron*. For example, in *Thomas Jefferson University v. Shalala*, the Supreme Court noted the "substantial deference [due] to an agency's interpretation of its own regulations,"[37] explaining: "Our task is not to decide which among several competing interpretations best serves the regulatory purpose. . . . [W]e must defer to the Secretary's interpretation unless an 'alternative reading is compelled by the regulation's plain language or by other indications of the Secretary's intent at the time of the regulation's promulgation.'"[38] The Court added that this "broad deference" is warranted especially where the regulation concerns a complex, technical regulatory program.[39] Perhaps the Court was convinced that agencies are better situated to understand their own ambiguous regulations as opposed to open-ended terms passed by Congress. Thus, *Seminole Rock* might be understood as "*Chevron*-plus" deference.

Despite this theoretical difference, the *Seminole Rock* and *Chevron* standards likely converge in practice. As the D.C. Circuit has noted:

> In the aftermath of *Chevron*, it may be that our deference to agency interpretations of ambiguous regulations is not different than that which we afford to interpretations of ambiguous statutes. It would

---

36. *Martin*, 499 U.S. at 151.
37. 512 U.S. at 512 (citations omitted).
38. *Id.* (quoting Gardebring v. Jenkins, 485 U.S. 415, 430 (1988)).
39. *Id.*

> seem that there are few, if any, cases in which the standard applicable under *Chevron* would yield a different result than the "plainly erroneous or inconsistent" standard set forth in *Bowles*.[40]

Similarly, the Supreme Court in *Martin v. OHSRC* implicitly invoked *Chevron* by admonishing courts to defer to agency interpretations of regulations "only if the Secretary's interpretation *is* reasonable. The Secretary's interpretation of an ambiguous regulation is subject to the same standard of substantive review as any other exercise of delegated lawmaking power."[41]

In one respect, however, it is clear that *Seminole Rock* deference goes beyond *Chevron* deference: the complicated "step zero" inquiry which narrows the reach of *Chevron* is absent in this setting; *Seminole Rock* extends to any authoritative agency interpretation. Consider the Supreme Court's other most-cited decision regarding such deference, *Auer v. Robbins*.[42] The dispute focused on a Department of Labor regulation fleshing out the meaning of the Fair Labor Standards Act's exemption for employees acting in "executive, administrative, or professional capacity."[43] The agency's regulation provided that an employee paid on a "salary basis" was exempt from the Act's protections.[44] That exception included employees whose wages were "not subject to reduction because of variations in the quality or quantity of the work performed."[45]

In litigation, the agency clarified that an employee would not be deemed to be paid on a "salary basis" if either there were an actual practice of taking deductions from pay for shoddy work or a "significant likelihood" that such deductions would occur if the employee violated pertinent work rules. Writing for a unanimous Court, Justice Scalia held that the agency's interpretation of the regulation, even though set out for the first time in a brief, was entitled to *Seminole Rock* deference and therefore was "'controlling unless "plainly erroneous or inconsistent with the regulation."'"[46] The Court explained that "[t]here is simply no reason to suspect that the interpretation does not reflect the agency's

---

40. Paralyzed Veterans of Am. v. D.C. Arena L.P., 117 F.3d 579, 584 (D.C. Cir. 1997).
41. 499 U.S. 144, 159 (1991) (emphasis original).
42. 519 U.S. 452 (1997).
43. 29 U.S.C. § 213(a)(1).
44. 29 C.F.R. § 541.1(f).
45. *Id.* § 54.118(a).
46. *Auer*, 519 U.S. at 461 (quoting Robertson v. Methow Valley Citizens Council, 490 U.S. 332, 359 (1989) (quoting *Seminole Rock*, 325 U.S. at 414)).

fair and considered judgment on the matter in question."[47] *Auer* suggests, therefore, that strong deference should be afforded any well-considered agency interpretation of any ambiguous regulations the agency has issued.[48]

Although *Seminole Rock*, *Auer*, and the *Blackletter Statement* lay out a well-settled doctrine that has been relied upon in numerous cases,[49] some commentators and jurists recently have called into question the propriety of strong deference in this setting. Some scholars object that empowering agencies to both make and interpret the law might endanger liberty.[50] In particular, when agencies both promulgate regulations and then interpret them, they have an incentive to issue overly vague rules, knowing that they can then flesh out the rules through interpretations that avoid stringent review.[51] Justice Scalia has endorsed this argument and articulated a willingness to overrule *Auer* (notwithstanding the fact that he is the author of the opinion).[52] Moreover, agencies can avoid rulemaking procedures merely by reinterpreting their own regulations in an enforcement action. Finally, some see placing the power to issue and to interpret regulations in the same hands as inconsistent with basic principles of separation of powers.[53]

---

47. *Id.* at 462.
48. *See also* Talk America, Inc. v. Michigan Bell Telephone Co., 131 S. Ct. 2254 (2011).
49. *See, e.g.*, *id.*; Chase Bank USA, N.A. v. McCoy, 131 S. Ct. 871, 880-81 (2011); Coeur Alaska v. SE Alaska Conservation Council, 557 U.S. 261, 277-78 (2009); Kennedy v. Plan Administrator for DuPont Sav. & Inv. Plan, 555 U.S. 285 (2009). Some commentators, however, have labeled the Supreme Court's application of *Auer* as sporadic. *See* William N. Eskridge, Jr. & Lauren E. Baer, *The Continuum of Deference: Supreme Court Treatment of Agency Statutory Interpretations from* Chevron *to* Hamdan, 96 Geo. L.J. 1083, 1103-04 (2008).
50. *See generally* Robert A. Anthony, *The Supreme Court and the APA: Sometimes They Just Don't Get It*, 10 Admin. L. J. Am. U. 1 (1996); John F. Manning, *Constitutional Structure and Judicial Deference to Agency Interpretations of Agency Rules*, 96 Colum. L. Rev. 612 (1996).
51. *See, e.g.*, Jonathan T. Molot, *The Judicial Perspective in the Administrative State: Reconciling Modern Doctrines of Deference with the Judiciary's Structural Role*, 53 Stan. L. Rev. 1, 105-07 (2000); Manning, *supra* note 50, at 655.
52. *Talk America, Inc.*, 131 S. Ct. at 2265-66 (Scalia, J., concurring) ("[D]eferring to an agency's interpretation of its own rule encourages the agency to enact vague rules which give it the power, in future adjudications, to do what it pleases.").
53. *See, e.g.*, Decker v. Northwest Environmental Defense Center, 133 S. Ct. 1326, 1340 (2013) (Scalia, J., concurring).

Commentators criticizing *Seminole Rock* argue that agency interpretations of their own regulations merit only the less generous deference accorded under *Skidmore v. Swift & Co.*[54] The *Skidmore* standard provides that an agency's interpretive position is "entitled to respect" and that the "weight of such a judgment in a particular case will depend upon the thoroughness evident in its consideration, the validity of its reasoning, its consistency with earlier and later pronouncements, and all those factors which give it power to persuade, if lacking power to control."[55] The more stringent review ex post would in turn sharpen the ex ante incentives for clearer rules.

Such arguments, however, are not fully persuasive. First, Congress possesses the same check of revising the delegation irrespective of whether the agency is interpreting a statute or a regulation. Congress can overrule or modify the one just as easily as the other. Second, even when a court overturns an agency's interpretation, the agency can respond in many instances by issuing a new regulation that embodies the interpretation rejected by the court. The agency, in other words, has more than one means to ensure that its preferred interpretation governs. Third, the separation-of-powers argument is not dispositive given that agencies widely interpret both statutes and regulations in enforcing their legislatively delegated tasks. Indeed, agencies exercise a mixture of functions in many contexts.[56] Fourth, one would think that agencies have greater expertise in divining the meaning of agency regulations than do courts. Courts construing regulations might supplant agencies as policymakers under delegated grants of authority from Congress. Although agencies can always issue a revised regulation, a judicial gloss raises the costs of maintaining the agency's preferred regulatory position. Finally, clearer rules may not always serve the public interest. A standard-like regulation may better protect the public than would judicially compelled bright-line rules.[57]

Although the Supreme Court as a whole has thus far been unmoved by the scholarly critique of *Auer*, it has declined to apply *Auer* in two contexts. First, in *Gonzales v. Oregon*[58] the Court considered the Attorney General's controversial decision to prohibit physicians from prescribing regulated drugs

---

54. 323 U.S. 134 (1944).
55. *Id.* at 140.
56. *Cf.* Withrow v. Larkin, 421 U.S. 35 (1975).
57. For a defense of *Seminole Rock*, see generally Scott H. Angstreich, *Shoring Up* Chevron*: A Defense of* Seminole Rock *Deference to Agency Regulatory Interpretations*, 34 U. C. Davis L. Rev. 49 (2000).
58. 546 U.S. 243 (2006).

for use in physician-assisted suicide even when sanctioned under state law. The AG based his decision on an interpretation of a Department of Justice regulation that required that prescriptions "be issued for a legitimate purpose,"[59] seeking *Seminole Rock* deference for that interpretation. The Court refused to defer because the regulation essentially tracked the statute.

> The CSA allows prescription of drugs only if they have a "currently accepted medical use"; requires a "medical purpose" for dispensing the least controlled substances of those on the schedules; and, in its reporting provision, defines a "valid prescription" as one "issued for a legitimate medical purpose." Similarly, physicians are considered to be acting as practitioners under the statute if they dispense controlled substances "in the course of professional practice." The regulation uses the terms "legitimate medical purpose" and "the course of professional practice," but this just repeats two statutory phrases and attempts to summarize the others. It gives little or no instruction on a central issue in this case . . . .[60]

The Court refused to allow the agency to bootstrap what was in essence an interpretation of *the statute* into *Seminole Rock* territory.

> Simply put, the existence of a parroting regulation does not change the fact that the question here is not the meaning of the regulation but the meaning of the statute. An agency does not acquire special authority to interpret its own words when, instead of using its expertise and experience to formulate a regulation, it has elected merely to paraphrase the statutory language.[61]

Second, in *Christopher v. Smithkline Beecham Corp.*[62] the Court departed from *Auer* when considering a Department of Labor interpretation of a regulation under the Fair Labor Standards Act[63] determining whether pharmaceutical sales representatives are exempt from overtime protections. According to the Court, the Department of Labor's interpretation of the ambiguous regulation was surprising and would have imposed "massive liabilities on

---

59. 21 C.F.R. § 1306.04a.
60. *Gonazales*, 546 U.S. at 257 (citations omitted).
61. *Id. See also* Federal Express Corp. v. Holowecki, 552 U.S. 389 (2008) (refusing to afford *Auer* deference to parroting language in a regulation); Northern California River Watch v. Wilcox, 633 F.3d 766 (9th Cir. 2011) (same).
62. 132 S. Ct. 2156 (2012).
63. 29 U.S.C. § 213(a)(1).

respondent for conduct that occurred well before that interpretation was announced. To defer to the agency's interpretation in this circumstance would seriously undermine the principle that agencies should provide regulated parties 'fair warning'."[64] Importantly, having determined that *Auer* did not apply, the Court invoked *Skidmore* (although it nonetheless rejected the agency's interpretation).[65]

The opinion in *Christopher* might hint at some further curtailment of *Seminole Rock*. Justice Alito asserted that "deference is likewise unwarranted when there is reason to suspect that the agency's interpretation does not reflect the agency's fair and considered judgment on the matter in question."[66] Signs of a lack of fair and considered judgment may include agency flip-flops on regulatory meaning and, more generally, evidence that an agency's regulatory interpretation is merely a "convenient litigating position" or "post hoc rationalization."[67] From a political process perspective, strong deference seems unwarranted if the agency interpretation has been hastily reached and little debated.[68] Pushed moderately hard, however, this stance has the potential seriously to undermine the scope of *Auer* deference. Most agency interpretations of regulations are not the outgrowth of any defined process, have not been tested by the crucible of public participation (through rulemaking or adjudication before the agency), and may reflect nothing more than the result of litigation pressures. Congress would not lightly imbue such interpretations

---

64. *Christopher*, 132 S. Ct. at 2167.
65. *Id.* at 2169. *See also* Independent Training & Apprenticeship Program v. Calif. Dep't of Indus. Relations, 730 F.3d 1024 (9th Cir. 2013) (also rejecting *Auer* deference because of notice concerns but applying *Skidmore* and *upholding* the agency's interpretation).
66. *Christopher*, 132 S. Ct. at 2166 (citation omitted).
67. *Id. See also* Akzo Nobel Salt, Inc. v. Fed. Mine Safety & Health Review Comm'n, 212 F.3d 1301, 1304-05 (D.C. Cir. 2000).
68. Exelon Generation Co. v. Local 15, IBEW, 676 F.3d 566 (7th Cir. 2012) (stating that affording *Auer* deference to ad hoc agency interpretations of regulations "would undermine democratic transparency and upset the settled expectations of regulated parties"); *see also* Matthew C. Stephenson & Miri Pogoriler, Seminole Rock*'s Domain*, 79 GEO. WASH. L. REV. 1449 (2011) (evaluating instability of *Auer* doctrine and weakness of its underlying assumptions).
69. This reading receives strong support from United States v. Mead Corp., 533 U.S. 218 (2001). There the Court held that *Chevron* deference applies only where Congress has delegated authority to the agency to act with the force of law and noted that relatively thorough procedural requirements were an indication that Congress had done so, but were not in themselves necessary or

with the presumption of correctness.[69] Heightening this tension, the interpretation in the *Auer* case itself—from which this type of deference obtained its modern name—was set forth in a brief, not a context suggesting focused consideration of the regulation's reach in future contexts.

As of this writing, the latest act in the *Seminole Rock* play is the Court's decision in *Decker v. Northwest Environmental Defense Center*.[70] The case involved whether the Clean Water Act and its implementing regulations required a permit for certain stormwater runoff from logging roads. EPA took the position in an amicus brief that a permit was not required and, in an opinion written by Justice Kennedy and joined by six others, the Court accepted that view, relying on *Auer* and noting that there was "no indication that [the agency's] current view is a change from prior practice or a post hoc justification adopted in response to litigation."[71] Writing only for himself, Justice Scalia concurred, agreeing that EPA's interpretation was correct but setting out his most full-throated attack on *Auer* yet.[72] Chief Justice Roberts, joined by Justice Alito, wrote briefly simply to note that the issue of whether *Auer* should be overruled had not been briefed or argued, but signaled that they would view such an argument with interest.

The future ambit of *Auer* remains unclear. For the time being, there is no indication that a majority of the Court is ready to overrule these longstanding precedents, and the *Blackletter Statement* accurately sets out current law.

In any event, *Auer*—irrespective of its ultimate scope—will not affect an agency's construction of its own interpretive rules and policy statements, as opposed to regulations. (The question of whether to defer to agency interpre-

---

sufficient to trigger *Chevron* deference. *See also* Robert A. Anthony, *Which Agency Interpretations Should Bind Citizens and the Courts?*, 7 YALE J. ON REG. 1, 39-40 (1990); *see generally* Lisa Bressman, *Beyond Accountability: Arbitrariness and Legitimacy in the Administrative State*, 78 N.Y.U.L. REV. 461 (2003). Courts by and large have not applied *Mead* to the *Auer* context, but may be emboldened by the *Christopher* decision.

70. 133 S. Ct. 1326 (2013).

71. *Id.* at 1337.

72. *Id.* at 1338-40 (Scalia, J., concurring). Largely tracking his opinion in *Talk America*, Justice Scalia rejected the intentionalist premises of an argument that the agency has special insight into the meaning of its own regulation, denied that expertise was relevant to *interpreting* (as opposed to *writing*) regulations, distinguished *Chevron* on the ground that it involved a setting where the law-maker and the law-interpreter were two different entities, and insisted that basic separation-of-powers principles required just that separation.

tations of informal rules such as policy statements or circulars will seldom arise given that so little turns on whether the agency interpretation is correct—the interpretive rules and policy statements themselves usually only warrant *Skidmore* deference.[73]) For example, in *Elgin Nursing and Rehabilitation Center v. Department of Health and Human Services*[74] the Fifth Circuit refused to grant *Auer* deference to an interpretation of an interpretive manual that interpreted a published regulation. The court rejected such "*Seminole Rock* squared" deference[75] on the grounds that it would (a) enable agencies not only to issue ambiguous regulations, but also to issue ambiguous interpretations thereof, (b) effectively insulated agencies from judicial review, and (c) allow sanctions without fair notice.[76]

---

73. *See, e.g.*, Shalala v. Guernsey Mem. Hosp., 514 U.S. 87, 99 (1995) (noting that interpretive rules "do not have the force and effect of law and are not accorded that weight in the adjudicatory process."); Hoctor v. United States Dep't of Agric., 82 F.3d 165 (7th Cir. 1996).
74. 718 F.3d 488 (5th Cir. 2013).
75. *Id.* at 493.
76. *Id.*

Chapter 7

JUDICIAL REVIEW OF ISSUES OF FACT

by Ronald M. Levin and Jim Rossi*

7.01 INTRODUCTION

The following standards apply, as specified herein, when courts review agencies' findings regarding purely factual questions. These standards also are commonly used to review agency findings that may be termed "factual" but actually embody a degree of normative judgment. (Such findings present what are sometimes called questions of "ultimate fact" or of "application of law to fact," or "mixed questions of law and fact.") In reviewing these findings, a court is likely to look exclusively to the standards expounded in this section if the meaning of the law is not in dispute. Where, however, the parties do disagree about the meaning of relevant law, the reviewing court must resolve that dispute using the appropriate test for adjudicating issues of law; if the agency action survives that scrutiny, the court then applies the appropriate standard stated in this section.

[Blackletter Statement, Part 3, § IV.]

* Ronald M. Levin is William R. Orthwein Distinguished Professor of Law, Washington University School of Law, and Jim Rossi is Professor of Law, Vanderbilt Law School.

Statutory review standards, as prescribed by section 706 of the Administrative Procedures Act (APA), provide the central reference point for judicial scrutiny of agency factual findings. The "substantial evidence" test applies to review of "formal" proceedings—those conducted pursuant to the APA's trial-type hearing proceedings.[1] This test "has not changed over the course of the century in which it has been applied by judges and by agencies" and is "among the most stable and satisfactory features of our system of administrative law."[2]

The APA incorporates, and the *Blackletter Statement* reflects, two primary exceptions to application of the substantial evidence test. First, findings of fact are subject to de novo review by a court where a statute or the Constitution requires independent review of facts.[3] Second, in the vast majority of "informal" proceedings, including notice-and-comment rulemaking, review of factual findings is considered a component of the "arbitrary and capricious" test and is not conducted separately under the substantial evidence standard.[4] Sections IV and V, below, discuss these two exceptions.

These standards also are commonly used to review agency findings that may be termed "factual" but actually embody a degree of normative judgment. Such findings present what are sometimes called questions of "ultimate fact," "application of law to fact," or "mixed questions of law and fact." In reviewing these findings, a court is likely to look exclusively to the standards expounded in this section if the meaning of the law is not in dispute. Where, however, the parties disagree about the meaning of relevant law, the reviewing court must resolve that dispute using the appropriate test for adjudicating issues of law;[5] most courts will resolve such legal questions first, reviewing factual issues under the appropriate standard stated in this section only if the agency action survives that scrutiny.

---

1. *See* 5 U.S.C. § 706(2)(E).
2. 2 Richard J. Pierce, Jr., Administrative Law Treatise § 11.2 at 979 (5th ed. 2010). *But see id.* at 984-88 (suggesting that the Court's opinion in *Allentown Mack Sales & Serv. Inc. v. NLRB*, 522 U.S. 359 (1998), which found a Board order to be unsupported by substantial evidence, has the potential to usher in a regime of less deferential review, although it probably will not do so).
3. 5 U.S.C. § 706(2)(F).
4. *Id.* § 706(2)(A). In *Citizens to Preserve Overton Park, Inc. v. Volpe*, 401 U.S. 402 (1971), the Court misread the APA as providing for substantial evidence review of informal rulemaking. *Id.* at 414. The Court later corrected its mistake. FCC v. Nat'l Citizens Comm. for Broadcasting, 436 U.S. 775, 803 (1977).
5. *See* Chapters Three, Four, Five, and Six, *supra*.

Although the substantial evidence test and its exceptions are well established, the test has provoked debate over the years. One debate centers on whether there is a difference between the degree of factual support necessary to satisfy the "substantial evidence" standard under the APA, on the one hand, and the "clearly erroneous" standard that applies to appellate review of factual findings by trial judges,[6] on the other. The substantial evidence test had its genesis in appellate court review of jury verdicts. Historically, jury verdicts have been reviewed less intensively than findings of judges without juries. Findings of judges were upheld unless "clearly erroneous," while juries were to be affirmed if they were supported by "substantial evidence." According to the leading analysis of the distinction between the two standards, "'clearly erroneous' permits a broader review than 'substantial evidence.'"[7] In *Dickinson v. Zurko*,[8] the Supreme Court noted that the difference between the tests "is a subtle one–so fine that (apart from the present case) we have failed to uncover a single instance in which a reviewing court conceded that the use of one standard rather than the other would in fact have produced a different outcome."[9] Nonetheless, in *Zurko* the Supreme Court reaffirmed that the clearly erroneous test is traditionally considered somewhat more searching than the substantial evidence test.[10]

Another longstanding debate among courts and commentators is whether there is any difference in the degree of factual support necessary to satisfy the "substantial evidence" test, on the one hand, and the "arbitrary and capri-

---

6. *See* FED. R. CIV. P. 52(a)(6).
7. Robert Stern, *Review of Findings of Administrators, Judges and Juries: A Comparative Analysis*, 58 HARV. L. REV. 70, 82 (1944).
8. 527 U.S. 150 (1999).
9. *Id.* at 163. Many agree with *Zurko*'s observation that there may be no difference in results under the two tests. *See, e.g.*, Int'l Bhd. of Elec. Workers v. NLRB, 448 F.2d 1127, 1142 (D.C. Cir. 1971) (Leventhal, J., dissenting) (noting that he had first thought this was the "case dreamed of by law school professors" in which the agency's conclusions were clearly erroneous but supported by substantial evidence, but later concluded that the agency's findings failed under both standards); Frank E. Cooper, *Administrative Law: The "Substantial Evidence" Rule*, 44 ABA J. 945, 947 (1958) (describing the difference between the tests as nothing more than a "label"). *But see* NLRB v. Universal Camera Corp., 179 F.2d 749, 754 (2d Cir. 1950) (L. Hand, J.) (upholding Board finding under substantial evidence test but stating that its sufficiency would have been "in doubt" if a judge had made it), *vacated and remanded on other grounds*, 340 U.S. 474 (1951).
10. *Zurko*, 527 U.S. at 153.

cious" test, on the other. Judicial authority on this issue has evolved considerably during the past few decades. The traditional view was that the arbitrary and capricious test is "more lenient."[11] Today, however, there is an "emerging consensus"[12] that the distinction "is 'largely semantic.'"[13] As stated in *Association of Data Processing Service Organizations v. Board of Governors*, a leading D.C. Circuit opinion by then-Judge Scalia, "in their application to the requirement of factual support the substantial evidence test and arbitrary or capricious test are one and the same. The former is only a specific application of the latter."[14] The D.C. Circuit has continued to assert this convergence between the two standards,[15] and at least eight other circuits have agreed.[16] Moreover, the Supreme Court has cited to the *Data Processing* reasoning and expressed no qualms about it.[17] However, one, or perhaps two, circuits have continued to echo the traditional view (albeit without displaying awareness of the developing rejection of it in other courts).[18]

---

11. Am. Paper Inst. v. Am. Elec. Power Serv. Corp. 461 U.S. 402, 412 n.7 (1983).
12. Ass'n of Data Processing Serv. Orgs., Inc. v. Bd. of Governors of the Fed. Reserve Sys., 745 F.2d 677, 684 (D.C. Cir. 1984) (quoting Pacific Legal Found. v. Dep't of Transp., 593 F.2d 1338, 1343 n.35 (D.C. Cir. 1979)).
13. *Id.* (quoting Aircraft Owners & Pilots Ass'n v. FAA, 600 F.2d 965, 971 n.28 (D.C. Cir. 1979)).
14. *Id.* at 683. That the two standards tend to "converge" was noted as early as 1973. Associated Indus. v. United States Dep't of Labor, 487 F.2d 342, 350 (2d Cir. 1973).
15. *See, e.g.*, CTS Corp. v. EPA, 759 F.3d 52, 59 n.1 (D.C. Cir. 2014); United Steel Workers Int'l Union v. PBGC, 707 F.3d 319, 325 (D.C. Cir. 2013); Butte County v. Hogen, 613 F.3d 190, 194 (D.C. Cir. 2010); Bangor Hydro-Electric Co. v. FERC, 78 F.3d 659, 663 n.3 (D.C. Cir. 1996); Consumers Union of the U.S. v. FTC, 801 F.2d 417, 422 (D.C. Cir. 1986).
16. Ace Tel. Ass'n v. Koppendrayer, 482 F.3d 876 (8th Cir. 2005); Bonnichsen v. United States, 367 F.3d 864, 880 n.19 (9th Cir. 2004); Sevoran v. Ashcroft, 290 F.3d 166, 174 (3d Cir. 2002); GTE South, Inc. v. Morrison, 199 F.3d 733, 745 n.3 (4th Cir. 1999); Lee v. Bd. of Govs. of Fed. Reserve Sys., 118 F.3d 905, 914 (2d Cir. 1997); Olenhouse v. Commodity Credit Corp., 42 F.3d 1560, 1575 n.25 (10th Cir. 1994); Tex. World Serv. Co. v. NLRB, 928 F.2d 1426, 1430 n.3 (5th Cir. 1991); Cruz v. Brock, 778 F.2d 62, 63-64 (1st Cir. 1985). *See also* Amusement & Music Operators Ass'n v. Copyright Royalty Tribunal, 676 F.2d 1144, 1151 & n.7 (7th Cir. 1982) (stating, prior to *Data Processing*, that the two criteria tend to converge in notice-and-comment rulemaking but possibly not in informal adjudication).
17. Dickinson v. Zurko, 527 U.S. 150, 158 (1999).
18. *See* Alabama Power Co. v. OSHA, 89 F.3d 740, 744 (11th Cir. 1996). The signals from the Federal Circuit have been mixed. *Compare* Consol. Bear-

The reluctance of most courts to distinguish between the stringency of these two standards is understandable, because it is difficult to perceive any justification for such a distinction. Traditionally, the two standards were regarded as inevitably different because substantial evidence review occurred on a "record."[19] Today, however, informal action is also reviewed on an administrative record;[20] thus, the basis for drawing a distinction between the two standards has largely disappeared. In addition, as agencies have increasingly used rulemaking and informal means of deciding matters that would previously have been handled through formal proceedings, courts have responded by importing the elements of substantial evidence analysis into "arbitrary and capricious" analysis.[21] For example, the judicial "hard look," originally enunciated in the context of substantial evidence review,[22] is now a fundamental aspect of the review of informal rulemaking.[23] Logically, there is no reason for judges to give a particular factual finding more critical scrutiny merely because the procedures through which it was reached were relatively elaborate.[24]

The *Blackletter Statement* uses the term "substantial support" to signify the quantum of support that an agency's factual determination must have in order to satisfy the arbitrary and capricious test. The term is intended to evoke the substantial evidence test while also recognizing that a reviewing court does not literally apply that test as it evaluates a decision reached after informal proceedings. Indeed, the phrase "substantial evidence" would be inapt when applied to the many informal settings in which "evidence" is never offered or taken.[25] Moreover, the arbitrary and capricious and substan-

---

ings Co. v. United States, 412 F.3d 1266 F.3d 1266, 1269 (Fed. Cir. 2005) (lack of substantial evidence would be an abuse of discretion), *with In re* Gartside, 203 F.3d 1305, 1312 (Fed. Cir. 2000) (arbitrary and capricious test is more deferential than substantial evidence). That circuit uses substantial evidence as the standard for review of factual findings by the Patent and Trademark Office, and at least one observer concludes that the result is that PTO findings are more readily reversed by the Federal Circuit than they would be if the arbitrary and capricious test were used. *See* Paul R. Gugliuzza, *The Federal Circuit as a Federal Court*, 54 WM. & MARY L. REV. 1791, 1821-22 (2013).

19. Abbott Labs., Inc. v. Gardner, 387 U.S. 136 (1967).
20. *See* § 7.04, *infra.*
21. *See* Ethyl Corp. v. EPA, 541 F.2d 1, 36 n.75 (D.C. Cir. 1976).
22. Greater Boston Television Corp. v. FCC, 444 F.2d 841, 851 (D.C. Cir. 1970).
23. *See* Chapter Eight, *infra.*
24. *Data Processing*, 745 F.2d at 685.
25. *See generally* Aircraft Owners & Pilots Ass'n v. FAA, 600 F.2d 965, 969-72 (D.C. Cir. 1979).

tial evidence tests *do* differ at least in their mechanics. In substantial evidence cases, a court seeks support for factual findings in the record of a formal hearing; in other cases, it does not.[26] Nevertheless, the terminology of the *Statement* should not be interpreted as implying that an agency needs to assemble more factual support to satisfy the substantial evidence test than to show that the action is not "arbitrary and capricious."[27]

7.02 FORMAL PROCEEDINGS

> **If the agency action resulted from a proceeding subject to APA §§ 556 and 557, or otherwise is reviewed on the record of an agency hearing provided by statute, the court determines whether the agency's factual finding or premise is supported by substantial evidence in the record as a whole. It is impossible to quantify "substantial evidence" precisely; one much-quoted Supreme Court formulation is "such evidence as a reasonable mind might accept as adequate to support a conclusion." This level of review is somewhat less intense than that employed when appellate courts review trial court findings of fact. In reviewing for substantial evidence, the court must consider the entire record, including the decision and factual findings of the Administrative Law Judge, if any, not just those portions of the record that support the agency's findings.**
>
> **[Blackletter Statement, Part 3, § IV.A.]**

The basic language of this section of the *Blackletter Statement* is drawn from § 706(2)(E) of the APA, which specifies that the substantial evidence test applies in formal proceedings. What, then, is "substantial evidence"?

26. Vt. Yankee Nuclear Power Corp. v. Natural Res. Def. Council, 435 U.S. 519, 547 (1978). More precisely, the usual significance of substantial evidence review is that a factual proposition that requires record support must be established through a trial-type adjudicative process, with all of the procedural opportunities that this entails. *See Data Processing*, 745 F.2d at 684. A few "anomalous" statutory schemes, however, prescribe substantial evidence review of decisions reached through informal rulemaking procedures. *See, e.g.*, Indus. Union Dep't, AFL-CIO v. Hodgson, 499 F.2d 467, 473 (D.C. Cir. 1974) (reviewing workplace safety standards issued under the Occupational Safety & Health Act).
27. *See* ABA Sect. of Admin. Law and Reg. Practice, *Comments on H.R. 3010, The Regulatory Accountability Act of 2011*, 64 Admin. L. Rev. 619, 670 (2012) (endorsing the *Data Processing* analysis).

Universal Camera Corp. v. NLRB[28] remains the leading statement on the meaning of the term. There the Court described substantial evidence as "more than a mere scintilla" and "such evidence as a reasonable mind might accept as adequate to support a conclusion."[29] Another standard formulation is that it is the amount of evidence necessary for a trial judge to deny a motion for directed verdict.[30] As the Court observed in *Universal Camera*, "[s]ince the precise way in which courts interfere with agency findings cannot be imprisoned within any form of words, new formulas attempting to rephrase the old are not likely to be more helpful than the old."[31] The precise quantum of evidence required can only be inferred from experience and the reading of many cases.

Other considerations are in play here beyond simply the amount of supporting evidence to be found in the record. First, an agency's findings may be upheld under the substantial evidence test if the determination is within the agency's expertise, even though cross-examination effectively destroys the testimony of expert witnesses supporting the agency's findings.[32] Second, as a corollary to *Chenery*'s requirement that an agency's decision must stand or fall on its stated rationale,[33] an agency's determination will be reversed under the substantial evidence test if the articulated basis for the agency's decision does not support its findings.[34] Third, the substantiality of the evidence must be determined by reference to the "whole record," not just the evidence supporting the agency.[35] Thus, evidence that would seem "substantial" standing alone—a particular document, say, or an individual witness's testimony—may not be "substantial" if it is contradicted or undermined by a raft of other evidence.

Finally, the Administrative Law Judge's decision is itself a part of the record and must be accorded "such probative force as it intrinsically com-

---

28. 340 U.S. 474 (1951).
29. *Id.* at 477 (quoting Consolidated Edison Co. v. Labor Board, 305 U.S. 197, 229 (1938)).
30. *Id.* (quoting NLRB v. Columbian Enameling & Stamping Co., 306 U.S. 292, 300 (1939)). Or, what amounts to the same thing: there must be sufficient evidence that it would have been possible for a reasonable jury to reach the agency's conclusion. Allentown Mack Sales & Service, Inc. v. NLRB, 522 U.S. 359, 366-67 (1998).
31. *Universal Camera*, 340 U.S. at 489.
32. *See* Elliot v. Commodity Futures Trading Comm'n, 202 F.3d 926, 933-35 (7th Cir. 2000).
33. *See* Chapter Nine, § 9.02, *infra*.
34. *See Allentown Mack,* 522 U.S. at 372-80.
35. *Universal Camera*, 340 U.S. at 487-88.

mands."[36] Accordingly, if the agency disagrees with the ALJ, that conflict is a factor undermining the agency's conclusion. This does not mean that an agency's findings are reviewed under a more stringent standard if they conflict with the ALJ's than if the two agree. In *Air Canada v. Department of Transportation*,[37] the D.C. Circuit noted "the substantial evidence standard is not modified in any way when an agency and an administrative law judge disagree; instead, where credibility of witnesses is at stake, an administrative law judge's evaluation of the witness' testimony may be an indicator of the substantiality of the evidence."[38] The court concluded: "Ultimately, where there is substantial evidence supporting its results, the Department's view governs."[39]

7.03 TRIAL DE NOVO

> **When the agency action resulted from a proceeding in which a statute or the Constitution requires that the facts shall be subject to trial de novo, the court makes its own, independent findings of fact and determines whether the agency action is warranted thereby. Trial de novo is available when a court reviews an agency's denial of a FOIA request, but is otherwise rare.**
>
> **[Blackletter Statement, Part 3, § IV.B.]**

This language from the *Blackletter Statement* resembles, but is significantly narrower than, § 706(2)(F) of the APA,[40] at least as that provision was originally conceived. The drafters of § 706(2)(F) contemplated a judicial trial of the facts in an unspecified, but presumably broad, range of circumstances, including review of informal administrative action.[41]

This state of affairs has been changed dramatically. In *Citizens to Preserve Overton Park, Inc. v. Volpe*,[42] the Supreme Court construed § 706(2)(F)

---

36. *Id.* at 495; *see generally id.* at 493-97.
37. 148 F.3d 1142 (D.C. Cir. 1998).
38. *Id.* at 1151 n.15 (citing Universal Camera Corp. v. NLRB, 340 U.S. 474, 496-97 (1951). *See also* Chen v. GAO, 821 F.2d 732, 734 (D.C. Cir. 1987); Nat'l Ass'n of Recycling Indus., Inc. v. Fed. Maritime Comm'n, 658 F.2d 816, 824-25 (D.C. Cir. 1980).
39. *Air Canada*, 148 F.3d at 1151 n.15 (citing Greater Boston Television Corp. v. FCC, 444 F.2d 841, 853 (D.C. Cir. 1970)).
40. 5 U.S.C. § 706(2)(F).
41. *See* Nathaniel L. Nathanson, *Probing the Mind of the Administrator*, 75 COLUM. L. REV. 721, 755 (1975).
42. 401 U.S. 402 (1971).

as applying only "when the action is adjudicatory in nature and the agency factfinding procedures are inadequate" or "when issues that were not before the agency are raised in a proceeding to enforce nonadjudicatory agency action."[43] Only one subsequent case has been found in which a court has explicitly found either of these criteria satisfied.[44] Thus, § 706(2)(F) has been reserved for truly extraordinary cases.[45] De novo factfinding by reviewing courts is largely confined to collateral matters, such as what the agency's rationale was and what materials the agency relied on.

The *Blackletter Statement* adapts the language of § 706(2)(F), limiting it to those few situations in which trial de novo is guaranteed by statute or by the Constitution. Perhaps the most important recurrent example consists of challenges to the denial of FOIA requests,[46] but other such settings also exist.[47]

7.04 OTHER CASES

> **In any other case, the court determines whether the factual premise has substantial support in the administrative record viewed as a whole (although the legal standard nominally being applied is the "arbitrary and capricious" test). APA § 706 (2)(A).**
> **[Blackletter Statement, Part 3, § IV.C.1.]**

Courts reviewing informal proceedings are willing to invalidate both rules and adjudicative orders because of inadequate factual support.[48] The

---

43. *Id.* at 415.
44. *See* Porter v. Califano, 592 F.2d 770, 782-84 (5th Cir. 1979) (involving an obviously biased agency adjudicator).
45. *See* Jifry v. FAA, 370 F.2d 1174 (D.C. Cir. 2004) (rejecting request for trial de novo of FAA determination based on classified information that pilots pose a security risk, instead reviewing this determination under the substantial evidence standard); Nat'l Org. for Women v. Soc. Security Admin., 736 F.2d 727, 744-46 (D.C. Cir. 1984). *See also* Dell v. Dep't of Commerce, 1999 WL 604217 (9th Cir. 1999) (unpublished mem. op.); JCI Metal Products v. U.S. Dep't of Navy, 2010 WL 2012006, at *3 (S.D. Cal. May 18, 2010).
46. 5 U.S.C. § 552(a)(4)(B).
47. *See, e.g.*, Agosto v. INS, 436 U.S. 748 (1978) (de novo trial of citizenship issue in deportation cases is guaranteed by statute and possibly by Constitution); Chandler v. Roudebush, 425 U.S. 840 (1976) (statutory guarantee of trial de novo of federal employees' Title VII claims).
48. *See, e.g.*, Nat'l Fuel Gas Supply Corp. v. FERC, 468 F.3d 831, 841-44 (D.C. Cir. 2006) (informal rulemaking); McGregor Printing Co. v. Kemp, 20 F.3d 1188, 1193-94 (D.C. Cir. 1994) (informal rulemaking); Timpinaro v. SEC, 2

Blackletter Statement's use of the term "substantial support" evokes the familiar "substantial evidence" test but avoids referring to "evidence" in recognition of the informal proceedings through which an administrative record is compiled. For all practical purposes, the stringency of the "substantial support" test is identical to that of the substantial evidence test.

> **For these purposes, the "administrative record" consists of a file of materials that the agency maintains as the exclusive basis for its decision; or, if no such file is maintained, it consists of all unprivileged materials that were actively considered by the agency or its staff (or that were submitted by outside parties) in connection with the action under review. Where procedural law so provides, the record must also disclose oral communications between decisionmakers and outside parties.**
>
> **[Blackletter Statement, Part 3, § IV.C.2.]**

Under the regime ushered in by *Overton Park*, the factual basis of an informal administrative action is usually reviewed on the "administrative record."[49] This principle was confirmed in *Camp v. Pitts*,[50] and was applied to informal rulemaking proceedings in *Vermont Yankee*.[51] Scholars have observed that the requirement of an exclusive record for review of informal actions was not contemplated by the framers of the APA.[52] However, the Supreme Court has described review on the basis of, and limited to, the administrative record as one of the "fundamental principles of judicial review of administrative action,"[53] and lower courts have accepted the principle

---

F.3d 453, 459 (D.C. Cir. 1993) (informal rulemaking); Davis v. Erdmann, 607 F.2d 917 (10th Cir. 1979) (informal adjudication); Antosh v. FEC, 599 F. Supp. 850 (D.D.C. 1984) (informal adjudication).

49. *Overton Park*, 401 U.S. at 419-20.

50. 411 U.S. 138 (1973).

51. Vt. Yankee Nuclear Power Co. v. Natural Res. Def. Council, 435 U.S. 519, 549 (1978).

52. *See, e.g.*, Nathanson, *supra* note 41, at 754-56; Stephen F. Williams, *"Hybrid Rulemaking" Under the Administrative Procedure Act: A Legal and Empirical Analysis*, 42 U. Chi. L. Rev. 401, 419-21 (1975); Gordon G. Young, *Judicial Review of Informal Agency Action on the Fiftieth Anniversary of the APA: The Alleged Demise and Actual Status of* Overton Park*'s Requirement of Judicial Review "On the Record,"* 10 Admin. L.J. Am. U. 179, 212-14 (1996).

53. Florida Power & Light Co. v. Lorion, 470 U.S. 729, 745 (1985).

as well.[54] The concept of a file or docket serving as a rulemaking record has not yet been enacted into general law,[55] but a 2013 recommendation by the Administrative Conference of the United States (ACUS) summarizes policies generally observed by federal agencies and recommends best practices.[56] Where an agency does not contemporaneously maintain a file or record for judicial review of a given action, the administrative record must be assembled after the fact, but in modern federal practice this situation arises only rarely.

The emergence of the "administrative record" concept does not mean that the agency must ensure that *all* factual assertions have support in a record. As discussed in Part V below, the requirement of record support has a variety of exceptions, regardless of whether the applicable standard of review is "arbitrary and capricious" or "substantial evidence."

The *Blackletter Statement*'s description of the contents of the administrative record refers to materials that the agency "actively considered," because there is no reason to burden the court with vast quantities of information that the agency fleetingly "considered" but ultimately disregarded for lack of relevance. The 2013 ACUS recommendation uses different language to express the same basic idea: the rulemaking record should contain "any material that the agency considered," but "[t]o say that material was considered … entails some minimum degree of attention to the contents of a document." The recommendation elaborates on this theme but acknowledges that "the concept resists precise definition."[57] In any event, the record on review should not be defined

---

54. *See, e.g.*, Simms v. Nat'l Highway Traffic Safety Admin., 45 F.3d 999 (6th Cir. 1995); Occidental Petroleum Corp. v. SEC, 873 F.2d 325, 338-39 (D.C. Cir. 1989).
55. Congress did take a step in this direction, however, in the E-Government Act of 2002, Pub. L. No. 107-347, 116 Stat. 2899 (2002). Section 206 of that legislation requires an agency to establish an electronic docket in notice-and-comment rulemaking. *Id.* § 206(d), codified at 44 U.S.C. § 3501 note (requiring, "[t]o the extent practicable," that agencies maintain an electronic docket that includes all submitted comments as well as "other materials that by agency rule or practice are included in the rulemaking docket").
56. ACUS Recommendation 2013-4, *The Administrative Record in Informal Rulemaking*, 78 Fed. Reg. 41,358 (2013); *see also* Leland E. Beck, *Agency Practices and Judicial Review of Administrative Records in Informal Rulemaking* (2013) (consultant's report supporting the recommendation), available at http://www.acus.gov/sites/default/files/documents/Agency%20Practices%20and%20Judicial%20Review%20of%20Administrative%20Records%20 in%20Informal%20Rulemaking.pdf.
57. ACUS Recommendation 2013-4, *supra* note 56, at 41,359.

as including only materials on which the agency "relied," because that standard would exclude information that tends to undercut the agency's conclusions.[58] Obviously, the determination of which items were "considered," or "actively considered," will be a contextual one; the courts rely primarily on the good faith of the agency, although, as is described below, occasionally more active judicial supervision will be deemed necessary.

The administrative record should include all submissions by outside parties in connection with the proceeding. Such material is part of the "whole record" and should be placed before the court regardless of whether the agency actually "considered" it.[59]

The administrative record may also include docket entries or other affirmative disclosure of oral communications between decisionmakers and interested parties, but such disclosure need not be made in every instance. The D.C. Circuit, which has generated most of the law on "ex parte contacts" in informal proceedings, has indicated that such disclosure is not essential to a court's substantive review function, so long as the agency is required to justify its action by reference to the record that the court does receive.[60] To be sure, various agencies operate under statutes or regulations that require public disclosure of written summaries of ex parte communications in certain circumstances. And this practice is required in formal proceedings.[61]

A few other details warrant mention. The administrative record should include materials considered by the agency staff, not just the agency head, because complex regulatory actions are often products of an "institutional decision" in which subordinates resolve many issues on their own, leaving only the most controversial or big-picture issues to be resolved by the official who bears formal responsibility for the action.[62] On the other hand, the

---

58. *See* A.O. Smith Corp. v. FTC, 403 F. Supp. 1000, 1008-09 (D. Del. 1975).
59. *See* Okoroha v. INS, 715 F.2d 380, 383-84 (8th Cir. 1983); *see also infra* note 75.
60. *See* Sierra Club v. Costle, 657 F.2d 298, 401, 403-04 (implicitly disapproving the contrary suggestion in Home Box Office, Inc. v. FCC, 567 F.2d 9, 54 (D.C. Cir. 1977)).
61. 5 U.S.C. § 557(d)(1)(C).
62. *See* Exxon Corp. v. Dep't of Energy, 91 F.R.D. 26, 35-37 (N.D. Tex. 1981); *A.O. Smith Corp.*, 403 F. Supp. at 1013 n.39. The language of recent cases is that the record must contain information that the agency considered "directly or indirectly." *E.g.*, Bar MK Ranches v. Yeutter, 994 F.2d 735, 739 (10th Cir. 1993); Fund for Animals v. Williams, 391 F. Supp. 2d 191, 196 (D.D.C. 2005).

administrative record that an agency forwards to a court for judicial review purposes need not contain privileged materials such as internal advice memoranda, as opposed to internally generated factual data,[63] or confidential information.[64] Communications from "outside parties" situated elsewhere in the federal government might also be treated as "privileged."[65] Some agencies furnish the reviewing court with a "privilege log" to disclose the existence of withheld material, but no single approach prevails at all agencies.[66] In any event, these privileges are qualified, not absolute; a court may use in camera inspection to ensure that critical facts are included in the record.[67]

> **The court may, upon a proper showing, allow discovery and other evidentiary proceedings in order to supervise the agency's compilation (but not the supplementation) of the administrative record.**
>
> **[Blackletter Statement, Part 3, § IV.C.3.]**

If necessary, courts will play an active role in overseeing the agency's assembly of an administrative record.[68] In a matter before a district court, this process is handled under the civil discovery rules or the Freedom of

---

63. *See* Nat'l Courier Ass'n v. Bd. of Govs. of Fed. Reserve Sys., 516 F.2d 1229, 1241-42 (D.C. Cir. 1975); Ad Hoc Metals Coalition v. Whitman, 227 F. Supp. 2d 134, 139-40 (D.D.C. 2002); Amfac Resorts, L.L.C. v. U.S. Dep't of Interior, 143 F. Supp. 2d 7, 12-13 (D.D.C. 2001). *But see* Miami Nation of Indians of Indiana v. Babbitt, 979 F. Supp. 771, 777-79 (N.D. Ind. 1996) (requiring the agency to include deliberative material in the record and then seek a protective order on the basis of the privilege); James N. Saul, Comment, *Overly Restrictive Administrative Records and the Frustration of Judicial Review*, 38 ENVTL. L. 1301, 1326-29 (2008) (endorsing the *Miami Nation* approach).
64. *See* Izaak Walton League of Am. v. Marsh, 655 F.2d 346, 369-71 (D.C. Cir. 1981). *See generally* Beck, *supra* note 56, at 32-40.
65. *See generally* Sierra Club v. Costle, 657 F.2d at 404-08; ACUS Recommendation 80-6, 1 C.F.R. § 305.80-6 (1985).
66. ACUS Recommendation 2013-4, *supra* note 56, at 41,360.
67. *Cf.* Jifry v. FAA, 370 F.2d 1174, 1181-82 (D.C. Cir. 2004) (examining in camera classified reports that the FAA had relied on ex parte in making a security risk determination that led to the suspension of pilots).
68. *See, e.g.,* Dopico v. Goldschmidt, 687 F.2d 644, 654 (2d Cir. 1982); Public Power Council v. Johnson, 674 F.2d 791, 794-95 (9th Cir. 1982); Natural Res. Def. Council v. Train, 519 F.2d 287, 291-92 (D.C. Cir. 1975); Tenneco Oil Co. v. Dep't of Energy, 475 F. Supp. 299, 317 (D. Del. 1979).

Information Act; in challenges brought originally in a court of appeals, the court may appoint a special master[69] or receive evidence itself.[70]

The agency's compilation of the administrative record is subject to a presumption of regularity.[71] Usually, therefore, an appeal will be resolved exclusively on the basis of the record tendered by the agency.[72] However, there are several recognized circumstances in which the court may examine extra-record evidence.[73] A common formulation is that of the Ninth Circuit in *Lands Council v. Powell*:

> In limited circumstances, district courts are permitted to admit extra-record evidence: (1) if admission is necessary to determine "whether the agency has considered all relevant factors and has explained its decision," (2) if "the agency has relied on documents not in the record," (3) "when supplementing the record is necessary to explain technical terms or complex subject matter," or (4) "when plaintiffs make a showing of agency bad faith."[74]

---

69. *See Public Power Council*, 674 F.2d at 796.
70. *See* National Nutritional Foods Ass'n v. FDA, 491 F.2d 1141, 1143-44 (2d Cir. 1974). *See generally* Richard McMillan, Jr. & Todd D. Peterson, *The Permissible Scope of Hearings, Discovery and Additional Factfinding During Judicial Review of Informal Action*, 1982 Duke L.J. 333, 343-50.
71. Citizens for Alternatives to Radioactive Dumping v. DOE, 485 F.3d 1091, 1097 (10th Cir. 2007) (citing Bar MK Ranches v. Yuetter, 994 F.2d 735, 740 (10th Cir. 1993)); Amfac Resorts, L.L.C. v. U.S. Dep't of Interior, 143 F. Supp. 2d 7, 12 (D.D.C. 2001).
72. IMS, P.C. v. Alvarez, 129 F.3d 618, 623-24 (D.C. Cir. 1997); San Luis Obispo Mothers for Peace v. Nuclear Reg. Comm'n, 751 F.2d 1287, 1327 (D.C. Cir. 1984).
73. *See generally* Beck, *supra* note 56, at 66-74; McMillan & Peterson, *supra* note 70; Young, supra note 52; Saul, *supra* note 63.
74. Lands Council v. Powell, 395 F.3d 1019, 1030 (9th Cir. 2005); *see* Ctr. for Biological Diversity v. U.S. Fish & Wildlife Serv., 450 F.3d 930, 943 (9th Cir. 2006) (similar); *see also* City of Dania Beach v. FAA, 628 F.3d 581, 590 (D.C. Cir. 2010) (endorsing, in substance, only the first two *Lands Council* settings); IMS, P.C. v. Alvarez, 129 F.3d at 618, 624. An earlier decision of the D.C. Circuit identified eight distinct exceptions. Esch v. Yeutter, 876 F.2d 976, 991 (D.C. Cir. 1989). However, recent decisions have called the *Esch* formula into question. *See, e.g.*, Axiom Res. Mgmt., Inc. v. United States, 564 F.3d 1374, 1378-81 (Fed. Cir. 2009) (and cases cited therein); *see also* Young, *supra* note 52, at 219-48 (critiquing the law review article on which *Esch* had relied).

There is little doubt about the legitimacy of the fourth *Lands Council* category, allowing courts to go outside the record in cases of agency bad faith, because it was recognized in *Overton Park* itself. In practice, however, courts have rarely been willing to find that the requisite showing of bad faith has been made.[75] Similarly, the second category, where the agency has failed to include in the record material on which it actually relied, is a natural corollary of the principle that the court must review the whole record on which the agency made its decision. In this connection, as noted above, the record should include documents the agency *considered* even if it does not *rely* on them;[76] indeed, a prominent goal of discovery is to uncover documents that may be adverse to the agency's position.[77]

The first category—the use of discovery to explore "whether the agency has considered all relevant factors and has explained its decision"—is not as expansive as one might at first think. Although in the abstract one could argue that these issues regarding the agency's reasoning might be suitable for discovery in almost any case, the reality is that the agency's explanation in the final rule or decision is usually the principal point of reference for evaluation of the rationality of the administrative decision.[78] If that explanation is inadequate, a remand is the preferred remedy,[79] with only occasional exceptions.[80]

---

75. See Air Transp. Ass'n v. NLRB, 663 F.3d 476 (D.C. Cir. 2011); Citizens for Alternatives, 485 F.3d at 1097. *But see* New York v. Salazar, 2011 WL 1938232 (N.D.N.Y. 2011), *affirming* 701 F. Supp. 2d 224 (N.D.N.Y. 2010) (Magistrate Judge's decision).
76. Ad Hoc Metals Coalition v. Whitman, 227 F. Supp. 2d 134, 139-40 (D.D.C. 2002); Saul, *supra* note 63, at 1310, 1313.
77. For examples of such review outside the record, see National Audubon Soc'y v. Hoffman, 132 F.3d 7, 14-15 (2d Cir. 1997) (NEPA context); Kent County v. EPA, 963 F.2d 391, 395-96 (D.C. Cir. 1992); Izaak Walton League v. Marsh, 655 F.2d 346, 368-69 (D.C. Cir. 1981) (NEPA context). *But see Amfac*, 143 F. Supp. 2d at 13-14.
78. Camp v. Pitts, 411 U.S. 138, 142 (1973); *Axiom Res. Mgmt.*, 564 F.3d at 1381; Olsen v. United States, 414 F.3d 144, 155 (1st Cir. 2005); Doraiswamy v. Sec'y of Labor, 555 F.2d 832, 842-43 (D.C. Cir. 1976).
79. Fla. Power & Light Co. v. Lorian, 470 U.S. 729, 744 (1985) (court must, "except in rare circumstances," review agency-compiled record or else remand case to agency).
80. For one such case, see Impresa Construzioni Geom. Domenico Garufi v. United States, 238 F.3d 1324, 1337-39 (Fed. Cir. 2001) (ordering deposition of agency official for fuller explanation of his decision).

The third category mentioned in *Lands Council* refers to a line of decisions, notably in the Ninth Circuit, that have allowed parties to submit evidence to a reviewing court for the purpose of enhancing the court's comprehension of technical matters underlying the agency action.[81] This category is also narrowly applied. Where a court perceives that supplemental technical information has been submitted in order to *dispute*, rather than *explain*, the factual premises of the action under review the material has been excluded or disregarded.[82]

Although it is natural for generalist judges to desire help in understanding complex problems of regulatory policy, the caution displayed by these cases seems justified. Just as parties to civil litigation are expected to introduce background facts in district court, rather than saving them for a court of appeals, the parties to an agency proceeding should not be encouraged to bypass building a record at the agency level.[83] Indeed, much seemingly innocuous "background" information may contain assumptions that would not have survived unchallenged if they had first been presented for the agency's consideration. To be sure, there is room for flexibility, especially in contexts where facts change rapidly.[84] Uncontroversial background information may be submitted to the court by joint stipulation,[85] and parties bring out judicially noticeable facts by merely inserting them in a brief.[86] But courts must

---

81. *See, e.g.*, Asarco, Inc. v. EPA, 616 F.2d 1153, 1159-60 (9th Cir. 1980); Bunker Hill Co. v. EPA, 572 F.2d 1286, 1292 (9th Cir. 1977); Indep. Meat Packers Ass'n v. Butz, 526 F.2d 228, 239, 241 (8th Cir. 1975). *See also* Young, *supra* note 52, at 233 n.212 (1996) (citing additional cases so stating in dictum).
82. *See* Kunaknana v. Clark, 742 F.2d 1145 (9th Cir. 1984); EDF v. Costle, 657 F.2d 275, 285-86 (D.C. Cir. 1981); *Asarco*, 616 F.2d at 1160-61.
83. *See* E.I. du Pont de Nemours & Co. v. Collins, 432 U.S. 46, 57 (1977) (criticizing Court of Appeals for relying on university professor to prepare reports and memoranda to assist it in understanding the record).
84. *See* Stuart Minor Benjamin, *Stepping Into the Same River Twice: Rapidly Changing Facts and the Appellate Process*, 78 TEX. L. REV. 269 (1999) (arguing that rapidly changing facts should, in certain circumstances, justify appellate factfinding).
85. *See* Walter O. Boswell Mem. Hospital v. Heckler, 749 F.2d 788, 794 (D.C. Cir. 1984).
86. *See* Am. Mining Congress v. Thomas, 772 F.2d 617, 627 (10th Cir. 1985) (court considered documents and reports that were not in the record, because "references to such extra-record items, we believe, are substantially akin to the practice of citation to scientific treatises in ordinary civil cases," but it did not incorporate them into the record).

avoid being drawn into making findings that the agency alone is authorized to make.[87] Background evidence submitted to a court should be used only for "clarification or . . . explanation of the original information before the Agency"—not "as a new rationalization either for sustaining or attacking the Agency's decision," or as proof "that the [decision was] not the product of reasoned decisionmaking."[88]

In *Verizon Communications Inc. v. Federal Communications Commission,* the Supreme Court upheld an agency rule against an arbitrary and capricious challenge based in part on evidence, not available at the time of rule adoption, of economic developments in the industry.[89] The rule had been challenged on the ground that it unreasonably failed to promote facilities-based investments in the telecommunications industry, but the Supreme Court rejected that challenge in light of evidence that competitive facilities-based investments had remained substantial subsequent to the rule's promulgation.[90] The evidence considered on review in *Verizon* is perhaps best understood as bolstering the agency's original explanation, which had been in part predictive, as opposed to offering a completely new explanation. Moreover, the challengers did not dispute the accuracy of the information. Nevertheless, the potential for tension with the *Chenery* principle–that judicial affirmation must rest on grounds articulated by the agency–seems obvious.

7.05 FINDINGS NOT SPECIFICALLY SUPPORTED BY THE RECORD

Notwithstanding the requirement of record support for agency findings in formal proceedings, an agency may, with notification to the parties and opportunity to rebut, rely on officially noticed facts in a proper case. In addition, in both formal and informal proceedings, an agency need not provide more support for predictive or other judgmental facts than it can fairly be expected to have gathered at the time of the action.

[Blackletter Statement, Part 3, § IV.D.]

---

87. *See* Fed. Power Comm'n v. Transcontinental Gas Pipe Line Corp., 423 U.S. 326, 333 (1976).
88. Ass'n of Pacific Fisheries v. EPA, 615 F.2d 794, 811-12 (9th Cir. 1980).
89. Verizon Commc'ns Inc. v. FCC, 535 U.S. 467 (2002).
90. *Id.* at 516-17.

7.051 Official Notice

In formal proceedings, the doctrine of official notice is a longstanding exception to the principle that the factual premises of an agency action must be supported by record *evidence*.[91] Discussions of official notice frequently focus upon the extent to which private parties have the right to controvert propositions of which official notice is taken. In many circumstances, such a right is guaranteed by the APA,[92] the rules of practice of many agencies,[93] as well as the due process clause.[94] Courts and scholars have devoted much effort to classifying various factual propositions into three categories: (1) facts that an agency may officially notice without allowing opposing parties a chance for rebuttal; (2) facts that an agency may officially notice if and only if a rebuttal is allowed; and (3) facts that are not subject to official notice and must instead be proven through the ordinary process of administrative litigation.[95] If an agency fails to permit adequate confrontation or rebuttal in its determination of adjudicative facts, its decision can, of course, be overturned for that reason alone.

From the standpoint of substantive review, relatively little difficulty arises when an agency takes official notice by relying on *openly disclosed* sources of information outside the formal record. By examining these extra-record authorities in light of any rebuttal material the opposing party has introduced, the court can proceed in the normal way to determine whether the agency's factual assertions rest upon "substantial evidence" (or have "substantial support"). For example, an agency may support a factual assertion by looking to the record of an earlier administrative proceeding, so long as this practice does not cause "substantial prejudice" to the procedural rights of the

---

91. *See* Market St. Ry. v. R.R. Comm'n, 324 U.S. 548 (1945).
92. 5 U.S.C. §556(e) ("When an agency decision rests on official notice of a material fact not appearing in the evidence in the record, a party is entitled, on the request, to an opportunity to show the contrary.").
93. For example, EPA's Rules of Practice provide:

> Official notice may be taken of any matter which can be judicially noticed in the Federal courts and of other facts within the specialized knowledge and experience of the Agency. *Opposing parties shall be given adequate opportunity to show that such facts are erroneously noticed.*

40 C.F.R. § 22.22(f) (emphasis added).

94. Ohio Bell Tel. Co. v. FCC, 301 U.S. 292 (1937).
95. *See* Ernest Gellhorn, *Rules of Evidence and Official Notice in Formal Administrative Hearings*, 1971 Duke L.J. 1, 42-49.

parties in the later proceeding.[96] Similarly, an agency's references to treatises, articles, etc., may qualify as substantial evidence if the opposing side has had an opportunity to rebut the contents of those sources.[97]

Much more troublesome are situations in which an agency takes official notice of a factual proposition but does not document it at all. An agency may take official notice of "'commonly acknowledged facts, [and] . . . technical or scientific facts that are within the agency's area of expertise,'"[98] so long as the agency provides an opportunity to show the contrary.[99] But agency attempts to advance broad factual claims on the basis of "experience" or undisclosed information in their files have been rejected by courts on the ground that this "precludes effective judicial review."[100] There is indeed a deep tension between official notice and the modern hard look doctrine, under which agencies have increasingly been obliged to furnish detailed justifications for the critical factual premises of their actions.[101]

It appears, then, that official notice without documentation can provide only fragile support for an agency's fact-findings (unless the fact is "judg-

---

96. United States v. Pierce Auto Freight Lines, Inc., 327 U.S. 515, 527-30 (1947); R.R. Comm'n v. United States, 765 F.2d 221, 229 (D.C. Cir. 1985). Such prejudice might exist if, for example, the challenger did not participate in the earlier proceeding, *see, e.g.*, Shell Oil Co. v. FERC, 707 F.2d 230 (5th Cir. 1983); Dayco Corp. v. FTC, 362 F.2d 180 (6th Cir. 1966), or if the challenger lacked fair notice that the record compiled in the earlier proceeding could be used in a later proceeding, *see, e.g.*, Pub. Serv. Comm'n v. Fed. Power Comm'n, 487 F.2d 1043, 1070 (D.C. Cir. 1973), or if circumstances appear to have changed since the earlier proceeding, *see, e.g.*, Air Prods. & Chems., Inc. v. FERC, 650 F.2d 687, 697 (5th Cir. 1981).
97. McDaniel v. Celebrezze, 331 F.2d 426, 428-29 (4th Cir. 1964).
98. Kapcia v. INS, 944 F.2d 702, 705 (10th Cir. 1991) (quoting McLeod v. INS, 802 F.2d 89, 93 n.4 (3d Cir. 1986)). *See also* Woldemeskel v. INS, 257 F.3d 1185, 1192 (10th Cir. 2001).
99. *Kapcia*, 944 F.2d at 706.
100. *Air Prods. & Chems., Inc.*, 650 F.2d at 699; United States Lines, Inc. v. Fed. Maritime Comm'n, 584 F.2d 519, 533-36 (D.C. Cir. 1978). *See also* Wilson v. Califano, 617 F.2d 1050, 1054 (4th Cir. 1980) (finding it "manifestly unfair" for ALJ in disability case to rely on his own knowledge rather than vocational expert witness, since "the claimant cannot, without reading the ALJ's mind, test or rebut" the "assumptions and 'facts'" on which the ALJ's decision rests).
101. *See* Baltimore & O.R.R. v. Aberdeen & Rockfish R.R., 393 U.S. 87, 91-92 (1968). On the hard look doctrine, see generally Chapter Eight, § 8.02, *infra*.

mental" in the sense discussed immediately below). If the opposing party responds with counter-evidence or at least some reason to doubt the agency's assertion, the agency will likely need to document the assertion if its ruling is to be upheld. On the other hand, if the party makes no such response, but simply objects that the agency's assertion lacks record support, the agency action has a good chance of surviving substantive (as distinct from procedural) review.[102]

Official notice is more likely to be upheld by a court if it addresses a matter of legislative as opposed to adjudicative fact.[103] (This distinction is reflected in Rule 201 of the Federal Rules of Evidence, which regulates judicial notice of adjudicative facts but includes no provision regarding judicial notice of legislative facts.[104]) For example, in an asylum case matters regarding the change of government in a foreign nation might be susceptible of official notice whereas matters involving the alien's particular circumstances would not.[105] Similarly, the "opportunity to show the contrary" required by the APA must be fuller for adjudicative than legislative facts. In a formal proceeding, "[w]hen facts are adjudicative, disputed, and critical, nothing less than the opportunity to present evidence at a hearing will normally suffice."[106]

7.052 "JUDGMENTAL FACTS"

So-called "judgmental facts" require only limited record support. The Supreme Court has sometimes declared that it is unnecessary for an agency to "prove" assertions that are predictive or are otherwise essentially incapable of

---

102. *See* Civil v. INS, 140 F.3d 52, 56 (1st Cir. 1998); Bonnaffons v. Dep't of Energy, 646 F.2d 548, 555 (Temp. Emer. Ct. App. 1981); McLamore v. Weinberger, 538 F.2d 572 (4th Cir. 1976); NLRB v. Milk Drivers & Dairy Employees Local 338, 531 F.2d 1162, 1165 (2d Cir. 1976); NLRB v. Selvin, 527 F.2d 1273 (9th Cir. 1975).
103. *See* Castillo-Villagra v. INS, 972 F.2d 1017, 1026 (9th Cir. 1992).
104. Fed. R. Evid. 201; *see id.* Advisory Committee's note (relying on the analysis of Professor K.C. Davis and explaining that "[t]he omission of any treatment [in the Rules] of legislative facts results from fundamental differences between adjudicative facts and legislative facts").
105. *See* Circu v. Gonzales, 450 F.3d 990 (9th Cir. 2006) (endorsing official notice of "legislative, indisputable and general" facts, such as a change in government, as opposed to "controversial or individualized" facts, such as whether that change eliminated the danger to a particular individual, which the applicant must be allowed to rebut); Castillo-Villagra v. INS, 972 F.2d at 1027-30.
106. 2 Pierce, *supra* note 2, § 10.6, at 959.

being definitely established. Such judgments are entitled to a greater level of deference than "simple findings of fact,"[107] especially when the agency's determinations are "at the frontiers of science"[108] or when the agency is making a "'forecast of the direction in which future public interest lies.'"[109] These principles of deference do not lose force, nor does the level of scrutiny of factual determinations increase, when the legislatively prescribed standard of review is substantial evidence.[110]

Courts take account of these principles as they enforce an agency's obligation, under the arbitrary and capricious standard, to "examine the relevant data and articulate a satisfactory explanation for its action."[111] For example, in *FCC v. Fox Television Stations, Inc.*, the Court determined that empirical evidence to support the notion that broadcast profanity has a harmful effect on children was unobtainable, and therefore the agency need not provide it in enforcement proceedings against broadcasters.[112] Similarly, the Court deferred to the agency's unsupported prediction (or assumption) that an exemption for fleeting expletives would lead to an increase in their occurrence.[113]

These judicial pronouncements should not be understood as meaning that certain broad categories of agency findings require *no* factual support. A court must still examine whatever factual materials have been placed in the record,

---

107. Baltimore Gas & Electric Co. v. Natural Res. Def. Council, 462 U.S. 87, 103 (1983).
108. *Id.*
109. FCC v. WNCN Listeners Guild, 450 U.S. 582, 595-96 (1981); FCC v. Nat'l Citizens Committee for Broadcasting, 436 U.S. 775, 813-14 (1978). *Cf.* Am. Airlines, Inc. v. Civil Aeronautics Bd., 359 F.2d 624, 632-33 (D.C. Cir. 1966) (en banc) (Leventhal, J.) ("It is the kind of issue where a month of experience will be worth a year of hearings.").
110. *See* Indus. Union Dep't, AFL-CIO v. Am. Petroleum Inst., 448 U.S. 607, 656 (1980) (plurality opinion); *id.* at 705-06 (Marshall, J., dissenting); FPC v. Florida Power & Light Co., 404 U.S. 453, 463-69 (1972); Indus. Union Dep't, AFL-CIO v. Hodgson, 499 F.2d 467, 475 (D.C. Cir. 1974).
111. Motor Vehicle Mfrs. Ass'n v. State Farm Mut. Automobile Ins. Co., 463 U.S. 29, 43 (1983).
112. FCC v. Fox Television Stations, Inc., 556 U.S. 502, 519 (2009) ("It is one thing to set aside agency action under the Administrative Procedure Act because of failure to adduce empirical data that can readily be obtained. [. . .] It is something else to insist upon obtaining the unobtainable.").
113. *Id.* at 521 ("But even in the absence of evidence, the agency's predictive judgment (which merits deference) makes entire sense. To predict that complete immunity for fleeting expletives, ardently desired by broadcasters, will lead to a substantial increase in fleeting expletives seems to us an exercise in logic rather than clairvoyance.").

both by the agency and by opposing parties.[114] In determining whether the record adequately supports findings as to judgmental facts, the court may take into account such considerations as the centrality of the conclusions to the agency's decision, the data available to but not offered by opposing parties, and the delay and expense that would be incurred if the agency were required to gather more data.[115] If an agency's factual premises are found to be unsupported by the kind of evidence that could fairly be expected, the basic principle of substantial evidence or substantial support requires reversal.[116]

---

114. One author contends that courts reviewing scientific findings have often played a useful role by "translating" complex technical determinations into terms that generalist readers can understand. *See* Emily Hammond Meazell, *Superdeference, the Science Obsession, and Judicial Review as Translation of Agency Science*, 109 MICH. L. REV. 733, 778-79 (2011). This practice, she suggests, is a constructive antidote to the possibility that the deference that courts must display toward judgmental fact findings gives agencies an incentive to "cloak their true reasoning behind an unassailable mantle of science." *Id.* at 763-64.

115. *Compare* Am. Textile Mfrs. Inst. v. Donovan, 452 U.S. 490, 528 (1981) (meager proof of feasibility was "substantial evidence" because industry prevented agency from developing better evidence) *with* Motor Vehicles Mfrs. Ass'n v. State Farm Mut. Auto. Ins. Co., 463 U.S. 29, 53-54 1983) (agency's conclusion that rule would have minimal safety benefits was arbitrary because agency completely ignored certain "grounds to believe" otherwise).

116. *See, e.g.*, Electricity Consumers Res. Council v. FERC, 747 F.2d 1511, 1516-18 (D.C. Cir. 1984); ILGWU v. Donovan, 722 F.2d 795, 818-26 (D.C. Cir. 1983); W. Va. Pub. Servs. Comm'n v. Dep't of Energy, 681 F.2d 847, 859-65 (D.C. Cir. 1982).

Chapter 8

JUDICIAL REVIEW OF AGENCY DISCRETION

by Lisa Schultz Bressman and Glen Staszewski*

8.01 INTRODUCTION

The court may set aside an agency action as an abuse of discretion (alternatively known in APA parlance as the "arbitrary and capricious" test), see APA § 706(2)(A), on any of several grounds. In practice, application of these grounds varies according to the nature and magnitude of the agency action. Thus, a court will typically apply the criteria rigorously during judicial review of

---

* Lisa Schultz Bressman is David Daniels Allen Distinguished Chair of Law, Vanderbilt Law School, and Glen Staszewski is Professor of Law and The A.J. Thomas Faculty Scholar, Michigan State University College of Law.

The authors are grateful for careful editing and helpful suggestions from Kathryn Watts, and outstanding research assistance from Ben Curl, Jessica Erickson, Emma Gardner, David Loudon, and Sarah Parker.

high-stakes rulemaking proceedings (a practice commonly termed "hard look" review), but much more leniently when reviewing a routine, uncomplicated action. A court may not impose its own policy preferences on the agency.

[Blackletter Statement, Part 3, § V.]

A court may set aside an agency action as an abuse of discretion under the "arbitrary and capricious" test.[1] The word "arbitrary" could suggest the deferential "rational basis" standard of review applicable to legislative policy decisions under the Due Process Clause. The precise standard of review—or more specifically, the precise level of deference—applicable to administrative policy decisions is not entirely clear, however. The Supreme Court has sent conflicting signals. It has described the arbitrary and capricious inquiry as "searching and careful"[2] and expressly held that it is more demanding than constitutional rational basis scrutiny.[3] At the same time, it has characterized "the ultimate standard of review as a narrow one"[4] and admonished courts not to "substitute [their] judgment for that of the agency."[5] Lower courts routinely invoke both of these sentiments, either ignoring the tension between them or eliminating the tension by emphasizing one or the other to fit the level of scrutiny ultimately applied.

Commentators also have debated the appropriate level of scrutiny.[6] Some have defended relatively stringent review as a cure for "capture" of the agency by the interests it is supposed to regulate[7] or as "a device, admittedly highly

---

1. *See* 5 U.S.C. § 706(2)(A) (2000) ("The reviewing court shall . . . hold unlawful and set aside agency action, findings, and conclusions found to be . . . arbitrary, capricious, [or] an abuse of discretion . . . .").
2. Citizens to Preserve Overton Park, Inc. v. Volpe, 401 U.S. 402, 416 (1971).
3. *See* Motor Vehicle Mfrs. Ass'n v. State Farm Mut. Auto Ins. Co., 463 U.S. 29, 42-43 & n.9 (1983).
4. *Overton Park*, 401 U.S. at 416.
5. *State Farm*, 463 U.S. at 32 (quoted in Judulang v. Holder, 132 S. Ct. 476, 483 (2011)).
6. *See generally* Patricia M. Wald, *Judicial Review in Midpassage: The Uneasy Partnership Between Courts and Agencies Plays On*, 32 TULSA L.J. 221, 258 (1996) ("After fifty years . . . we have yet to agree on how this review should operate in practice. We are still struggling with where to draw the line between obsequious deference and intrusive scrutiny.").
7. *See, e.g.*, Thomas W. Merrill, *Capture Theory and the Courts: 1967-1983*, 72 CHI.-KENT. L. REV. 1039, 1093-95 (1997); Mark Seidenfeld, *A Civic Republican Justification for the Bureaucratic State*, 105 HARV. L. REV. 1512, 1569-70 (1992).

imperfect, for reducing the risk that agency decisions will result from 'political' considerations that are sometimes illegitimate and at any rate ought not to be concealed."[8] Others have argued for minimal review on the theory that agency decisions appropriately reflect political judgments that courts should respect rather than impede[9] or expertise that courts lack.[10]

More recently, the debate over the level of deference due administrative policy judgments has shifted to the question of whether intrusive judicial review causes "ossification" of the rulemaking process. Many commentators have claimed that intensive judicial review forces agencies to devote excessive resources to insulating their policy decisions from reversal (or to rehabilitating those policy decisions on remand) and often discourages agencies from issuing such decisions at all.[11] Others have disputed this claim as an empirical matter.[12] Still others have acknowledged the risk of agency paraly-

---

8. Cass R. Sunstein, *Deregulation and the Hard-Look Doctrine*, 1983 Sup. Ct. Rev. 177, 211 (1983).
9. *See* Antonin Scalia, *Chairman's Message, Separation of Functions: Obscurity Preserved*, 34 Admin. L. Rev. v (1982).
10. Richard J. Pierce, Jr., *Seven Ways to Deossify Agency Rulemaking*, 47 Admin. L. Rev. 59, 68-71 (1995). For a brief discussion of recent scholarship that revives certain aspects of these fundamental debates, *see infra* § 8.03.
11. *See, e.g.*, Stephen Breyer, Breaking the Vicious Circle: Toward Effective Risk Regulation 48 (1993); Jerry L. Mashaw & David L. Harfst, The Struggle for Auto Safety, 19, 199, 224-55 (1990); Thomas O. McGarity, *The Courts and the Ossification of Rulemaking: A Response to Professor Seidenfeld*, 75 Tex. L. Rev. 525 (1997); Thomas O. McGarity, *Some Thoughts on "Deossifying" the Rulemaking Process*, 41 Duke L.J. 1385 (1992); Richard J. Pierce, Jr., *Judicial Review of Agency Actions in a Period of Diminishing Agency Resources*, 49 Admin. L. Rev. 61 (1997); Richard J. Pierce, Jr., *Two Problems in Administrative Law: Political Polarity on the District of Columbia Circuit and Judicial Deterrence of Agency Rulemaking*, 1988 Duke L.J. 300 (1988).
12. *See, e.g.*, Jason Webb Yackee & Susan Webb Yackee, *Testing the Ossification Thesis: An Empirical Examination of Federal Regulatory Volume and Speed, 1950-1990*, 80 Geo. Wash. L. Rev. 1414 (2012); William S. Jordan, III, *Ossification Revisited: Does Arbitrary and Capricious Review Significantly Interfere with Agency Ability to Achieve Regulatory Goals Through Informal Rulemaking?*, 94 Nw. U. L. Rev. 393 (2000). *But see* Richard J. Pierce, *Rulemaking Ossification is Real: A Response to Testing the Ossification Thesis*, 80 Geo. Wash. L. Rev. 1493 (2012).

sis but have maintained that the risk is worth running to improve the quality of rulemaking.[13]

This debate aside, one aspect of arbitrary-and-capricious review has become relatively certain. In practice, the grounds for setting aside an agency action under the arbitrary-and-capricious test vary according to the nature and magnitude of that action. Thus, a court typically will apply the criteria set forth in this chapter rigorously during judicial review of high-stakes rulemaking proceedings (a practice commonly termed "hard look" review), but much more leniently when reviewing, for example, an adjudicative matter that an agency would be expected to dispose of quickly.[14]

---

13. *See, e.g.*, Jim Rossi, *Redeeming Judicial Review: The Hard Look Doctrine and Federal Regulatory Efforts to Restructure the Electric Utility Industry*, 1994 WIS. L. REV. 763 (1994); Thomas O. Sargentich, *The Critique of Active Judicial Review of Administrative Agencies: A Reevaluation*, 49 ADMIN. L. REV. 599 (1997); Mark Seidenfeld, *Demystifying Deossification: Rethinking Recent Proposals to Modify Judicial Review of Notice and Comment Rulemaking*, 75 TEX. L. REV. 483 (1997) [hereinafter, "Seidenfeld, *Demystifying Deossification*"]; Patricia M. Wald, *Judicial Review in the Time of Cholera*, 49 ADMIN. L. REV. 659 (1997). *Cf.* Mark Seidenfeld, *Why Agencies Act: A Reassessment of the Ossification Critique of Judicial Review*, 70 OHIO ST. L.J. 251 (2009) (recognizing that hard-look judicial review is beneficial when it discourages agencies from taking unjustified action, and claiming that its normative value is therefore highly contextual).
14. *Compare* Motor Vehicle Mfrs. Ass'n v. State Farm Mut. Auto. Ins. Co., 463 U.S. 29, 43 (1983) (applying the requirement that an agency explain the basis for its decision stringently to NHTSA's rescission of its passive restraint rule), *with* Camp v. Pitts, 411 U.S. 138, 142-43 (1973) (applying the requirement less stringently to the Comptroller of the Currency's action on an application for a certificate authorizing organization of a new national bank), *and* Dunlop v. Bachowski, 421 U.S. 560, 572-75 (1975) (applying the requirement less stringently to the Secretary of Labor's determination not to sue to set aside an allegedly invalid labor union election). *See also* Jerry L. Mashaw, *Rethinking Judicial Review of Administrative Action: A Nineteenth Century Perspective*, 32 CARDOZO L. REV. 2241, 2242 (2011) ("Of course, administrative lawyers have long understood that the verbal formulae for the scope of review of administrative actions seldom control individual cases."). For an argument that arbitrary-and-capricious review should be understood as a variety of distinct inquiries into particular components of agency decision making, see Louis J. Virelli III, *Deconstructing Arbitrary and Capricious Review*, 92 N.C. L. REV. 721 (2014).

One other general issue deserves mention at the outset. That is the relationship between the arbitrary-and-capricious test and *Chevron* step two. *Chevron* step two directs courts to defer to "reasonable" agency interpretations of ambiguous statutory provisions. Such "interpretations" constitute policy decisions of the sort to which the arbitrary-and-capricious test also applies.[15] The question arises whether the *Chevron* step two "reasonableness" test incorporates, overlaps, or remains distinct from the arbitrary-and-capricious test. This question is addressed in Chapter Three, which discusses a growing consensus that step two is and should be essentially identical to arbitrary-and-capricious review.[16] Indeed, many cases applying the arbitrary-and-capricious test that are discussed in this chapter are assessing the "reasonableness" of an agency interpretation as part of the *Chevron* step-two inquiry.

A court may set aside an agency action under the arbitrary-and-capricious test on any of several grounds. As one lower court has aptly noted, "the 'arbitrary or capricious' concept, needless to say, is not easy to encapsulate in a single list of rubrics because it embraces a myriad of possible faults and depends heavily upon the circumstances of the case."[17] There are "rules of thumb," however.[18] In *State Farm*, the Court said that "the agency must examine the relevant data and articulate a satisfactory explanation for its action including a 'rational connection between the facts found and the choice made.'"[19] In reviewing that explanation, the Court continued, "we must 'consider whether the decision was based on a consideration of the relevant factors and whether there has been a clear error of judgment.'"[20] Furthermore, the Court stated:

> an agency rule would be arbitrary and capricious if the agency has relied on factors which Congress has not intended it to consider, entirely failed to consider an important aspect of the problem, offered an explanation for its decision that runs counter to the evidence before the agency, or is so implausible that it could not be ascribed to a difference in view or the product of agency expertise.[21]

---

15. *See* 5 U.S.C. § 706 (2000).
16. *Accord* Judulang v. Holder, 132 S. Ct. 476, 483 n.7 (2011).
17. P.R. Sun Oil Co. v. EPA, 8 F.3d 73, 77 (1st Cir. 1993).
18. *Id.*
19. 463 U.S. at 43 (quoting Burlington Truck Lines, Inc. v. United States, 371 U.S. 156, 168 (1962)).
20. *Id.* (quoting Bowman Transp., Inc. v. Ark.-Best Freight Sys., 419 U.S. 281, 285 (1975) (citing Citizens to Preserve Overton Park, Inc. v. Volpe, 401 U.S. 402, 416 (1971)).
21. *Id.*

It also would be arbitrary and capricious if the agency failed to consider certain policy alternatives.[22] The following subsections organize and amplify this language.

8.02 BASES FOR REVERSAL OF AGENCY ACTION

Commonly applied bases for reversal are discussed in this Part.

8.021 Impermissible Factors

> **[An agency action will be set aside as arbitrary and capricious if] the agency relied on factors that may not be taken into account under, or ignored factors that must be taken into account under, any authoritative source of law. (The caselaw often describes this ground as an element of the "arbitrary and capricious" test, although it seems more properly understood as a component of the court's legal analysis.)**
>
> **[Blackletter Statement, Part 3, § V.A.]**

As the *Blackletter Statement* observes, this basis for reversal is more properly understood as a part of an analysis of whether the agency has considered all relevant *legal* factors. Nonetheless, the issue is further addressed in the following section's discussion of *Massachusetts v. EPA*. The *Massachusetts* case represents an important, recent opinion in which the Supreme Court found agency action arbitrary and capricious based on the agency's failure to properly apply the relevant statute.

8.022 Relationship to Statutory Purposes or Requirements

> **[An agency action will be set aside as arbitrary and capricious if] the action does not bear a reasonable relationship to statutory purposes or requirements.**
>
> **[Blackletter Statement, Part 3, § V.B.]**

Some judicial pronouncements suggest that courts should invalidate agency actions that are—in the courts' view—just plain wrong. Thus, *Overton Park* instructs courts to determine whether the agency has made a "clear error of judgment,"[23] and *State Farm* refers to an agency rule that is "so implausible

---

22. *Id.* at 51.

23. *Overton Park*, 401 U.S. at 416 (stating that to uphold agency choice "the court must consider . . . whether there has been a clear error of judgment"). The *Overton Park* phraseology should not be confused with similar language in

that it could not be ascribed to a difference in view or the product of agency expertise."[24] Yet courts rarely overturn an agency action simply on the ground that the substance of that decision is unacceptable or unwise. Perhaps they refrain from doing so because the Supreme Court has warned them not to "substitute [their] judgment for that of the agency."[25] In any event, courts clearly prefer to rely on the less overtly value-laden rationales described in later subsections. Although courts once examined whether an agency had made an unpalatable discretionary choice as a core part of "arbitrary and capricious" review,[26] they no longer perform this function vigorously.

Nonetheless, courts occasionally will invalidate an action that does not bear a reasonable relationship to *statutory* purposes or requirements and is, in this sense, irrational or unacceptable.[27] It is possible to re-characterize some

---

Federal Rule of Civil Procedure 52, under which district court findings of fact must stand unless they are "clearly erroneous." Nothing in *Overton Park* suggests that the similarity is more than mere coincidence. Furthermore, courts and commentators long have recognized that Rule 52 criteria are out of place in this context. *See* NAACP v. FCC, 682 F.2d 993, 998 n.4 (D.C. Cir. 1982); J. Skelly Wright, *The Courts and the Rulemaking Process: The Limits of Judicial Review*, 59 CORNELL L. REV. 375, 392 n.84 (1974). *See also* STEPHEN G. BREYER ET AL., ADMINISTRATIVE LAW AND REGULATORY POLICY 366 (4th ed. 1998) ("[O]n the conventional view, reviewing courts should be more deferential to agency policy decisions than to findings of fact by lower courts.").

24. Motor Vehicle Mfrs. Ass'n v. State Farm Mut. Auto. Ins. Co., 463 U.S. 29, 43 (1983).
25. *Overton Park*, 401 U.S. at 416.
26. *See, e.g.*, ICC v. Ill. Cent. R.R., 215 U.S. 452, 470 (1910) (reviewing agency policy choice for "unreasonableness" as distinct from constitutional or statutory violations).
27. *See, e.g.*, Judulang v. Holder, 132 S. Ct. 476, 483-87 (2011) (invalidating BIA's approach for determining whether an alien was eligible for discretionary relief from deportation as arbitrary and capricious because the agency's approach was irrelevant to the merits of the petitioner's fitness to reside in this country); Athens Cmty. Hosp., Inc. v. Shalala, 21 F.3d 1176, 1179-80 (D.C. Cir. 1994); Dugan v. Ramsay, 727 F.2d 192, 196 (1st Cir. 1984); Conway v. Watt, 717 F.2d 512, 514-17 (10th Cir. 1983); Cmty. Nutrition Inst. v. Bergland, 493 F. Supp. 488, 494-95 (D.D.C. 1980). *See also* Verizon Commc'ns, Inc. v. FCC, 535 U.S. 467, 542 (2002) (Breyer, J., concurring and dissenting) (citing *State Farm*, 463 U.S. at 56, somewhat loosely, for the proposition that an agency must "show a 'rational connection' between the regulations and the statute's purposes," and arguing that the FCC regulations under review were arbitrary and capricious because they would actually harm rather than advance overall statutory goals).

of these cases under other subsections. To the extent these cases focus on *statutory* purposes, they are another instance of what is really a *legal* analysis occurring under the arbitrary and capricious rubric. It also is possible to break them out to the extent they find fatal substantive flaws in the rules rather than potentially curable process defects, such as reliance on flawed reasoning.[28]

In *Massachusetts v. EPA*, the Court reviewed the agency's denial of a rulemaking petition seeking the regulation of greenhouse gas emissions from new motor vehicles under the Clean Air Act ("CAA").[29] The statute provided, in relevant part, as follows:

> The Administrator shall by regulation prescribe . . . standards applicable to the emission of any air pollutant from any class . . . of new motor vehicles or new motor vehicle engines, which in his judgment cause, or contribute to, air pollution which may reasonably be anticipated to endanger public health or welfare . . . .[30]

EPA denied the petition on the grounds that it lacked statutory authority to regulate greenhouse gas emissions under the CAA and, in the alternative, that it would be unwise to exercise such authority at that time.[31] In reaching the latter conclusion, the agency claimed that a causal link between increased greenhouse gas emissions and rising global surface temperatures "cannot be

---

The difference in wording between the "Restatement" adopted by the Administrative Law Section in 1986 and the "Blackletter Statement" adopted 15 years later is telling. The earlier version stated that courts would set aside an agency action that "rests upon a policy judgment that is so unacceptable as to render the action arbitrary." Section of Administrative Law, American Bar Association, *A Restatement of Scope-of-Review Doctrine*, 38 ADMIN. L. REV. 235, 235 (1986). That language implies a more aggressive and policy-based judicial role than does the later version, which implicitly acknowledges congressional primacy with regard to policy. Under this formulation, the "arbitrariness" or irrationality of the agency action is its wrong-headedness not in light of general principles but rather in light of particular statutory policies.

28. *See infra* § 8.024.
29. 549 U.S. 497, 510-14 (2007).
30. 42 U.S.C. § 7521(a)(1) (2006).
31. *Massachusetts v. EPA*, 549 U.S. at 511; 68 Fed. Reg. 52922, 52929-30 (2003).

unequivocally established,"[32] and explained that a piecemeal approach to climate change would conflict with President George W. Bush's comprehensive approach to the problem and interfere with his "ability to persuade key developing countries to reduce greenhouse gas emissions."[33]

After concluding that the Commonwealth of Massachusetts had standing,[34] the Court explicitly adopted the D.C. Circuit's long-held view that denials of rulemaking petitions are subject to an "extremely limited" and "highly deferential" form of judicial review.[35] The Court proceeded to hold that greenhouse gases are "air pollutants" that fall within EPA's regulatory authority under the CAA,[36] and that the agency's rationale for declining to make an endangerment finding was arbitrary and capricious.[37] The Court rejected the agency's rationale for declining to take regulatory action[38] on the

32. 68 Fed. Reg. 52922, 52930 (quoting COMMITTEE ON THE SCIENCE OF CLIMATE CHANGE, NATIONAL RESEARCH COUNCIL, CLIMATE CHANGE SCIENCE: AN ANALYSIS OF SOME KEY QUESTIONS 17 (National Academy Press ed., 2001)).
33. *Massachusetts v. EPA*, 549 U.S. at 513-14.
34. *Id.* at 514-27.
35. *Id.* at 527-28 (quoting Nat'l Customs Brokers & Forwarders Ass'n, Inc. v. United States, 883 F.2d 93, 96 (D.C. Cir. 1989)). *See also* Am. Horse Prot. Ass'n, Inc. v. Lyng, 812 F.2d 1, 3-4 (D.C. Cir. 1987).
36. *Massachusetts v. EPA*, 549 U.S. at 528-32.
37. *Id.* at 532-35.
38. The majority seemed uncertain as to whether to characterize the issue as a review of EPA's decision not to regulate or as a review of EPA's decision to decline to make the judgment that would be a prerequisite to regulation. *Compare id.* at 504 (identifying the issue as whether EPA's stated reasons for refusing to regulate greenhouse gas emissions from new motor vehicles are consistent with the statute) *with id.* at 532 (holding that "EPA has offered no reasoned explanation for its refusal to decide whether greenhouse gases cause or contribute to climate change"). While this distinction was functionally irrelevant because EPA's denial of the rulemaking petition meant that the agency was declining to regulate greenhouse gas emissions (at least for the time being), the distinction has formal legal significance, and was in fact the primary basis for Justice Scalia's dissenting opinion. *See infra* notes 46-50 and accompanying text.

Scholars have, of course, previously recognized that formalism and functionalism are jurisprudential differences with a profound impact on administrative law. *See, e.g.*, Peter L. Strauss, *Formal and Functional Approaches to Separation-of-Powers Questions–A Foolish Inconsistency?*, 72 CORNELL L. REV. 488 (1987). *Massachusetts* could, of course, also be explained by the competing political or ideological preferences of the Justices. *See* Richard J. Pierce, Jr., *What Factors Can an Agency Consider in Making a Decision?*, 2009 MICH. ST. L. REV. 67, 86-87 (2009). *See also* Thomas J. Miles &

grounds that it "rest[ed] on reasoning divorced from the statutory text."[39] The Court emphasized that the EPA must regulate an air pollutant under the statute when the agency finds that it "cause[s], or contribute[s] to, air pollution which may reasonably be anticipated to endanger public health or welfare,"[40] and the Court suggested that EPA's decision regarding *whether to make this judgment* must be based on similar technical or scientific considerations.[41] Thus, the Court explained:

> [u]nder the clear terms of the Clean Air Act, EPA can avoid taking further action only if it determines that greenhouse gases do not contribute to climate change or if it provides some reasonable explanation as to why it cannot or will not exercise its discretion to determine whether they do.[42]

Because the "laundry list" of policy reasons that EPA provided for declining to regulate had "nothing to do with whether greenhouse gas emissions contribute to climate change," and did not "amount to a reasoned justification for declining to form a scientific judgment," the Court held that EPA's denial of the rulemaking petition was arbitrary and capricious under the judicial review provisions of the statute.[43] It explicitly held "that EPA must ground its reasons for action or inaction in the statute."[44]

Cass R. Sunstein, *The Real World of Arbitrariness Review*, 75 U. Chi. L. Rev. 761 (2008) (examining the influence of judicial policy preferences on the operation of hard look judicial review).

39. *Massachusetts v. EPA*, 549 U.S. at 532.
40. *Id.* at 532-33.
41. *See id.* at 533 (recognizing that EPA has substantial discretion regarding how and when to act, "[b]ut once EPA has responded to a petition for rulemaking, its reasons for action or inaction must conform to the authorizing statute"). *See also* Jody Freeman & Adrian Vermeule, Massachusetts v. EPA*: From Politics to Expertise*, 2007 Sup. Ct. Rev. 51, 80 (2007) ("Crucially, the same statutory factors that govern the agency's decision about whether or not a pollutant meets the endangerment standard also govern its decision about whether or not to make that judgment in the first place.") (emphasis omitted).
42. *Massachusetts v. EPA*, 549 U.S. at 533. *See also id.* at 534 ("If the scientific uncertainty is so profound that it precludes EPA from making a reasoned judgment as to whether greenhouse gases contribute to global warming, EPA must say so."); *id.* ("The statutory question is whether sufficient information exists to make an endangerment finding.").
43. *Id.* at 533-34.
44. *Id.* at 535.

Justice Scalia dissented on the ground that EPA had provided a lawful explanation for refusing to make an endangerment finding.[45] He agreed with the Court that once "the Administrator *makes* a judgment whether to regulate greenhouse gases, that judgment must relate to whether they are air pollutants that 'cause, or contribute to, air pollution which may reasonably be anticipated to endanger public health or welfare.'"[46] Justice Scalia pointed out, however, that it was undisputed that the Administrator had not made the requisite judgment in this case, and had instead deferred this decision.[47] Justice Scalia emphasized that "the statute says *nothing at all* about the reasons for which the Administrator may *defer* making a judgment—the permissible reasons for deciding not to grapple with the issue at the present time."[48] Moreover, "[t]he reasons the EPA gave are surely considerations executive agencies *regularly* take into account (and *ought* to take into account) when deciding whether to consider entering a new field: the impact such entry would have on other Executive Branch programs and on foreign policy."[49] Accordingly, Justice Scalia would have upheld the agency's decision to refuse to take action at this time. He would also have deferred to EPA's conclusion that it lacked statutory authority to regulate greenhouse gases under the Clean Air Act.[50]

The Court could arguably be excused for not making too much of the formal distinction between EPA's refusal to regulate greenhouse gases and its deferral of the decision to make a judgment (which could, in turn, require it to regulate greenhouse gases) because the end result was the same (*i.e.*, no regulation of greenhouse gases).[51] Nonetheless, commentators are skeptical that *Massachusetts* should be understood to stand for the proposition that agencies must ground their reasons for action or inaction exclusively in their authorizing statutes as a general principle of administrative law. For example, it is widely understood that agencies have limited resources and must therefore establish priorities.[52] It is doubtful that an agency's refusal to take action based on a reasoned decision to prioritize some aspects of its statutory re-

---

45. *Id.* at 549 (Scalia, J., dissenting).
46. *Id.* at 552 (quoting 42 U.S.C. § 7521(a)(1)).
47. *See id.* at 549-52.
48. *Id.* at 552.
49. *Id.*
50. *See id.* at 555-60.
51. *See supra* note 38.
52. *See, e.g.*, Eric Biber, *The Importance of Resource Allocation in Administrative Law*, 60 ADMIN. L. REV. 1 (2008).

sponsibilities over others would be deemed arbitrary and capricious, even if the factors that led to this decision were not explicitly set forth in the relevant statutory provisions, as long as they were otherwise logically relevant. Similarly, it is widely accepted that agencies should ordinarily consider the costs and benefits of proposed regulatory initiatives unless they are precluded by law from doing so.[53] Yet a decision regarding whether to proceed that was based on cost-benefit considerations would not necessarily be "grounded in the statute" if the statute is silent on the permissible role of cost-benefit analysis. Commentators have therefore sought to identify ways in which *Massachusetts* is unique, or at least unusual, so that lower courts can avoid invalidating agency decisions that are based on logically relevant factors that are not addressed in their authorizing statutes as a matter of course.[54]

Some commentators have suggested that the Court's unusually stringent review was likely a function of the tremendous importance of the issue of climate change.

> In other words, there are petitions—and then there are *petitions*. When an agency denies a petition for rulemaking on a relatively small issue, such as an issue that involves only a narrow kind of economic regulation, the reviewing court is unlikely to be as troubled by the denial, even when denials are based on policy considerations. But when an agency is presented with very big issues that impact public health or safety—such as the EPA being presented with what is, according to many commentators, the most important environmental issue of the century—the courts might be willing to review the agency's decision more closely.[55]

While this explanation would be difficult to capture in doctrinal terms or to administer in consistent or predictable ways,[56] it is consistent with the observation that the stringency of arbitrary-and-capricious review varies in practice based on the nature and perceived significance of the agency's deci-

---

53. While the weight that should be given to cost-benefit analysis and the role of the White House in reviewing agency decisions are certainly controversial, most commentators agree that the costs and benefits of regulation are typically *relevant* to agency decision making.
54. *See* Pierce, *supra* note 38, at 79.
55. Kathryn A. Watts & Amy J. Wildermuth, Massachusetts v. EPA: *Breaking New Ground on Issues Other Than Global Warming*, 102 Nw. U. L. Rev. Colloquy 1, 14 (2007).
56. *See id.* at 15.

sion.[57] Commentators have also argued that *Massachusetts* is best understood as a form of "expertise-forcing," whereby the Court is attempting "to ensure that agencies exercise expert judgment free from outside political pressures, even or especially political pressures emanating from the White House."[58] From this perspective, "the Court seems to adopt a kind of anti-circumvention principle: agencies cannot perpetually defer the threshold decisions necessary to trigger regulation if doing so would undermine the main purposes of the statute."[59] Finally, some commentators have suggested that the Court's decision could be understood to turn on the highly circumscribed or "mandatory" nature of regulation under the Clean Air Act, and that the denial of a rulemaking petition could be based on other policy considerations when an agency's authorizing statute is written in more discretionary terms.[60]

Massachusetts is likely unique in the sense that it presented all of the factors described above. In other words, the decision involved an unusually important problem, which was resolved (or deferred) by an agency under a statute that was written in "action-forcing" terms, in circumstances where the Court might reasonably have been suspicious of undue politicization. Accordingly, it is perhaps not surprising that the decision does not appear to have had a profound impact on the work of the lower courts. Some lower courts have cited *Massachusetts* for the proposition that denials of rulemaking petitions are subject to an exceptionally deferential form of judicial review.[61] Moreover, there are some examples of lower court decisions that appear to adopt an "expertise-forcing" reading of the decision,[62] or turn on the non-

57. *See supra* note 14 and accompanying text.
58. Freeman & Vermeule, *supra* note 41, at 52.
59. *Id.* at 53.
60. *See* Pierce, *supra* note 38, at 82-84. *See also* Freeman & Vermeule, *supra* note 41, at 98 ("Crucial to the holding is the point that § 202(a) excludes nonscientific and nontechnical factors from the agency's initial decision-making calculus. Some statutes can plausibly be read to share that feature; others presumably cannot.").
61. *See, e.g.*, N.Y. v. U.S. Nuclear Regulatory Comm'n, 589 F.3d 551, 554 (2d Cir. 2009). *Cf.* Conservancy of Sw. Florida v. U.S. Fish & Wildlife Serv., 677 F.3d 1073, 1085 (11th Cir. 2012) (holding that the denial of the petition at issue was committed to agency discretion by law, but recognizing that denials of rulemaking petitions "may often be reviewable" in light of *Massachusetts v. EPA*).
62. *See, e.g.*, Upper Blackstone Water Pollution Abatement Dist. v. EPA, 690 F.3d 9, 23-24 (1st Cir. 2012) (upholding effluent limitations imposed by EPA in a permit, and relying on *Massachusetts* for the proposition that "EPA is required to exercise its judgment even in the face of some scientific uncer-

discretionary nature of the relevant statutory language.[63] Of course, the long-term impact of the decision on judicial review of agency discretion remains to be seen. As explained below, however, *Massachusetts* raises fundamental questions about the appropriate role of "political reasons" in agency decision-making and judicial review of agency discretion, which have been the focus of recent scholarship.[64]

In sum, it is impossible to generalize as to when a court is likely to find that an action does not bear a reasonable relationship to statutory purposes or requirements. The inquiry obviously is subjective and context dependent. (Indeed, this is true of the inquiries in the remaining subsections as well.) The important point for present purposes is that this type of review is available to courts, even though they rarely use it.

8.023 Inadequate Factual Premise

> **[An agency action will be set aside as arbitrary and capricious if] the asserted or necessary factual premises of the action do not withstand scrutiny under the relevant standard of review.**
> **[Blackletter Statement, Part 3, § V.C.]**

This provision of the *Blackletter Statement* essentially is a cross-reference to Chapter Seven, which addresses in detail the standards of review for factual issues. It is included here for the sake of completeness.

---

tainty"); Miami-Dade Cnty. v. EPA, 529 F.3d 1049, 1065 (11th Cir. 2008) (upholding the agency's final rule, and relying on *Massachusetts* for the proposition that "the EPA is compelled to exercise its judgment in the face of scientific uncertainty unless that uncertainty is so profound that it precludes any reasoned judgment"). *See also* George v. Bay Area Rapid Transit, 577 F.3d 1005, 1011 (9th Cir. 2009) (upholding DOT regulations and distinguishing *Massachusetts* on the grounds that the challenged judgment "has everything to do with [the decision makers'] specific areas of technical expertise").

63. *See, e.g.*, WildEarth Guardians v. EPA, 751 F.3d 649 (D.C. Cir. 2014) (deferentially reviewing, and upholding, denial of petition asking EPA to regulate greenhouse gases from landfills); United States v. Divens, 650 F.3d 343, 347 (4th Cir. 2011). *See also In re* MDL-1824 Tri-State Water Rights Litig., 644 F.3d 1160, 1192-98 (11th Cir. 2011) (invalidating an agency's denial of a water supply request on the grounds that it was based on "a clear error of law").

64. *See infra* § 8.03.

The "necessary" factual premises of an agency action are derived from substantive law—almost always, the statute that authorizes and constrains the agency action in question. For example, in *Industrial Union Department, AFL-CIO v. American Petroleum Institute* (the *Benzene Case*),[65] the Supreme Court held that the Occupational Safety and Health Act required OSHA to demonstrate that exposure to a toxic substance presented a "significant risk" of harm before regulating that substance. After the *Benzene Case*, the existence of a "significant risk" is a prerequisite to any OSHA toxic substance regulation. Were OSHA to adopt such a rule without a finding of significant risk, that rule would be arbitrary.

The "asserted" factual premises are determined by the agency itself. When an agency actually relies on a factual finding in defending its action, courts subject that finding to scrutiny under the standards set forth in Chapter Seven—regardless of whether the finding is "necessary," as defined above. The requirement that "asserted" factual findings pass muster follows from the principle that an agency action can be sustained only on the grounds upon which the agency relied.[66]

8.024 Explanation and Reasoning

> **[An agency action will be set aside as arbitrary and capricious if] the action is unsupported by any explanation or rests upon reasoning that is seriously flawed.**
>
> **[Blackletter Statement, Part 3, § V.D.]**

Even when an agency's factual premises themselves are sustainable, the agency must show a "rational connection between the facts found and the choice made," and may not "offer[] an explanation for its decision that runs counter to the evidence" before it.[67] At the same time, a court must "uphold a decision of less than ideal clarity if the agency's path may be reasonably discerned."[68] As one common formulation puts it, an agency "'must inform the court and the petitioner of the grounds of the decision and the essential facts upon which the administrative decision was based.'"[69]

---

65. 448 U.S. 607 (1980).
66. *See* Part Three, § VI of the *Blackletter Statement*, reprinted in Appendix A, *infra*.
67. Motor Vehicle Mfrs. Ass'n v. State Farm Mut. Auto Ins. Co., 463 U.S. 29, 43 (1983) (quotations omitted).
68. Bowman Transp., Inc. v. Ark.-Best Freight Sys., Inc., 419 U.S. 281, 286 (1974).
69. United States v. Dierckman, 201 F.3d 915, 926 (7th Cir. 2000) (quoting Bagdonas v. Dep't of the Treasury, 93 F.3d 422, 426 (7th Cir. 1996)).

At bottom, this category covers instances in which an agency provides an explanation for its policy choice that is inadequate to suggest reasoned decisionmaking. An "inadequate explanation" is the most commonly offered reason for invalidating an agency policy decision. It covers a variety of errors and takes a variety of forms. The easiest to spot occurs when an agency fails to provide any explanation whatsoever for its policy choice.[70] At a minimum, the absence of any explanation leaves courts without the ability to judge whether the agency has engaged in reasoned decisionmaking.

Even when an agency does provide an explanation for its policy choice, that explanation may fail to satisfy the demands of reasoned decision-making. Sometimes an explanation relies on unconvincing or implausible reasoning.[71] Sometimes it relies on illogical reasoning.[72] Other times it simply offers insufficient reasoning.[73] It also may rely on inconsistent

---

70. *See, e.g.*, Greater Yellowstone Coal., Inc. v. Servheen, 665 F.3d 1015, 1029-30 (9th Cir. 2011); William Gas Processing-Gulf Coast Co. v. FERC, 475 F.3d 319, 322, 328-30 (D.C. Cir. 2006); Am. Petroleum Inst. v. EPA, 216 F.3d 50, 57-58 (D.C. Cir. 2000); United Transp. v. ICC, 52 F.3d 1074, 1079 n.9 (D.C. Cir. 1995); Allied-Signal, Inc. v. NRC, 988 F.2d 146, 150 (D.C. Cir. 1993); Nat'l Tank Truck Carriers, Inc. v. EPA, 907 F.2d 177, 184-85 (D.C. Cir. 1990); United Mine Workers v. Dole, 870 F.2d 662, 673 (D.C. Cir. 1989).
71. *See, e.g.*, Ky. Riverkeeper, Inc. v. Rowlette, 714 F.3d 402, 408-13 (6th Cir. 2013); Friends of Back Bay v. U.S. Army Corps of Eng'rs, 681 F.3d 581, 588-89 (4th Cir. 2012); Barnes v. U.S. Dep't of Transp., 655 F.3d 1124, 1137 (9th Cir. 2011); Fresno Mobile Radio, Inc. v. FCC, 165 F.3d 965, 969-70 (D.C. Cir. 1999); Time Warner Entm't Co. v. FCC, 56 F.3d 151, 209-10 (D.C. Cir. 1995); Bldg. & Constr. Trades Dep't, AFL-CIO v. Brock, 838 F.2d 1258, 1277 (D.C. Cir. 1988); Alltel Corp. v. FCC, 838 F.2d 551, 558-59 (D.C. Cir. 1988).
72. *See, e.g.*, Gamefly, Inc. v. Postal Regulatory Comm'n, 704 F.3d 145, 148-49 (D.C. Cir. 2013); Sorenson Commc'ns, Inc. v. FCC, 567 F.3d 1215, 1220-23 (10th Cir. 2009); Advocates for Highway and Auto Safety v. Fed. Motor Carrier Safety Admin., 429 F.3d 1136, 1146 (D.C. Cir. 2005); Exxon Co., U.S.A. v. FERC, 182 F.3d 30, 42 (D.C. Cir. 1999). *See also* Am. Fed'n of Gov't Emps. v. FLRA, 470 F.3d 375, 380 (D.C. Cir. 2006) (internal quotation marks omitted) (quoting IRS v. FLRA, 963 F.2d 429, 439 (D.C. Cir. 1992)) ("Certainly, if the result reached is illogical on its own terms, the Authority's order is arbitrary and capricious.").
73. *See, e.g.*, Coburn v. McHugh, 679 F.3d 924, 933-34 (D.C. Cir. 2012); Cablevision Sys. Corp. v. FCC, 649 F.3d 695, 719-23 (D.C. Cir. 2011); Arrington v. Daniels, 516 F.3d 1106, 1114 (9th Cir. 2008); Miccosukee Tribe of Indians v. United States, 566 F.3d 1257, 1275 (11th Cir. 2009); Air Transp.

reasoning.[74] Or it may rely on skewed or biased reasoning.[75] Many of these categories overlap. Moreover, they are intended to be illustrative rather than exhaustive.

Two recurrent issues are of specific concern to scientific or technical policy decisions: (1) the extent to which agencies are entitled to rely on predictive judgments, and (2) the extent to which agencies are entitled to rely on broad models or tests. Courts routinely state that agencies are entitled to significant latitude with respect to scientific or technical decisions.[76] Thus, agencies are entitled to rely on predictive judgments when they possess an imperfect basis for more concrete judgments.[77] And they are entitled to rely

---

Ass'n of Am. v. Dep't of Transp., 119 F.3d 38, 44-45, *amended on reh'g*, 129 F.3d 625 (D.C. Cir. 1997); Petroleum Commc'ns., Inc. v. FCC, 22 F.3d 1164, 1172-73 (D.C. Cir. 1994); Am. Mining Cong. v. EPA, 907 F.2d 1179, 1190 (D.C. Cir. 1990); Hazardous Waste Treatment Council v. EPA, 886 F.2d 355, 365-66 (D.C. Cir. 1989).

74. *See, e.g.*, Catawba County, NC v. EPA, 571 F.3d 20, 51-52 (D.C. Cir. 2009); Venetian Casino Resort, L.L.C. v. EEOC, 530 F.3d 925, 934-35 (D.C. Cir. 2008); Engine Mfrs. Ass'n v. EPA, 20 F.3d 1177, 1182 (D.C. Cir. 1994); Ill. Bell Tel. v. FCC, 911 F.2d 776, 784 (D.C. Cir. 1990).

75. *See, e.g.*, Humane Soc'y of U.S. v. Locke, 626 F.3d 1040, 1048-54 (9th Cir. 2010); Natural Res. Def. Council v. U.S. Forest Serv., 421 F.3d 797, 806-13 (9th Cir. 2005); Sierra Club v. Thomas, 105 F.3d 248, 251-53 (6th Cir. 1997), *vacated on other grounds sub nom.* Ohio Forestry Ass'n v. Sierra Club, 523 U.S. 726 (1998).

76. *See, e.g.*, Balt. Gas & Elec. Co. v. Natural Res. Def. Council, 462 U.S. 87, 103 (1983); Nat'l Envtl. Dev. Ass'n's Clean Air Project v. EPA, 686 F.3d 803, 810 (D.C. Cir. 2012); Defenders of Wildlife v. Bureau of Ocean Energy Mgmt., 684 F.3d 1242, 1250 (11th Cir. 2012); Coal. for Responsible Regulation, Inc. v. EPA, 684 F.3d 102, 120 (D.C. Cir. 2012), *aff'd in part and rev'd in part on other grounds*, 134 S. Ct. 2427 (2014); N. Plains Res. Council, Inc. v. Surface Trans. Bd., 668 F.3d 1067, 1075 (9th Cir. 2011); Am. Iron & Steel Inst. v. EPA, 115 F.3d 979, 1006 (D.C. Cir. 1997); Am. Legion v. Derwinski, 54 F.3d 789, 795 (D.C. Cir. 1995). For a comprehensive evaluation and critique of the "super-deference" that federal courts purportedly give to scientific and technical determinations, see Emily Hammond Meazell, *Super Deference, the Science Obsession, and Judicial Review as Translation of Agency Science*, 109 MICH. L. REV. 733 (2011).

77. *See, e.g.*, FCC v. Fox Television Stations, Inc., 556 U.S. 502, 521 (2009) (accepting agency's prediction that allowing broadcasters to air fleeting expletives would lead to an increased use of expletives, one at a time – a prediction that was not based on any evidence but made sense as "an exercise in logic rather than clairvoyance"); Upper Blackstone Water Pollution Abatement Dist. v. EPA, 690 F.3d 9, 20-25 (1st Cir. 2012); League of Wilderness

on broad models or tests when faced with a wide range of potential applications.[78] At the same time, courts do not allow agencies to rely on mere speculation or unsubstantiated predictions[79] or on models or tests that lack a rational relationship to their specific applications.[80] These divergent strains leave agencies without much guidance on when a court will reject the use of a predictive judgment or a general model.[81]

This observation recalls a more general point made above: simply identifying the components of the inquiry does not indicate when a court is likely to reject an agency action under that inquiry. A determination that a particular policy decision suffers from any of the general defects specified in this subsection inevitably varies from case to case. Furthermore, it varies from

---

Defenders-Blue Mountains Biodiversity Project v. U.S. Forest Serv., 689 F.3d 1060, 1076-77 (9th Cir. 2012); *Defenders of Wildlife*, 684 F.3d at 1248-49; Town of Winthrop v. FAA, 535 F.3d 1, 13-14 (1st Cir. 2008); Chamber of Commerce of U.S. v. SEC, 412 F.3d 133, 142-43 (D.C. Cir. 2005); Cellnet Commc'ns., Inc. v. FCC, 149 F.3d 429, 441 (6th Cir. 1998); California v. FCC, 75 F.3d 1350, 1359 (9th Cir. 1996); Am. Postal Workers Union v. U.S. Postal Serv., 891 F.2d 304, 314 (D.C. Cir. 1989), *rev'd on other grounds*, 498 U.S. 517 (1991).

78. *See, e.g.*, Or. Natural Res. Council Fund v. Goodman, 505 F.3d 884, 896-97 (9th Cir. 2007) (deferring to the Forest Service's analysis where the statute did not require the "best scientific methodology available" and the agency disclosed the potential weaknesses of its model); *Am. Iron & Steel Inst.*, 115 F.3d at 1004-05; Eagle-Picher Indus., Inc. v. EPA, 759 F.2d 905, 921-22 (D.C. Cir. 1985).

79. *See, e.g.*, Dow Agrosciences L.L.C. v. Nat'l Marine Fisheries Serv., 707 F.3d 462, 469-75 (4th Cir. 2013); *Goodman*, 505 F.3d at 892-93 (holding that the agency failed to adequately discuss the environmental impact of two related projects because "generalized, conclusory assertions from agency experts are not sufficient; the agency must provide the underlying data supporting the assertion in language intelligible to the public"); Tripoli Rocketry Ass'n, Inc. v. Bureau of Alcohol, Tobacco, Firearms, and Explosives, 437 F.3d 75, 81-84 (D.C. Cir. 2006); Cincinnati Bell Tel. Co. v. FCC, 69 F.3d 752, 760 (6th Cir. 1995); Am. Mining Cong. v. EPA, 907 F.2d 1179, 1188 (D.C. Cir. 1990).

80. *See, e.g.*, *Dow Agrosciences*, 707 F.3d at 470-72; Greater Yellowstone Coal, Inc. v. Servheen, 665 F.3d 1015, 1029 (9th Cir. 2011); Leather Indus. of Am., Inc. v. EPA, 40 F.3d 392, 402-03, 404-05 (D.C. Cir. 1994); Chem. Mfrs. Ass'n v. EPA, 28 F.3d 1259, 1265-66 (D.C. Cir. 1994); Edison Elec. Inst. v. EPA, 2 F.3d 438, 446-47 (D.C. Cir. 1993); Anne Arundel Cnty., Md. v. EPA, 963 F.2d 412, 413-14 (D.C. Cir. 1992).

81. *See* Chapter Seven, *supra*.

judge to judge, depending on the particular judge's general posture toward arbitrary-and-capricious review. This realization exposes judges "to the charge that the results of [their] review are inconsistent and reflect political or philosophical preference of the judges on the panel rather than any objective standard."[82] And this charge, in turn, fuels much of the debate over the ossification of agency rulemaking. An agency aware that different judges in different cases will deem different factors sufficient to undermine its rationale may commit too many resources to immunizing that rationale from challenge or may decline to take any action at all. Whether the solution to this problem, to the extent it exists, is relaxing scrutiny or improving it is a question that continues to occupy the thinking of scholars and judges. In any event, this problem counsels courts to refrain from overzealous inquiry into allegedly flawed administrative reasoning.

8.025 Failure to Consider Key Aspects of the Issue Presented

> **[An agency action will be set aside as arbitrary and capricious if] the agency failed, without adequate justification, to give reasonable consideration to an important aspect of the problems presented by the action, such as the effects or costs of the policy choice involved, or the factual circumstances bearing on that choice. [Blackletter Statement, Part 3, § V.E.]**

This type of error concerns an agency's failure "to consider an important aspect of the problem."[83] This deficiency is similar to the ones identified in subsection 8.024 above in that it arises in relation to the agency's explanation. Specifically, it arises when an agency fails to demonstrate in its explanation that it has considered all of the significant issues affecting its policy choice. But this shortcoming differs from those in subsection 8.024 in that it occurs when the explanation or analysis is *incomplete* rather than internally weak. Although there may be nothing irrational in what the agency actually has said, it has not said enough (or done enough) because it has failed to consider a relevant issue. This distinction is admittedly fine. In many "inadequate explanation" cases, the charge is that the agency has failed to consider or articulate all of the ramifications of its policy decisions. Nonetheless, courts

---

82. Wald, *supra* note 6, at 234. For a recent empirical investigation of this issue, see Miles & Sunstein, *supra* note 38.

83. Motor Vehicle Mfrs. Ass'n v. State Farm Mut. Auto Ins. Co., 463 U.S. 29, 43 (1983).

occasionally identify failure "to consider an important aspect of the problem" rather than "inadequate explanation" as the defect in an agency policy decision.[84] This type of agency error is not to be confused with an agency's failure to consider a relevant *legal* factor. Rather, it addresses instances in which the agency has not taken into account all the effects of its policy decision,[85] the full costs or benefits of its policy decision,[86] or the full range of facts affecting its policy decision.[87]

As with all arbitrary-and-capricious inquiries, courts possess a considerable amount of latitude in determining when an agency has failed to consider

---

84. *See, e.g.*, N. Plains Res. Council, Inc. v. Surface Transp. Bd., 668 F.3d 1067, 1085 (9th Cir. 2011); Ohio River Valley Envtl. Coal., Inc. v. Kempthorne, 473 F.3d 94, 102-03 (4th Cir. 2006).

85. *See, e.g.*, Ctr. for Biological Diversity v. U.S. Bureau of Land Mgmt., 698 F.3d 1101, 1119-24 (9th Cir. 2012); *N. Plains Res. Council*, 668 F.3d at 1077-79; *Ohio River Valley Envtl. Coal., Inc.*, 473 F.3d at 102-03; *Am. Iron & Steel Inst.*, 115 F.3d at 997; P.R. Sun Oil Co. v. EPA, 8 F.3d 73, 73 (1st Cir. 1993).

86. *See, e.g.*, Ctr. for Biological Diversity v. Nat'l Highway Traffic Safety Admin., 538 F.3d 1172, 1198-1203 (9th Cir. 2008) (holding that NHTSA's failure to monetize the benefits of a reduction in greenhouse gas emissions in setting fuel economy standards was arbitrary and capricious); Timpinaro v. SEC, 2 F.3d 453 (D.C. Cir. 1993). *Cf.* Bus. Roundtable v. SEC, 647 F.3d 1144, 1146 (D.C. Cir. 2011) (holding that a rule promulgated by the SEC violated the APA, "because, among other reasons, the Commission failed to consider the rule's effect upon efficiency, competition, and capital formation, as required by Section 3(f) of the Exchange Act and Section 2(c) of the Investment Company Act of 1940"); Chamber of Commerce of U.S. v. SEC, 412 F.3d 133, 142-44 (D.C. Cir. 2005) (concluding that the SEC violated its statutory obligation to consider whether an action "will promote efficiency, competition, and capital formulation," and thus violated its obligations under the APA, when it failed adequately to consider the costs imposed upon funds by the two challenged conditions) (citation omitted) (internal quotation marks omitted). For a critique of these decisions, see James D. Cox & Benjamin J.C. Baucom, *The Emperor Has No Clothes: Confronting the D.C. Circuit's Usurpation of SEC Rulemaking Authority*, 90 TEX. L. REV. 1811 (2012).

87. *See, e.g.*, Ctr. for Biological Diversity v. U.S. Bureau of Land Mgmt., 698 F.3d 1101, 1121-25 (9th Cir. 2012); W. Watersheds Project v. Kraayenbrink, 632 F.3d 472, 491-95 (9th Cir. 2011); Advocates for Highway & Auto Safety v. Fed. Motor Carrier Safety Admin., 429 F.3d 1136, 1145-47 (D.C. Cir. 2005); NAACP v. Donovan, 765 F.2d 1178 (D.C. Cir. 1985).

an important aspect of the problem.[88] As a result, there is a risk that courts will over-emphasize marginal issues and effectively "substitute [their] judgment for that of the agency."[89] And, again, it permits them to increase the costs of rulemaking. Courts should remain cognizant of these difficulties and moderate their review accordingly.[90]

8.026 Unexplained Inconsistency with Prior Actions

> **[An agency action will be set aside as arbitrary and capricious if] the action, where inconsistent with prior agency policies or precedents, fails to display an awareness of the change in position, fails to explain a changed view of the facts, or fails to consider serious reliance interests that its prior policy engendered. [Blackletter Statement, Part 3, § V.F.]**

Reviewing courts have long held that an agency action that is inconsistent with prior actions, without good reason, is "arbitrary." As stated in one early decision: "An agency's view of what is in the public interest may change, either with or without a change in circumstances. But an agency changing its course must supply a reasoned analysis indicating that prior policies and standards are being deliberately changed, not casually ignored . . . ."[91] The Supreme Court applied this doctrine to adjudicative orders in *Atchison, Topeka & Santa Fe Railway Co. v. Wichita Board of Trade.*[92] Ten years later, it extended the doctrine to rules in *State Farm.* There the Court held that when an agency departs from settled policy by amending or rescinding a rule, it must provide an explicit justification for the change.[93]

Agencies are not categorically forbidden from changing prior policy. Indeed, the *State Farm* Court was careful to "recognize that 'regulatory agencies do not establish rules of conduct to last forever,' and that an agency must be given ample latitude to 'adapt their rules and policies to the demands of

---

88. *See* Seidenfeld, *Demystifying Deossification*, *supra* note 13, at 510-11.
89. Motor Vehicle Mfrs. Ass'n v. State Farm Mut. Auto Ins. Co., 463 U.S. 29, 43 (1983).
90. *Cf.* Arkansas v. Oklahoma, 503 U.S. 91, 113-14 (1992) (rejecting lower court conclusion that agency failed to consider an important aspect of the problem as based on overly aggressive construction of statute).
91. Greater Bos. Television Corp. v. FCC, 444 F.2d 841, 852 (D.C. Cir. 1970) (footnotes omitted).
92. 412 U.S. 800, 808 (1973).
93. *State Farm*, 463 U.S. at 41-42.

changing circumstances.'"[94] However, agencies must explain any such change. Moreover, as *State Farm* demonstrates, the explanation must be adequate; not just any explanation will do.[95]

The precise nature of the explanation that is required to justify an agency's change in policy was addressed by the Court in *FCC v. Fox Television Stations, Inc.*[96] While federal law prohibits the broadcasting of "any . . . indecent . . . language,"[97] the FCC had long taken the position that it would not take enforcement action against the broadcast of isolated or fleeting expletives. However, the Commission changed its position in a series of orders, and held that the "nonliteral (expletive) use of the F- and S-words could be actionably indecent, even when the word is used only once."[98] Fox TV and other broadcasters challenged the FCC's decision on constitutional grounds, and they also claimed that the decision was arbitrary and capricious in violation of the APA.[99] The Second Circuit invalidated the orders on the grounds that the FCC's reasoning was inadequate based, in part, on circuit precedent that required agencies that change policy to explain "why the original reasons for adopting the displaced rule or policy are no longer dispositive as well as why the new rule effectuates the statute as well as or better than the old rule."[100] A sharply divided Supreme Court reversed the Second Circuit's decision, and remanded the matter for consideration of the constitutional questions.

---

94. *State Farm*, 463 U.S. at 42 (quoting Am. Trucking Ass'ns v. Atchison, T. & S.F.R. Co., 387 U.S. 397, 416 (1967), and Permian Basin Area Rate Cases, 390 U.S. 747, 784 (1968)). By the same token, if an agency has changed its policy, it may be permissible to decline to apply this new policy to pending cases; again, the result turns on whether the agency has a rational reason for relying on the older policy in the particular case. Consol. Edison Co. of N.Y. v. FERC, 315 F.3d 316, 323-24 (D.C. Cir. 2003).
95. *See State Farm*, 463 U.S. at 41-42. *See also* Am. Hosp. Ass'n v. NLRB, 499 U.S. 606, 618-19 (1991) ("The question whether the Board has changed its view about certain issues or certain industries does not undermine the validity of a rule that is based on substantial evidence and supported by a 'reasoned analysis.'") (quoting *State Farm*, 463 U.S. at 42, 57); Robertson v. Methow Valley Citizens Council, 490 U.S. 332, 355-56 (1989) (an agency's new position is entitled to deference as long as "there appears to have been good reason for the change").
96. 556 U.S. 502 (2009).
97. 18 U.S.C. § 1464.
98. *See Fox TV*, 556 U.S. at 507.
99. *See id.* at 510-11.
100. *Id.* at 514 (internal citations and references omitted).

Justice Scalia's opinion for a five-Justice majority rejected the notion that an agency's change in policy is subject to "more searching" judicial review than the agency's initial policy decision.[101] Rather, he described the agency's obligation under the APA as follows:

> [T]he requirement that an agency provide reasoned explanation for its action would ordinarily demand that it display awareness that it *is* changing position. An agency may not, for example, depart from a prior policy *sub silentio* or simply disregard rules that are still on the books. And of course the agency must show that there are good reasons for the new policy. But it need not demonstrate to a court's satisfaction that the reasons for the new policy are *better* than the reasons for the old one; it suffices that the new policy is permissible under the statute, that there are good reasons for it, and that the agency *believes* it to be better, which the conscious change of course adequately indicates.[102]

While agencies do not always need to provide "a more detailed justification" for changing a policy than for adopting a policy in the first instance, Justice Scalia acknowledged that a more thorough explanation would be required "when, for example, [the agency's] new policy rests upon factual findings that contradict those which underlay its prior policy; or when its prior policy has engendered serious reliance interests that must be taken into account."[103] The Court explained that "[i]t would be arbitrary or capricious to ignore such matters"—not because the agency changed its position, but rather because "a reasoned explanation is needed for disregarding facts and circumstances that underlay or were engendered by the prior policy."[104]

Justice Kennedy concurred in the bulk of the majority's decision, but he refused to sign on to a portion of the opinion that criticized the dissenters' view of the nature of an agency's obligation to explain a policy change.[105] He agreed with the dissenters that under some circumstances, "the agency must explain why 'it now rejects the considerations that led it to adopt [the] initial policy.'"[106] Nonetheless, Justice Kennedy concluded that the question of whether

101. *Id.* at 514-15.
102. *Id.* at 515 (internal citation omitted).
103. *Id.* (internal citation omitted).
104. *Id.* at 515-16.
105. *Id.* at 535 (Kennedy, J., concurring).
106. *Id.* (quoting *id.* at 550 (Breyer, J., dissenting)).

an agency must provide "a more-reasoned explanation" for a change in policy is not susceptible to a single correct answer.[107] In his view:

> [t]he question in each case is whether the agency's reasons for the change, when viewed in light of the data available to it, and when informed by the experience and expertise of the agency, suffice to demonstrate that the new policy rests upon principles that are rational, neutral, and in accord with the agency's proper understanding of its authority.[108]

Thus, an agency would, for example, be required to provide a reasoned explanation for deviating from its prior factual findings.[109] Justice Kennedy concluded, however, that the FCC's explanation was adequate in this case because its new policy was based on a reasoned change in its legal position, rather than a different view of the relevant facts.[110]

Justice Breyer dissented on the ground that the FCC "failed adequately to explain *why* it *changed* its indecency policy from a policy permitting a single 'fleeting use' of an expletive, to a policy that made no such exception."[111] He described the obligation of an agency to explain a change in policy as follows:

> To explain a change requires more than setting forth reasons why the new policy is a good one. It also requires the agency to answer the question, "Why did you change?" And a rational answer to this question typically requires a more complete explanation than would prove satisfactory were change itself not at issue.[112]

Justice Breyer claimed that this approach would not impose "a heightened standard of review," but it would recognize that an agency's change in policy would ordinarily be *a relevant consideration* that must be addressed under the arbitrary and capricious standard.[113] Accordingly, an agency must "focus upon the reasons that led [it] to adopt the initial policy, and explain why it now comes to a new judgment."[114] Justice Breyer concluded that the FCC failed to satisfy this requirement because it "failed to consider two criti-

---

107. *Id.* at 535 (Kennedy, J., concurring).
108. *Id.* at 536.
109. *See id.* at 537-38.
110. *See id.* at 538.
111. *Id.* at 546-47 (Breyer, J., dissenting).
112. *Id.* at 549.
113. *Id.* at 550 (emphasis omitted) (internal quotation marks omitted).
114. *Id.*

cally important aspects of the problem that underlay its initial policy judgment"[115]—namely, the potential for a chilling effect on constitutionally protected speech and the potentially detrimental impact of the new policy on local broadcasters.[116]

The sharp divisions in *Fox TV* should not obscure the fact that there are significant areas of agreement.[117] First, the Justices agreed that an agency must "display awareness that it is changing position,"[118] and that it may not engage in stealth overruling of its previous policy determinations.[119] Second, the Justices agreed that an agency must provide a reasoned explanation for disregarding the data or factual findings that underlay its initial policy choices.[120] Third, the Justices agreed that an agency must address any serious reliance interests that were generated by its earlier policy decisions when it decides to change course.[121]

The Justices' disagreement therefore seemed to center primarily on the nature of an agency's obligation to explain policy changes that are based on changes in the agency's legal positions (and, in particular, changes to the agency's view of relevant constitutional doctrines or norms) or differences in "values" or other political considerations.[122] As to the first, Justice Scalia's

---

115. *Id.* at 553.
116. *See id.* at 553-62.
117. *See* Ronald M. Levin, *Hard Look Review, Policy Change, and* Fox Television, 65 U. MIAMI L. REV. 555, 564-67 (2011).
118. *Fox TV*, 556 U.S. at 515 (emphasis omitted).
119. *Cf.* Barry Friedman, *The Wages of Stealth Overruling (With Particular Attention to* Miranda v. Arizona*)*, 99 GEO. L.J. 1 (2010) (describing and criticizing the use of this technique by the Court).
120. *Fox TV*, 556 U.S. at 515-16; *id.* at 536 (Kennedy, J., concurring); *id.* at 550-51 (Breyer, J., dissenting).
121. *Id.* at 515 (majority opinion); *id.* at 536 (Kennedy, J., concurring) ("Reliance interests in the prior policy may also have weight in the analysis."); *id.* at 549 (Breyer, J., dissenting) (providing a hypothetical example of an agency that changed its policy from requiring driving on the right side of the road to driving on the left side of the road, and claiming that the agency would need to explain why it changed its position even if the initial decision was properly based on the flip of a coin).
122. *See* Levin, *supra* note 117, at 555-56 (claiming that "one lesson that seems to emerge from *Fox* is that when courts evaluate the rationality of an agency's change in policy, the nature of the agency's explanation for its decision can be crucial," and explaining that fact-based determinations will "cry out for explanation" in a way that might not be true when "the agency changes its policy for reasons that could be better described as a value judgment"); Richard Murphy, *Politics and Policy Change in Administrative Law*, 28

majority opinion rejected the notion that a "more stringent" form of judicial review applies to agency action that implicates constitutionally protected liberties (such as freedom of speech), and he stated that the validity of agency action under the arbitrary-and-capricious test presents "a separate question" from its constitutionality.[123] The majority was doubtful that an agency's decision could be deemed arbitrary or capricious merely because the agency failed to provide an adequate discussion of relevant Supreme Court precedent, and Justice Scalia pointed out that the FCC provided an extensive explanation for why it believed that its new fleeting expletives policy was consistent with the First Amendment.[124] Similarly, Justice Kennedy agreed with the judgment of the Court because the FCC's new policy was based on a different reading of the relevant judicial precedent rather than a changed view of the relevant facts.[125] In contrast, Justice Breyer argued that "where an agency rested its

---

WINDSOR Y.B. ACCESS TO JUST. 325, 336-39 (2010) (analyzing the opinions and explaining that "the difference revolves around treatment of policy choices based on evolving political preferences in the absence of any technocratic cover"). The Justices also seemed to disagree about whether changes in policies by independent agencies should be subject to less deference than changes made by executive agencies. *Compare Fox TV*, 556 U.S. at 525-26 (plurality opinion) (pointing out that the APA does not distinguish between executive and independent agencies, and claiming that "[t]here is no reason to magnify the separation-of-powers dilemma posed by the Headless Fourth Branch by letting Article III judges—like jackals stealing the lion's kill—expropriate some of the power that Congress has wrested from the unitary Executive") (internal citations omitted); *with id.* at 541 (Stevens, J., dissenting) (claiming that independent agencies are best viewed as agents of Congress, and that "[t]here should be a strong presumption that the FCC's initial views, reflecting the informed judgment of independent commissioners with expertise in the regulated area, also reflect the views of the Congress that delegated the Commission authority to flesh out details not fully defined in the enacting statute"); *and id.* at 547 (Breyer, J., dissenting) (claiming that an independent "agency's comparative freedom from ballot-box control makes it all the more important that courts review its decisionmaking to assure compliance with applicable provisions of law-including law requiring that major policy decisions be based upon articulable reasons"). For a more extensive discussion of this issue, see Randolph J. May, *Defining Deference Down, Again: Independent Agencies,* Chevron *Deference, and* Fox, 62 ADMIN. L. REV. 433 (2010).

123. *Fox TV*, 556 U.S. at 516 (refusing to apply "the avoidance canon" of statutory interpretation "to limit the scope of authorized executive action").

124. *See id.* at 526 (plurality opinion).

125. *Id.* at 538 (Kennedy J., concurring).

prior policy on its view of the governing law," the agency should be expected to focus on its previous legal views "and explain why they are no longer controlling."[126] He therefore concluded that the FCC's new policy was arbitrary or capricious because the agency never explained why it changed its legal position.[127]

The Justices also expressed starkly divergent views on the nature of an agency's obligation to justify policy changes that are based on different values or other political considerations. In this regard, the majority expressed a willingness to uphold changes in agency policy as long as the challenged decision is permissible under the statute and supported by "good reasons."[128] While the agency must also *believe* that the new policy is better than the old policy, this is adequately indicated by the agency's "conscious change of course."[129] The agency need not explain *why* it believes that the new policy is better or "demonstrate to a court's satisfaction that the reasons for the new policy are better than the reasons for the old one."[130] Accordingly, agencies are freely allowed to change policies whenever *they like* the new policy better than the old policy, as long as the new policy is consistent with law and supported by good reasons, and agencies are not obligated to explain *why* they like the new policy better.[131] This gives agencies significant leeway to change policies based on different values, and perhaps to change policies based on other political considerations. Indeed, Justice Scalia's opinion for a plurality candidly pointed out that "the precise policy change at issue here was spurred by significant political pressure from Congress."[132]

Justice Breyer argued, in contrast, that broad discretionary authority "does not permit [agencies] to make policy choices for purely political reasons nor to rest them primarily upon unexplained policy preferences."[133] On the contrary, arbitrary-and-capricious review under the APA "helps assure agency decision-making based upon more than the personal preferences of the decisionmakers."[134] While Justice Breyer recognized "that *sometimes* the ulti-

---

126. *Id.* at 550-51 (Breyer, J., dissenting).
127. *See id.* at 552-56.
128. *Id.* at 515 (majority opinion).
129. *Id.*
130. *Id.* (emphasis omitted).
131. *See* Murphy, *supra* -note 122, at 338 ("The short of the matter is that Justice Scalia and his fellow conservatives believe that political preferences may justify any agency choice among reasonable alternatives.").
132. *Fox TV*, 556 U.S. at 523.
133. *Id.* at 547 (Breyer, J., dissenting).
134. *Id.* at 548.

mate explanation for a change may have to be, 'We now weigh the relevant considerations differently,'" he claimed that an agency often "can and should say more."[135] Justice Breyer therefore expressed concern that the majority's decision could significantly change judicial review of agency action for the worse:

> After all, if it is *always* legally sufficient for the agency to reply to the question "why change?" with the answer "we prefer the new policy" (even when the agency *has not considered* the major factors that led it to adopt its old policy), then why bother asking the agency to focus on the fact of change? More to the point, *why* would the law exempt this and no other aspect of an agency decision from "arbitrary, capricious" review? Where does, and why would, the APA grant agencies the freedom to change major policies on the basis of nothing more than political considerations or even personal whim?[136]

While one cannot be sure, it appears that Justice Kennedy may have agreed with Justice Breyer on this score;[137] otherwise, it would be difficult to explain why he refused to join all of Justice Scalia's opinion.

Thus far, lower courts have not treated Justice Kennedy's concurring opinion as controlling precedent, as some commentators have urged.[138] Nor have they devoted sustained attention to the areas of disagreement reflected in the opinions. Rather, lower courts have simply followed the majority's view that

---

135. *Id.* at 550. *See also id.* at 567 (claiming that even if elected officials can justify policy changes merely by saying that they "like the new policy better," this kind of answer is frequently inadequate for administrative agencies).

136. *Id.* at 551-52.

137. *Id.* at 535 (Kennedy, J., concurring) (agreeing with Justice Breyer that in some circumstances, "the agency must explain why 'it now rejects the considerations that led it to adopt [the] initial policy'") (quoting *id.* at 550 (Breyer, J., dissenting)). *See also* text accompanying *supra* note 106; Murphy, *supra* note 122, at 336 (pointing out that Justice Kennedy "joined Justice Breyer's discussion of the proper framework for arbitrariness review of agency policy shifts, which thus attracted a majority vote").

138. *See* Toby Coleman, *Limiting Judges: Placing Limits on Judges' Power in Hard-look Review*, 88 U. DET. MERCY L. REV. 883, 911-12 (2011) (recognizing the potential significance of Justice Kennedy's concurring opinion and the difficulty of predicting its precedential value in the lower courts); Brian J. Shearer, Comment, *Out*foxing Alaska Hunters*: How Arbitrary and Capricious Review of Changing Regulatory Interpretations Can More Efficiently Police Agency Discretion*, 62 AM. U. L. REV. 167, 184 (2012).

an agency's policy change does not ordinarily require a more detailed explanation than the adoption of an initial policy, and they have essentially interpreted *Fox TV* as establishing the following test: "The new policy must be permissible under the statute; there must be good reasons for it; and the agency must believe that the new policy is better, 'which the conscious change of course adequately indicates.'"[139] Lower courts have also emphasized that agencies must *acknowledge* their policy changes, and they have therefore invalidated unexplained deviations from prior agency precedent in several cases.[140] When agencies have acknowledged their policy changes, the lower courts have generally focused on whether the agency's explanation for its new policy was reasonable,[141] and the D.C. Circuit has recently described this as a "low bar."[142] The lower courts have also recognized that under *Fox TV* agencies must explain their rejection of prior factual findings,[143] and they must address any serious reliance interests that would be upset by their changes in policy.[144]

8.027 Failure to Consider Alternative Solutions

> **[An agency action will be set aside as arbitrary and capricious if] the agency failed, without an adequate justification, to con-**

---

139. Handley v. Chapman, 587 F.3d 273, 282 (5th Cir. 2009) (quoting *Fox TV*, 556 U.S. at 515). *See also* Am. Elec. Power Serv. Corp. v. FCC, 708 F.3d 183, 186 (D.C. Cir. 2013); Modesto Irrigation Dist. v. Gutierrez, 619 F.3d 1024, 1034 (9th Cir. 2010); Ad Hoc Shrimp Trade Action Comm. v. United States, 596 F.3d 1365, 1372 (Fed. Cir. 2010).
140. *See* CBS Corp. v. FCC, 663 F.3d 122, 124 (3d Cir. 2011); Jicarilla Apache Nation v. U.S. Dept. of Interior, 613 F.3d 1112, 1119-20 (D.C. Cir. 2010); Dillmon v. Nat'l Transp. Safety Bd., 588 F.3d 1085, 1089-91 (D.C. Cir. 2009).
141. *See, e.g.*, *Modesto*, 619 F.3d at 1033-38.
142. Inv. Co. Inst. v. Commodity Futures Trading Comm'n, 720 F.3d 370, 377 (D.C. Cir. 2013).
143. *See, e.g.*, *Modesto*, 619 F.3d at 1034. *Cf.* Humane Soc'y of U.S. v. Locke, 626 F.3d 1040, 1047-53 (9th Cir. 2010) (invalidating a decision as arbitrary or capricious based on the agency's failure to address inconsistent factual findings that were rendered in a closely related matter).
144. *See, e.g.*, Quest Corp. v. FCC, 689 F.3d 1214, 1224-25, 1227-31 (10th Cir. 2012) (upholding an agency's change in policy despite the fact that it "engaged in some goalpost-moving" on the issue); Huvis Corp. v. United States, 570 F.3d 1347, 1355-56 (Fed. Cir. 2009) (upholding an agency's policy change and concluding that the plaintiff did not "detrimentally rely" on the agency's prior approach to the problem).

sider or adopt an important alternative solution to the problem addressed in the action.

[Blackletter Statement, Part 3, § V.G.]

Just as a decision should, under subsection 8.026, be "rational" in the broader context of an agency's past regulatory efforts, it should be "rational" when viewed in light of alternative solutions that the agency might have adopted. Agencies must consider significant alternatives when making policy decisions. Like subsection 8.025 (consideration of important aspects), this subsection requires the agency to demonstrate consideration of these alternatives in the explanation it provides for its ultimate policy choice. Failure to do so renders the agency's explanation incomplete and its policy decision arbitrary.

The difficult question is which policy alternatives the agency must consider. In *State Farm*, the Supreme Court cautioned that "a rulemaking 'cannot be found wanting simply because the agency failed to include every alternative device and thought conceivable by the mind of man . . . regardless of how uncommon or unknown that alternative may have been . . . .'"[145] In short, agencies do not have to consider every conceivable option. Such a requirement surely would inhibit or prevent them from issuing policy decisions by increasing the transaction costs of such action.

In *State Farm*, the Court required the agency to consider alternatives "within the ambit of the existing standard."[146] NHTSA had failed to consider an airbags-only requirement as an alternative to rescinding a rule requiring automobile manufacturers to install either airbags *or* automatic seatbelts at their choosing. Because the agency already had considered requiring airbags in the context of adopting its broader passive restraint standard, it would not have imposed undue burdens or consumed excessive resources for the agency to consider mandating airbags alone before rescinding the standard entirely.[147]

Lower courts have imposed a broader obligation on agencies not only to consider those alternatives that are a subset of the decision made but also others that are significant or important. Thus, lower courts have required agencies to consider alternatives that "appear[] to serve precisely the agency's

---

145. Motor Vehicle Mfrs. Ass'n v. State Farm Mut. Auto Ins. Co., 463 U.S. 29, 51 (1983) (quoting Vt. Yankee Nuclear Power Corp. v. Natural Res. Def. Council, 435 U.S. 519, 551 (1977)).

146. *Id.*

147. *Id.*

purported goals,"[148] those that are "plausible,"[149] and those that represent "less restrictive, yet easily administered" measures.[150]

Often an agency does not utterly fail to consider relevant alternatives but instead gives them limited or minimal consideration. Courts should review such consideration applying the normal arbitrary and capricious factors.[151] They should not evaluate the rationality of the rejection or the ultimate policy choice according to their own independent judgment. Thus, this part of the inquiry—like the subsection 8.026 inquiry—is best understood as a specific application of the criteria in earlier provisions of this report rather than an addition.

8.028 Failure to Respond to Relevant Arguments or Comments

> **[An agency action will be set aside as arbitrary and capricious if] the agency failed to consider substantial arguments, or respond to relevant and significant comments, made by the participants in the proceeding that gave rise to the agency action.**
> **[Blackletter Statement, Part 3, § V.H.]**

---

148. Office of Commc'n of the United Church of Christ v. FCC, 779 F.2d 702, 714 (D.C. Cir. 1985). *See also* Wilderness Watch, Inc. v. U.S. Fish & Wildlife Serv., 629 F.3d 1024, 1036-39 (9th Cir. 2010) (invalidating agency's approval of construction of water structures in wilderness area to conserve bighorn sheep when "the record demonstrates that many alternative actions not prohibited by the Wilderness Act very well could have attained the Service's goal," and the Service failed to consider whether the new water structures were necessary at all in light of those alternatives) (emphasis omitted).
149. Qwest Commc'ns. Int'l, Inc. v. FCC, 229 F.3d 1172, 1183 (D.C. Cir. 2000). *Cf.* Se. Alaska Conservation Council v. Fed. Highway Admin., 649 F.3d 1050, 1056-59 (9th Cir. 2011) (invalidating an agency's decision for failing to consider a "reasonable" alternative under NEPA); Chamber of Commerce of U.S. v. SEC, 412 F.3d 133, 144-45 (D.C. Cir. 2005) (holding that the SEC's failure to consider a "disclosure alternative" was arbitrary and capricious when the alternative proposal was "a familiar tool in the Commission's tool kit" and "was neither frivolous nor out of bounds").
150. Cincinnati Bell Tel. Co. v. FCC, 69 F.3d 752, 761 (6th Cir. 1995).
151. *See, e.g.*, *Se. Alaska Conservation Council*, 649 F.3d at 1058; *Qwest Commc'ns*, 229 F.3d at 1184; Farmers Union Cent. Exch., Inc. v. FERC, 734 F.2d 1486, 1511-21 (D.C. Cir. 1984); Pub. Citizen v. Steed, 733 F.2d 93, 99 (D.C. Cir. 1984).

This subsection concerns the agency's consideration of the arguments of the parties participating in the proceeding before it. Like the preceding two subsections, it describes a specific application of the agency's general obligation to provide an explanation for its policy choice that demonstrates reasoned decisionmaking.

The difficulty under this subsection, as with subsections 8.025 (consideration of important aspects) and 8.027 (consideration of important alternative solutions), is determining which submissions require a response. Courts have long held that an agency must respond to "relevant" and "significant" comments but not to "speculative" ones.[152] Thus, the agency is not required to discuss every fact or opinion submitted to it.[153] Instead, the agency need only enable the reviewing court "to see what major issues of policy were ventilated . . . and why [it] reacted to them as it did."[154] Furthermore, the agency need not respond to comments that are "purely speculative and do not dis-

---

152. Home Box Office, Inc. v. FCC, 567 F.2d 9, 35 n.58 (D.C. Cir. 1977). *See also* United States v. N.S. Food Prods. Corp., 568 F.2d 240, 252-53 (2d Cir. 1977) (relying both on the arbitrary-and-capricious standard and on the APA's requirement that the agency accompany a final rule with a "concise general statement of basis and purpose") (quoting Auto. Parts & Accessories Ass'n v. Boyd, 407 F.2d 330, 338 (D.C. Cir. 1968)); Portland Cement Ass'n v. Ruckelshaus, 486 F.2d 375, 394 (D.C. Cir. 1973) (stating that once a comment is "significant enough to step over a threshold requirement of materiality," the "lack of agency response or consideration becomes of concern"). For recent examples of courts applying these principles, see Ass'n of Private Sector Colls. & Univs. v. Duncan, 681 F.3d 427, 441, 448-49 (D.C. Cir. 2012); Sierra Club v. Van Antwerp, 661 F.3d 1147, 1156-57 (D.C. Cir. 2012); Cape Cod Hosp. v. Sebelius, 630 F.3d 203, 211-17 (D.C. Cir. 2011). *See also* W. Watersheds Project v. Kraayenbrink, 632 F.3d 472, 492-95 (9th Cir. 2011) (holding that a decision was arbitrary and capricious in violation of NEPA because "the BLM failed to address concerns raised by its own experts, FWS, the EPA, and state agencies").

153. *See, e.g.*, Nat'l Shooting Sports Found., Inc. v. Jones, 716 F.3d 200, 215-17 (D.C. Cir. 2013); Sherley v. Sebelius, 689 F.3d 776, 784-85 (D.C. Cir. 2012); Earth Island Inst. v. Carlton, 626 F.3d 462, 472-73 (9th Cir. 2010); Am. Mining Cong. v. EPA, 907 F.2d 1179, 1187-91 (D.C. Cir. 1990); Thompson v. Clark, 741 F.2d 401, 408 (D.C. Cir. 1984).

154. Auto. Parts & Accessories Ass'n v. Boyd, 407 F.2d 330, 338 (D.C. Cir. 1968). *See also* City of Portland, Or. v. EPA, 507 F.3d 706, 714 (D.C. Cir. 2007); Mortg. Investors Corp. of Ohio v. Gober, 220 F.3d 1375, 1379 (Fed. Cir. 2000); Int'l Fabricare Inst. v. EPA, 972 F.2d 384 (D.C. Cir. 1992); South Carolina *ex rel.* Tindal v. Block, 717 F.2d 874, 886 (4th Cir. 1983).

close the factual or policy basis on which they rest,"[155] or those that are remote or insignificant.[156] Of course, these general pronouncements hardly predict concrete applications.

A special problem occurs when an agency fails to make a preliminary disclosure of the theories, data, or studies upon which it bases its action, thereby depriving interested persons of a full opportunity to comment. The issue is whether these circumstances justify reduced confidence in the rationality of the agency action. Some courts have so held.[157] Other courts have cautioned against requiring agencies to "subject each and every study to notice and comment."[158] These decisions:

> reflect the commonsense recognition that Congress, in providing for notice and comment under the APA, could not have intended to subject the agencies—and the public on whose behalf they regulate—to the sort of interminable back-and-forth petitioners [who seek an op-

155. *Home Box Office, Inc.*, 567 F.2d at 35 n.58.
156. Ctr. for Auto Safety v. Peck, 751 F.2d 1336, 1355 n.14 (D.C. Cir. 1985). *See also Nat'l Shooting*, 716 F.3d at 215-17; *Sherley*, 689 F.3d at 784-85; Ecology Ctr. v. Castaneda, 574 F.3d 652, 668 (9th Cir. 2009); *City of Portland, Or.*, 507 F.3d at 714-15; *Pub. Citizen, Inc.*, 988 F.2d at 197; City Nat'l Bank v. Smith, 513 F.2d 479, 484 (D.C. Cir. 1975).
157. *See, e.g.*, Am. Radio Relay League, Inc. v. FCC, 524 F.3d 227, 236-40 (D.C. Cir. 2008); Owner-Operator Indep. Drivers Ass'n v. Fed. Motor Carrier Safety Admin., 494 F.3d 188, 199-203 (D.C. Cir. 2007); Aqua Slide 'N' Dive Corp. v. CPSC, 569 F.2d 831, 842-43 (5th Cir. 1978); *N.S. Food Prods. Corp.*, 568 F.2d at 252-53; *Portland Cement Ass'n*, 486 F.2d at 392-93. *Cf.* Solite Corp. v. EPA, 952 F.2d 473, 499-500 (D.C. Cir. 1991) (agency's reliance on new data and calculations that had not been available at proposed rule stage deprives private parties of opportunity to comment). *Cf.* Chamber of Commerce v. SEC, 443 F.3d 890, 899-908 (D.C. Cir. 2006) (holding that on remand from an earlier decision of the D.C. Circuit, the Commission violated the comment requirement of section 553, because it "relied on extra-record material critical to its costs estimates without affording an opportunity for comment to the prejudice of the Chamber").
158. *Int'l Fabricare*, 972 F.2d at 399 (citation omitted); Cmty. Nutrition Inst. v. Block, 749 F.2d 50, 57-58 (D.C. Cir. 1984). *See also* Echostar Satellite L.L.C. v. FCC, 457 F.3d 31, 40 (D.C. Cir. 2006) (concluding that it was unnecessary to provide further opportunity for comment on the agency's data and analysis because the relevant statements merely involved "the agency staff's own cogitations upon the evidence in the record," and explaining that if parties were

portunity to comment on withheld information after the promulgation of the final rule] would have [the court] require.[159]

There are other reasons to reject this back-and-forth with respect to rulemaking as well as other agency action. The APA, the Due Process Clause, and other procedural mandates already require agencies to provide notice of the issues in controversy in both rulemaking[160] and adjudicative proceedings.[161] Furthermore, a heightened disclosure requirement, taken to its logical extreme, would pressure agencies to issue tentative decisions even in adjudicative and ratemaking proceedings, although those decisions would be of little interest to the public at large. It also would come close to constituting a judicially created procedural requirement, which *Vermont Yankee Nuclear Power Corp. v. NRDC*[162] forbids. Some courts have recognized the potential *Vermont Yankee* problem,

---

"entitled to comment upon every observation an agency staff member draws from the record it accrues, rulemaking proceedings would be interminable"); *Chamber of Commerce*, 443 F.3d at 900 (explaining that "further notice and comment are not required when additional fact gathering merely supplements information in the rulemaking record by checking or confirming prior assessments without changing methodology, by confirming or corroborating data in the rulemaking record, or by internally generating information using a methodology disclosed in the rulemaking record") (internal citations omitted).

159. *Int'l Fabricare*, 972 F.2d at 399 (citing City of Stoughton, Wis. v. EPA, 858 F.2d 747, 753 (D.C. Cir. 1988)).

160. *See, e.g.*, 5 U.S.C. § 553(b)(3) (2000); Ass'n of Private Sector Colls. & Univs. v. Duncan, 681 F.3d 427, 441, 461-63 (D.C. Cir. 2012); Prometheus Radio Project v. FCC, 652 F.3d 431, 449-53 (3d Cir. 2011); Global Van Lines, Inc. v. ICC, 714 F.2d 1290, 1297-98 (5th Cir. 1983); Am. Standard, Inc. v. United States, 602 F.2d 256, 268 (Ct. Cl. 1979). For discussion of notice requirements in federal rulemaking, see Jeffrey S. Lubbers, A Guide to Federal Agency Rulemaking (3d ed. 1998).

161. *See, e.g.*, 5 U.S.C. § 554(b)(3) (2000); Bowman Transp., Inc. v. Ark.-Best Freight Sys., Inc., 419 U.S. 281, 288 n.4 (1974); Goldberg v. Kelly, 397 U.S. 254, 267-68 (1970); *In re* Biedermann, 733 F.3d 329, 336-39 (Fed. Cir. 2013); Indep. Elec. Contractors of Hous., Inc. v. NLRB, 720 F.3d 543, 552-54 (5th Cir. 2013); Soule Glass & Glazing Co. v. NLRB, 652 F.2d 1055, 1073-75, 1100-02 (1st Cir. 1981); Golden Grain Macaroni Co. v. FTC, 472 F.2d 882, 885-87 (9th Cir. 1972). For a discussion of notice requirements in federal agency adjudications, see A Guide to Federal Agency Adjudication § 4.01 (Michael Asimow ed. 2003).

162. 435 U.S. 519 (1978).

treating the disclosure requirement as an implementation of APA § 553 or similar legislation rather than as a freestanding principle of judicial review.[163]

8.029 Disproportionate Sanctions

> **[An agency action will be set aside as arbitrary and capricious if] the agency has imposed a sanction that is greatly out of proportion to the magnitude of the violation.**
>
> **[Blackletter Statement, Part 3, § V.I.]**

Courts sometimes will vacate or modify a sanction imposed by an agency because it deems the remedy too broad or too severe in relation to the violation.[164] Courts also will assess whether a remedy is unfairly retroactive.[165] In such cases, it is hard to see the courts as doing anything other than declaring that the agency has made an improvident discretionary decision. Of course, this judicial power should be restricted to correction of "arbitrary" errors and does not extend to every case where a court disagrees with an agency's choice of remedy.[166]

---

163. *See, e.g.*, Am. Radio Relay League, Inc. v. FCC, 524 F.3d 227, 236-40 (D.C. Cir. 2008) (holding that "the Commission . . . failed to comply with the APA by not disclosing in full certain studies by its staff upon which the Commission relied in promulgating the rule," and arguing that its decision did not violate the *Vermont Yankee* principle because "the court does not impose any new procedures for the regulatory process, but merely applies settled law to the facts"); Ass'n of Data Processing Serv. Orgs., Inc. v. Bd. of Govs., 745 F.2d 677, 684-85 (D.C. Cir. 1984); Wash. Trollers Ass'n v. Kreps, 645 F.2d 684, 686 (9th Cir. 1981).
164. *See, e.g.*, FTC v. Royal Milling Co., 288 U.S. 212, 217-18 (1933); Morall v. Drug Enforcement Admin., 412 F.3d 165, 181-84 (D.C. Cir. 2005) (holding that revocation of a physician's license to dispense controlled substances for recordkeeping failures was arbitrary and capricious when failures occurred during brief time period of personal stress, physician had expressed regret, and DEA had declined to revoke registration of any other physician in comparable situation); Chrysler Corp. v. FTC, 561 F.2d 357, 364 (D.C. Cir. 1977) (selectively rejecting particular provisions in overbroad cease-and-desist order); Spiegel, Inc. v. FTC, 540 F.2d 287, 295-97 (7th Cir. 1976) (narrowing cease-and-desist order).
165. *See, e.g.*, Buccaneer Point Estates, Inc. v. United States, 729 F.2d 1297 (11th Cir. 1984); McDonald v. Watt, 653 F.2d 1035 (5th Cir. 1981); NLRB v. E & B Brewing Co., 276 F.2d 594 (6th Cir. 1960). *See also supra* notes 91, 118-21, 140 and accompanying text (recognizing an agency's obligation to address serious reliance interests when it changes policies).
166. *See* Butz v. Glover Livestock Comm'n Co., 411 U.S. 182 (1973).

8.0210 Other Shortcomings

> **[An agency action will be set aside as arbitrary and capricious if] the action fails in other respects to rest upon reasoned decisionmaking.**
>
> **[Blackletter Statement, Part 3, § V.J.]**

This is a catchall category. This subsection might be seen to extend to cases in which courts conclude that an agency has not thought about the issues seriously enough to make its decision "rational."[167] However, for the most part, such cases are subsumed in prior subsections. One exception, perhaps, is *National Lime Association*, in which the court implied that the agency had acted arbitrarily by exercising its discretion on the basis of something less than a full-dress policy analysis.[168] As Ron Levin has pointed out, this type of thinking was the product of a climate "in which lower courts broadly asserted that they may 'intervene [when] the agency has not really taken a "hard look" at the salient problems and has not genuinely engaged in reasoned decisionmaking.'"[169] Courts now counter this notion or its equivalent with the sentiment from *Overton Park* and *State Farm* characterizing "the ultimate standard of review [as] a narrow one"[170] and admonishing courts not to "substitute [their] judgment for that of the agency."[171] And in reviewing an agency's rationale, they search for the specific shortcomings identified in *State Farm* and described in the prior subsections rather than searching for a general failure to engage in reasoned decision making, as in *National Lime Association*. Nonetheless, "a general failure of reasoned decision making" may continue to be the only way to capture certain cases that cannot be explained in any other way.

---

167. That is the characterization offered by Ron Levin in discussing identical language in the Administrative Law Section's 1986 "Restatement." *See* Ronald M. Levin, *Scope-of-Review Doctrine Restated: An Administrative Law Section Report*, 38 ADMIN. L. REV. 239, 259 (1986) (citing United States v. Garner, 767 F.2d 104, 116-18 (5th Cir. 1985); Md. People's Counsel v. FERC, 761 F.2d 768 (D.C. Cir. 1985); Nat'l Lime Ass'n v. EPA, 627 F.2d 416, 431 (D.C. Cir. 1980); Cent. Fl. Enters., Inc. v. FCC, 598 F.2d 37, 50 (D.C. Cir. 1978)).
168. *See Nat'l Lime Ass'n*, 627 F.2d at 452-53.
169. Levin, *supra* note 167, at 259 (quoting Greater Bos. Television Corp. v. FCC, 444 F.2d 841, 851 (D.C. Cir. 1970)).
170. Citizens to Preserve Overton Park, Inc. v. Volpe, 401 U.S. 402, 416 (1971)
171. *Id.*; Motor Vehicle Mfrs. Ass'n v. State Farm Mut. Auto Ins. Co., 463 U.S. 29, 43 (1983).

Another possible application of this general catchall category may require agencies to supply standards guiding and limiting the exercise of their delegated regulatory authority. In *Whitman v. American Trucking Associations*,[172] the Supreme Court rejected the D.C. Circuit's attempt to use the nondelegation doctrine, which in theory bars delegation of legislative power to agencies, to require agencies to supply such standards limiting their own discretion to within constitutional limits. The Court held that agency-promulgated standards by definition cannot cure an excessive congressional delegation, only Congress can provide the constraint required under the nondelegation doctrine.[173] Although *Whitman* rejected the idea that the nondelegation doctrine requires agencies to limit their discretion, it left open the issue of whether agencies must limit their discretion to avoid arbitrary decision-making. The D.C. Circuit has so held in at least one case, finding that the arbitrary-and-capricious test required an agency to define specific criteria to guide and limit its discretion.[174] Some commentators have embraced this use of the arbitrary-and-capricious test as an effort to democratize delegation by, among other things, preventing arbitrary administrative lawmaking and reducing the influence of private interest groups at the administrative level.[175] Others have argued, in the context of a constitutionally mandated administrative standards requirement, that such a requirement would impair administrative flexibility.[176]

8.03 POLITICAL REASONS AND JUDICIAL REVIEW OF AGENCY DISCRETION

Judicial review of agency discretion "has gotten relatively little attention during the past two decades or so, because both courts and commentators have devoted themselves instead to exploring, somewhat obsessively, the intricacies of judicial review of issues of law . . . primarily through elaboration of the so-

---

172. 531 U.S. 457 (2001).

173. *Id.* at 472-76.

174. *See* Pearson v. Shalala, 164 F.3d 650, 660-61 (D.C. Cir. 1999).

175. *See* Lisa Schultz Bressman, *Disciplining Delegation after* Whitman v. American Trucking Ass'ns, 87 CORNELL L. REV. 452, 457-69 (2002); Lisa Schultz Bressman, Schechter Poultry *at the Millennium: A Delegation Doctrine for the Administrative State*, 109 YALE L.J. 1399, 1417-18, 1422-24 (2000); Cass R. Sunstein, *Is the Clean Air Act Unconstitutional?* 98 MICH. L. REV. 303, 369-70 (1999).

176. *See* Mark Seidenfeld & Jim Rossi, *The False Promise of the "New" Nondelegation Doctrine*, 76 NOTRE DAME L. REV. 1 (2000).

called *Chevron* doctrine."[177] Courts and scholars have begun to devote renewed attention to this subject, however, partly because the Supreme Court's decisions in *Massachusetts v. EPA* and *Fox TV* raise fundamental questions about the proper role of "political reasons" in agency decisionmaking and judicial review of agency discretion,[178] which turn in part on one's theory of the democratic legitimacy of administrative discretion in the modern regulatory state.[179] The dominant theories of administrative legitimacy have gradually evolved from the traditional notion that agencies merely served as a "transmission belt" for implementing the policy choices of Congress, to the New Deal era's view that discretionary authority enabled agencies to solve social problems identified by the legislature through the application of "neutral expertise." When society lost faith in the notion that agencies could objectively solve social problems through the application of neutral expertise, and agency policymaking came to be viewed as inherently political, the interest-group representation model of administrative legitimacy emerged. Market failures in the political process of agency decision-making led, in turn, to a general recognition that the administrative process could not be "perfected" in a manner that would reliably reflect the pre-political preferences of all of the relevant interests.

Thus, beginning in the early 1980s, the "political control model" emerged as the dominant theory of the legitimacy of the regulatory state.[180] This model "focuses on the ability of elected officials to supervise and control the discretionary policy choices of regulatory agencies as the basis for democratic le-

---

177. Levin, *supra* note 117, at 556.

178. *See supra* §§ 8.022 & 8.026. The proper definition of "political reasons" is contested in the recent scholarly literature. For example, some scholars define political reasons as any reasons that emanate from elected officials or high-level members of their staffs, while other scholars define political reasons as political preferences that are not directly relevant to the merits of the policy decision at issue. *See* Glen Staszewski, *Political Reasons, Deliberative Democracy, and Administrative Law*, 97 IOWA L. REV. 849, 860-61 (2012) (discussing the competing definitions and following the latter approach).

179. For some leading sources on the intellectual history of the democratic legitimacy of administrative discretion, see, e.g., Lisa Schultz Bressman, *Beyond Accountability: Arbitrariness and Legitimacy in the Administrative State*, 78 N.Y.U. L. REV. 461, 469-91 (2003); Elena Kagan, *Presidential Administration*, 114 HARV. L. REV. 2245, 2272-83 (2001); Richard B. Stewart, *The Reformation of American Administrative Law*, 88 HARV. L. REV. 1669, 1671-88 (1975).

180. *See* Bressman, *supra* note 179, at 485-92; Kathryn A. Watts, *Proposing a Place for Politics in Arbitrary and Capricious Review*, 119 YALE L.J. 2, 35-39 (2009).

gitimacy."[181] The central idea is that if agencies are following the preferences of elected officials who are politically accountable to voters, then agencies' policy decisions will be democratically legitimate because they will presumably reflect the will of the people and achieve the consent of the governed.[182] Although such political control could be exercised by Congress, most scholars have concluded that the President is better situated to perform this function as the only nationally elected official in the United States, and "the one person who speaks for the entire nation."[183] If the President strays from the people's will, she (or her party) can be held politically accountable at the next election.[184] From this perspective, "Congress's delegation of broad policymaking authority to regulatory agencies . . . can be legitimized if agency decisions are subject to the control of the Chief Executive who is politically accountable to all of the nation's voters."[185]

If administrative discretion is ultimately justified by presidential or political control of agency decision making, it arguably makes little sense for agencies and courts to ignore those political influences when agencies explain their policy decisions. Yet, this is precisely what has happened under the conventional understanding of hard-look judicial review, which posits that "agencies should explain their decisions in technocratic, statutory, or scientifically driven terms, *not* political terms."[186] Several prominent scholars have therefore recently argued that political reasons should play a larger and more transparent role in administrative decisionmaking, and that federal courts should give agencies credit for providing political reasons for their policy decisions in a variety of contexts.[187]

---

181. Staszewski, *supra* note 178, at 856. *See also* Watts, *supra* note 180, at 35.
182. *See, e.g.*, McNollgast, *The Political Economy of Law*, *in* 2 Handbook of Law and Economics 1651, 1663 (A. Mitchell Polinsky & Steven Shavell eds., 2007); Matthew C. Stephenson, *Optimal Political Control of the Bureaucracy*, 107 Mich. L. Rev. 53, 56-58 (2008).
183. Bressman, *supra* note 179, at 490. *See also* Staszewski, *supra* note 178, at 858-59 (describing the presidential control model). For a thorough analysis of congressional influences on agency action, see Jack M. Beermann, *Congressional Administration*, 43 San Diego L. Rev. 61 (2006).
184. *See* Bressman, *supra* note 179, at 491.
185. Staszewski, *supra* note 178, at 859.
186. Watts, *supra* note 180, at 5.
187. *See* Nina A. Mendelson, *Disclosing "Political" Oversight of Agency Decision Making*, 108 Mich. L. Rev. 1127, 1173-75 (2010); Watts, *supra* note 180, at 32-45. *See also* Christopher F. Edley, Jr., Administrative Law: Rethinking Judicial Control of Bureaucracy 190-92 (1990) (advocating "a judicial insistence that agencies frankly acknowledge the role of political, ideological, or

Around the same time that the political control model of administrative legitimacy was developing, courts and scholars also began to emphasize the role that the deliberative process can perform in legitimizing agency discretion from the standpoint of democracy.[188] In contrast to political control theories, which maintain that government should ascertain and implement the pre-political preferences of citizens or their representatives, deliberative models of administrative legitimacy focus on the obligation of public officials to engage in reasoned deliberation on which courses of action will promote the public good.[189] From this perspective, agency officials must engage in a decision-making process that considers a broad range of interests and views,[190] and they must provide reasoned explanations for their decisions that could reasonably be accepted by free and equal citizens with fundamentally competing perspectives.[191] Agency decisions adopted pursuant to these criteria are democratically legitimate because each interest and perspective is treated with equal respect, and arbitrary decisionmaking is prohibited.[192] A deliberative

---

subjective analyses in their reasons and findings," and suggesting that courts should give credit to politics "as an acceptable and even desirable element of decision making" in appropriate circumstances); Kagan, *supra* note 179, at 2380 (advocating a relaxation in "the rigors of hard look review when demonstrable evidence shows that the President has taken an active role in, and by so doing has accepted responsibility for, the administrative decision in question"); Pierce, *supra* note 38, at 72-73 (claiming that agencies should be able to rely on any logically relevant factor that is not precluded from consideration by statute in making their decisions).

188. *See, e.g.*, Seidenfeld, *supra* note 7; Cass R. Sunstein, *Interest Groups in American Public Law*, 38 STAN. L. REV. 29 (1985). For examples of more recent work that develops this perspective, see Evan J. Criddle, *Fiduciary Administration: Rethinking Popular Representation in Agency Rulemaking*, 88 TEX. L. REV. 441 (2010); HENRY S. RICHARDSON, DEMOCRATIC AUTONOMY: PUBLIC REASONING ABOUT THE ENDS OF POLICY (2002); Mark Seidenfeld, *The Role of Politics in a Deliberative Model of the Administrative State*, 81 GEO. WASH. L. REV. 1397 (2013) [hereinafter, "Seidenfeld, *Role of Politics*"]; Staszewski, *supra* note 178; Glen Staszewski, *Reason-Giving and Accountability*, 93 MINN. L. REV. 1253 (2009).
189. Staszewski, *supra* note 178, at 857-58.
190. *See, e.g.*, RICHARDSON, *supra* note 188, at 213.
191. For influential statements of this requirement in deliberative democratic theory, *see, e.g.*, AMY GUTMANN & DENNIS THOMPSON, DEMOCRACY AND DISAGREEMENT 52-94 (1996); Joshua Cohen, *Democracy and Liberty*, *in* DELIBERATIVE DEMOCRACY 185, 193-94 (Jon Elster ed., 1998).
192. *See* Staszewski, *supra* note 188, at 1282-84, 1291 (discussing the capacity of reason giving to promote the legitimacy of governmental authority in a democracy).

model of administrative legitimacy is based on broader theories of deliberative democracy, which seek to eliminate arbitrary governmental action and reach the best decisions on the merits in light of the available information and fundamental differences of opinion.

Deliberative models of administrative legitimacy are more concerned with the substantive merits of particular arguments, positions, or policy choices than with the status or identity of the advocates of a particular position or how many people hold a certain view. Therefore, the proponents of such models tend to share the traditional view that arbitrary-and-capricious review is a process that should focus on the merits of an agency's policy choice rather than other political considerations.[193] Moreover, judges and scholars who are sympathetic to this perspective would naturally view proposals to alter hard look review by giving agencies credit for justifying their decisions based on political reasons as highly problematic and potentially quite destabilizing to the basic quality and legitimacy of the modern regulatory state. On the other hand, political preferences are not necessarily irrelevant to administrative decisionmaking under the principles of deliberative democratic theory. Accordingly, scholars have recently addressed the more limited role that would be appropriate for political reasons in administrative law from this theoretical perspective.[194]

The Supreme Court has neither settled on one theory of legitimacy for the administrative state nor adopted a uniform attitude toward the value of political reasons in judicial review of agency discretion. Rather, the Court's disagreement or ambivalence on these fundamental questions of administrative law has resulted in co-existing lines of precedent that are in some philosophical tension with one another on these issues. Justice Rehnquist's partial dissent in *State Farm* pointed out that the agency's challenged position "seems to be related to the election of a new president of a different political party," and suggested that "[a] change in administration brought about by the people casting their votes is a perfectly reasonable basis for an executive agency's reappraisal of the costs and benefits of its programs and regulations."[195] Be-

---

193. *See, e.g.*, Mark Seidenfeld, *The Irrelevance of Politics for Arbitrary and Capricious Review*, 90 WASH. U. L. REV. 141 (2012) (claiming that while agencies may properly consider certain political influences in making their decisions, those political influences may not be considered by courts under the arbitrary and capricious standard of review); Staszewski, *supra* note 178, at 891-93.

194. *See, e.g.*, Seidenfeld, *Role of Politics*, *supra* note 188; Staszewski, *supra* note 178.

195. Motor Vehicle Mfrs. Ass'n v. State Farm Mut. Auto Ins. Co., 463 U.S. 29, 59 (1983) (Rehnquist, J., concurring in part and dissenting in part).

cause the Court declined to address this aspect of Justice Rehnquist's opinion and invalidated the agency's decision on the merits, the conventional wisdom is that *State Farm* rejected the notion that political reasons can justify an agency's discretionary policy choices under the arbitrary and capricious standard.[196] *State Farm* is therefore far more compatible with the deliberative model of administrative legitimacy than with a political control model.[197] Conversely, the Court justified judicial deference to administrative interpretations of ambiguous statutory provisions in *Chevron* by characterizing the requisite decisions as policy choices, and stating that "an agency to which Congress has delegated policy-making responsibilities may, within the limits of that delegation, properly rely upon the incumbent administration's views of wise policy to inform its judgment."[198] The Court emphasized that "[w]hile agencies are not directly accountable to the people, the Chief Executive is, and it is entirely appropriate for this political branch of the Government to make such policy choices."[199] *Chevron* is therefore widely understood to reflect the presidential control model of administrative legitimacy and embrace political influences on agency decision making.[200]

A quarter century later, the Court rejected political reasons emanating from the White House as a valid justification for the EPA's refusal to regulate greenhouse gases, and remanded the matter for the agency to reconsider its decision in light of technocratic considerations.[201] Jody Freeman and Adrian Vermeule have therefore characterized the Court's approach as "expertise-forcing," and aptly described *Massachusetts* as "*State Farm* for a new generation."[202] Meanwhile, Justice Scalia's opinion in *Fox TV* upheld an agency's decision that was admittedly based upon political pressure from Congress,

---

196. *See* Watts, *supra* note 180, at 19 (explaining that *State Farm* "has been widely read over time to represent the triumph of expertise to the exclusion of politics").
197. *See* Staszewski, *supra* note 178, at 891-92.
198. Chevron U.S.A., Inc. v. Natural Res. Def. Council, Inc., 467 U.S. 837, 865 (1984).
199. *Id.*
200. *See* Watts, *supra* note 180, at 37-38.
201. *See supra* notes 38-44 and accompanying text.
202. *See* Freeman & Vermeule, *supra* note 41, at 98. *Cf.* Murphy, *supra* note 122, at 328, 333-39 (providing an insightful analysis of *Fox TV*, and arguing that "[w]here a reviewing judge has reason to think that strong political preferences (or pressure) are affecting agency judgment, that judge should scrutinize the agency's explanation for a decision with a sharper eye—or dare one say—a harder look").

and excused agencies from providing thorough explanations for changing their positions whenever agencies evidently preferred their new policies based on differences in values.[203] While Justice Breyer was concerned about the corrosive effect that this decision could have on the quality of agency deliberations,[204] Justice Scalia's opinion could aptly be described as "*Chevron* for a new generation."

These are, of course, not minor or obscure judicial decisions that have been overlooked by lower courts or scholars. They are instead some of the greatest hits of modern administrative law. The fact that these decisions reflect fundamentally different attitudes toward "political reasons" and the democratic legitimacy of the modern regulatory state suggests that the best justification for administrative discretion may ultimately be an essentially contested concept.

---

203. *See supra* notes 128-132 and accompanying text. *See also* Levin, *supra* note 117, at 555 (recognizing that *Fox TV* "will at least slightly broaden the capacity of an administration to pursue an agenda of change" based on differences in value judgments, and arguing "that this development is, on the whole, salutary").

204. *See* FCC v. Fox Television Stations, Inc., 556 U.S. 502, 551-52 (Breyer, J., dissenting).

Chapter 9

ANCILLARY ISSUES CONCERNING AGENCY EXPLANATIONS

by Harold J. Krent*

9.01 INTRODUCTION

In order to decide whether an agency action violates applicable standards of review, as set forth above, courts examine material portions of the agency's own proffered rationale. They normally will allow an agency to defend its action only on the basis of reasons articulated prior to judicial review and will not supply their own rationale for discretionary agency conduct or speculate as to the conceivable purposes underlying the action. A court may deem an error in reasoning to be harmless error if the agency clearly would have reached the same result even if it had not made the error.

[Blackletter Statement, Part 3, § VI.]

9.02 THE AGENCY'S CONTEMPORANEOUS EXPLANATION

An explanation issued contemporaneously with an agency action is treated as containing the agency's actual rationale for taking the action, unless the party challenging the action impeaches the explanation with a strong showing of bad faith or improper behavior.

[Blackletter Statement, Part 3, § VI, ¶ 1.]

The validity of any agency's exercise of discretion typically turns on the rationale used by the agency at the time of its action. The Supreme Court in

* Dean and Professor of Law, IIT Chicago-Kent College of Law.

SEC v. Chenery Corp.[1] held that discretionary administrative action will be upheld only on grounds articulated by the agency in the administrative record.[2] The *Chenery* rule preserves in agencies authority to exercise the discretion delegated by Congress, preventing courts from substituting their own policy views for those of the agency. At the same time, *Chenery* limits agency power to make policy outside of public scrutiny.

In *Chenery*, the SEC conditioned its approval of a public utility holding company's reorganization on an agreement by its officers to disgorge shares of preferred stock in the new corporation that they had purchased during the reorganization period. The SEC had not found any wrongdoing, but thought its ruling compelled by court cases exploring the common law duty of fiduciaries. The Supreme Court vacated the SEC's decision, holding that the agency had misread the judicial precedents.[3] The Court refused to speculate regarding other possible justifications for the agency's conclusion: "The grounds upon which an administrative order must be judged are those upon which the record discloses that its action was based."[4] Accordingly, a court must assess agency action based on the rationales put forward by the agency itself at the time of its decision: "[C]ourts may not accept appellate counsel's post hoc rationalizations for agency action."[5] The *Chenery* decision has been widely followed.[6]

---

1. 318 U.S. 80 (1943).
2. The *Chenery* rule applies both to formal and informal proceedings, but they implicate different concepts of the "record." *See* 5 U.S.C. § 556(e) (defining the "record" for formal proceedings to include, among other things, the "transcript of testimony and exhibits"). *Cf.* Association of Data Processing Serv. Orgs., Inc. v. Board of Governors of Fed. Reserve Sys., 745 F.2d 677, 684 (D.C. Cir. 1984) (explaining that the administrative record in informal proceedings consists "of what [the administrator] had before him when he acted").
3. 318 U.S. at 89.
4. *Id.* at 87. In reviewing the SEC's action after remand, the Court explained that "a reviewing court, in dealing with a determination or judgment which an administrative agency alone is authorized to make, must judge the propriety of such action solely by the grounds invoked by the agency. If those grounds are inadequate or improper, the court is powerless to affirm the administrative action by substituting what it considers to be a more adequate or proper basis." SEC v. Chenery Corp., 332 U.S. 194, 196 (1947).
5. Burlington Rock Lines v. United States, 371 U.S. 156, 168-69 (1962).
6. *See, e.g.*, Caterpillar Logistics Servs. v. Solis, 674 F.3d 705, 709-10 (7th. Cir. 2012); Forest Guardians v. United States Forest Service, 641 F.3d 423, 435-36 (10th Cir. 2011); Ass'n of Civilian Technicians v. FLRA, 269 F.3d 1112, 1116 (D.C. Cir. 2001); Navas v. INS, 217 F.3d 646, 658 n.16 (9th Cir. 2000); Massachusetts *ex rel.* Div. of Marine Fisheries v. Daley, 170 F.3d 23, 31 (1st Cir. 1999).

The *Chenery* doctrine has three principal interrelated benefits. First, it serves as a check on agency action, preventing agencies from making policy outside of public scrutiny; second, it prevents courts from substituting their own views of policy for those of the agency; and third, it helps senior agency officials exercise control over staff and counsel by privileging only those agency rationales proffered by the agency itself at the time of its decision.

Reviewing courts generally will allow agencies to defend their actions only on the basis of reasons articulated prior to judicial review. As conditions or personnel change, agencies cannot substitute a different rationale without reopening proceedings. If agencies reopen the proceedings, then they must subject their new reasoning to challenge by interested parties in either a rulemaking proceeding or an adjudication. A continuity requirement prevents circumvention of the process checks that control administrative action.

In this respect the *Chenery* doctrine is akin to the warrant requirement limiting administrative and traditional law enforcement searches. The need for a warrant constrains enforcement discretion by mandating that officials assert the purposes and aims of the search *before* the search takes place. By creating a record prior to the search, the warrant requirement prevents law enforcement personnel from changing the justification for, and the permissible scope of, the search once it is under way. The ex ante requirement of a particularized warrant demands continuity—the search generally is limited to the purposes, places, and individuals detailed in the warrant. Like the warrant requirement, therefore, the *Chenery* doctrine forces agencies to precommit to particular rationales for agency action.

The record requirement permits judges to check agency decisions by assessing whether the asserted rationales are sufficient. Under the arbitrary-and-capricious standard of review, a court will set aside an action based on a rationale that is internally inconsistent, is incoherent,[7] or departs without explanation from an agency's prior policies and precedents.[8] But for the *Chenery*

---

7. *See, e.g.*, Motor Vehicle Mfrs. Ass'n v. State Farm Mut. Auto. Ins. Co., 463 U.S. 29, 43 (1983) (requiring agency to show "a rational connection between the facts found and the choice made") (quoting Burlington Truck Lines v. United States, 371 U.S. 156, 168 (1962)).
8. *See, e.g.*, FCC v. Fox Television Stations, Inc., 556 U.S. 502, 515 (2009); Atchison, Topeka & Santa Fe Ry. v. Wichita Bd. of Trade, 412 U.S. 800, 808 (1973). For detailed discussion of the arbitrary-and-capricious standard of review, see generally Chapter 8, *supra*. The default remedy for arbitrary action is vacation. Courts will, however, remand without vacation under limited circumstances to avoid disruption of agency policies. For discussion of this alternative remedy, see Chapter 10, *infra*.

principle, such judicial review would be far less meaningful, because the agency would always be able to polish or adjust a problematic rationale.

At the same time, the *Chenery* doctrine prevents courts from supplying their own rationales for the agency decision. In contrast to rational basis review of legislative action, courts cannot speculate as to the conceivable government purposes underlying the action.

On the surface, it would seem that agencies should prefer rational basis review because reviewing courts more frequently would uphold their determinations. Courts would not set aside agency action even when the agency's explanation was wanting, as long as they could conceive of an adequate alternative justification. Congress has no quarrel with such deferential review as applied to legislation.

Yet, in the administrative context, the court-supplied rationale might result in less authority for the administrative agency in the future, or it might conflict with some other agency priority. Consider the facts of *Chenery* itself. Instead of remanding the reorganization petition back to the agency, the Court might have upheld the action on the ground that *all* preferred stock must always be disgorged before a reorganization can be approved, or on the ground that *no* stock can be acquired by directors during a reorganization period. Either hypothetical ruling would have gone far beyond what the agency in fact held on remand, and would have led to results in other cases that the agency might well have disapproved.

Finally, the *Chenery* doctrine reserves policymaking authority to senior agency officials. Only rationales reflected in the record, as opposed to ex ante or ex post justifications by staff (or counsel), will be considered. Although agencies at times would prefer that decisions be upheld on any ground—even if articulated by counsel or staff—the agency may not wish to be bound by such justifications in the future. Thus, the *Chenery* doctrine preserves agency policymaking both from courts and subordinate agency officials.

Application of *Chenery* is straightforward when an explanation of the agency action is articulated before or at the same time the action is taken. As the Supreme Court noted in *Camp v. Pitts*,[9] where there is a "contemporaneous explanation of the agency decision . . . [t]he validity of the . . . action . . . must stand or fall on the propriety of that finding." Only a "strong showing of bad faith or improper behavior"[10] will prompt a court to look behind the agency's articulated explanation for its own action.[11]

---

9. 411 U.S. 138, 143 (1973).
10. Citizens to Preserve Overton Park v. Volpe, 401 U.S. 402, 420 (1971).
11. *See, e.g.*, San Luis Obispo Mothers for Peace v. United States Nuclear Regulatory Comm'n, 789 F.2d 25, 44-45 (D.C. Cir. 1986) (en banc) (refusing to

Post hoc rationalizations, therefore, are not generally considered.[12] A rationale articulated by agency counsel in litigation may not reflect the agency's view, may have been hastily developed with an eye only toward prevailing in the litigation, and will not have been subject to the input of parties in either a rulemaking or adjudication.[13]

Several exceptions to *Chenery* nevertheless have been recognized. First, a reviewing court may uphold the agency decision on a rationale different from but closely related to the one relied on by the agency if "it is clear that . . . the agency would have reached the same ultimate result" on remand.[14] If the agency inescapably would reach the same decision, then neither the courts nor agency staff has supplanted the agency from its assigned policymaking task.

For instance, in *Ward v. MSPB*,[15] the Merit Systems Protection Board had rejected a federal employee's claim that his failure to be promoted violated the Whistleblower Protection Act. The agency reasoned that the employee's complaint about a colleague's travel to a conference did not constitute "whistleblowing" because a single employee's travel could not involve a "gross waste of funds" as required to come within the protections of the Act.[16] Without reaching that issue, the Federal Circuit held that, under the circumstances, there was no way that the travel in question could have in-

---

supplement the agency record with transcripts of agency deliberative proceedings that petitioners claimed would prove bad faith).

12. *Overton Park*, 401 U.S. at 419; Burlington Truck Lines v. United States, 371 U.S. 156, 168-169 (1962).
13. *Cf.* FLRA v. United States Dep't of Treasury, 884 F.2d 1446, 1455 (D.C. Cir. 1989) ("[A] position established only in litigation may have been developed hastily, or under special pressure, or without an adequate opportunity for presentation of conflicting views.").
14. Spiva v. Astrue, 628 F.3d 346, 353 (7th. Cir. 2010) (noting that harmless error rule applies to *Chenery* objection where it is "predictable with great confidence that the agency will reinstate its decision on remand because the decision is overwhelmingly supported by the record though the agency's original opinion failed to marshal that support"); Mengistu v. Ashcroft, 355 F.3d 1044, 1047 (7th. Cir. 2004) (similar); Osmani v. INS, 14 F.3d 13, 15 (7th. Cir. 1994) (noting exception to *Chenery* where "it is clear what the agency's decision has to be"); Consolidation Coal Co. v. Smith, 837 F.2d 321, 323 n.3 (8th Cir. 1988); Salt River Project Agric. Improvement & Power Dist. v. United States, 762 F.2d 1053, 1060 n.8 (D.C. Cir. 1985).
15. 981 F.2d 521 (Fed. Cir. 1992).
16. *Id.* at 524-25.

volved a "gross waste of funds." The court reasoned that its decision dealing "with particular travel by a particular individual" was safely within the framework set by the agency because it reflected "a narrower application of the agency's interpretation of the statute."[17] Presumably, the agency would have endorsed the narrower approach on remand. Thus, the court upheld the agency without having to reach the broader question of whether one employee's travel could ever constitute a "gross waste of funds."[18]

Second, the *Chenery* doctrine protects agency discretion; where no agency discretion exists, *Chenery* should not apply. Accordingly, *Chenery* does not prevent a court from upholding an agency decision "based on another ground within the power of the [reviewing] court to formulate" rather than on a factual or policy determination that "the agency alone is authorized to make."[19] Such judicial determinations do not interfere with the discretion Congress delegated to agencies. As such, a court can and should affirm an agency decision if it concludes that the decision was compelled by law—even though the agency's own reasons for taking the action were mistaken.[20]

Applying this principle, courts have sometimes broadly stated that *Chenery* applies solely to agency factfinding and policymaking functions, not to statutory construction.[21] This proposition does not necessarily hold, however, where *Chevron* deference applies to a court's review of an agency's construction of a statute that it administers.[22] Simplifying, the *Chevron* doctrine recognizes

---

17. *Id.* at 527.
18. *Id.* at 527-28.
19. *Chenery*, 318 U.S. at 88.
20. *See, e.g.*, Morgan Stanley Capital Group v. Public Util. Dist. No. 1, 554 U.S. 527, 544-45 (2008) (holding *Chenery* inapplicable where the agency "lucked out" because Supreme Court precedent required the result that the agency had reached); Koyo Seiko Co. v. United States, 95 F.3d 1094, 1099-1101 (Fed. Cir. 1996) (holding *Chenery* inapplicable where "the plain language of the statute compels the conclusion"); Shea v. Director, Office of Workers' Comp. Programs, 929 F.2d 736, 739 n.4 (D.C. Cir. 1991); Chae-Sik Lee v. Kennedy, 294 F.2d 231, 234 (D.C. Cir. 1961).
21. *See, e.g.*, Ark. AFL-CIO v. FCC, 11 F.3d 1430, 1440 (8th. Cir. 1993) ("[T]he Supreme Court clearly limited *Chenery* to situations in which the agency failed to make a necessary determination of fact or of policy.").
22. *See* Chevron, U.S.A., Inc. v. Natural Res. Def. Council, 467 U.S. 837, 842-43 (1984). For general discussion of the *Chevron* doctrine, see Chapters 3 and 4, *supra*. For discussion of the interaction of *Chevron* and *Chenery*, see Richard Murphy, Chenery *Unmasked: Reasonable Limits on the Duty to Give Reasons,* 80 U. Cin. L. Rev. 817, 870-74 (2012); Kevin Stack, *The Constitutional Foundations of* Chenery, 116 Yale L. J. 952, 1008-13 (2007); Michael Herz,

that an agency will often have discretionary power to choose among reasonable statutory constructions based on policy concerns. Courts give effect to this power by applying the famous *Chevron* two-step. At step one, a reviewing court determines for itself whether Congress has spoken to the precise issue of statutory construction in play. If Congress has done so, courts (and agencies) should of course give effect to congressional will. If not, then the court proceeds to step two, where it should uphold the agency's statutory construction so long as the agency gave a reasonable explanation for its choice.

Given this structure, *Chenery* is inapplicable to step-one issues because courts, not agencies, have final authority to resolve them.[23] The exception that *Chenery* does not apply where a case can be resolved on a "ground within the power of the [reviewing] court to formulate,"[24] operates with full force.

Step two, by contrast, contemplates agency discretion to make a reasoned choice among available statutory constructions, and this discretion, as courts sometimes have recognized, leaves room for application of *Chenery*.[25] Following this logic, courts applying step two should not rely upon a post

---

Deference Running Riot: Separating Interpretation and Lawmaking Under Chevron, 6 Admin. L.J. Am. U. 187 (1990).

23. Bank of America, N.A. v. FDIC, 244 F.3d 1309, 1319 (11th. Cir. 2001) (concluding that the *Chenery* principle does not apply "to agency post-hoc rationalizations involving the kind of pure questions of statutory analysis that are involved under the first prong of the *Chevron* analysis"; discussing authority).
24. *Chenery*, 318 U.S. at 88.
25. *See* America's Cmty. Bankers v. F.D.I.C., 200 F.3d 822, 835 (D.C. Cir. 2000) (noting that the *Chenery* principle "applies as well to our review of statutory interpretations under the second prong of *Chevron*"); Environmental Def. Fund, Inc. v. Administrator of U.S.E.P.A., 898 F.2d 183, 189 (D.C. Cir. 1990) (citing *Chenery* for the proposition that the court "cannot sustain an action merely on the basis of interpretive theories that the agency might have adopted and findings that (perhaps) it might have made"). *See also* ICC v. Brotherhood of Locomotive Eng'rs, 482 U.S. 270, 283 (1987) (observing in dicta that *Chenery* instructs that a court "may not affirm on a basis containing any element of [agency] discretion—including discretion to find facts and interpret statutory ambiguities"). *See generally* Stack, *supra* note 22, at 1008-13 (discussing and approving this approach to *Chenery*'s relation to *Chevron*). *But see* Church of Scientology v. IRS, 792 F.2d 153, 166 (D.C. Cir. 1986) (Silberman, J., concurring) (concluding that, at least for informal adjudications, the *Chenery* rule should not bar reliance on arguments proffered by counsel "at the first moment when it was appropriate and relevant to do so," which may be during judicial review).

hoc justification to save an agency's statutory construction that was based on an otherwise inadequate contemporaneous rationale. Suppose, for example, that an agency determines that a statute inescapably means *X*—in *Chevron* terms, the statute compels result *X* in step one. The reviewing court determines that the statute is actually ambiguous and could reasonably support either meaning *X* or meaning *Y* at step two,[26] but agency counsel offers a reasonable, post hoc justification for the agency's favored construction. Rather than rely on this post hoc justification, the court generally should vacate and remand, giving the agency a chance to make this discretionary choice itself with a proper understanding of the scope of its authority.[27] *Chenery* should permit a court, however, to rely on post hoc legal arguments insofar as they do not threaten agency discretion. Along these lines, the D.C. Circuit has advised that a court can properly consider post hoc legal arguments that support rather than improperly replace an agency's discretionary choice.[28]

9.03 UNEXPLAINED ACTIONS

Where an agency action is not accompanied by a contemporaneous explanation, the court at times may investigate the agency's rationale by receiving evidence. Under these circumstances there is no presumption as to whether the post hoc explanation tendered by the agency to the court expresses the agency's original

---

26. *See* Herz, *supra* note 22 (discussing this example). Anachronistically, one might describe *Chenery* itself as a case in which the agency thought that it confronted a step-one issue but the Court determined that the agency faced a step-two issue. The SEC concluded that the law governing fiduciaries compelled its treatment of the stock purchases by insiders during a corporate reorganization. The Court explained that the agency had misunderstood this law, effectively leaving the agency with discretion to choose how to address these purchases as a matter of statutory construction. *See* SEC v. Chenery Corp., 332 U.S. 194, 198-99 (1943).
27. *See* Negusie v. Holder, 555 U.S. 511 523 (2009) (declaring, albeit without citing *Chenery*, that, where an agency "has not yet exercised its *Chevron* discretion to interpret the statute in question, the proper course, except in rare circumstances, is to remand to the agency for additional investigation or explanation") (quotation marks and citations omitted).
28. *See* America's Cmty. Bankers v. F.D.I.C., 200 F.3d 822, 835 (D.C. Cir. 2000) (holding that, although *Chenery* applies to *Chevron* step-two review, it did not block the court from considering FDIC's post hoc argument that its statutory construction was reasonable in light of the apparent meaning of another, related portion of the statute).

rationale. In attempting to identify the agency's actual, though not contemporaneously articulated, rationale, courts generally avoid direct scrutiny of the agency's decisionmaking process and rely on the representations of counsel, affidavits from relevant officials, and extrinsic evidence rather than depositions, interrogatories, and courtroom testimony.

[Blackletter Statement, Part 3, § VI, ¶ 2.]

As explained above, absent a strong showing of bad faith, courts presume that an agency's contemporaneous *articulated* rationale for an action is, in fact, its *actual* rationale. The courts' favorable treatment of contemporaneous explanations creates a strong incentive for agencies to offer them, even where they are not statutorily required, as is often the case with informal adjudications under the APA. If an agency's explanation for an action is inadequate, then the default remedy is for the court to vacate the action and remand for further agency proceedings.[29] The court generally will not allow agency officials to be dragged through burdensome discovery and hearings during judicial review to obtain information regarding the agency's rationale that was not included in the administrative record. In limited circumstances, however, courts will accept extra-record evidence supplied through less intrusive means to explicate the agency's contemporaneous rationale for its action.

A foundational case is *Citizens to Preserve Overton Park v. Volpe*,[30] in which the Supreme Court reviewed the Secretary of Transportation's decision to approve an interstate highway through a park. As this decision was an informal adjudication, the APA did not require formal findings, and the Secretary had not offered any. The Court explained that arbitrary-and-capricious review nonetheless required assessment of the agency's rationale. It added

29. *See* Pension Benefit Guar. Corp. v. LTV Corp., 496 U.S. 633, 654 (1990) (clarifying that "remanding to the agency in fact is the preferred course" where an agency does not provide an adequate basis for review); Florida Power & Light Co. v. Lorion, 470 U.S. 729, 744, (1985) ("[I]f the reviewing court simply cannot evaluate the challenged agency action on the basis of the record before it, the proper course, except in rare circumstances, is to remand to the agency for additional investigation or explanation"); Camp v. Pitts, 411 U.S. 138, 143 (1973). Note, however, that courts will sometimes remand an agency action without vacating it where they determine that an agency's explanation for its action is inadequate, the agency can likely address the inadequacy and vacation would be unduly disruptive. For discussion of this alternative remedy, see Chapter 10, *infra*.

30. 401 U.S. 402 (1971).

that, where an agency fails to provide this information through a contemporaneous explanation, the agency might be required to do so after the fact during judicial review. Parties could attempt to demonstrate the agency's rationale at the time of its decision through discovery, relying on documentary evidence and testimony of agency officials to reconstruct the bases for the agency action. The record created in this way would, however, have to be viewed with suspicion because post hoc rationalizations of agency officials would be inevitable.

Overton Park's threat of discovery during judicial review ran counter to longstanding judicial criticism of the undesirable side effects of such efforts to probe agency decisionmaking. Forcing agency officials to participate in depositions or to answer interrogatories saps resources. Moreover, such probing of the agency's decisionmaking process is antithetical to the respect owed senior agency officials. The lead case on this point has for many decades been *United States v. Morgan*,[31] in which the Supreme Court addressed the perplexing difficulties arising out of the lack of an administrative record. The controversy in that case stemmed from a Secretary of Agriculture order fixing the maximum rates for buying and selling livestock at the Kansas City stockyards. Morgan alleged that the Secretary never personally heard or examined the relevant evidence and arguments presented in the case. When the case originally was heard in the Supreme Court, the Court held that the allegation, if proven, would violate the statutory right to a "full hearing," and the Court interpreted the statute to require the decisionmaker personally to consider the evidence and arguments.[32] The district court on remand permitted the plaintiff to question the Secretary about his personal role in setting the prices. On appeal, the Supreme Court reversed on unrelated grounds, but observed that "it was not the function of the court to probe the mental processes of the Secretary."[33] After a third appeal, the Secretary issued a new rate order. Morgan once again challenged the order, alleging that the Secretary was not sufficiently involved, and deposed the Secretary to determine the extent of his involvement. The Supreme Court this time condemned the examination: "[T]he Secretary should never have been subjected to this examination. . . . Just as a judge cannot be subjected to such a scrutiny . . . so the integrity of the administrative process must be equally respected."[34] This prin-

31. 313 U.S. 409 (1941) (*Morgan III*).
32. Morgan v. United States, 298 U.S. 468, 481 (1936).
33. Morgan v. United States, 304 U.S. 1, 18 (1938).
34. *Morgan III*, 313 U.S. at 422. *See also* Florida Power & Light Co. v. Lorion, 470 U.S. 729, 744 (1985).

ciple reflects a fundamental reality of decisionmaking in a large, hierarchical bureaucracy. Agency heads typically have far too many demands placed upon them to focus on the details of every action taken by the agencies that they lead. Given this fact, deposing the Secretary, in addition to draining time and resources, is likely to embarrass the administrative process rather than usefully illuminate it.

These sorts of concerns have not disappeared since the day of *Morgan*, and they quickly led the Court to dial back *Overton Park*'s threat of intrusive discovery in *Camp v. Pitts*.[35] In this case, the Comptroller of the Currency denied an applicant's request to organize a national bank. The explanation for the denial took the form of a very brief, conclusory letter. The court of appeals ordered a de novo trial to investigate the agency's grounds for the denial. The Supreme Court reversed in a per curiam opinion in which it explained that a de novo hearing is appropriate only where "there are inadequate factfinding procedures in an adjudicatory proceeding, or where judicial proceedings are brought to enforce certain administrative actions."[36] In all other contexts, where an agency offers a contemporaneous explanation for its discretionary action, even one as "curt" as the Comptroller's in *Camp*, the validity of the action must "stand or fall" based on the propriety of that explanation judged in light of the administrative record.[37]

Camp added, however, that where there has been "such failure to explain administrative action as to frustrate effective judicial review," a court may "obtain from the agency, either through affidavits or testimony, such additional explanation of the reasons for the agency decision as may prove necessary." To limit the scope of this exception—and ease its tension with the general rule disfavoring extra-record evidence—courts have held that such supplemental materials "should be merely explanatory of the original record and should contain no new rationalizations."[38] Thus, an agency official might

35. 411 U.S. 138 (1973).
36. *Id.* at 142.
37. *Id.* at 143.
38. Yale-New Haven Hosp. v. Leavitt, 470 F.3d 71, 82 (2d Cir. 2006) (supplementation of record pursuant to *Camp* exception allowable "only if the proffered evidence illuminates the original record and does not advance new rationalizations for the agency's action"); Sierra Club v. Marsh, 976 F.2d 763, 773-74 (1st Cir. 1992) (noting that "new material . . . should be explanatory of the decisionmakers' action at the time it occurred"); Bunker Hill Co. v. EPA, 572 F.2d 1286, 1292 (9th Cir.1977) (requesting supplementation by the parties to help the court "make sense of complex technical" materials in the record). Courts have also indicated that acceptance of extra-record evidence may be

supply extra-record details explaining the agency's contemporaneous rationale for its action.[39] If, however, this explanation "is not sustainable on the record itself, the proper judicial approach has been to vacate the action and to remand the matter back to the agency for further consideration."[40] Also, as the Court opined in *Overton Park*, any such explanation "will, to some extent, be a 'post hoc rationalization' and thus must be viewed critically."[41]

---

appropriate where it is necessary for determining whether an agency's analysis was complete. *See* National Audubon Society v. Hoffman, 132 F.3d 7, 14-15 (2d Cir. 1997) (noting that deviation from the record rule occurs more frequently in NEPA cases because a reviewing court must determine whether an agency analysis has satisfied NEPA's requirement of a "comprehensive analysis of the potential environmental impacts").

39. *See, e.g.*, Bagdonas v. Dep't of Treasury, 93 F.3d 422, 426-27 (7th Cir. 1996) (approving agency efforts to supplement record by providing "the court with an explanation for the agency's action submitted by the officer who had the authority to act on the application").
40. Environmental Defense Fund, Inc. v. Costle, 657 F.2d 275, 285 (D.C. Cir. 1981).
41. Citizens to Preserve Overton Park, Inc. v. Volpe, 401 U.S. 402, 420 (1970); Women Involved in Farm Economics v. United States Dep't of Agric., 876 F.2d 994, 999 (D.C. Cir. 1989).

Chapter 10

JUDICIAL REMEDIES

by Ronald M. Levin*

As noted in the foregoing chapters, in general a reviewing court will set aside agency action that does not meet the standards described, instead of mandating a specific disposition of its own design. When an agency's exercise of discretion cannot be upheld on the basis of the agency's rationale, or no rationale can be discerned, or if the agency so requests, the court will almost always remand the action so that the agency can provide further justification. When remanding, a court normally will vacate the agency's action, except in special circumstances. Such circumstances may exist where (1) the court discerns a substantial probability that the agency can cure its error on remand and (2) the challenging party's interest in obtaining relief from the agency's decision is clearly outweighed by the substantial adverse impact that vacation would have on private persons who have reasonably relied on the agency action being remanded.

[Blackletter Statement, Part 3, § IX.]

As a general rule, when an agency action fails the standards of judicial review, the court is expected to set the action aside and remand it to the agency for further consideration.[1] The court should ordinarily not mandate a specific disposition of its own design. A judicial determination that the government erred in its initial effort "does not impliedly foreclose the adminis-

* William R. Orthwein Distinguished Professor of Law, Washington University School of Law.

1. *See, e.g.*, FPC v. Transcontinental Gas Pipe Line Corp., 423 U.S. 326, 331 (1976) ("If the decision of the agency 'is not sustainable on the administrative record made, then the . . . decision must be vacated and the matter remanded . . . for further consideration.'") (quoting Camp v. Pitts, 411 U.S. 138, 143 (1973)).

trative agency, after its error has been corrected, from enforcing the legislative policy committed to its charge."[2]

For example, when a reviewing court decides that an agency included an improper condition in granting a license, the court may not modify the license by eliminating the condition; instead, the court should remand the case to allow the agency to decide whether to drop the condition or issue no license at all.[3] As the Supreme Court explained in *FPC v. Idaho Power Co.*, the court of appeals' statutory power "to 'affirm, modify, or set aside' the order of the Commission 'in whole or in part' . . . is not power to exercise an essentially administrative function."[4] Similarly, in *NLRB v. Food Store Employees Union, Local 347*,[5] the Court held that the court of appeals could not modify the Board order under review by awarding the union reimbursement of litigation expenses, as a recent Board precedent arguably indicated would be appropriate. Instead, the court had to give the Board an initial opportunity to decide whether to apply or distinguish the precedent.[6] Furthermore, the reviewing court usually will not specify the procedures that the agency is to employ during post-remand proceedings.[7]

These decisions seem to rest primarily on inferences drawn from the very existence of delegated authority. When Congress empowers an agency to implement a program, it presumably intends to reap the benefits of some institutional advantage that it thinks the agency in question possesses, such as administrators' capacity to develop specialized experience or expertise, or to stay in touch with the political process. Thus, a judicially designed remedy could amount to an exercise of authority that Congress entrusted to the agency instead.[8] These remedial principles are closely related to the *Chenery* doc-

2. FCC v. Pottsville Broadcasting Co., 309 U.S. 134, 145 (1940). *See generally* Ronald M. Levin, *"Vacation" at Sea: Judicial Remedies and Equitable Discretion in Administrative Law*, 53 Duke L.J. 291, 364-68 (2003).
3. FPC v. Idaho Power Co., 344 U.S. 17, 20 (1952).
4. *Id.* at 21.
5. 417 U.S. 1 (1974).
6. *Id.* at 8-10; *see also* Neb. Dep't of Health & Human Servs. v. Dep't of Health & Human Servs., 435 F.3d 326 (D.C. Cir. 2006).
7. *Transcontinental Gas Pipe Line Corp.*, 423 U.S. at 333 (holding that "[a]t least in the absence of substantial justification for doing otherwise, a reviewing court may not . . . proceed by dictating to the agency the methods, procedures, and time dimension of the needed inquiry" on remand).
8. *See, e.g.*, Sure-Tan, Inc. v. NLRB, 467 U.S. 883, 898-906 (1984).

trine, under which a discretionary decision may be upheld only on the basis of the agency's rationale.[9]

The above generalizations have limited exceptions.[10] Courts have, for example, been willing to prescribe affirmative relief predicated on "a violation of 'nondiscretionary' duties," or on a "determination that the agency had repeatedly rejected the only rational course available for protecting statutory beneficiaries."[11] These cases typically involve situations in which the agency's action was, in the perception of the reviewing court, substantively unreasonable or contrary to law, as opposed to being undone by inadequate analysis or explanation.[12] In addition, in "'truly extraordinary situations,'" such as an agency's repeated inability to justify an action, a court will order an agency proceeding terminated immediately, instead of giving the agency another chance to rehabilitate the action.[13]

An agency that recognizes an apparent defect in a rule or order may voluntarily ask the court to remand it without actually resolving the merits of the appeal. A court normally has discretion to grant this sort of relief, although its advisability can vary with the circumstances.[14]

Within the constraints of its obligation to respect the agency's delegated authority, a reviewing court has significant discretion in framing its remedial orders.[15]

When remanding an action for further consideration, courts sometimes exercise discretion in deciding whether to vacate the action pending the re-

---

9. *See supra* Chapter 9. *See generally* Kevin M. Stack, *The Constitutional Foundations of* Chenery, 116 YALE L.J. 952 (2007).
10. *See* Levin, *supra* note 2, at 368-70.
11. Merrick B. Garland, *Deregulation and Judicial Review*, 98 HARV. L. REV. 507, 572 (1985).
12. *Id.* at 570-71.
13. Checkosky v. SEC, 139 F.3d 221, 226 (D.C. Cir. 1998) (quoting Tenn. Gas Pipeline Co. v. FERC, 926 F.2d 1206, 1214 (D.C. Cir. 1991)).
14. *See* Ford Motor Co. v. NLRB, 305 U.S. 364 (1939); Citizens Against Pellissippi Parkway Extension, Inc. v. Mineta, 375 F.3d 412 (6th Cir. 2004); Ctr. for Native Ecosystems v. Salazar, 795 F. Supp. 2d 1236 (D. Colo. 2011); Toni M. Fine, *Agency Requests for "Voluntary" Remand: A Proposal for the Development of Judicial Standards*, 28 ARIZ. ST. L.J. 1079 (1996).
15. *See Ford Motor Co.*, 305 U.S. at 373 ("The jurisdiction to review the orders of the [NLRB] is vested in a court with equity powers, and while the court must act within the bounds of the statute and without intruding upon the administrative province, it may adjust its relief to the exigencies of the case in accordance with the equitable principles governing judicial action.").

mand proceedings. A decision not to do so is sometimes known as "remand without vacation." The legality of this device has not been definitively resolved. Some individual judges read § 706 of the Administrative Procedure Act, which provides that a court "shall . . . set aside" an agency action that violates any of the review standards codified in that section, to prohibit remand without vacation.[16] Nevertheless, no majority opinion has so held, the Administrative Conference of the United States has endorsed the practice,[17] and it remains in common use in the D.C. Circuit and elsewhere.[18]

The last sentence of the *Blackletter Statement* passage set out at the beginning of this chapter states in condensed form an August 1997 resolution of the ABA House of Delegates, which suggested criteria to guide judicial practice in this area:

> In exercising this discretion, a reviewing court should normally strike the balance in favor of vacating the agency's action, unless special circumstances exist. Such special circumstances may be most often found to exist where, in the context of the proceeding as a whole:
>
> (a) the agency's error did not preclude fair public consideration of a central issue in a rulemaking or a fair hearing on the necessary findings in an adjudication or other agency proceeding;

---

16. *See* Comcast Corp. v. FCC, 579 F.3d 1, 10-12 (D.C. Cir. 2009) (Randolph, J., concurring); Milk Train, Inc. v. Veneman, 310 F.3d 747, 757-58 (D.C. Cir. 2002) (Sentelle, J., dissenting); Checkosky v. SEC, 23 F.3d 452, 490-93 (D.C. Cir. 1994) (opinion of Randolph, J.).
17. Administrative Conference of the U.S., *Recommendation 2013-6, Remand Without Vacatur* ¶ 1, 78 Fed. Reg. 76,272 (2013) [hereinafter *ACUS Recommendation*].
18. *E.g.*, National Ass'n of Clean Water Agencies v. EPA, 734 F.3d 1115 (D.C. Cir. 2013); N. Air Cargo v. USPS, 674 F.3d 852, 860-61 (D.C. Cir. 2012); *Milk Train*, 310 F.3d 747; Nat'l Org. of Veterans' Advocates, Inc. v. Sec'y of Veterans Affairs, 260 F.3d 1365, 1380-81 (Fed. Cir. 2001); Cent. Me. Power Co. v. FERC, 252 F.3d 34, 48 (1st Cir. 2001); Cent. & S.W. Servs., Inc. v. EPA, 220 F.3d 683, 692 (5th Cir. 2000). One study found that the D.C. Circuit remanded without vacating in 73 cases between 1972 and 2013; 41 of those were decided between 2000 and 2013. Stephanie J. Tatham, The Unusual Remedy of Remand Without Vacatur 21 (2014) (report to the Administrative Conference of the United States). *See also id.* at 54-58 (listing the cases).

(b) the court finds a substantial likelihood that the agency, after further consideration, will be able to remedy its error and reach a similar overall result on a valid basis; and

(c) the challenging party's interest in obtaining relief from the agency's decision is clearly outweighed by the substantial and adverse impact that vacation of the agency's action would have on

(i) persons other than the Government who over time have reasonably relied on the agency action being remanded, or

(ii) persons other than the Government, during the interim period before agency action on remand to cure the error has become final,

and such impact cannot be remedied after such interim period.[19]

Although this resolution was written in prescriptive terms, it largely coincides with the case law.[20] According to the leading case, *Allied-Signal, Inc. v. USNRC*,[21] the court's decision about whether to vacate, in addition to remanding, depends on "the seriousness of the order's deficiencies (and thus the extent of doubt whether the agency chose correctly) and the disruptive consequences of an interim change that may itself be changed."

As *Allied-Signal* indicates, a court is relatively likely to resort to remand without vacation if it perceives that the agency has a good chance of curing its previous error with, at most, minor changes to its rule or order.[22] Conversely, a court normally will vacate an action if the agency's chances of being able to rehabilitate its prior action look poor.[23] A fortiori, remand without vacation is inappropriate if the violation that the court has found is one that the agency could not possibly cure, such as a violation of a flat statutory ban on regulation of a particular subject area. Of course, on remand the

---

19. 122-2 ABA Ann. Rep. 45-46, at ¶ 1 (1997) (hereinafter *ABA Resolution*).
20. Levin, *supra* note 2, at 377-78.
21. 988 F.2d 146, 150-51 (D.C. Cir. 1993).
22. *N. Air Cargo*, 674 F.3d at 861; La. Fed. Land Bank Ass'n v. Farm Credit Admin., 336 F.3d 1075, 1085 (D.C. Cir. 2003); *Milk Train*, 310 F.3d 747; Engine Mfrs. Ass'n v. EPA, 20 F.3d 1177, 1184 (D.C. Cir. 1994).
23. *Comcast Corp.*, 579 F.3d at 8-10; Am. Bioscience, Inc. v. Thompson, 269 F.3d 1077, 1083-84 (D.C. Cir. 2001); Ill. Pub. Telecomm. Ass'n v. FCC, 123 F.3d 693, 693 (D.C. Cir. 1997); Indep. U.S. Tanker Owners Comm. v. Dole, 809 F.2d 847, 855 (D.C. Cir. 1987).

agency does not have to attempt to salvage its prior action; it can, instead, reconsider the whole of its original decision.[24]

Pursuant to the *Allied-Signal* formula, the court should also take account of any "disruptive consequences" that would ensue from vacation of the agency's action.[25] Under this reasoning, courts have utilized remand without vacation to avoid such short-term harms to the public as an interruption in coverage by a rule governing disposal of PCBs,[26] impairment of the operation of the Clean Air Act in California,[27] and interruption of the federal food stamp program.[28] As the ABA resolution suggests, the need to protect private reliance interests can be an additional factor militating against vacation of the action.[29] Conversely, the absence of likely disruption militates in favor of vacating the action.[30] The court will also find it relevant if no party actually seeks vacation.[31] Finally, and intertwined with several of the foregoing considerations, courts will consider whether the interests of the party or parties who prevailed against the agency would be served by allowing the challenged action to remain in place.[32]

---

24. Flying J Inc. v. FERC, 363 F.3d 495, 497 (D.C. Cir. 2004).
25. *N. Air Cargo*, 674 F.3d at 861.
26. *Cent. & S.W. Servs.*, 220 F.3d at 692.
27. W. Oil & Gas Ass'n v. EPA, 633 F.2d 803, 813 (9th Cir. 1980).
28. Rodway v. USDA, 514 F.2d 809 (D.C. Cir. 1975).
29. A.L. Pharma, Inc. v. Shalala, 62 F.3d 1484, 1492 (D.C. Cir. 1995) ("vacating the rule approving the [new animal drug application] would prove disruptive to [the drug's manufacturer], which has relied on it in good faith for over thirteen years"); City of Brookings Mun. Tel. Co. v. FCC, 822 F.2d 1153, 1171-72 (D.C. Cir. 1987).
30. Council Tree Commc'ns, Inc. v. FCC, 619 F.3d 235, 258 (3d Cir. 2010) (finding that, assuming arguendo that remand without vacation is lawful, it would not be warranted under the circumstances).
31. *See, e.g.*, Mississippi v. EPA, 744 F.3d 1344, 1362 (D.C. Cir. 2013). The Administrative Conference recommends that "[w]hen a court has decided to remand an agency action, it should consider hearing parties' views on whether to vacate the agency action and on any related remedial issues." *ACUS Recommendation*, *supra* note 17, ¶ 6.
32. *See, e.g.*, Envtl. Def. Fund v. EPA, 898 F.2d 183, 190 (D.C. Cir. 1990) (remanding without vacatur because "no party to this litigation asks that the court vacate the EPA's regulations, and to do so would at least temporarily defeat petitioner's purpose, the enhanced protection of environmental values covered by the" statutory provisions it relied on). The ACUS recommendation lists this criterion as one of three relevant considerations, along with the *Allied-Signal* considerations of ease of cure and potential for disruption. *ACUS Recommendation*, *supra* note 17, ¶ 5.

Remand without vacation does increase the risk that an agency may drag its feet in responding to the remand, because the practical pressure to find a substitute for a vacated rule is absent. To encourage prompt action, courts will sometimes direct the agency to take action to repair the remanded rule within a specified period of time.[33]

---

33. *See In re* Core Commc'ns., 531 F.3d 849, 861 (D.C. Cir. 2008); *id.* at 862-63 (Griffith, J., concurring) (strongly recommending this practice as a general matter); *ABA Resolution, supra* note 19, ¶ 2 (recommending that courts give "serious consideration" to this option); Levin, *supra* note 2, at 384 n.421 (citing additional case law).

Chapter 11

AGENCY OVERSIGHT BY THE POLITICAL BRANCHES

by William Funk*

11.01 SCOPE

> **This Chapter concerns procedures relating to the management of administrative functions across agencies, particularly requirements for agencies to submit proposed actions for advance review and opportunities for executive and congressional supervision or correction of agency decisionmaking.**
> **[Blackletter Statement, Part 6, § I.]**

The previous chapters in this book relate to judicial review of agency action under the Administrative Procedure Act. This Chapter covers procedures relating to the management of agency actions across agencies. Specifically, it covers requirements, whether imposed by statute or executive order,

* Lewis & Clark Distinguished Professor of Law, Lewis and Clark Law School.

for agencies to submit their proposed actions to some non-judicial entity with authority to review or supervise those actions. It does not cover requirements that are simply additional rulemaking requirements, such as the Unfunded Mandates Reform Act's requirement that agencies' major rules contain cost-benefit analyses[1] or the National Environmental Policy Act's requirement that agencies' rules having a significant effect on the human environment be accompanied by an Environmental Impact Statement.[2] Nor does it cover requirements for agencies to coordinate their activities in particular ways, such as the Fish and Wildlife Coordination Act's requirement that agencies engaged in water development projects coordinate with the Fish and Wildlife Service.[3]

11.02 CONGRESSIONAL MANAGEMENT OF AGENCY ACTION

The Constitution prohibits members or houses of Congress, or Congress itself, from being, appointing, or removing officers of the United States, or from vetoing an agency action other than through the enactment of legislation. Therefore, Congress has no power of direct supervision or management over agencies even though its power to define and limit an agency's authority is virtually plenary within the bounds of the Constitution.

Nevertheless, Congress has the recognized constitutional authority to oversee agency action for a number of purposes, especially for determining whether new legislation is necessary or appropriate. Congress's ultimate control over the agency's budget and its organic statute means that congressional views will have influence with the agency. Also, inherent in the legislative power is a power of inquiry, including the power to subpoena witnesses and documents (subject to applicable privileges, including an executive privilege of uncertain scope) and to enforce compliance therewith through the contempt power. Congressional investigation and public hearings can lead to public scrutiny and political pressure on the agency.

Attempts by members or committees of Congress to influence the outcome of an agency proceeding are subject to the APA's constraints on ex parte communications and other restrictions that apply to such attempts by private persons. Beyond those requirements, however, congressional attempts to

1. *See* 2 U.S.C. § 1532.
2. *See* 42 U.S.C. § 4332(2)(C).
3. *See* 16 U.S.C. § 1662(a).

influence agency proceedings are largely unregulated. Use of the congressional hearing power to try to influence the outcome of a pending formal adjudication has been held a violation of due process, although hearings to explore policy issues that might be involved in an adjudication can be permissible and appropriate if properly managed. Outside the context of formal or other on-the-record proceedings, a court is not likely to set aside an agency decision because of alleged congressional influence unless the evidence shows that the pressure brought to bear caused the agency action to be affected by factors that are not relevant under the governing statute.

Under the Congressional Review Act, 5 U.S.C. §§ 801-808, a rule cannot take effect if Congress passes a joint resolution disapproving the rule. The act exempts rules relating to agency management or personnel or agency organization, procedure, or practice, as well as rules of particular applicability. Before a rule can take effect, the promulgating agency must submit a copy of the rule and a concise general statement relating thereto to both Houses of Congress and the comptroller general. A joint resolution of disapproval must be introduced within sixty days of such submission and is considered according to expedited procedures set out in the act. A *major* rule *cannot* take effect for sixty days after it has been submitted to Congress, a delay designed to ensure Congress has time to disapprove the rule. Major rules include any rule (other than one promulgated under the Telecommunications Act of 1996 and its amendments) that the administrator of the Office of Management and Budget's Office of Information and Regulatory Affairs (OIRA) finds will result in an annual effect on the economy of $100 million or more; a major increase in costs or prices; or significant adverse effects on competition, employment, investment, productivity, or the ability of U.S.-based enterprises to compete with foreign enterprises.

[Blackletter Statement, Part 6, § II.]

The Constitution establishes many obstacles to congressional management of agency action. It expressly prohibits members of Congress from being officers of the United States.[4] Likewise it does not allow Congress to

4. U.S. Const. art. I, § 6, cl. 2. *See also* Buckley v. Valeo, 424 U.S. 1 (1976) (persons performing significant public duties must be officers of the United

appoint officers of the United States.[5] The Supreme Court has held that Congress cannot except by impeachment remove officers of the United States.[6] In *Immigration and Naturalization Service v. Chadha*,[7] the Court held that Congress cannot retain for itself a veto over agency action other than through enacting new legislation.

While Congress may have no power of direct supervision or management over agencies performing public functions, Congress can exercise oversight over them.[8] First, it can investigate, and obtain information from, agencies. The power of inquiry is deemed inherent in the legislative power, because Congress needs to gather information to determine whether to enact new legislation.[9] Congress is deemed to have the power to subpoena witnesses and documents and to enforce compliance through the use of the contempt power.[10] Occasionally, the congressional power to investigate runs into invocations of executive privilege by executive officers. The constitutional basis of executive privilege, like the congressional power of inquiry, is not express but inferred. In *United States v. Nixon*,[11] the Supreme Court said the privilege was "constitutionally based" to the extent that it "relates to the effective discharge of a President's powers." The Court has never ruled on a conflict between the congressional power of investigation and the President's executive privilege, and lower courts have assiduously avoided deciding such a case on the merits.[12] In all probability, the issue is not justiciable as a political question. In practice, these disputes have been resolved politically, rather than judicially.

States); Metropolitan Washington Airport Auth. v. Citizens for the Abatement of Aircraft Noise, Inc., 501 U.S. 252 (1991) (Congress may not invest itself or its members with executive or judicial powers).

5. *See* U.S. Const. art. II, § 2, cl. 2.
6. *See* Bowsher v. Synar, 478 U.S. 714 (1986).
7. 462 U.S. 919 (1983).
8. A useful overview of the many tools of congressional oversight and influence is Jack M. Beermann, *Congressional Administration*, 43 San Diego L. Rev. 61 (2006).
9. *See* Eastland v. United States Servicemen's Fund, 421 U.S. 491, 503-07 (1975); Barenblatt v. United States, 360 U.S. 109, 111 (1959); Watkins v. United States, 354 U.S. 178, 187 (1957); McGrain v. Daugherty, 273 U.S. 135, 174-75 (1927).
10. *See, e.g.*, *McGrain*, 279 U.S. 135.
11. 418 U.S. 683, 711 (1974).
12. *See, e.g.*, Senate Select Committee on Presidential Campaign Activities v. Nixon, 498 F.2d 725 (D.C. Cir. 1974).

The Government Accountability Office (formerly the General Accounting Office), which is generally considered an arm of Congress,[13] is authorized by statute to "investigate all matters related to the receipt, disbursement, and use of public money"[14] and to "evaluate the results of a program or activity the Government carries out under existing law."[15] Such investigations of executive branch agencies can raise the same sort of problems raised by congressional committee investigations. Again, however, courts have generally not rendered decisions resolving these disputes.[16]

Second, either as a body or through any of its committees or members, Congress can express a view concerning an agency's performance of its functions. Again as a practical matter, these views can, depending upon the political power of the person or entity expressing them, have significant persuasive power on agencies. The legal limits on the exercise of these political, persuasive powers are unclear.

There are apparently only two reported cases in which congressional interference in administrative action has been held unlawful. One involved a congressional inquiry into a formal adjudication that was *sub judice* before the agency at the time of the inquiry, and the court held that the clear attempt by the congressional committee to influence the agency's decision violated the due process rights of the parties to the adjudication.[17] The court held that it was not necessary to determine whether the decisionmakers *actually* were influenced by the committee's importunings, because the appearance of fairness was an essential element of due process in a quasi-judicial proceeding. As a result, members of Congress and committee staffers generally avoid interfering in pending agency adjudications. The other case involved a committee chair's attempt to influence a decision regarding the siting of a bridge. The D.C. Circuit held that two conditions must be present before it is improper for members of Congress to attempt to influence an administrative decision that is neither judicial nor quasi-judicial: the pressure brought to

---

13. *See, e.g.*, *Bowsher*, 478 U.S. at 727.
14. 31 U.S.C. § 712(1).
15. *Id.* § 717(b).
16. *See* Walker v. Cheney, 230 F. Supp. 2d 51 (D.D.C. 2002) (holding that Comptroller General lacked standing to sue Vice President to obtain information regarding a national energy task force he chaired). *But see* Committee on the Judiciary of the United States House of Representatives v. Miers, 558 F. Supp. 2d 53 (D.D.C. 2008) (enforcing congressional subpoena), *voluntarily dismissed*, 2009 WL 3568649 (D.C. Cir. 2009).
17. Pillsbury Co. v. FTC, 354 F.2d 952 (5th Cir. 1966).

bear must be irrelevant to the factors to be considered under the governing statute and the decisionmaker must be affected by these extraneous considerations.[18] It distinguished the earlier case, saying that when an agency proceeding is not an on-the-record public proceeding, the mere appearance of unfairness is not enough to void a decision; there must be an actual effect of the influence. As a result of these two cases and the cases interpreting them, congressional influence on agency rulemaking is not considered improper if "Congressmen keep their comments focused on the substance of the proposed rule," and the comments "are not designed to force [the agency] to decide upon factors not made relevant by Congress in the applicable statute," i.e. "extraneous considerations."[19]

Third, because Congress may control agency action by enacting new legislation, Congress may require an agency to suspend the effective date of a particular action for a specified period of time in order to allow Congress to consider possible legislation. Congress has included such "report-and-wait" provisions in a number of statutes, and all legislative veto provisions are construed to be report-and-wait provisions subsequent to *Chadha*. More generally, the 1996 Congressional Review Act[20] requires that agencies send all rules to each house of Congress and to the Comptroller General with a concise general statement relating to the rule. In the case of a major rule, this must occur at least 60 legislative days before the rule's effective date, giving Congress time to adopt a Joint Resolution of Disapproval if it is so inclined. In practice, this mechanism is almost wholly ineffective; even if Congress is arrayed against the agency, a joint resolution requires the President's signature (or the override of his veto) which will almost always be impossible to obtain. Since its passage the Act has only been used successfully once—to repeal the Occupational Safety and Health Administration's Ergonomics Rule.[21]

11.03 PRESIDENTIAL MANAGEMENT OF AGENCY ACTION

11.031 The President's Constitutional Authority

Two provisions of Article II are conceived to be the primary sources of the President's authority to manage agency action. The first,

18. D.C. Federation of Civic Ass'ns v. Volpe, 459 F.2d 1231 (D.C. Cir. 1971).
19. Sierra Club v. Costle, 657 F.2d 298, 408-10 (D.C. Cir. 1981).
20. 5 U.S.C. §§ 801-08. *See generally* Jeffrey S. Lubbers, A Guide to Federal Agency Rulemaking 163-69 (5th ed. 2012).
21. *See* Ergonomics Rule Disapproval, Pub. L. No. 107-5, 115 Stat. 7 (2001) (invalidating Ergonomics Program, 65 Fed. Reg. 68,262 (Nov. 14, 2000)).

known as the Vesting Clause, states that the "executive power" shall be vested in the President. U.S. Const., Art. II, Sec. 1, cl. 1. The second, known as the "Take Care Clause," states that the President "shall take care that the laws be faithfully executed." U.S. Const., Art. II, Sec. 3. In addition, the President may "require the opinion, in writing, of the principal officer in each of the executive departments, upon any subject relating to the duties of their respective offices." U.S. Const., Art. II, Sec. 2, cl. 1 These provisions furnish authority to the President to supervise, consult with, and obtain information from executive officers in the performance of their statutory duties. For these purposes, an executive department includes cabinet departments, independent executive agencies, and independent regulatory commissions.

However, most statutes place rulemaking and adjudicatory authority in the agency head or the agency itself, not in the President. The extent to which the President can order agency officials to take actions within the officials' delegated authority is uncertain.

In practice, the President's exercise of his supervisory power has largely correlated with his ability on the one hand to appoint, with the advice and consent of the Senate, principal officers, U.S. Const., Art. II, Sec. 2, cl. 2, and on the other hand to remove agency officials who ignore his direction. While the Constitution may be read to preclude any statutory limitation on the President's appointment power, it is not uncommon for a statute creating an agency to place some limits on whom the President may appoint to head the agency. No cases have addressed the constitutionality of such limits, but Presidents since Ronald Reagan have issued signing statements to the effect that some such limitations are an unconstitutional restriction on the President's appointment powers.

The Constitution, other than in the impeachment clause, does not address who may remove executive officers or on what basis, but impeachment is by no means the only permissible route to removal of executive officers. Where statutes do not address removal of particular officers, it is presumed that the President may remove them at will, except perhaps when their sole function is the adjudication of administrative cases. Thus, under these circumstances, the President may remove an official simply for failure to follow supervision.

A number of statutes provide that an officer may be removed only for cause. Exactly what kind of conduct can constitute "cause" is unclear, but in practice removals on this basis are rare, and the Court has never directly addressed the issue. However, in a case involving the ability of Congress to remove the Comptroller General for "inefficiency," "neglect of duty," and "malfeasance," it characterized these terms as very broad and said they could be interpreted to include "any number of actual or perceived transgressions of the legislative will."

The validity of "for cause" removal provisions is not well defined by case law. Even with respect to purely executive officers, such a provision may be valid if it does not impede the President's ability to perform his constitutional duties. This does not necessarily mean, however, that Congress could constrain the President's ability to remove a principal officer, such as the Secretary of State, whose job involves execution of authorities granted by the Constitution to the President. Moreover, in some circumstances, "dual for-cause" provisions (whereby a principal officer can be removed only for cause and an inferior officer can be removed only for cause by that principal officer) unconstitutionally constrain the President's ability to oversee the executive branch.

[Blackletter Statement, Part 6, § II.A.]

Article II vests the executive power in the President,[22] and requires the President to "take care that the laws be faithfully executed."[23] These general duties furnish authority to the President to supervise executive officers in the performance of their statutory duties. More specifically, the President may "require the opinion, in writing, of the principal officer in each of the executive departments, upon any subject relating to the duties of their respective offices."[24]

The President's practical ability to supervise or influence high-level executive officers begins with his appointment power.[25] While the Constitution specifies that the President nominates and appoints (with the consent of the Senate) all principal officers, Congress has limited the president's discretion by placing some limitations on the qualifications for certain positions. These limitations may be quite broad or fairly specific. For example, the Secretary

22. U.S. Const. art. II, § 1, cl. 1.
23. *Id.* at § 3.
24. *Id.* at § 2, cl. 1.
25. *Id.* at cl. 2.

of Defense must be a civilian,[26] while the Director of the Federal Emergency Management Agency must have a demonstrated ability in and knowledge of emergency management and homeland security, and not less than 5 years of executive leadership and management experience in the public or private sector.[27] At some uncertain point, such requirements might unconstitutionally restrict the President's appointment authority, but so far Congress has not constrained presidential discretion in a problematic way. It seems unlikely that the issue could ever be brought to a court for resolution.

Equally or more important to the President's practical ability to supervise agencies is his power to remove agency heads. The relevant caselaw suggests that in the absence of a statutory limitation on removal the President may remove executive officials at will,[28] at least when the official is not engaged in purely adjudicatory functions.[29] This would imply that the President can likewise supervise such officials without restriction. One question that has not been judicially considered is whether the President can direct such an executive official to exercise her discretion in a particular manner on a matter that a statute has placed within the responsibility of the officer. For example, may the President direct the Administrator of the EPA to exercise her discretion in a particular manner with respect to a Clean Air Act regulation? It seems clear that the President may tell the Administrator his preferences and remove the Administrator if she acts inconsistently with them. Some would argue, however, that notwithstanding the President's ability to remove the Administrator at will, it would be inconsistent with the statute placing responsibility for the rulemaking in the Administrator for the President to direct her to exercise her discretion in a particular manner.[30] Others would disagree.[31]

---

26. 10 U.S.C. § 113(a).
27. 6 U.S.C. § 313(c)(2).
28. *See* Myers v. United States, 272 U.S. 52 (1926).
29. *See* Wiener v. United States, 357 U.S. 349 (1958).
30. *See, e.g.*, Peter L. Strauss, *Overseer, or "the Decider"? The President in Administrative Law*, 75 GEO. WASH. L. REV. 696 (2007).
31. *See* Elena Kagan, *Presidential Administration*, 114 HARV. L. REV. 2245 (2001) (arguing that when Congress chooses not to limit the President's removal power, as a matter of statutory construction the placement of legal authority in the head of the agency should not be read to preclude the President from issuing directives to that person); Steven G. Calabesi & Saikrishna B. Prakash, *The President's Power To Execute The Laws*, 104 YALE L.J. 541, 549, 593–97 (1994) (arguing that any limitation on the President's power to direct subordinate officers is unconstitutional).

The President should also be able to supervise officials whom he may only remove for cause, as is the case with most independent regulatory agency members, at least to the extent of ensuring their "faithful execution" of the laws. If such an official did not follow that supervision, removal would clearly be justified if the official's action amounted to nonfeasance or malfeasance independent of the failure to follow the President's supervision. For example, in *Morrison v. Olson*,[32] the Court said:

> This is not a case in which the power to remove an executive official has been completely stripped from the President, thus providing no means for the President to ensure the "faithful execution" of the laws. Rather, because the independent counsel may be terminated for "good cause," the Executive, through the Attorney General, retains ample authority to assure that the counsel is competently performing his or her statutory responsibilities in a manner that comports with the provisions of the Act.[33]

It is unclear how broadly this power of supervision/removal extends, and there are virtually no judicial decisions on the question of what constitutes "cause" as a basis for Presidential removal of an officer. In *Morrison v. Olson*, the Court said that it was clear that "misconduct" in office would suffice.[34] In *Bowsher v. Synar*,[35] however, the Court interpreted broadly the statutory provision allowing for congressional removal of the Comptroller General for neglect of duty or malfeasance, saying it "could sustain removal of the Comptroller General for any number of actual or perceived transgressions of the legislative will."[36] This might support a broad reading of the President's authority to remove an executive official for cause.

It is also unclear how far Congress can go in limiting the President's ability to remove executive officers. In *Morrison v. Olson*, the Court stated that Congress could not impose a limitation on the President's removal power that interfered with his ability to perform his constitutional duty, particularly the obligation to ensure faithful execution of the laws.[37] Earlier, in *Humphrey's Executor v. United States*,[38] the Court held that a "for cause" removal limita-

---

32. 487 U.S. 654 (1988).
33. *Id.* at 692.
34. 487 U.S. at 692.
35. 478 U.S. 714 (1986).
36. *Id.* at 729.
37. *Morrison*, 487 U.S. at 690-93.
38. 295 U.S. 602 (1935).

tion applicable to Commissioners of the Federal Trade Commission was constitutional, and in *Morrison* the Court re-affirmed the validity of that holding, if not its particular rationale. Consequently, one would conclude that Congress could impose a "for cause" removal limitation even on some Cabinet officers, whose functions are largely indistinguishable from those of members of so-called independent regulatory commissions. Nevertheless, one would also conclude that such a restriction would exceed constitutional limits if applied to officers performing on the President's behalf functions constitutionally lodged in the President.

In *Free Enterprise Fund v. Public Company Accounting Oversight Board*,[39] the Court found that double "for cause" protection (*i.e.*, an officer who can only be removed for cause by a superior who in turn can only be removed for cause by the President) unconstitutionally restricted the President's ability to perform his core functions.

11.032 Regulatory Review

Although the specifics have varied with each administration, all Presidents since Richard Nixon have required executive agencies to perform certain analyses and submit proposed rules to an office in the Executive Office of the President for its review. Since President Reagan's E.O. 12,291 (1981), responsibility for such review has been lodged with OIRA.

The relevant executive orders have also included provisions concerning regulatory planning, including the semiannual publication of a Unified Regulatory Agenda, identifying and describing all regulations each agency has under development or review. Under the most recent of these, President Clinton's E.O. 12,866, agencies must prepare an annual Regulatory Plan, submitted to OIRA and included in the Unified Regulatory Agenda, describing and justifying the most important "significant regulatory actions" that the agency reasonably expects to issue in proposed or final form in that fiscal year or thereafter. Under E.O. 12,866, but not under its predecessors, these planning requirements extend to independent as well as executive agencies.

Current Executive Orders, which are by definition subject to rescission or revision by successive administrations, also require or encourage the pursuit of specific substantive policies by

39. 561 U.S. 477 (2010).

requiring agencies to (a) prepare a cost-benefit analysis for significant regulatory actions, (b) pursue the most cost-effective regulatory alternative, and (c) consider the impacts of proposed regulations on certain specified interests, including federalism, the environmental health and safety of children, Indian tribal governments, and takings of private property.

Most executive orders governing agency rulemaking provide, as they must under the Constitution, that their provisions apply only "to the extent permitted by law." A violation of their requirements does not affect the validity of the rule or provide a basis for judicial review. Enforcement of the provisions of the oversight orders is left to the political process.

[Blackletter Statement, Part 6, § II.B.]

Starting with President Nixon's "Quality of Life Review" in 1971,[40] Presidents have imposed requirements that agencies perform certain analyses and submit proposed rules to an office in the Executive Office of the President for its review. President Ford's review mechanism required agencies to prepare economic impact statements[41] for "major" rules, which were reviewed by the Council on Wage and Price Stability (COWPS). COWPS adopted criteria for determining "major" rules, which included rules having an impact of over $100 million in one year. COWPS could then jawbone the agency if it believed the rule would have too great an economic impact. President Carter built on this system in his Executive Order 12,044, issued in 1978.[42] In addition to performing what were now called "regulatory analyses" of "major" rules, agencies also were required to identify "significant" rules, evaluate their need, and choose the "least burdensome of the acceptable alternatives."[43] In place of COWPS, President Carter established the Regulatory Analysis Review Group (RARG) to review the regulatory analyses for certain major rules. RARG would submit public comments during the notice-and-comment period, as COWPS had before it, as well as jawbone. RARG consisted of members of the major economic

---

40. *See* Subcomm. on Oversight and Investigations of the House Comm. on Interstate and Foreign Commerce, 94th Cong., Federal Regulation and Regulatory Reform (Subcomm. Print 1976).

41. These were first denominated "inflation impact statements," but in 1975 were relabeled "economic impact statements." *See* OMB Circular No. A-107, § 4(d) (Jan. 28, 1975).

42. Exec. Order No. 12,044, 43 Fed. Reg. 12,661 (1978).

43. *Id.* § 2(d).

and regulatory agencies, but its four-member executive committee, which in fact directed RARG's activities, consisted of representatives from OMB, the Council of Economic Advisors, and two positions that rotated among cabinet departments and EPA. Staff was drawn from the CEA and COWPS. RARG reviewed only a very limited number of rules under E.O. 12,044. In addition, President Carter established the Regulatory Council, charged with coordinating agency rulemaking to avoid duplication or conflict. Finally, President Carter required agencies to publish semi-annual agendas of their current and future rulemaking activities.

Shortly after entering office President Reagan issued Executive Order 12,291, rescinding Executive Order 12,044[44] but building upon it. Whereas each of the preceding orders had left to the agencies the primary responsibility for implementing the substantive policies and regulatory reform measures in the orders, with COWPS and RARG having only peripheral influence except on a very limited number of rules, E.O. 12,291 placed significant responsibility in the Office of Information and Regulatory Affairs in the Office of Management and Budget.[45] The Reagan Administration initially considered applying the order to independent regulatory agencies as well as executive agencies, and the Department of Justice opined that such an extension would be lawful. Nevertheless, President Reagan applied the order only to executive agencies, while "inviting" independent regulatory agencies to comply—an invitation that was universally ignored.

The order instructed agencies, "to the extent authorized by law," not to adopt a regulation "unless the potential benefits to society from the regulation outweigh the potential costs to society" and to choose the regulatory alternative with the least net costs to society.

In addition, there were procedural requirements. Agencies were required first to conduct preliminary regulatory impact analyses of all proposed major rules, still defined largely as those with an annual impact of $100 million. An analysis was to include a description of the costs and benefits of the proposed rule, a determination of the net benefits of the proposed rule, a description of alternative regulatory approaches that could achieve the same goal at lower cost, and the identification of any legal requirements that would preclude

44. Exec. Order No. 12,291, 46 Fed. Reg. 13,193 (1981).

45. This office was created administratively in the Carter Administration, but the Paperwork Reduction Act statutorily established it in 1980. *See* Pub. L. No. 96-511, 94 Stat. 2812 (1980). In 1986, the Act was amended to provide for presidential appointment of the Director with the advice and consent of the Senate. *See* 44 U.S.C. § 3503.

adoption of the rule that would maximize net benefits for society. *All* proposed rules (including interpretive rules and statements of policy that would not be subject to notice-and-comment rulemaking) and any associated preliminary regulatory impact analyses were to be submitted to OMB prior to their public proposal–60 days before publication of the notice of proposed rulemaking for major rules and 10 days before publication of the notice of proposed rulemaking for other rules. During this period, OMB would review the rule and any analysis, but OMB could (and in fact often did) extend the period of review and delay publication of the proposed rule indefinitely in order to study the rule fully and communicate with the agency. Essentially the same drill applied to preparation of the final rule, with the agency submitting the proposed final rule to OMB together with any associated final regulatory impact analysis prior to publication. Again, OMB was provided time to review the final rule and analysis prior to publication, and OMB could extend this time in order to further discuss the rule with the agency.

E.O. 12,291 continued the semi-annual regulatory agenda instituted under President Carter's executive order.

Finally, E.O. 12,291 authorized the Presidential Task Force on Regulatory Relief, headed by then Vice President Bush, to identify already existing regulations for reconsideration under the procedures of the executive order.

In his second term, President Reagan expanded the oversight program by issuing Executive Order 12,498.[46] It was responsive to a concern that by the time that agencies began the rulemaking process they had already invested so much time and effort into the policy behind the rule that it was difficult to turn them from their course. Consequently, E.O. 12,498 required agencies to undertake an annual regulatory planning process. Agencies would plan what significant regulatory actions they intended to take during the upcoming year and would submit that draft plan to OMB. OMB then would review the draft plan and discuss it with the agency. In the event of disagreements, the Order provided that the Director of OMB or the agency head could appeal to the President or an appropriate Cabinet Council.[47] Once the administration's Regulatory Program for the year was established, if an agency desired to take a regulatory action that was not previously submitted for review under E.O. 12,498 or if an action materially differed from that described in the agency's

46. Exec. Order No. 12,498, 50 Fed. Reg. 1,036 (1985).

47. Cabinet Councils were a management tool used by the Reagan administration. Cabinet Councils were essentially subsets, organized by broad subject area, of the cabinet, which could coordinate administration policy on various subjects.

final Regulatory Program, the agency was required to advise the Director immediately and submit the action to the Director for review. Unless the matter was responsive to an emergency or subject to statutory or judicial deadlines, the agency was required to refrain from taking the proposed regulatory action until OMB's review was complete. Moreover, the Order authorized OMB to "return for reconsideration" (meaning "reject") any such unreviewed action absent "unusual circumstances, such as new statutory or judicial requirements or unanticipated emergency situations."

While on its face E.O. 12,291 sought only to increase regulatory efficiency, maximizing the net benefits to society of regulation, it, together with E.O. 12,498 and the Presidential Task Force on Regulatory Relief, reflected a strong skepticism about regulation generally. Thus, the Presidential review mechanism tended to reduce regulation and allow for it only when its net benefits were clearly significant or when regulation could not be legally or politically avoided. Observers, whether supportive or critical of the review process, appeared convinced that it had a significant effect on what agencies actually adopted as regulations.

A major criticism of the early workings of E.O. 12,291 was that the review process occurred behind closed doors and OMB's communications with the agency were not on the public record. There was a concern that OMB was being used as a conduit for private communications from regulated parties arguing against various regulations in a process that gave a "second bite of the apple" to preferred interests (generally regulated entities) while excluding others (generally regulatory beneficiaries). In 1986, in response to congressional pressure, the administration agreed to a procedure that in effect required OMB to make public any written communications between OMB and agencies.

Still later in his administration, President Reagan issued three more executive orders governing agency regulatory activities: E.O. 12,606,[48] E.O. 12,612,[49] and E.O. 12,630.[50] Executive Order 12,606 required agencies to assess the effects of proposed regulatory actions on the family by responding to a specified series of questions in a written submission to OMB. Executive Order 12,612 required agencies to consider federalism issues before taking regulatory actions. Substantively, the order directed that agency regulations

---

48. Exec. Order No. 12,606, 52 Fed. Reg. 34,188 (1987), *rescinded by* Exec. Order No. 13,045, 62 Fed. Reg. 19,885 (1997).
49. Exec. Order No. 12,612, 52 Fed. Reg. 41,685 (1987), *rescinded by* Exec. Order No. 13,132, 64 Fed. Reg. 43,225 (1999).
50. Exec. Order No. 12,630, 53 Fed. Reg. 8,859 (1988).

not preempt state law unless the authorizing statute expressly authorized issuance of preemptive regulations or there was some other "firm and palpable evidence compelling the conclusion that the Congress intended [to authorize preemption]."[51] Procedurally, the order required that, before issuing any rule having federalism implications, agencies were to coordinate with state and local governments and to conduct Federalism Assessments, which would be submitted to OMB with other documents under E.O. 12,291. Executive Order 12,630 required agencies to assess the implications of their regulatory actions under the Takings Clause of the Fifth Amendment to the Constitution. The order implied that OMB could reject a proposed action if the action would result in an unbudgeted expenditure of funds to pay for a "taking."

As a practical matter, none of these three orders had much impact on agency rulemaking. Each was perceived as having been issued to appeal to particular interest groups, and, once the orders were issued, neither agencies nor OMB seemed to place much importance on furthering their particular objectives. In addition, guidance from the Attorney General implementing E.O. 12,630 effectively reduced that order to a nullity, as virtually all regulatory actions were determined to be simply not subject to the requirement of a specific "takings" assessment.

President George H.W. Bush did not alter the Reagan orders, although he did effectively replace the Task Force on Regulatory Relief with the Council on Competitiveness chaired by Vice President Quayle.

In 1993 President Clinton issued Executive Order 12,866, Regulatory Planning and Review, replacing President Reagan's Executive Orders 12,291 and 12,498.[52] Like those orders before it, E.O. 12,866 built upon the preceding orders. It begins with a lengthy statement of the principles of regulation. These bear a resemblance to the principles expressed in E.O. 12,291 that is startling, given the different political backgrounds of Presidents Clinton and Reagan, although E.O. 12,866 makes a particular point of requiring agencies to consider both quantifiable and unquantifiable costs and benefits.[53] It retains the $100 million trigger level for those rules subject to agency cost/benefit analyses, although now those rules are denominated "significant regulatory actions" rather than "major rules."[54] As had been the case under E.O. 12,291, E.O. 12,866 requires agencies to conduct cost-benefit analyses for these significant regulatory actions.

---

51. Exec. Order No. 12,612, *supra* note 49, at § 4(b).
52. *See* Exec. Order No. 12,866, 58 Fed. Reg. 51,735 (1993).
53. *See id.* § 1.
54. *Id.* § 3(f).

Despite the similarities to E.O. 12,291, E.O. 12,866 did make certain changes. First, not all proposed and final rules had to be sent to OMB for review before they were published. Interpretive rules and statements of policy were not included within the scope of the Order at all. In addition, each agency provided OMB with a list of its proposed regulatory actions, indicating those it believed were significant. Thereafter, only those listed as significant had to be submitted to OMB for review, unless OMB specifically requested to review an action listed as non-significant or the non-significant action materially changed. Second, strict timelines were established to ensure that OMB review was not used to delay a regulatory action indefinitely. Third, the Order included requirements for ensuring that the review process was transparent—limiting those who could communicate with private interests, making public the facts surrounding any such communications, maintaining a public log of the status of all matters under OMB review, and making public (after the regulatory action has occurred) all documents exchanged between OMB and the agency.

E.O. 12,866 also included provisions relating to regulatory planning to replace the similar provisions in E.O. 12,498. As with the earlier order, agencies were required to make annual determinations concerning possible or proposed significant regulatory actions, to submit them to OMB for review, and to make public the final determinations. Again, however, there were also a few changes. First, E.O. 12,866 broadened its reach by extending its planning requirements to independent regulatory agencies, not just to executive agencies. Second, there was no comparable suggestion that an agency's failure to include an action in its planning document would interfere with going forward with that action later.

In place of Presidents Reagan and Bush's Task Force on Regulatory Relief and Council on Competitiveness, with their mandated reviews of existing regulations, E.O. 12,866 required the OIRA Administrator to convene a Regulatory Working Group consisting of representatives of the heads of each agency having significant domestic regulatory responsibility, the Vice President, and advisors to the President. The Regulatory Working Group was charged with assisting agencies in analyzing regulatory issues and working with the Administrator of OIRA in identifying existing regulations that impose significant burdens or have outlived their usefulness. The Vice President was named as the President's principal advisor on regulatory policy. The Order also institutionalized previous Presidents' directives to agencies to review existing rules with an eye to eliminating unnecessary ones.[55]

55. *See id.* § 6.

Observers of the review process under E.O. 12,866 naturally compare it to the process under E.O. 12,291. There appears to be consensus that under the Clinton Administration the E.O. 12,866 review process was quicker and less confrontational than the process under E.O. 12,291. At the same time some observers believe that the reviews under E.O. 12,866 were less effective precisely because they were not as intrusive or skeptical of the agency. Critics believed that OIRA review had become toothless, noting that in the last three years of the Clinton administration OIRA had returned no rules to agencies requiring further analysis or explanation. It is not clear whether the lack of returns in the latter years of the Clinton administration was due to a lack of rigor in OIRA reviews, or to agencies learning what satisfied OIRA, and/or to reliance on less formal mechanisms of de facto rejection.[56] Although the Office of Information and Regulatory Affairs issued annual reports attesting to the reductions in regulatory burdens and increases in net benefits resulting from E.O. 12,866 activity, even a supporter must take these reports with a grain of salt.

Just as President Reagan had not limited his regulatory reform to the program contained in E.O. 12,291, issuing additional orders on particular subjects, President Clinton likewise supplemented E.O. 12,866 with additional orders. Over his two terms, he replaced two of the additional Reagan orders, substituting his own federalism order[57] and replacing the order requiring consideration of the impact on families with one requiring consideration of the impacts on the environmental health and safety of children.[58] In addition, President Clinton issued an order on civil justice reform that required agencies in promulgating regulations to draft those regulations so as to minimize litigation and provide clear legal standards,[59] and he issued orders requiring agencies to take account of the effect of their regulations on Indian

---

56. The Obama administration has eschewed the use of return letters in favor of informal consultations, issuing only one in the first six years of the administration. *See* OIRA Return Letters, *available at* http://www.reginfo.gov/public/do/eoReturnLetters.
57. Exec. Order No. 13,132, 64 Fed. Reg. 43,255 (1999).
58. Exec. Order No. 13,045, 62 Fed. Reg 19,885 (1997). Congress responded to the rescission of the order relating to impacts on families by enacting its requirements into law. *See* Omnibus Consolidated & Emergency Supplemental Appropriations Act, Pub. L. No. 105-277, Div. A, Title VI, § 654, 112 Stat. 2681-480, 2681-528 (1998), codified at 5 U.S.C. § 601 note.
59. Exec. Order No. 12,988, 61 Fed. Reg. 4,729 (1996).

tribal governments and to make tribal impact statements.[60] Commentators have been uniformly critical of the proliferation of specialized impact studies and regulatory analyses,[61] believing that it has added to the ossification of rulemaking with little or no marginal benefit beyond those already obtained by E.O. 12,866 and its predecessors.

President George W. Bush retained President Clinton's Executive Order, except that he eliminated the role of the Vice President.[62] Retention of the Order, however, does not mean there was no change. Particularly in the early years of the Bush presidency, two changes were particularly notable. First, in the first year of the Bush administration, OIRA returned 13 rules or analyses to agencies.[63] The next year, though, the number dipped to five, followed by two the following year, and averaged only one in each of the remaining years in his administration.[64] It was suggested by some that under President Clinton, OIRA used oral, informal means to achieve changes in agency regulations, hence the lack of formal return letters. Under President Bush, OIRA used formal return letters that explicitly detailed the nature of the problem OIRA found with the rule or analysis, resulting in a meaningful increase in transparency. Second, OIRA instituted what is known as a "prompt letter." Whereas OIRA previously had acted only in reaction to agency proposed rules, in writing a prompt letter OIRA took the initiative, suggesting that an agency undertake regulation where it had not proposed to do so. Instituted with some fanfare in September 2001, OIRA had sent seven prompt letters within a year.[65] However, as with return letters, the number of prompt letters then

---

60. Exec. Order No. 13,084, 63 Fed. Reg. 27,655 (1998), *rescinded and replaced by* Exec. Order No. 13,175, 65 Fed. Reg. 67,249 (2000).
61. *See, e.g.*, ABA Sec. Admin. L. & Reg. Prac., *Improving the Administrative Process: A Report to the President-Elect of the United States*, 61 ADMIN. L. REV. 235, 239-40 (2008) ("Over time, both Congress and the executive have laden the process of informal rulemaking with multiple requirements for regulatory analysis. Viewed in isolation, a good case can be made for each of these requirements. Their cumulative effect, however, has been unfortunate."); Richard B. Stewart, *Administrative Law in the Twenty-First Century*, 78 N.Y.U. L. REV. 437, 447 (2003) ("OMB regulatory analysis and other forms of regulatory impact review have also contributed to 'paralysis by analysis.'"); *see generally* Mark Seidenfeld, *A Table of Requirements for Federal Administrative Rulemaking*, 27 FLA. ST. U. L. REV. 533 (2000).
62. Exec. Order No. 13,258, 67 Fed. Reg. 9385 (2002).
63. OIRA Return Letters, *supra* note 56.
64. *Id.*
65. OIRA Prompt Letters, *available at* http://www.reginfo.gov/public/jsp/EO/promptLetters.jsp.

took a notable downturn. There were five the following year and none thereafter, save for a lone missive from 2006.[66]

In addition to his initial executive order eliminating the role of the Vice President in the regulatory review process,[67] President Bush issued a later order that made at least one significant change, extending the review process (in somewhat diluted form) not only to rules with legal effect but also to significant guidance documents.[68]

Immediately upon taking office, President Obama rescinded both George W. Bush orders amending E.O. 12,866.[69] However, shortly thereafter, the Director of OMB sent a memorandum to heads of departments and agencies directing them to continue to submit significant guidance documents to OIRA, thereby effectively reinstating a portion of the order the President had recently rescinded.[70] In 2011, President Obama also issued his own order on "Improving Regulation and Regulatory Review," which largely tracks and reaffirms, without superseding, E.O. 12,866.[71]

As mentioned earlier, most statutes place rulemaking and adjudicatory authority in the head of an executive agency or in the agency itself in the case of an independent regulatory agency. On their face, none of the oversight orders has raised any problem in this regard. None have authorized any person to substitute their judgment for that of the agency official responsible for the action. Actual practice, however, seems to have subverted this limitation.[72]

These orders have imposed requirements that are mandatory on agency officials, such as the procedural requirement to send certain rules to OMB before they are published in the Federal Register. A violation of these requirements, however, does not affect the validity of the rule, nor does it provide a basis for judicial review. The orders have expressly provided that they are intended to "improve the internal management of the Federal Government and [do] not create any right or benefit, substantive or procedural, enforceable at law or equity by a party against the United States . . . ."[73] Courts have respected

66. *Id.*
67. Exec. Order No. 13,258, 67 Fed. Reg. 9385 (2002).
68. Exec. Order No. 13,422, 72 Fed. Reg. 2763 (2007).
69. Exec. Order No. 13,497, 74 Fed. Reg. 6113 (2009).
70. *See* http://www.whitehouse.gov/sites/default/files/omb/assets/memoranda_fy2009/m09-13.pdf.
71. Exec. Order No. 13,563, 76 Fed. Reg. 3821 (2011).
72. *See* Lisa Heinzerling, *Inside EPA: A Former Insider's Reflections on the Relationship Between the Obama EPA and the Obama White House*, 31 Pace Envtl. L. Rev. 325 (2014).
73. *See, e.g.*, Exec. Order No. 12,866, *supra* note 52, § 10.

these provisions or determined independently that compliance with the orders is not subject to judicial review under general principles.[74] Accordingly, enforcement of the oversight orders is left to the political process.

If courts have been unwilling to enforce the provisions of the orders, they have occasionally been willing in limited cases to override the provisions of the orders when they conflict with statutory requirements. This has invariably been when OIRA review would result in delays beyond a statutory deadline.[75] Challenges to alleged *substantive* interference by OIRA in agency decisionmaking through the regulatory review mechanism of the orders have been unsuccessful.[76]

Although elements of OIRA review have caused some controversy from time to time, it seems firmly established, having been adopted by a succession of Presidents of both parties. Similarly, the requirement that agencies perform cost-benefit analyses in assessing how or what to regulate, at least where a statute allows for consideration of costs and benefits in adopting regulations, also seems well entrenched, with bipartisan support. Nevertheless, "progressives" continue to object to making a regulation's stringency turn on a monetized cost-benefit analysis,[77] "Conservatives" would make maximizing net benefits a legal requirement for all regulations and would make cost-benefit analyses subject to judicial review.

11.04 STATUTORY REQUIREMENTS

11.041 The Paperwork Reduction Act

The Paperwork Reduction Act of 1980, which covers essentially all agencies (including independent regulatory agencies and the Executive Office of the President) except the Government Accountability Office (GAO) and the Federal Election Commission, applies to agency "collection of information." This term

---

74. *See, e.g.*, Trawler Diane Marie, Inc. v. Brown, 918 F. Supp. 921 (E.D.N.C. 1995).

75. *See* Am. Lung Ass'n v. Browner, 884 F. Supp. 345 (D. Ariz. 1994); Environmental Defense Fund v. Thomas, 627 F. Supp. 566 (D.D.C. 1986); NRDC v. Ruckelshaus, 1984 WL 6092 (D.D.C. 1984).

76. *See, e.g.*, Public Citizen Health Research Grp. v. Tyson, 796 F.2d 1479, 1507 (D.C. Cir. 1986) (finding it unnecessary to decide if OIRA acted unlawfully).

77. *See, e.g.*, Frank Ackerman & Lisa Heinzerling, Priceless: On Knowing the Price of Everything and the Value of Nothing (2004).

includes an agency's (1) collecting facts or information from ten or more persons, (2) requiring ten or more persons to disclose facts or opinions to the public or third parties, (3) requiring ten or more persons to maintain records, (4) collecting information from federal agencies or employees for statistical purposes. It does not include the collection of information as part of criminal investigations, civil or administrative proceedings to which the government is a party, or intelligence activities.

Before an agency may engage in the collection of information, it must:

(1) undertake an internal review to evaluate the need for the information, describe the information to be collected, create a plan for its collection, and estimate the burden on private parties that the collection will impose;
(2) publicly announce its reasons for collecting the information, the way in which the information will be used, the burden its collection will impose, whether responses are voluntary or mandatory, and the fact that in the absence of a valid control number a person is not bound to respond to any collection requirement;
(3) submit the proposal for public notice and comment; and
(4) submit the proposal and an accompanying justification to OIRA, which then seeks public comment on the agency's submission for thirty days.

If OIRA takes no action within 60 days, the proposed collection of information is deemed approved. In the case of a collection of information that is not part of or required by a rule that goes through notice and comment, OIRA may disapprove the collection if it determines that it is "unnecessary for any reason." In the case of a collection of information that is part of or required by a rule that goes through notice and comment, OIRA must submit comments as part of that proceeding and may disapprove the collection of information only if the agency's response to OIRA's comments was unreasonable. An independent regulatory commission may override an OIRA disapproval by majority vote. The Paperwork Reduction Act states that OIRA's approval (or failure to act on) a proposed collection of information is not subject to judicial review, but it is silent as to judicial review of disapprovals. Presumably, therefore, judicial review by persons adversely affected by a disapproval would be available under the APA subject to conventional requirements for judicial review.

When OIRA approves a collection of information, it assigns a control number to the collection. No one is subject to any penalty for failing to comply with an agency's collection of information requirement that does not display a valid control number. The absence of a valid control number, however, is no defense to a penalty for filing false information or for failing to file information required to be filed by statute.

[Blackletter Statement, Part 6, § IV.A.]

11.0411 The Paperwork Reduction Act

Even before adoption of the APA, Congress had enacted the Federal Reports Act of 1942,[78] which generally required agencies to obtain the approval of the Bureau of the Budget (later, the Office of Management and Budget) before collecting information from the public.[79] In 1973, Congress transferred the review function with regard to the independent regulatory agencies to the then General Accounting Office.[80] Criticism of the adequacy of these reviews led to the passage of the Paperwork Reduction Act in 1980.[81]

The Paperwork Reduction Act applies to, among other things, the "collection of information."[82] This term has several different facets. It includes an agency collecting facts or opinions from ten or more persons, whether through mandatory or voluntary responses, and it also includes requiring ten or more persons to disclose facts or opinions to the public or third parties or requiring ten or more persons to maintain records. It also applies to the collection of information by agencies from federal agencies or employees for statistical purposes.[83] The term does not apply, however, to the collection of information as part of a criminal investigation, a civil or administrative proceeding to which the government is a party, or intelligence activities, or to compulsory

---

78. Pub. L. No. 77-831, 56 Stat. 1078 (1942).
79. For a history of the practice under the Federal Reports Act, see Raymond T. Bowman, *Administration of the Federal Reports Act*, 18 ADMIN. L. REV. 109 (1965).
80. *See* Pub. L. No. 93-153, § 409, 87 Stat. 576, 593 (1973).
81. *See* Pub. L. No. 96-511, 94 Stat. 2812 (1980), codified at 44 U.S.C. §§ 3501-20. For discussion of the criticism, see COMM'N OF FEDERAL PAPERWORK, FINAL SUMMARY REPORT (Oct. 3, 1977). For a legislative history of the Paperwork Reduction Act, see William Funk, *The Paperwork Reduction Act: Paperwork Reduction Meets Administrative Law*, 24 HARV. J. ON LEGIS. 1 (1987).
82. *See* 44 U.S.C. § 3502(3).
83. *Id.*

process under the Antitrust Civil Process Act and section 13 of the FTC Improvements Act.[84] In addition, the Act exempts certain specific activities.[85] Finally, OMB regulations clarify that the term does not apply to "general solicitations" (such as Federal Register notices),[86] the solicitation of facts or opinions at public meetings,[87] or "like items."[88] OMB understands these exceptions to extend to most agency on-line and social media activity.[89]

The Act applies to both executive agencies (including the Executive Office of the President) and independent regulatory agencies.[90] The only exceptions are the Government Accountability Office, the Federal Election Commission, the governments of the District of Columbia and territories and possessions of the United States, and government-owned contractor-operated facilities.[91]

Before an agency may engage in the collection of information, it must undertake a number of steps. It must make an internal review to evaluate the need for the information, functionally describe the information to be collected, create a plan for its collection, and provide an objectively supported estimate of the burden on private parties that the collection will impose.[92] In

---

84. *Id.* § 3518(c)(1).
85. *See, e.g.*, 49 U.S.C. § 5108(i) (registration of transportation of hazardous materials); Agricultural Risk Protection Act, Pub. L. No. 106-224, Title II, § 263, 114 Stat. 358, 427 (2000) (Secretary of Agriculture and Commodity Credit Corporation activities under price support programs).
86. 5 C.F.R. § 1320.3(h)(4).
87. *Id.* § 1320.3(h)(8).
88. *Id.* § 1320.3(h)(10).
89. *See generally* Memorandum from Cass R. Sunstein, OIRA Administrator, to the Heads of Executive Departments and Agencies and Independent Regulatory Agencies regarding Social Media, Web-based Interactive Technologies, and the Paperwork Reduction Act (April 7, 2010), available at http://www.whitehouse.gov/sites/default/files/omb/assets/inforeg/SocialMediaGuidance_04072010.pdf. In particular, "[f]or purposes of the PRA, OMB considers interactive meeting tools—including but not limited to public conference calls, webinars, blogs, discussion boards, forums, message boards, chat sessions, social networks, and online communities—to be equivalent to in-person public meetings." *Id.* at 5.
90. 44 U.S.C. § 3502(1).
91. *Id.* In addition, Kuzma v. U.S. Postal Service, 798 F.2d 29 (2d Cir.1986), interpreted the Act not to apply to the United States Postal Service.
92. The Act defines "burden" as the "time, effort, or financial resources expended by persons to generate, maintain, or provide information to or for a Federal agency." 44 U.S.C. § 3502(2). "Burden" specifically includes reviewing instructions, searching data sources, and acquiring and installing necessary technology. *Id.* However, practice under the Act has evolved into reporting burden virtually solely in terms of "burden hours."

addition, the agency must publicly announce the reasons for collecting the information, the way the information will be used, the burden the collection will impose, whether responses are voluntary or mandatory, and the fact that no one is required to respond to any collection requirement that lacks a valid control number.[93] The proposed collection of information must also go through public notice and comment.[94] Finally, the agency must send the proposed collection of information requirement to the Office of Information and Regulatory Affairs.[95] In this submission, the agency must certify that the collection (1) is "necessary for the proper performance of the functions of the agency"; (2) is not unnecessarily duplicative; (3) reduces burdens "to the extent practicable and appropriate," including the possible use of differential requirements for small entities; (4) is written in "plain, coherent, and unambiguous terminology"; (5) is designed to be compatible to the maximum extent practicable with respondents' existing reporting or recordkeeping practices; (6) specifies the length of time persons are required to keep records; (7) has been developed by an office concerned with efficient and effective use of the information; (8) uses appropriate statistical survey methodology, where applicable; and (9) to the maximum extent practicable uses information technology to reduce burdens and improve efficiency.[96] The agency must at the same time publish a notice in the Federal Register stating that it has made the submission to OIRA and including the title for and summary of the proposed collection, a brief description of the need and proposed use for the information, a description of the likely respondents and frequency of response, an estimate of the burden caused by the collection, and a notice that comments may be submitted to the agency and OIRA.

If OIRA takes no action on the proposed collection of information submitted to it within 60 days, the proposed collection of information is deemed

---

93. *See id.* § 3506(c)(1)(B)(iii).
94. *See id.* § 3506(c)(2).
95. *See id.* § 3507(a)(1)(C). (To be precise, the Act actually places all responsibilities in the Director of OMB, *see id.* § 3504, but then he is directed to delegate all his authorities under the Act to the OIRA Administrator, *see id.* § 3503(b)).The Act authorizes delegation of the review function over all or a portion of an agency's collection activities to a senior official in the agency itself. *See id.* § 3507(i). To date, OIRA has only delegated such authority to the Federal Reserve Board and, with respect to certain existing collections, to the Managing Director of the Federal Communications Commission. *See* 5 C.F.R. Part 1320, App. A.
96. 44 U.S.C. § 3506(c)(3).

approved.[97] Otherwise, OIRA's responsibilities differ depending on whether the proposed collection of information is contained in a proposed rule or not. If the collection of information is *not* part of or required by a rule that goes through notice and comment, OIRA may disapprove the collection if it "determines that the collection of information . . . is unnecessary for any reason."[98] If the collection of information is part of a rule that goes through notice and comment, OIRA cannot disapprove the collection of information if it does not comment on the rule within 60 days of the notice of proposed rulemaking,[99] unless the agency failed to submit the proposed collection and other information to OIRA at the time of the notice of proposed rulemaking or the agency made a substantial modification in the final rule without giving OIRA at least 60 days to consider the modification.[100] If OIRA does comment on the proposed rule, it may disapprove the collection of information only if the agency's response to OIRA's comments was unreasonable.[101]

If OIRA disapproves a collection of information proposed by an independent regulatory agency, the independent regulatory agency may override that disapproval by a majority vote of the members of the agency.[102]

In practice, OIRA rarely disapproves proposed collections of information either by executive agencies or independent regulatory agencies. As it does under E.O. 12,866, OIRA uses the power of its influence and high administration support to "convince" agencies to make changes, so that the need to disapprove a particular collection of information is rarely an issue.

Decisions to disapprove a collection of information or to instruct an agency to make a "substantive or material change" to a collection of information must be made publicly available together with an explanation of reasons.[103] Any communication between OIRA and a person outside the federal government regarding a proposed collection of information must also be made publicly available, unless disclosure "could lead to retaliation or discrimination against the communicator."[104]

An approval of a collection of information cannot extend for longer than three years.[105] The Act requires an agency essentially to go through the entire

---

97. *Id.* § 3507(c)(3)(A).
98. *Id.* § 3508.
99. *Id.* § 3507(d)(3).
100. *Id.* § 3507(d)(4).
101. *Id.* § 3507(d)(4)(C).
102. *Id.* § 3507(f).
103. *Id.* § 3507(e)(1).
104. *Id.* §§ 3507(e)(2), (3)(B).
105. *Id.*. § 3507(g).

agency, public, and OIRA review process again, prior to the expiration of the three-year period, in order to obtain an extension.[106]

Whenever OIRA approves a collection of information, it assigns a control number to the collection. This is important because the "public protection" provision of the Act states that no one is subject to any penalty for failing to comply with a collection of information that does not display a valid control number.[107] This provision does not protect persons who submit false information, even if the collection of information lacks a valid control number.[108] Moreover, the provision does not protect someone who fails to comply with a *statutory* reporting or recordkeeping requirement, even if the regulatory implementation of that requirement lacks a valid control number.[109] In this circumstance, the person cannot be penalized for failing to utilize the form provided in the regulations (e.g., the 1040 form for reporting income tax), but the person can be penalized for violating the underlying statutory requirement (e.g., to report annually their income). What constitutes a "penalty" under the Act is not without some question. OIRA's regulations indicate that a penalty includes denial of a license, privilege, right, grant, or benefit.[110] A decision by the D.C. Circuit is consistent with that interpretation, finding that an agency's denial of a license for failure to comply with an information requirement that had not received OMB clearance was a penalty under the Act.[111] On the other hand, the Tenth Circuit held that the imposition of interest for unpaid federal taxes was not a penalty.[112]

The 1995 Amendments to the Paperwork Reduction Act[113] added to the public protection provision a statement that the protection of the section can be raised as a complete defense, bar, or otherwise at any time during the agency administrative process or judicial action.[114]

The extent to which courts can enforce the requirements of the Paperwork Reduction Act, other than the public protection provision when raised as a defense to a government penalty action, is unclear. Section 3507 (d)(6)

---

106. *Id.* § 3507(h).
107. *Id.* § 3512.
108. *E.g.*, United States v. Sasser, 974 F.2d 1544, 1554-55 (10th Cir. 1992).
109. *E.g.*, United States v. Wunder, 919 F.2d 34, 38 (6th Cir. 1990). *See also* United States v. Ionia Management S.A., 498 F. Supp. 2d 477, 487-89 (D. Conn. 2007).
110. 5 CFR § 1320.3(j).
111. *See* Saco River Cellular, Inc. v. FCC, 133 F.3d 25 (D.C. Cir. 1998).
112. Springer v. Commissioner, 580 F.3d 1142 (10th Cir. 2009).
113. Pub. L. No. 104-13, 109 Stat.163 (1995).
114. 44 U.S.C. § 3512 (b).

explicitly states that OMB's decision "to approve or not act upon a collection of information contained in an agency rule shall not be subject to judicial review."[115] Much, however, is left unsaid. For example, may courts review an OMB decision to *disapprove* a collection of information in a rule or otherwise? Without directly addressing that issue, the Supreme Court has reviewed an *agency's decision* to modify its rules due to an OMB disapproval, and indeed the Court in that case overturned the agency's modification because the rules did not require "collection of information" within the meaning of the Act and thus were outside OMB's jurisdiction.[116] Similarly, the D.C. Circuit has also reviewed an agency's decision to modify its regulations due to an OMB rejection, and the court in that case reviewed (and sustained) OMB's reasoning in making the rejection. [117]

If OMB has approved a collection of information in a rule, may someone challenge *the agency action* as violative of the Paperwork Reduction Act, as opposed to challenging OMB's decision? The cases uniformly reject such challenges.[118] This conclusion is probably correct, because the explicit bar of review of OMB's decision should likewise insulate the agency's action in reliance on that decision; that is, judicial review of the agency action seems implicitly precluded by statute.[119] Unfortunately, this rationale has not been the basis of the decided cases. Rather, they have stated simply that the PRA does not provide a private cause of action. While it may be true that the Act

---

115. *Id.* § 3507(d)(6).

116. *See* Dole v. United Steelworkers of America, 494 U.S. 26 (1990) (holding that agency-imposed labeling requirement was not subject to OMB review under the Paperwork Reduction Act because the requirement was not an information collection requirement).

117. Action Alliance of Senior Citizens of Greater Philadelphia v. Bowen, 846 F.2d 1449, 1454 (D.C. Cir. 1988) (reviewing OMB's rejection and holding that OMB "pushed the magic button as well as it needed to" in rejecting the agency's information collection requirement), *vacated*, 499 U.S. 1001 (1990); Action Alliance of Senior Citizens of Greater Philadelphia v. Sullivan, 930 F.2d 77, 83 (D.C. Cir. 1991) (noting on remand that prior panel opinion retains "precedential weight" because the Supreme Court did not disapprove its holdings).

118. *See* Ass'n of Am. Physicians & Surgeons, Inc. v. U.S. Dep't of Health & Human Servs., 224 F. Supp. 2d 1115 (S.D. Tex. 2002) (refusing to consider claim that alleged undercounting of burden hours made regulation invalid); Tozzi v. EPA, 148 F. Supp. 2d 35 (D.D.C. 2001) (refusing to hear claim that agency's submission to OMB was incomplete and therefore violated the Act).

119. 5 U.S.C. § 701(1).

itself does not provide a private right of action,[120] this is beside the point in a case brought under the APA or another statute that does create a private cause of action against a government agency for actions that adversely affect or aggrieve a person within the meaning of a relevant statute.[121] This error has consequences when a person challenges a collection of information as violative of the Act precisely because it was never submitted to OMB for approval and never received approval; that is, when OMB has neither approved nor disapproved the collection. Here the Act's preclusive language clearly does not apply. Nevertheless, some courts have likewise denied review here on the basis that the Act does not provide a private cause of action.[122] At least one court has rejected that view and held that a person can sue for violations of the Act in an APA action.[123] It is fair to say that no court has given the issue close analytical consideration. The Paperwork Reduction Act claim is often the last of several claims and combined with clearly spurious claims, so that the courts' treatment of it is not deeply considered.

The success of the Act in reducing paperwork burdens imposed on the public may be presumed. The emphasis the Act places on such reductions clearly has inspired both agencies and OIRA to be more circumspect in their collection requirements than had previously been the case, except with rare exceptions, under the Federal Reports Act. Quantifying the Act's success, however, is difficult despite annual reports required under the Act.[124] As en-

---

120. *See* Sutton v. Providence St. Joseph Medical Center, 192 F.3d 826 (9th Cir. 1999). In this case, a prospective employee was not hired by a hospital because he refused to provide his social security number as required by federal regulations. He sued the hospital on the grounds that the federal requirement for him to provide his social security number violated the Paperwork Reduction Act. The court held that there was no private right of action to enforce the Act.
121. *See* Chrysler Corp. v. Brown, 441 U.S. 281 (1979) (although 18 U.S.C. § 1905 did not provide a private cause of action, adversely affected persons could sue under the APA for an agency violation of that statute).
122. *See* Council on Regulatory and Info. Mgt., Inc. v. U.S. Dep't of Labor, 1993 WL 544303 (D.D.C. 1993). *See also* Teledyne, Inc. v. United States, 50 Fed. Cl. 155, 190 (Fed. Cl. 2001) (appeal by government contractor of agency determination that contractor owed over $100 million, alleging rule requiring payment had not been submitted to OMB as required by Paperwork Reduction Act, dismissed because Act does not provide a private cause of action).
123. Livestock Mktg. Ass'n v. U.S. Dept. of Agric., 132 F. Supp. 2d 817, 831 (D.S.D. 2001).
124. 44 U.S.C. § 3514(a)(1). Despite the requirement for annual reports, annual reports have not always been issued.

acted, the PRA specified mandatory percentage burden reductions; since 2001, it has simply required agencies to set annual burden reduction goals.[125] While paperwork burdens include more than just burden hours,[126] the only two quantified measurements have been burden hours, calculated since before the Act passed, and financial costs, which have been calculated only for a few years. Despite the mandated reduction of burdens—and, until recently, the routine reporting of results that were better than the mandate—the reported burden hours imposed on the public have increased from 1.5 billion burden hours in FY 1981[127] to approximately 9.14 billion burden hours in FY 2011.[128] There are a number of reasons for this discrepancy,[129] most importantly factors beyond agencies' control, such as increased population and new legislation requiring additional collections of information. Moreover, burden hours viewed in isolation are not the best measure of actual burden on the public. For example, substitution of an information disclosure requirement in place of a command-and-control regulation might well reduce substantially the burden of regulation on regulated entities but increase burden hours under the Paperwork Reduction Act. In addition, the fact that approximately 75 percent of all paperwork burdens are attributable to the Treasury Department, the vast majority of which results from Internal Revenue Service reporting and recordkeeping requirements, suggests that paperwork reductions will always be marginal.

11.0412 The Information Collection Budget

In 1979 President Carter initiated the concept of an information collection budget. By executive order he required each executive agency to prepare an annual paperwork budget using burden hours as the standard of measurement.[130] While OMB had been reviewing individual information collection requests for years under the Federal Reports Act, this process focused on the

---

125. *Id.* § 3505(a)(1).
126. *See id.* § 3502(2).
127. *See* U.S. Office of Management and Budget, Information Collection Budget of the United States Government: Fiscal Year 1981.
128. *See* U.S. Office of Management and Budget, Information Collection Budget of the United States Government: 2012, *available at* http://www.whitehouse.gov/sites/default/files/omb/inforeg/icb/icb_2012.pdf.
129. *See* Funk, *supra* note 81 (describing the same phenomenon fifteen years earlier).
130. Exec. Order No. 12,174, 44 Fed. Reg. 69,609 (1979), *rescinded by* Exec. Order No. 12,291, 46 Fed. Reg. 13,193 (1981).

trees and could be said to have missed the forest. An annual review of the entire mass of federal information requests promised a valuable overview of federal paperwork requirements. The production of an annual Information Collection Budget has continued ever since.[131] Although the Paperwork Reduction Act did not specifically require the production of an Information Collection Budget, its requirement to reduce paperwork burdens annually presupposed an accounting of those burdens and plans to limit them.

Unlike a financial budget, however, the budget of burden hours for particular agencies lacks any actual limiting force on the information collections proposed by those agencies or approved by OIRA. Moreover, the Information Collection Budget obscures, rather than highlights, the overall burden-hour impacts of federal information collections, because it focuses on instances where burden hours have been either reduced or increased. Instead of concentrating on the number of burden hours, the Clinton administration concentrated on "improving how agencies collect information."[132] This included "streamlining regulations," "eliminating redundancy," "simplifying forms," "changing statutes," and "using information technology."[133] In the administration of George W. Bush, OIRA focused on eliminating Paperwork Reduction Act violations, reducing the violation rate from over 150 per year during the Clinton administration to just over 50 per year in 2003,[134] and on its E-Government strategy to reduce burdens.[135]

The Obama administration inaugurated a look-back review of existing regulations and information collections that resulted in eliminating "tens of millions of hours of paperwork burden."[136] In particular, there has been an emphasis on shifting from paper reporting to electronic reporting.

---

131. *See* 5 CFR § 1320.17.

132. *See* U.S. Office of Management and Budget, Information Collection Budget of the United States Government: Fiscal Year 2000, at 2, *available at* http://www.whitehouse.gov/omb/inforeg/icbfy2000.pdf.

133. *Id.* at 4-10.

134. *See* U.S. Office of Management and Budget , Managing Information Collection and Dissemination, FY 2003, at 12, *available at* http://www.whitehouse.gov/sites/default/files/omb/inforeg/icb/2003_info_coll_dism.pdf.

135. *Id.* at 7.

136. *See* U.S. Office of Management and Budget, Information Collection Budget of the United States Government: 2012, *available at* http://www.whitehouse.gov/sites/default/files/omb/inforeg/icb/icb_2012.pdf.

11.042 The Regulatory Budget and the Regulatory Right to Know Act

Perhaps inspired by President Carter's Information Collection Budget, in 1979 the Joint Economic Committee of Congress recommended consideration of the adoption of a "regulatory budget" that would set an annual limit on the costs imposed on the economy by government regulations.[137] As described by Fix and Eads,

> the concept of a regulatory budget is closely analogous to that of a financial budget. Costs and benefits would be estimated in dollar terms for all proposed regulations. Through a process akin to that employed in putting together a financial budget, agencies would be allotted ceilings representing the total regulatory costs they would be permitted to impose on the economy. Once these ceilings were set, the precise details of how regulations were written and imposed would be left to the agencies.[138]

In 1981, E.O. 12,291 required the Presidential Task Force on Regulatory Relief and the Office of Management and Budget to "develop procedures for estimating the annual benefits and costs of agency regulations, on both an aggregate and economic or industrial sector basis, for purposes of compiling a regulatory budget." In 1985-86, the Administrative Conference of the United States studied this concept, but no recommendation or report resulted. Several bills in Congress were introduced that included required agency regulatory budgets, but none passed. Ultimately, most people involved in the process came to believe that a regulatory budget was probably not an effective tool for managing the federal regulatory process. Not only would the process of determining the costs of regulation be daunting and the results highly debatable, but also the idea of limiting regulations on the basis of their "costs" without regard to their "benefits" seemed counterproductive.

Nevertheless, Congress did include as riders to several appropriation bills a requirement for OMB to "estimate the total annual costs and benefits (including quantifiable and nonquantifiable effects) of Federal rules and paper-

---

137. *See* Christopher C. DeMuth, *The Regulatory Budget*, 4 Regulation 29, 30 (1980), *cited at* Robert V. Percival, *Checks Without Balance: Executive Office Oversight of the Environmental Protection Agency*, 54 Law & Contemp. Probs. 127, 147 n.115 (1991).

138. Michael Fix & George C. Eads, *The Prospects for Regulatory Reform: The Legacy of Reagan's First Term*, 2 Yale J. on Reg. 293, 312 (1985).

work" in the aggregate, by agency and agency program, and by major rule.[139] This requirement is now codified and is popularly known as the Regulatory Right-to-Know Act.[140] This estimate must go through public notice and comment[141] as well as peer review[142] and is then submitted to Congress as part of OMB's annual budget package.[143] Although the Act suggests that the estimate is to cover all federal rules for the prior year, OMB has traditionally reported the estimated average annual costs and benefits for the prior ten years of those "major" rules for which agencies monetized costs and benefits. The most recent final report, covering FY2003-2012, estimated that the 115 rules considered would produce benefits of between $192.7 billion and $799.7 billion and impose costs of between $56.6 billion and $83.7 billion.[144] These results are generally consistent with the findings of previous years' reports. Although OMB's reports have stimulated substantial debate over the proper methodology to be used in making any such accounting, the impact of the reports' quantified and unquantified costs and benefits of regulations seems to have been slight. That is, no statutory or regulatory changes appear to have resulted from the published reports of costs and benefits.

11.043 The Government Performance and Results Act

The Government Performance and Results Act of 1993, as amended by the GPRA Modernization Act of 2010, requires agencies to prepare a strategic plan and performance plan annually, and to post these plans on the agency's website and notify the President and Congress of their availability.

The strategic plan must include a mission statement, a general statement of goals, a description of how those goals are to

---

139. *See, e.g.*, Treasury & General Government Appropriations Act, Pub. L. No. 106-58, § 628(a), 113 Stat 430, 472 (1999); Omnibus Consolidated & Emergency Supplemental Appropriations Act, Pub. L. No. 105-277, Div. A, Title VI, § 638(a), 112 Stat. 2681, 2681-526 (1998).
140. Consolidated Appropriations Act of 2001, Pub. L. No. 106-554, § 1(a)(3) & App. C § 624, 114 Stat. 2763, 2763, 2763A-161 (2000) (published as a note to 31 U.S.C.A. 1105).
141. *Id.* § 624(b).
142. *Id.*§ 624(d).
143. *Id.*§ 624(a).
144. *See* U.S. Office of Management and Budget, 2013 Report to Congress on the Benefits and Costs of Federal Regulations and Unfunded Mandates on State, Local, and Tribal Entities, *available at* http://www.whitehouse.gov/sites/default/files/omb/inforeg/2013_cb/2013_cost_benefit_report.pdf.

be achieved, a description of obstacles to their achievement, and a description of how the agency's performance goals contribute to its strategic goals, among other statements. The performance plan must establish performance goals, express those goals in objective, quantifiable, and measurable form (unless the director of OMB determines it is not feasible to do so), describe how these goals contribute to the agency's strategic plan and the federal government's performance goals, identify how these goals are to be achieved, provide a basis for measuring its performance, and identify low-priority activities, among other statements. The agency head must also make available updates on performance, comparing actual performance achievements with the agency's performance goals, not less than 150 days after the end of the fiscal year, and more frequently if it can do so at a reasonable level of administrative burden. These updates must provide a detailed review and assessment of the agency's successes and failures in achieving its performance goals. OMB must make an annual determination of whether the agency met its performance goals, and report on unmet goals to the head of the agency, the House Committee on Oversight and Governmental Reform, and the GAO. If the agency's activities have not met its performance goals as determined by OMB for one fiscal year, the agency must designate a senior official to oversee its performance improvement and must submit a performance improvement plan to OMB. If OMB determines the agency's activities have not met its performance goals for two consecutive years, the agency head must submit to Congress a description of the actions the administration will take to improve performance, and describe any additional funding the agency will obligate to achieve the goal. If OMB determines the agency has not met its performance goals for three consecutive fiscal years, OMB shall submit recommendations to Congress on actions to improve the agency's performance, including reauthorization proposals, statutory changes, and planned executive actions.

The director of OMB must coordinate with agencies to improve the performance of the federal government and to establish priority goals, and every two years, or as otherwise determined by the director of OMB, the head of each agency shall identify a set of priority goals.

[Blackletter Statement, Part 6, § IV.B.]

If the actualization of a regulatory budget proved problematic, Congress provided a substitute in the Government Performance and Results Act of 1993.[145] The purpose of the Act was to improve government performance by requiring agencies to set quantifiable performance goals and then to assess their performance against their goals. The Act initially required all agencies not later than September 30, 1997, to make a "strategic plan" for their program activities covering a period of not less than five years.[146] As amended by the GPRA Modernization Act of 2010,[147] this plan is to include a comprehensive mission statement for all major functions and operations, general goals and objectives for these functions and operations, a description of how the goals and objectives contribute to the federal government's priority goals, a description of how the goals and objectives will be achieved, a description of how the goals and objectives reflect consideration of congressional suggestions, a description of how the performance goals identified in the performance plan (see below) contribute to the goals in the strategic plan, an identification of those external factors beyond the agency's control that might impede achievement of the goals and objectives, and a description of the program evaluations used in establishing the goals and objectives.[148]

This strategic plan is the backdrop for the additional requirement that each agency prepare an annual "performance plan" for each program activity contained in its budget.[149] The performance plan must establish performance goals for each program activity, which goals are to be objective, quantifiable, and measurable.[150] The performance plan also describes how the performance goals contribute to the goals of the agency's strategic plan as well as the federal government's performance goals, and it identifies which goals have priority.[151] Moreover, it describes how the goals will be achieved, including the processes and resources necessary to meet the goals and clear milestones; establishes performance indicators for measuring outcomes; provides a basis for comparing program goals with program results; and describes the means

---

145. Government Performance & Results Act, Pub. L. No. 103-62, 107 Stat. 285 (1993) (codified in scattered sections of Titles 5 and 31 of the United States Code). The Act is variously referred to as "GPRA" (pronounced "gipra") and the "Results Act."
146. *See* 5 U.S.C. § 306.
147. Pub. L. No. 111-352, 124 Stat 3866 (2011).
148. 5 U.S.C. § 306.
149. 31 U.S.C. § 1115(b).
150. *Id.* § 1115(b)(1)-(2).
151. *Id.* § 1115(b)(3).

to be used to verify the measured values.[152] The plan is also to identify major management challenges and how the agency plans to address those challenges.[153] The Act authorizes the Director of OMB to waive the requirement that the performance goals be in an objective, quantifiable, and measurable form if it is not feasible to so express them and to provide instead an alternative form.[154] The Act also requires the Director of OMB to include "a Federal Government performance plan" in the annual budget.[155]

The agency performance plans become the benchmarks for required annual program "performance reports."[156] Each agency is to post on its website and report to the President and Congress a report on program performance for the previous year.[157] This report describes the extent of the success in meeting the performance goals for the previous year, evaluates the new performance plan in light of the performance achieved under the previous performance plan, and explains why any program goal was not achieved and how to remedy the situation.[158] Both the annual performance plan and the annual performance report are required to be prepared by federal employees,[159] thereby preventing agencies from contracting out these activities.

These requirements have generated a lot of paperwork. The actual impact on agency activity seems not so great, though few empirical studies have been done to identify any such impact. A 2001 General Accounting Office study found that in only seven of twenty-eight agencies did a majority of federal grant-making officers attempt to follow the Act's procurement guidelines.[160] A more recent GAO report identifies a number of areas in which agencies have failed to implement the Act fully.[161]

---

152. *Id.* §§ 1115(b)(4)-(8).
153. *Id.* § 1115(b)(9).
154. *Id.* § 1115(c).
155. *Id.* § 1115(a).
156. *Id.* § 1116.
157. *Id.* § 1116(a).
158. *Id.* § 1116(b).
159. *Id.* §§ 1115(f), 1116(e).
160. Gen. Accounting Office, Managing For Results: Federal Managers' Views on Key Issues Vary Widely Across Agencies 10 (GAO-01-592, 2001).
161. *See* Gov't Accountability Office, Managing For Results: Executive Branch Should More Fully Implement the GPRA Modernization Act to Address Pressing Governance Challenges (GAO-13-518, 2013).

11.044 Regulatory Flexibility Act

The Regulatory Flexibility Act of 1980, 5 U.S.C. §§ 601-612, requires agencies to consider the special needs and concerns of small entities in the regulatory process. Small entities include small businesses as defined in the Small Business Act, 15 U.S.C. §§ 631 et seq.; not-for-profit organizations that are not dominant in their field; and governmental jurisdictions with a population of less than 50,000.

1. Unified Agenda

In October and April of each year, each agency must publish a "regulatory flexibility agenda" in the *Federal Register* that identifies and describes all rules under consideration that are likely to have a significant economic impact on a substantial number of small entities. The agenda must be submitted to the chief counsel for advocacy of the Small Business Administration (SBA) for comment.

2. Regulatory Flexibility Analysis

When proposing a regulation subject to notice-and-comment requirements, whether under the APA or any other law, an agency must make available for public comment an initial regulatory flexibility analysis (IRFA), unless the agency head certifies that the proposed rule will not have a significant economic impact on a substantial number of small entities. Courts have interpreted the significant economic impact as being limited to the direct costs of having to comply with a regulation and not including the indirect economic effects on small entities that may result from a regulation. The IRFA must be submitted to the chief counsel for advocacy of the Small Business Administration, and either a copy of the IRFA or a summary must be published in the *Federal Register*. An IRFA must contain a description of the reasons why the agency is considering the rule, a statement of the objectives of and legal basis for the rule, a description of and (where feasible) an estimate of the number of small entities to which the rule will apply, a description of any reporting or record-keeping requirements contained in the rule, an identification of other federal rules that may duplicate or overlap with the rule, and a description of significant alternatives to the rule that would accomplish

the stated objectives while minimizing economic effects on small entities. The Consumer Financial Protection Bureau must also include a discussion of those alternatives, a description of any increase in the cost of credit for small entities resulting from the proposed rule, a description of the alternatives to the proposed rule that accomplish the stated objectives of applicable statutes and minimize any increase in the cost of credit for small entities, and advice for small entities regarding impacts of the proposed rule on the cost of credit.

In the case of rules issued by the Environmental Protection Agency, the Consumer Financial Protection Bureau, or the Occupational Safety and Health Administration, the agency must, prior to publication of the IRFA, notify the chief counsel for advocacy of the potential impacts of the proposed rule on small entities, so that he may identify representatives of the likely affected small entities for their advice and recommendations about the potential impacts. Unless this requirement is waived by the chief counsel for advocacy, these agencies must then convene a review panel consisting of employees from the agency, OIRA, and the chief counsel's office to review the proposed regulation, any other material developed in connection with the proposed rule, and the comments of the small-entity representatives. Within sixty days, the review panel must publicly report on the comments and its findings on the issues discussed in the IRFA. Other agencies *may* in their discretion also utilize this procedure if they wish.

Unless the agency head certifies that the final rule will not have a significant economic impact on a substantial number of small entities, it must be published with a final regulatory flexibility analysis (FRFA). The FRFA must contain a statement of the need for and objectives of the rule; a statement of and response to significant issues raised by the comments received (including in particular those of the chief counsel for advocacy of the SBA); a description of the small entities to which the rule will apply and an estimate of their number; a description of any reporting or recordkeeping requirements; a description of the steps the agency has taken to minimize the economic impact on small entities, including a statement of the reasons for adopting the alternative selected and for not adopting other alternatives; and, in the case of the Consumer Financial Protection Bureau, a description of the steps the agency has taken to minimize any additional cost of credit for small entities. If a rule is a response to an

emergency, the head of an agency may delay the completion of the FRFA until not later than 180 days after the publication of the final rule. If the FRFA is not published within 180 days, the rule automatically lapses and has no effect.

Neither the chief counsel nor a Regulatory Review Panel has authority to veto or reject an agency proposal or regulatory flexibility analysis. The chief counsel is required to report annually to the President and to relevant congressional committees on agency compliance with the act and is authorized to appear as amicus curiae in any action seeking judicial review of a rule.

3. Periodic Review of Rules

The Regulatory Flexibility Act also requires agencies to engage in a ten-year review cycle of their regulations that have a significant economic effect on a substantial number of small entities. Each year agencies are to publish in the *Federal Register* the list of such rules that are to be reviewed in the following twelve months.

4. Judicial Review

A small entity adversely affected or aggrieved by final agency action may obtain judicial review under the APA of an agency's compliance with the requirements applicable to FRFAs, the validity of any certification that a rule will not have a significant economic effect on a substantial number of small entities, and an agency's compliance with the requirement for periodic review of its rules. The Act establishes a maximum statute of limitations for such actions at one year from the date of the final agency action. The act allows a court, in addition to or in lieu of its other remedial powers under the APA, to defer the enforcement of a rule against small entities.

[Blackletter Statement, Part 6, § IV.C.]

The Regulatory Flexibility Act imposes special rulemaking requirements on agencies when their rules would have a significant economic impact on a substantial number of small entities. Most importantly, agencies must prepare an initial regulatory flexibility analysis (IRFA) to accompany any such proposed rule (including proposed interpretive rules issued by the Internal Revenue Service)[162] and a final regulatory flexibility analysis (FRFA) to accompany

162. 5 U.S.C. § 603.

the final rule.[163] The IRFA must contain a description of the reasons why the agency is considering the rule, a statement of the objectives of and legal basis for the rule, a description of and (where feasible) an estimate of the number of small entities to which the rule will apply, a description of any reporting or recordkeeping requirements contained in the rule, an identification of other federal rules that may duplicate or overlap with the rule, and a description of significant alternatives to the rule that would accomplish the stated objectives while minimizing economic effects on small entities. The FRFA must contain a statement of the need for and objectives of the rule, a statement of and response to significant issues raised by the comments received (including in particular those of the Chief Counsel for Advocacy of the Small Business Administration (SBA)), a description of the small entities to which the rule will apply and an estimate of their number, a description of any reporting or recordkeeping requirements, and a description of the steps the agency has taken to minimize the economic impact on small entities, including a statement of the reasons for adopting the alternative selected and for not adopting other alternatives.

The Act imposes additional requirements on the Environmental Protection Agency (EPA), the Consumer Financial Protection Bureau (CFPB), and the Occupation Safety and Health Commission (OSHA). Before these agencies publish their IRFAs, they must inform the Chief Counsel of the SBA of the potential impacts of their proposed rules on small entities and the type of small entities that might be affected.[164] Within fifteen days the Chief Counsel is to identify representatives of affected small entities in order to obtain their advice and recommendations about the potential impacts of the proposed rule.[165] In addition, unless waived by the Chief Counsel after consultation with the Administrator of OIRA and the representatives of small entities,[166] the agency must convene a review panel consisting of persons in the agency responsible for the rule and staff from the Office of Management and Budget and the Chief Counsel's office. The panel reviews the proposed rule and the comments and recommendations of the representatives of the small entities in light of the considerations contained in the IRFA and provides a report of its findings.[167]

A CFPB IRFA must also include a description of any projected increase in the cost of credit for small entities and any significant alternatives to the proposed rule which accomplish the stated objectives of applicable statutes

163. *Id.* § 604.
164. *Id.* §§ 609(b), (d).
165. *Id.* § 609(b)(2).
166. *Id.* § 609(e).
167. *Id.* §§ 609(b)(3)-(5).

and which minimize any increase in the cost of credit for small entities.[168] A CFPB FRFA must include a description of the steps the agency has taken to minimize any additional cost of credit for small entities.[169]

All of the above requirements may be avoided if the head of the agency certifies that the proposed or final rule will not have a significant economic impact on a substantial number of small entities.[170] Such a certification must be published in the Federal Register with the proposed or final rule with a statement explaining the basis for the certification. The certification and statement must also be sent to the Chief Counsel for Advocacy of the Small Business Administration.

The above requirements also may be avoided if the agency is not required to publish a notice of proposed rulemaking. However, IRS interpretive rules concerning the internal revenue laws *are* subject to the Act even though they might not require a notice of proposed rulemaking.[171]

The Act also requires agencies to publish in the Federal Register a "regulatory flexibility agenda" in October and April of each year.[172] For each rule expected to be issued or proposed by an agency that is likely to have a significant economic effect on a substantial number of small entities the agenda must set out: a description of the subject area involved; a summary of the rule, including its objectives and legal basis and a schedule for completing action on any rule for which a notice of proposed rulemaking has been issued; and the name and telephone number of an agency official knowledgeable concerning the rule. The agenda is also to be sent to the Chief Counsel for Advocacy of the Small Business Administration. Under E.O. 12,866, the information required for the regulatory flexibility agenda may be used as part of the Unified Agenda required by the Order.[173]

In addition, the Act requires agencies to engage in the periodic review of their rules that have a significant economic impact on a substantial number of small entities.[174] By July 1981, each agency was required to publish in the Federal Register a plan under which all such rules would be reviewed within ten years and any rules issued after July 1981 would be reviewed within ten years of their issuance. The Act authorizes the head of any agency to extend the ten-year period in one-year increments for a time not to exceed five years

---

168. *Id.* § 603(d).
169. *Id.* § 604(a)(6).
170. *Id.* § 605(b).
171. *Id.* § 603(a).
172. *Id.* § 602.
173. *See* Exec. Order No. 12,866, § 4b, 58 Fed. Reg. 51,735 (1993).
174. 5 U.S.C. § 610.

if the head of the agency certifies that completion is not feasible within ten years. Each year the agency must publish in the Federal Register the list of the rules that will be reviewed in the coming year. The purpose of the review is to assess whether existing rules should be retained, amended, or rescinded in order to minimize their economic impact on small entities consistent with the objectives of the statutes under which the rules are promulgated. The Act directs that agencies reviewing a rule should consider the continued need for the rule; the nature of any complaints or comments received from the public about the rule; the complexity of the rule; the extent to which the rule overlaps or conflicts with other rules; the length of time since the agency has evaluated the rule; and the extent to which technological, economic, or other factors have changed since the last evaluation.

As originally enacted, the Act expressly prohibited judicial review of agency compliance with any of its requirements. Accordingly, most courts limited review to a determination under the APA of the reasonableness of a final rule based on the record before the agency, which included the regulatory flexibility analysis and any comments from small entities expressing the hardships associated with a proposed rule.[175]

In 1996, after noting that agencies were too often ignoring the requirements of the Act, Congress amended the Act to provide judicial review to small entities adversely affected or aggrieved by a final agency action. The amended Act permits review of agency compliance with certain sections of the Act and, without expressly precluding other relief, specifies the possibility of remanding the rule to the agency or deferring enforcement against the entity.[176]

Courts are instructed to conduct their review in accordance with Chapter 7 of the APA.[177] Several courts have read this cross-reference to mean that the standard of review is reasonableness, meaning that the agency must have made a reasonable, good-faith effort to carry out the requirements of the statute.[178] Under the reasonableness standard, an FRFA need only consider

---

175. *See, e.g.*, State of Michigan v. Thomas, 805 F.2d 176 (6th Cir. 1986); Thompson v. Clark, 741 F.2d 401 (D.C. Cir. 1984).

176. *See* 5 U.S.C. § 611. *See also* U.S. Telecom Ass'n v. FCC, 400 F.3d 29 (D.C. Cir. 2005) (remanding rule to agency to prepare a FRFA and staying enforcement of the rule against small entities pending its preparation and publication).

177. 5 U.S.C. §§ 611(a)(1), (2), (4).

178. *See* Associated Fisheries of Me., Inc. v. Daley, 127 F.3d 104, 114 (1st Cir. 1997); *see also* S. Offshore Fishing Ass'n v. Daley, 995 F.Supp. 1411 (M.D. Fla. 1998).

significant alternatives to a rule, rather than all alternatives.[179] Similarly, an agency must make a reasonable effort to facilitate participation by small entities, but the method and manner of accomplishing this is left to agency discretion, since the Act only offers suggestions.[180] One case applied the reasonableness standard and concluded that the agency's certification of no significant economic impact on a substantial number of small entities was unsatisfactory, because the evidence contradicted many of the assumptions upon which the certification was based.[181] Other cases have found that the agency's certification was reasonable.[182]

In several cases, a party has challenged the adequacy of an agency certification of no significant impact on the ground that the agency failed to consider the impact of the proposed rule on an entity *affected* by the rule but not actually *regulated* by it. The first such case, *Mid-Tex Electric Cooperative, Inc. v. FERC*,[183] determined that the certification was appropriate because the agency need only consider the rule's direct impact on regulated entities and not the indirect impacts of the rule on entities not regulated by the agency. More recent cases have affirmed *Mid-Tex's* holding.[184]

The Act specifies that judicial review of its provisions can only be had under the terms of the Act,[185] and the Act does not provide for review of compliance with all of its provisions. Notably, it does not provide review for compliance with the IRFA requirements or the special requirements for the EPA, CFPB, and OSHA to consult with Chief Counsel and representatives of small entities or to convene a review panel.[186] At least one court has held that persons who are not themselves "small entities" cannot sue to enforce the Act's provisions.[187]

---

179. *See Associated Fisheries*, 127 F.3d at 116.
180. *See id.* at 117.
181. *See Southern Offshore*, 995 F. Supp. at 1436.
182. *See, e.g.*, Nat'l Restaurant Ass'n v. Solis, 870 F. Supp. 2d 42 (D.D.C. 2012); Boatmen v. Gutierrez, 429 F. Supp. 2d 543 (E.D.N.Y. 2006).
183. 773 F.2d 327 (D.C. Cir. 1985).
184. *See, e.g.*, Cement Kiln Recycling Coalition v. EPA, 255 F.3d 855 (D.C. Cir. 2001); Motor & Equipment Mfrs. Ass'n v. Nichols, 142 F.3d 449, 467 (D.C. Cir. 1998); United Distribution Cos. v. FERC, 88 F.3d 1105, 1170 (D.C. Cir. 1996); State of Colo. *ex rel.* Colo. State Banking Bd. v. Resolution Trust, 926 F.2d 931 (10th Cir. 1991); *but see* Federal Aeronautical Repair Station Ass'n, Inc. v. FAA, 494 F.3d 161 (D.C. Cir. 2007).
185. *See* 5 U.S.C. § 611(c).
186. *See* 5 U.S.C. § 611(a)(1).
187. *See* Western Wood Preservers Inst. v. McHugh, 925 F. Supp. 2d 63 (D.D.C. 2013).

11.045 Attorney General Supervision of Litigation

> **By statute, the Department of Justice authorizes and handles most litigation involving agencies, including both enforcement actions that an agency wishes to bring and challenges to agency action under the APA. Even where an agency does have independent litigating authority, the attorney general and the solicitor general, with rare exceptions, have the exclusive authority to pursue and conduct litigation in the Supreme Court on behalf of the agency. By controlling the agency's litigation, the Department is able to affect the manner in which agencies perform their statutory duties.**
>
> **[Blackletter Statement, Part 6, § IV.D.]**

By statute, the Attorney General is responsible for supervising "all litigation to which the United States, an agency, or officer thereof is a party," unless otherwise provided by law.[188] As a result, the Department of Justice controls the large majority of litigation involving federal agencies, including both enforcement actions brought by the agency and challenges to agency action under the APA.[189] In the former, if the Department of Justice does not approve, the agency cannot bring the enforcement action. In the latter, if the Department will not defend the agency (which is extraordinarily rare), it may confess judgment against the agency. While normally the Department makes decisions on a case-by-case basis, there have been occasions when the Attorney General has made generic determinations with respect to classes of cases. For example, during the Clinton administration, the Attorney General issued a memorandum to all agencies stating that the Department would not defend suits against an agency brought

---

188. 28 U.S.C. § 516 ("Except as otherwise authorized by law, the conduct of litigation in which the United States, an agency, or officer thereof is a party, or is interested, and securing evidence therefor, is reserved to officers of the Department of Justice, under the direction of the Attorney General."); *see also id.* § 519 ("Except as otherwise authorized by law, the Attorney General shall supervise all litigation to which the United States, an agency, or officer thereof is a party, and shall direct all United States attorneys, assistant United States attorneys, and special attorneys appointed under section 543 of this title in the discharge of their respective duties.").

189. A useful description and assessment is Neal Devins & Michael Herz, *The Uneasy Case for Department of Justice Control of Federal Litigation*, 5 U. PA. J. CONST. L. 558 (2003).

under the Freedom of Information Act to disclose records exempt from disclosure unless the agency "reasonably foresees that disclosure would be harmful to an interest protected by that exemption."[190] That is, the Department would not defend suits for disclosure of even exempt records unless harm from disclosure was reasonably foreseeable. Shortly after the Bush administration came into office, however, Attorney General Ashcroft rescinded the Clinton Attorney General memorandum, issuing a new one that assured agencies that Justice would defend their nondisclosure of exempt documents.[191] When the Obama administration took office, the Attorney General rescinded the Ashcroft memorandum and essentially reinstated the Clinton era policy.[192]

There are exceptions to the Attorney General's supervision of litigation. Some independent regulatory agencies have independent litigating authority under certain circumstances,[193] as does the Tennessee Valley Authority.[194] Among executive agencies, such authority is much rarer, though the Department of Labor is one example,[195] and EPA has, but never uses, authority to represent itself under some of its statutes if the Attorney General refuses to do so.[196]

Separate from the Attorney General's general responsibility for supervising all litigation to which the United States or an agency is a party, the

---

190. Memorandum from Attorney General Janet Reno to the Heads of Departments and Agencies (Oct. 4, 1993), available at http:// www.usdoj.gov/oip/foia_updates/Vol_XIV_3/page3.htm.
191. Memorandum from Attorney General John Ashcroft to the Heads of All Federal Departments and Agencies (Oct. 12, 2001), *available at* http://www.justice.gov/archive/oip/foiapost/2001foiapost19.htm.
192. *See* Memorandum from Attorney General Eric Holder to the Heads of All Federal Departments and Agencies (March 19, 2009), *available at* http://www.justice.gov/ag/foia-memo-march2009.pdf.
193. *See, e.g.*, 16 U.S.C. § 823b(d)(6) (Federal Energy Regulatory Commission); 15 U.S.C. § 56 (Federal Trade Commission).
194. *See, e.g.*, Tenn. Valley Auth. v. EPA, 278 F.3d 1184 (11th Cir. 2002).
195. *See* 29 U.S.C. § 663 (providing that except in the Supreme Court "the Solicitor of Labor may appear for and represent the Secretary in any civil litigation brought under [the Occupational Safety and Health Act] but all such litigations shall be subject to the direction and control of the Attorney General"); *id.* § 2005(b) (providing that Solicitor may represent the Secretary in actions under the Employee Polygraph Protection Act); *id.* § 2617(e) (providing same for actions under the Family and Medical Leave Act).
196. Clean Air Act § 305, 42 U.S.C. § 7605; Clean Water Act § 506, 33 U.S.C. § 1366; Safe Drinking Water Act § 1450(f), 42 U.S.C. § 300j-9(f).

Attorney General and Solicitor General are, absent specific legislation,[197] the only officers authorized to represent the interests of the United States in the Supreme Court, the Court of Federal Claims, the Federal Circuit, and the Court of International Trade.[198]

---

197. *See, e.g.*, 15 U.S.C. § 56(a)(3) (Federal Trade Commission).
198. *See* 28 U.S.C. § 518.

Appendix

A BLACKLETTER STATEMENT OF FEDERAL ADMINISTRATIVE LAW (EXCERPTS)

PART THREE
SCOPE OF REVIEW

I. GENERAL

Except where a statute § 7provides otherwise, courts generally review agency action according to the principles set forth below. These principles collectively constitute a judicial gloss on § 706 of the APA, although courts do not always describe them as such. In applying these principles, a court should distinguish among the agency's legal, factual, and policy conclusions, because different standards of review apply to each category.

If a particular challenge has not been properly preserved at the administrative level, the reviewing court has discretion not to address it. If the unpreserved challenge relates to an issue of fact or policy, the court typically is not permitted to adjudicate it (see *infra* § VI).

II. STANDARDS OF REVIEW: STATUTORY ISSUES

A. In General

The court will set aside an agency action if it finds that the action exceeds the authority granted, or violates limitations imposed, by a federal statute. APA § 706(2)(C).

B. Determining Statutory Requirements—The *Chevron* Doctrine

Where Congress has delegated to an agency the power to speak with the force of law, and the agency has, in the course of exercising that power, interpreted ambiguity in the statute that it administers, the reviewing court must afford some deference to the agency's reasonable statutory interpretation. Such deference is provided by the two-part "*Chevron* test." See *Chevron U.S.A., Inc. v. NRDC*, 467 U.S. 837 (1984).

Under step one of the *Chevron* test, the reviewing court determines whether the statutory meaning with respect to the precise issue before it is "clear" (and thus, not "ambiguous"). Step one of *Chevron* does not dictate that courts use any particular method of statutory interpretation. However, the court should use "the traditional tools of statutory construction" to determine whether the meaning of the statute is clear with respect to the precise issue before it. For most judges, these tools include examination of the text of the statute, dictionary definitions, canons of construction, statutory structure, legislative purpose, and legislative history.

If the statutory meaning on the precise issue before the court is not clear, or if the statute is silent on that issue, the court is required to defer to the agency's interpretation of the statute if that interpretation is "reasonable" or "permissible" (step two of *Chevron*).

While there is no single, established method of conducting the step two analysis, two interrelated approaches are most prominent. First, courts regularly examine the same statutory materials relied on in step one, seeking to determine whether the statute, even if subject to more than one interpretation, can support the particular interpretation adopted by the agency. For example, the court might find that the statutory context, viewed as a whole, clearly rules out the option the agency selected, or a premise on which it relied. (Some courts, however, make essentially the same inquiry within step one when they determine whether the agency interpretation violates the clear meaning of the statute. As a practical matter, the court's review of these legal issues is not affected by which step is deemed to be involved. In either case, the court is measuring the interpretation against congressionally established limitations.)

Second, in addition to engaging in conventional statutory construction, or in some cases instead of engaging in it, courts at step two of *Chevron* evaluate whether the agency, in reaching its interpretation, reasoned from statutory premises in a well-considered fashion. Courts may look, for example, to whether the interpretation is supported by a reasonable explanation and is logically coherent, or they may ask whether the agency interpretation is arbitrary or capricious in substance. In this regard, the step two inquiry tends to merge with review under the "arbitrary and capricious" standard (see *infra* § V).

C. The Scope of *Chevron*

(1) *Chevron* principles apply to an agency's interpretation of a statute the agency administers, where
  a. the interpretation is embodied in a rule that has the force of law;
  b. the interpretation was developed in the course of formal adjudication, except where the adjudicating agency's lawmaking power is limited by virtue of a "split-enforcement" statutory scheme, in which lawmaking authority over the same subject has been vested in an enforcing agency;
  c. the interpretation was developed in the course of informal agency action if the agency's conferred authority and other statutory circumstances demonstrate that "Congress would expect the agency to be able to speak with the force of law" in taking such action, *United States v. Mead Corp.*, 533 U.S. 218, 229 (2001); or
  d. the interstitial nature of the legal question, the related expertise of the agency, the importance of the question to administration of the statute, the complexity of that administration, and the careful consideration the agency has given the question over a long period of time indicate that *Chevron* deference is appropriate.

(2) *Chevron* principles do not apply to agency interpretations
  a. of statutes that apply to many agencies and are specially administered by none, such as the APA, Freedom of Information Act (FOIA), or the National Environmental Policy Act (although *Chevron* may apply to interpretations of statutes administered by two or a few agencies);

b. of criminal statutes where the agency's power with respect to the statute consists solely of the power to prosecute offenses in court;

c. that contradict the interpretation of a statute given in a controlling judicial decision if that court's opinion indicates that its interpretation follows from the unambiguous terms of the statute and thus leaves no room for agency discretion;

d. that represent merely the agency's litigating posture developed after the agency's decision; or

e. that are embodied in policy statements, manuals, enforcement guidelines, interpretive rules, and other such documents unless the agency's conferred authority and other statutory circumstances demonstrate that "Congress would expect the agency to be able to speak with the force of law" in taking such action.

(3) Although in general courts have extended *Chevron* deference to agencies' interpretations of the boundaries of their own statutory jurisdiction, *Chevron* principles have uncertain application to an agency interpretation that significantly expands the agency's previously recognized jurisdiction.

D. *Skidmore* Deference

Even in situations in which *Chevron* principles do not apply, such as those just mentioned, courts ordinarily will give some deference or weight to an agency's interpretation of a statute that it administers. In these circumstances, as the Supreme Court ruled in *Skidmore v. Swift & Co.*, 323 U.S. 134 (1944), the agency's view can have "power to persuade," as distinguished from "power to control." In determining whether and to what extent an agency interpretation deserves *Skidmore* deference, courts are guided by such factors as the thoroughness evident in its consideration, the validity of its reasoning, and its consistency with earlier and later pronouncements.

In various circumstances, the rigor of a court's scrutiny when it applies *Skidmore* sometimes appears to resemble *Chevron* deference, but at other times it appears significantly more intrusive. No clear pattern emerges from the cases. When faced with uncertainty as to whether its review should be governed by *Chevron* or *Skidmore*, a court will sometimes declare that it does not need to choose, because it would uphold, or would reject, the agency's interpretation under either standard.

III. STANDARDS OF REVIEW: NONSTATUTORY LEGAL ISSUES

A. The court will set aside an agency action if it finds that the action exceeds the authority granted, or violates limitations imposed, by
   1. the Constitution;
   2. an agency rule having the force of law (as opposed to, for example, internal operating procedures);
   3. federal common law, in the rare cases in which it applies;
   4. any other source of law that is binding upon the agency, including a consent decree or other judicial order, international law, and (to the extent applicable and enforceable by their terms) executive orders.

   See APA §§ 706(2)(A) (requiring invalidation of agency action "not in accordance with law"), 706(2)(B) (requiring invalidation of agency action that is "contrary to constitutional right, power, privilege, or immunity").

B. Except as provided in subsection C, below, in resolving legal issues arising under the foregoing sources of law, courts have no established tradition of deference to any agency, although they occasionally give some weight to the agency's views.

C. Pursuant to what is sometimes called "*Auer*" or "*Seminole Rock*" deference, a court must accept an agency's interpretation of its own regulation unless the agency's interpretation is "plainly erroneous or inconsistent with the regulation." *Auer v. Robbins*, 519 U.S. 452, 461 (1997) (quoting *Bowles v. Seminole Rock & Sand Co.*, 325 U.S. 410, 414 (1945)). The Supreme Court has applied *Auer* deference to agency interpretations, as in litigation briefs, that are not the outgrowth of any formal process within the agency as long as it appears that the interpretation reflects the agency's fair and considered judgment. A lesser degree of deference is sometimes considered appropriate where Congress has not delegated lawmaking authority to the agency or where an agency seeks deference for an interpretation of a regulation that merely parrots the language of the statute.

IV. STANDARDS OF REVIEW: ISSUES OF FACT

The following standards apply, as specified herein, when courts review agencies' findings regarding purely factual questions. These standards also are commonly used to review agency findings that may be termed "factual" but actually embody a degree of normative judgment. (Such findings present what are sometimes called questions of "ultimate fact" or of "application of law to fact," or "mixed questions of law and fact.") In reviewing these findings, a court is likely to look exclusively to the standards expounded in this section if the meaning of the law is not in dispute. Where, however, the parties do disagree about the meaning of relevant law, the reviewing court must resolve that dispute using the appropriate test for adjudicating issues of law (see *supra* §§ II, III); if the agency action survives that scrutiny, the court then applies the appropriate standard stated in this section.

A. Formal Proceedings

If the agency action resulted from a proceeding subject to 5 U.S.C. §§ 556 and 557, or otherwise is reviewed on the record of an agency hearing provided by statute, the court determines whether the agency's factual finding or premise is supported by substantial evidence in the record as a whole. APA § 706(2)(E). It is impossible to quantify "substantial evidence" precisely; one much-quoted Supreme Court formulation is "such evidence as a reasonable mind might accept as adequate to support a conclusion." This level of review is somewhat less intense than that employed when appellate courts review trial court findings of fact. In reviewing for substantial evidence, the court must consider the entire record, including the decision and factual findings of the ALJ, if any, not just those portions of the record that support the agency's findings.

B. Trial De Novo

When the agency action resulted from a proceeding in which a statute or the Constitution requires that the facts shall be subject to trial de novo, the court makes its own, independent findings of fact and determines whether the agency action is warranted thereby. See APA § 706(2)(F). Trial de novo is available when a court reviews an agency's denial of a FOIA request, but it is otherwise rare.

C. Other Cases

(1) In any other case, the court determines whether the factual premise has substantial support in the administrative record viewed as a whole (although the legal standard nominally being applied is the "arbitrary and capricious" test). APA § 706(2)(A).

(2) For these purposes, the "administrative record" consists of a file of materials that the agency maintains as the exclusive basis for its decision; or, if no such file is maintained, it consists of all unprivileged materials that were actively considered by the agency or its staff (or that were submitted by outside parties) in connection with the action under review. Where procedural law so provides, the record must also disclose oral communications between decisionmakers and outside parties.

(3) The court may, upon a proper showing, allow discovery and other evidentiary proceedings in order to supervise the agency's compilation (but not the supplementation) of the administrative record.

D. Findings Not Specifically Supported by the Record

Notwithstanding the requirement of record support for agency findings in formal proceedings, an agency may, with notification to the parties and opportunity to rebut, rely on officially noticed facts in a proper case. APA § 556(e). In addition, in both formal and informal proceedings, an agency need not provide more support for predictive or other judgmental facts than it can fairly be expected to have gathered at the time of the action.

V. REVIEW OF THE EXERCISE OF AGENCY DISCRETION

The court may set aside an agency action as an abuse of discretion (alternatively known in APA parlance as the "arbitrary and capricious" test), see APA § 706(2)(A), on any of several grounds. In practice, application of these grounds varies according to the nature and magnitude of the agency action. Thus, a court will typically apply the criteria rigorously during judicial review of high-stakes rulemaking proceedings (a practice commonly termed "hard look" review), but much more leniently when reviewing a routine, uncomplicated action. A court may not impose its own policy preferences on the agency. Commonly applied bases for reversal include the following:

A. The agency relied on factors that may not be taken into account under, or ignored factors that must be taken into account under, any authoritative source of law. (The case law often describes this ground as an element of the "arbitrary and capricious" test, although it seems more properly understood as a component of the court's legal analysis. See *supra* §§ II, III.)

B. The action does not bear a reasonable relationship to statutory purposes or requirements.

C. The asserted or necessary factual premises of the action do not withstand scrutiny under the relevant standard of review (see *supra* § IV).

D. The action is unsupported by any explanation or rests upon reasoning that is seriously flawed.

E. The agency failed, without adequate justification, to give reasonable consideration to an important aspect of the problems presented by the action, such as the effects or costs of the policy choice involved, or the factual circumstances bearing on that choice.

F. The action, where inconsistent with prior agency policies or precedents, fails to display an awareness of the change in position, fails to explain a changed view of the facts, or fails to consider serious reliance interests that its prior policy engendered.

G. The agency failed, without an adequate justification, to consider or adopt an important alternative solution to the problem addressed in the action.

H. The agency failed to consider substantial arguments, or respond to relevant and significant comments, made by the participants in the proceeding that gave rise to the agency action.

I. The agency has imposed a sanction that is greatly out of proportion to the magnitude of the violation.

J. The action fails in other respects to rest upon reasoned decisionmaking.

VI. ANCILLARY ISSUES CONCERNING AGENCY EXPLANATIONS

In order to decide whether an agency action violates applicable standards of review, as set forth above, courts examine material portions of the agency's own proffered rationale. They normally will allow an agency to defend its action only on the basis of reasons articulated prior to judicial review and will not supply their own rationale for discretionary agency conduct or speculate as to the conceivable purposes underlying the action. A court may deem an error in reasoning to be harmless error if the agency clearly would have reached the same result even if it had not made the error.

The court ascertains the agency's rationale as follows:

(1) An explanation issued contemporaneously with an agency action is treated as containing the agency's actual rationale for taking the action, unless the party challenging the action impeaches

the explanation with a strong showing of bad faith or improper behavior.

(2) Where an agency action is not accompanied by a contemporaneous explanation, the court may investigate the agency's rationale by receiving evidence, though this is rare. Under these circumstances there is no presumption as to whether the post hoc explanation tendered by the agency to the court expresses the agency's original rationale. In attempting to identify the agency's actual, though not contemporaneously articulated, rationale, courts generally avoid direct scrutiny of the agency's decision-making process and rely on the representations of counsel, affidavits from relevant officials, and extrinsic evidence rather than depositions, interrogatories, and courtroom testimony.

VII. PROCEDURAL ISSUES

The foregoing standards also apply to allegations that an agency violated procedural law in taking the action under review, see APA § 706(2)(D), with the applicable standard of review depending on whether the allegation rests on the agency's organic statute, the APA, agency regulations, etc. The court presumes the procedural regularity of agency action, but a person may come forward with facts to prove the contrary. An action will not be set aside because of a procedural error that plainly did not influence the outcome of the agency proceeding. APA § 706 (final sentence).

VIII. AGENCY DELAY

A court will compel agency action unlawfully withheld or unreasonably delayed, APA § 706(1), though such a claim can proceed only where a plaintiff asserts that an agency failed to take a discrete action that it is *required* to take. An agency's delay in completing a pending action for which there is no statutory deadline may not be held unlawful unless the delay is unreasonable in light of such considerations as the agency's need to set priorities among lawful objectives, the challenger's interest in prompt action, and any relevant indications of legislative intent. In considering such challenges, courts are deferential to agencies' allocations of their own limited resources.

IX. REMEDY

As noted in the foregoing sections, in general a reviewing court will set aside agency action that does not meet the standards described, instead of mandating a specific disposition of its own design. When an agency's exercise of discretion cannot be upheld on the basis of the agency's rationale, or no rationale can be discerned, or if the agency so requests, the court will almost always remand the action so that the agency can provide further justification. When remanding, a court normally will vacate the agency's action, except in special circumstances. Such circumstances may exist where (1) the court discerns a substantial probability that the agency can cure its error on remand and (2) the challenging party's interest in obtaining relief from the agency's decision is clearly outweighed by the substantial adverse impact that vacation would have on private persons who have reasonably relied on the agency action being remanded.

PART FOUR
THE AVAILABILITY OF JUDICIAL REVIEW OF ADMINISTRATIVE ACTION

I. OVERVIEW OF PREREQUISITES TO JUDICIAL REVIEW

A. Statutory Basis for Subject Matter Jurisdiction and Venue

The APA itself does not provide jurisdiction in suits seeking review of federal administrative action, but the federal-question statute, 28 U.S.C. § 1331, generally does. General federal-question jurisdiction in district court does not apply, however, where special jurisdictional statutes such as the Hobbs Act, 28 U.S.C. § 2342, provide exclusive jurisdiction for review of specified classes of cases in the courts of appeals.

Under the generally applicable venue statute, 28 U.S.C. § 1391(e), venue is proper for a suit against an officer, an agency, or the United States "in any judicial district in which: (1) a defendant in the action resides, or (2) the cause of action arose, or (3) any real property involved in the action is situated, or (4) the plaintiff resides if no real property is involved in the action." This is a default provision that may be superseded by venue provisions in a special jurisdictional statute.

B. Waiver of Sovereign Immunity

Section 702 of the APA waives sovereign immunity of the federal government for judicial review of agency action where the plaintiff is seeking relief other than money damages. This waiver applies regardless of whether a petitioner invokes the APA's cause of action or some other cause of action. It also permits a suit seeking a financial award that does not technically constitute "money damages."

A claimant seeking money damages from the federal government must invoke a waiver of sovereign immunity other than § 702. Examples of such waivers include (a) provisions in agency enabling acts that authorize an agency to "sue and be sued"; (b) the Federal Tort Claims Act (FTCA), 28 U.S.C. §§ 1346(b), 2671–80, which waives sovereign immunity for certain tort claims; and (c) the Tucker Act, 28 U.S.C. § 1491, which applies, most importantly, to contract and takings claims.

C. Official Immunity

A suit against an agency official in her official capacity is functionally identical to a suit against the government and is subject to the same principles of sovereign immunity.

A suit against an agency official in her personal capacity implicates a different set of immunity doctrines. As injunctive relief is generally available directly against the government under § 702 of the APA, the primary significance of personal-capacity suits is that they create a potential path for plaintiffs to seek money damages.

The Federal Employees Liability Reform and Tort Compensation Act of 1988 (the "Westfall Act") provides that federal officials are immune from common-law tort liability for actions taken within the scope of their employment. 28 U.S.C. § 2679(b)(1). Where the attorney general certifies that the defendant was acting within the scope of her employment, the United States is substituted as defendant. 28 U.S.C. § 2679(d)(1). Whether the United States has waived sovereign immunity is then determined according to the terms of the FTCA.

The Westfall Act does not immunize officials from constitutional torts or from claims that they have violated federal statutes that authorize a cause of action. Executive officials, however, are generally protected from suits for civil damages for such claims by the doctrine of "qualified immunity." This doctrine blocks claims for damages arising from an official's performance of discretionary functions so long as the official's conduct did not violate clearly established statutory or constitutional rights. A right is clearly established for the purpose of this test if a reasonable officer should have understood that her conduct was illegal given the particular facts she confronted. Courts have accorded absolute immunity to certain officials in light of their special functions. For instance, administrative law judges enjoy absolute immunity from damages liability allegedly arising from their judicial acts.

D. Cause of Action or Defense

Many specific statutes authorize judicial review of particular types of federal agency action. An agency's enabling act may, for instance, contain a set of provisions establishing parameters for review of rules issued pursuant to that act's authority. Review pursuant to such provisions is sometimes characterized as a "special statutory proceeding." Often, the jurisdictional provisions for a special statutory review proceeding assign subject matter jurisdiction to courts of appeals (especially the D.C. Circuit).

In the absence of a special statutory review scheme, parties may seek review under APA §§ 702–704, which provide a general cause of action for parties "adversely affected or aggrieved by agency action" for which "there is no other adequate remedy in court."

Where neither a specific statute nor the APA provides a cause of action, parties may obtain review by seeking various forms of relief, including equitable relief under a federal court's general equity jurisdiction, 28 U.S.C. § 1331, declaratory relief under the Declaratory Judgment Act, 28 U.S.C. § 2201, and mandamus under 28 U.S.C. § 1361. (These forms of review, as well as review sought under the APA without authorization by a more specific statute, are sometimes described as instances of "nonstatutory review." This usage is misleading, however, because almost all of these forms of review rest on a statutory foundation.)

In rare circumstances, a plaintiff may sue an agency official in her *personal* capacity for a constitutional tort in a "*Bivens* action." See *Bivens v. Six Unknown Named Agents of Federal Bureau of Narcotics*, 403 U.S. 388 (1971). The Supreme Court has narrowly defined the availability of the

Bivens cause of action, and it is not available where Congress has provided an adequate statutory alternative.

Rather than challenge an agency action affirmatively, under many circumstances a party may instead raise the invalidity of an agency action as a defense in a subsequent enforcement proceeding based on that agency action. The existence of a prior, adequate, and exclusive opportunity for judicial review may, however, cut off this right to raise the invalidity of the agency action as a defense in an enforcement proceeding. Cf. § II.D, Statutory Deadlines.

E. Reviewability

Doctrines of reviewability block judicial review of certain types of claims that would otherwise appear to fall within the scope of the APA's general cause of action. More particularly: (a) the APA's cause of action applies only to challenges to "agency action"—and not everything an agency does satisfies the APA's technical meaning of this phrase; (b) Congress may by statute preclude review of certain types of agency action; and (c) courts regard some agency actions as unreviewable because they are "committed to agency discretion by law." See § III, Reviewability.

F. Timing Doctrines

A complex set of timing doctrines limits access to the courts for judicial review of agency action. These include the following:

Finality: In general, courts will review only final agency actions. Agency action is final if it (1) is consummated and (2) determines rights or obligations or otherwise carries legal consequences.

Exhaustion: Parties generally must pursue available intra-agency remedies, such as an appeal to higher agency authorities, before seeking judicial review.

Ripeness: Courts will normally not review a matter that is not "ripe," meaning that the issues raised in the case must be "fit" for review, and delaying review must cause hardship to the plaintiff.

Statutory deadlines: Many agency enabling acts limit the time period for petitioning for review of agency actions. However, courts generally construe such statutes to mean that even after the deadline has passed, the defendant in an enforcement proceeding may challenge a rule on the grounds that it is unconstitutional or exceeds the agency's statutory authority.

Primary jurisdiction: Courts sometimes invoke this doctrine to stay proceedings that fall within their original jurisdiction, so as to permit an agency to examine an issue that falls within its special competence but that it has not yet addressed.

For further discussion of these timing doctrines, see § II.

G. Standing—Constitutional, Prudential, and Statutory

The term "standing" covers three quite different concepts. First, for a challenge to administrative action to proceed in federal court, at least one plaintiff must demonstrate *constitutional standing*. To do so, a plaintiff must show that she has suffered an "injury in fact"—a legally cognizable injury. She must also show that this injury is fairly traceable to the defendant's conduct and that a favorable court order would likely redress it. Second, in certain circumstances, judge-made *prudential standing* doctrines deny standing to a plaintiff who satisfies constitutional standing requirements, as, for example, when the plaintiff sues to protect the rights of a third party rather than her own. Third, the doctrine of *statutory standing* inquires whether a statute authorizes a particular type of plaintiff to seek judicial review of agency action. Most important, a litigant may invoke the APA's cause of action under § 702 only if she is "adversely affected or aggrieved by agency action within the meaning of the relevant statute."

For further discussion of these standing doctrines, see § IV.

II. TIMING OF JUDICIAL REVIEW

A. Finality

Administrative law presumes that judicial review should await final agency action; interlocutory review is generally unavailable. The APA codifies this presumption at § 704, which provides, "[a]gency action made reviewable by statute and final agency action for which there is no adequate remedy in a court are subject to judicial review."

Agency action is "final" for APA purposes if two conditions are met. First, the action must not be tentative or interlocutory, but rather the "consummation" of the agency's decisionmaking. Issuance of an administrative complaint, for example, does not satisfy this first condition.

Second, the action must determine rights or obligations, or create legal consequences. This condition implicates the following problem: certain types of agency rules—interpretive rules and policy statements—do not carry the force of law. It might seem that such rules cannot constitute "final agency action" because they do not carry legal consequences. In practice, however, interpretive rules and policy statements often have significant impact on both regulated parties and the beneficiaries of regulation. This fact suggests that the finality requirement should not immunize these types of agency action from judicial review. Thus, agency actions have sometimes been deemed "final" for judicial review purposes where the decision appears binding as a practical matter—even if the agency has characterized the decision as nonbinding (e.g., by labeling it as "informal guidance").

Where an agency action is not final and no specific statute authorizes interlocutory review, a party may obtain review of the action in two ways. First, the party may be able to seek so-called nonstatutory review outside of the APA, but only if the agency action is clearly in excess of the agency's delegated powers or the ongoing action plainly cannot result in a valid agency order. Otherwise, the party may obtain review of all preliminary, procedural, or intermediate agency action or rulings on review of the final agency action.

B. Exhaustion of Administrative Remedies

An agency action may be considered "final" even though opportunities remain for seeking further review of the action within the agency itself. Nonetheless, where the *exhaustion* doctrine applies, it requires a plaintiff to seek relief from all available and adequate administrative remedies, including intra-agency appellate remedies, prior to seeking judicial review.

In some contexts, Congress specifies exhaustion requirements by statute. Where Congress has not done so, courts determine whether to require exhaustion by balancing the needs of the reviewing court for judicial economy and an adequate record, the needs of the agency for autonomy and for a fair opportunity to apply its expertise, and the hardship to the plaintiff of denying review. The ordinary litigation cost of exhausting the administrative remedy is not sufficient hardship to render that remedy inadequate.

The Supreme Court has identified several sets of circumstances in which a plaintiff's interest in prompt judicial review strongly favors excusing exhaustion. These include (1) where requiring exhaustion would cause undue prejudice, perhaps due to unreasonable deadlines for administrative review; (2) where the agency lacks authority to grant effective relief; and (3) where the administrative body is biased or has predetermined the issue.

Section 704 of the APA carves out an exception to the courts' "common-law" authority to impose an exhaustion requirement on plaintiffs invoking the APA's cause of action. Unless expressly required by statute, a party seeking review pursuant to the APA of otherwise final agency action need not pursue any process for agency reconsideration of its decision. However, an agency may require exhaustion of any intra-agency appeals, provided (1) it imposes this requirement by rule and (2) it provides that the agency action is inoperative during the time of the appeal. In practice, most agencies do make use of this option when it is available.

In both APA and non-APA cases, the courts have frequently refused to consider issues that were not first raised before the agency. Courts enforce such *issue exhaustion* more stringently where the parties are expected to develop the issues in an adversarial proceeding than in circumstances in which they review the results of nonadversarial, informal hearings.

Some courts have also applied the issue-exhaustion doctrine to the notice-and-comment rulemaking process. Under this approach, a party that fails to raise an objection to a rule during notice and comment may not press that objection on direct judicial review of the rule unless (1) another party made the objection or (2) the agency's decision indicates that it did in fact consider the issue.

Even where courts do not apply the issue-exhaustion doctrine, because the review of agency action under the "arbitrary and capricious" standard of § 706(2)(A) is limited to the record before the agency at the time of its decision, the agency's action may well be deemed reasonable in the absence of an argument that was not presented to the agency. Thus, the absence of an argument at the administrative level may affect the substance, if not the availability, of review.

C. Ripeness

To determine whether agency action is ripe for judicial review, courts balance (1) "the fitness of the issues for judicial decision" and (2) "the hardship to the parties of withholding court consideration." The Supreme Court has also advised courts to consider whether judicial intervention would unduly interfere with subsequent agency action.

The *fitness* inquiry largely turns on whether delaying judicial review until a rule has been applied to a particular, concrete situation could develop a factual record that would aid judicial resolution of the legality of the rule. Purely legal issues are thus typically, though not always, "fit" for review.

The *hardship* inquiry largely turns on whether a rule requires an immediate and costly change to a regulated party's "primary conduct"—i.e., its day-to-day business. Thus, a rule requiring pharmaceutical firms to change their labeling practices or face possible civil and criminal penalties satisfied the hardship prong of ripeness. By contrast, a rule specifying that manufacturers of color additives must permit regulators to inspect their facilities on request did not.

Mere uncertainty on the challenger's part about the legality of a rule does not constitute hardship for the purpose of ripeness analysis.

Agency statements concerning how to implement or interpret a statute that the agency does not administer are unlikely to constitute hardship for the purpose of demonstrating ripeness.

D. Statutory Deadlines for Review of Rules

Many enabling acts provide for short time limits (e.g., sixty days) for review of agency action—especially rules. In the absence of such a time limit, a six-year statute of limitations generally applies to challenges to agency action. Courts nonetheless allow post-deadline judicial review of agency rules under some circumstances. The availability of judicial review depends on whether the challenge is substantive or procedural as well as on whether the statutory time limit at issue expressly precludes untimely review.

Even after a statutory deadline has run, courts permit parties defending against application of a rule in an enforcement proceeding to challenge the rule on the substantive grounds that it is unconstitutional or exceeds the agency's statutory authority.

At least in those cases where a statutory time limit does not expressly preclude later judicial review, a party may also pursue these types of substantive challenges after a statutory deadline by making them the basis for a petition to revise or revoke the rule. If the agency denies this rulemaking petition, the party may then seek review of this denial. Such review is limited to issues considered in the denial decision and thus usually does not encompass factual or discretionary determinations underlying the original rule.

By contrast, courts generally bar post-deadline procedural challenges to rules, regardless of whether they are raised first as a defense in an enforcement proceeding or via a petition for a new rulemaking.

Courts have held that a statutory deadline for review does not begin to run until a rule is ripe for review. A party wishing to challenge a rule should at least try to do so within the statutory time period, because courts have also held that mere speculation that a challenge is unripe does not excuse an untimely petition.

An agency may restart an expired statutory time limit on judicial review by "reopening" its consideration of an earlier action by either explicitly or implicitly undertaking to reexamine it.

E. Primary Jurisdiction

Primary jurisdiction applies when claims properly cognizable in court contain one or more issues within the special competence of an administrative agency. In such cases, the court enables a referral to the agency, staying further proceedings so as to give the parties reasonable opportunity to seek an administrative ruling. In cases of mandatory primary jurisdiction, an agency ruling is required, and the court cannot proceed with the case until the agency has acted. In cases where an agency ruling is not required but the court might benefit from the expertise of the agency, the court may make a referral but also provide that if the agency has not ruled after a certain time the court will proceed without the agency ruling.

In determining whether to invoke the doctrine of primary jurisdiction, courts consider (1) whether the issues in a case implicate an agency's expertise or discretion, (2) whether the issues need a uniform resolution that the agency is best situated to provide, and (3) whether the referral to the administrative agency will impose undue delays or costs on the litigants.

III. REVIEWABILITY

A. "Agency Action" as a Limit on Review

The APA's cause of action applies only to "agency action." Section 551(13) defines "agency action" as including "the whole or a part of an agency rule, order, license, sanction, relief, or the equivalent or denial thereof, or failure to act." Given this expansive list, the APA's definition of "agency action" rarely blocks judicial review of an agency's affirmative action or its denial of a request for action (e.g., review of a rule or a denial of a petition for rulemaking).

The APA cause of action cannot be invoked to make a broad, programmatic attack on an agency's general work as opposed to an attack on a specific "agency action." For instance, an environmental group could not invoke the APA to challenge a Bureau of Land Management "program" in the absence of a specific agency action pursuant to that program.

The APA's inclusion of "failure to act" in the definition of "agency action" presents an interpretive challenge. At any given time, any given agency is failing to take an infinite number of actions—not all of which should count as "agency actions" subject to judicial review under the APA. The Supreme Court has solved this puzzle by holding that "failure to act" as used by § 551(13) includes only failures to take the "discrete" types of agency actions listed earlier in that subsection (e.g., failure to adopt a rule or to issue an order).

B. Statutory Preclusion or Limitation of Review

Section 701(a)(1) of the APA recognizes that Congress may by statute preclude judicial review. The Supreme Court has never decided whether the Constitution limits this preclusive power. In part to avoid that question, courts will often work hard to interpret statutory language to avoid preclusive effect, requiring "clear and convincing evidence of a contrary legislative intent" to overcome the general presumption of judicial review.

Statutory preclusion of judicial review need not be expressed so long as the requisite congressional intent to preclude is "fairly discernible" from a statutory scheme. The Court has found implicit preclusion where judicial review on behalf of a particular group would "severely disrupt" a complex and delicate administrative scheme.

Courts are especially reluctant to find statutory preclusion where review implicates constitutional questions or the legality of a rule. By contrast, courts are quicker to find preclusion where only issues of fact or of application of law to fact are at issue.

Where Congress restricts judicial review to particular courts or times by adopting special statutory review procedures, courts generally presume that Congress intends these procedures to be the exclusive means for review.

C. Matters Committed to Agency Discretion

Section 701(a)(2) of the APA recognizes that the APA's cause of action is not available "to the extent that . . . agency action is committed to agency discretion by law." This exception to the APA's general presumption of review is narrow. The Supreme Court has stated that this exception applies where statutes are written in such broad terms that there is, in effect, "no law to apply." More broadly, the Court has recognized that there are certain categories of administrative decision that are unreviewable as a matter of tradition. Functional inquiries regarding the desirability of judicial review also come into play—though not always expressly.

For example, agency decisions regarding how to allocate lump-sum appropriations are committed to agency discretion by law. In reaching this conclusion, the Supreme Court cited tradition and also noted that such allocations require complicated balancing of many factors and determining agency priorities—tasks best handled by agencies, not courts.

Likewise, agency decisions declining to initiate enforcement actions are presumptively committed to agency discretion by law. This presumption is based on judicial respect for prosecutorial discretion and for an agency's discretion in allocating its resources. Congress can, however, overcome this presumption by providing sufficient standards limiting agency enforcement discretion to guide review in a particular case. Also, where an agency refusal to initiate an enforcement action is based on statutory interpretation, the agency's inaction can usually be reviewed, at least if it is expressed in a written policy. (Notably, the presumption against review of nonenforcement does not apply to denial of a petition for rulemaking.)

Section 701(a)(2)'s exemption to review applies only "to the extent" that agency action is committed to agency discretion. As a result, some issues raised by an action may be reviewable while others are not. The Supreme Court has, for instance, held that a constitutional claim raised in connection with termination of a government employee was reviewable but that a statutory claim was not. Similarly, even where the substance of an agency's decision is committed to agency discretion, the procedure applicable to the action may not be.

IV. STANDING

A. Overview

The doctrine of "standing" determines whether a particular litigant is entitled to an adjudication of the particular claims asserted. These requirements are imposed by the Constitution, the courts as a matter of judicial discretion, and Congress.

B. Constitutional Requirements

Article III's limitation of the judicial power to "cases" and "controversies" implies three standing requirements. First, the plaintiff must have suffered an "injury in fact"—an invasion of a legally protected interest that is (a) concrete and particularized and (b) actual or imminent, not conjectural or hypothetical. Second, there must be a causal connection between the conduct complained of and the injury—the injury has to be fairly traceable to the challenged action of the defendant, and not the result of the independent action of some third party not before the court. Third, it must be likely that the injury will be redressed by a favorable decision.

1. *Injury*

a. The Constitutional Injury-in-Fact Requirement: In General

The basic Article III requirement is "injury in fact." Constitutionally cognizable injuries include not only harms to person or property and economic harm but also harm to nonmonetary intangible interests. For example, so long as it is individually experienced, harm to environmental, recreational, or aesthetic interests can support standing. The injury must be actual or imminent, not conjectural or hypothetical. Mere ideological objection to government action does not constitute a constitutionally cognizable injury.

In addition to the kinds of harm that would have been recognized at common law, violations of some rights created by statute can also qualify as injury for purposes of standing. For example, violation of a statutory right to obtain certain information can constitute injury. However, not all rights created by statute can so qualify. For example, denial of a statutory right to comment on a proposed rule is not injury sufficient for standing.

The right of a prevailing party to claim a statutory bounty satisfies the injury-in-fact requirement; entitlement to attorney's fees or litigation costs does not.

The Supreme Court has suggested that when states are plaintiffs suing on their own behalf, as opposed to *parens patriae*, special concerns are involved that may lessen traditional standing requirements.

b. Injury from Violation of Procedural Requirements

When a challenged agency action harms an underlying substantive interest of the plaintiff, the plaintiff has standing to challenge the agency's failure to follow legally required procedures even though she cannot prove that the procedural error actually changed the substantive outcome. For example, a taxpayer whose tax liability is increased by a new regulation can challenge the adequacy of the notice of proposed rulemaking, even though it cannot be shown that adequate notice would have resulted in a more favorable regulation. However, she may be required to show that a more favorable regulation is possible. Cognizable injury cannot arise from a procedural violation without a showing that the action taken harms or endangers a concrete substantive interest of the plaintiff.

Apparently, the statutory right to attend meetings and otherwise have access to government proceedings, such as under the Government in the Sunshine Act and the Federal Advisory Committee Act, are sufficiently similar to substantive rights to be treated as such. FOIA rights and voter rights to certain information under the Federal Election Campaign Act are also substantive rights, denial of which will support standing without regard to proof of harm to a particular, underlying substantive interest.

c. Generalized Grievances vs. Harm to Informational Rights and Other Broadly Shared Interests

A "generalized grievance" is not injury sufficient to confer standing. Thus, harm to the general interest shared by all citizens in the government conforming its conduct to law is not a judicially cognizable injury. Accordingly, a statute purporting to allow "any person" to challenge agency action cannot authorize suit by a plaintiff without some distinct, constitutionally cognizable injury. However, a person who suffers a concrete, particularized harm does satisfy the injury requirement even though many other persons do or could suffer the same harm. Statutes can create and/or protect broadly shared interests, harm to which can constitutionally support standing. For example, individual voters can vindicate a concrete, though widely shared, right to election-finance information required by statute to be made public. Similarly, an individual denied access to government information or to an agency meeting has standing to challenge the denial, even though all citizens have an identical right of access. The widely shared injury, while satisfying constitutional standing requirements, may raise prudential standing concerns.

d. Risk as Injury

The extent to which risk of harm can constitute injury for standing purposes is not clear. On the one hand, the Supreme Court has denied standing to an organization to sue on behalf of its members when it did not show that a *specific* member was threatened with an imminent concrete harm, even though it was virtually certain that *some* member would suffer a concrete harm in the foreseeable future. On the other hand, the Court found standing on behalf of organic alfalfa farmers to challenge the deregulation of genetically modified alfalfa because of the significant risk that the lack of regulation would lead to contamination of the farmers' crops. The fact that the farmers had already undertaken activities and expended funds to avoid the risk was apparently important to the Court's conclusion. In yet a third case, the Court dismissed a claim by persons challenging the constitutionality of a statute authorizing certain government electronic surveillance because it was not "certainly impending" that they would be subject to it, even though there was clearly a significant risk that they would be. The lower courts' decisions regarding risk as injury are in tension, with the D.C. Circuit holding that for increased risk to support standing there must be both (i) a substantial increase in the risk of harm and (ii) a substantial probability of actual harm with that increase taken into account. Other circuits have generally been more receptive to considering any significant increase in risk of physical harm as sufficient cognizable injury.

e. *Taxpayer Standing*

In general, a taxpayer does not suffer cognizable injury because the federal government spends money in a manner objectionable to the taxpayer. The one limited exception involves federal appropriations for religious purposes. Although the doctrinal basis for this exception has been undermined over the years, the foundational decision has continually been distinguished rather than overruled.

2. *Causation and Redressability*

The constitutional requirements of *causation* and *redressability*—often together referred to as "nexus"—ensure that there is at least a reasonable probability that the plaintiff's injury was caused by the defendant and will be remedied by the relief requested from the court.

Although stated as distinct requirements, causation and redressability are typically analyzed in tandem because it is rare that one exists without the other. However, if the court's remedial options are limited by statute or other law, the injury may indeed be traceable to the defendant's action, but not redressable by the available remedies. For example, a plaintiff who has suffered an environmental injury caused by the defendant will be denied standing on redressability grounds where the wrongdoing had ceased before the suit was filed, the plaintiff cannot demonstrate a reasonable likelihood that it will recur, and the only statutory remedies are prospective injunctive relief and civil penalties payable to the government.

Analysis of causation and redressability tends to be very fact specific, and in general there is no ready formula for predicting when a court will conclude that the causal chain has become too uncertain or attenuated. Cases attempting to challenge either favorable tax treatment of a third party or decisions not to prosecute appear to follow a pattern of dismissal on the basis of an absence of either causation or redressability.

Whether causation and redressability exist can be highly dependent upon how the injury is defined. For example, if the harm to a plaintiff challenging an affirmative-action program is defined as not obtaining the relevant position or contract, the plaintiff will rarely have standing, since almost never would a particular disappointed applicant be able to show it would have obtained the benefit but for the challenged program. However, the Court instead defines the injury in such cases as a lack of opportunity to compete for the desired outcome according to permissible criteria, a definition that eliminates problems of causation or redressability.

A similar definitional issue is posed by the suggestion, advanced by some judges, that complaints by regulatory beneficiaries categorically present difficult causation and redressability problems not faced by regulated entities. For example, it has been argued that consumers who can satisfy the particularized injury requirement and wish to challenge an agency's failure to adopt more rigorous fuel economy standards for automobiles must also show that if a more demanding rule were adopted, manufacturers would change their designs rather than pay noncompliance penalties. Because the standard for redressability is only that the favorable court decision would "likely" redress (or avoid) the injury, the plaintiff should have to show only that it is likely that the manufacturer will comply with the law.

Complaints about procedural violations provide another example. If the injury is defined as the actual agency decision, the plaintiff will normally not satisfy standard nexus requirements, since it will be possible, even likely, that the agency could have reached, and on remand will reach, the same outcome even following proper procedures. The Court, however, has made clear that when the alleged violation is procedural, the normal standards for redressability do not apply. It suffices if the procedures exist to protect a concrete interest of the plaintiff and a favorable outcome on the merits will be possible if the correct procedures are followed.

Redressability issues can also arise under citizen suit provisions that provide only injunctive relief and payment of civil penalties to the government when the complained-of action has ceased after filing of the action, making an injunction inappropriate. While arguably, paying civil penalties to the government does not redress the injury to the citizen plaintiff, the Court has said that such penalties deter future violations and therefore satisfy the redressability requirement.

C. Associational Standing

An association has standing in its own right if it satisfies the above constitutional tests. In addition, an association has standing to sue on behalf of its members when (a) one or more identified members would have standing to sue in their own right; (b) the interests it seeks to protect are germane to the organization's purpose; and (c) neither the claim asserted nor the relief requested requires the participation of individual members in the lawsuit. The second of these criteria is construed very leniently. The third effectively limits associations suing on behalf of their members to declaratory or injunctive relief, because if the redress required the payment of monetary damages, the persons to whom the damages would be paid would have to be parties themselves.

D. Prudential Standing Requirements

Three judicially self-imposed "prudential" restrictions further limit standing beyond the constitutional minima. Congress may, by statute, override prudential restrictions on standing.

First, parties cannot raise claims or defenses that rest on a third party's legal rights (the *jus tertii* limitation). The *jus tertii* prohibition plays an important role in constitutional litigation but has not been very significant in limiting judicial review of agency action under the APA or specific organic statutes. A litigant attempting to challenge government action on grounds that it violates the constitutional rights of a third party may be prohibited from doing so unless (1) the litigant has suffered an injury in fact; (2) the litigant and the third party stand in some close relationship; and (3) "some hindrance" impedes the third party's ability to assert her own rights.

Second the plaintiff's interests must be within the "zone of interests" regulated or protected by the constitutional or statutory provision relied upon. In challenges to agency action, this requirement is subsumed under the APA requirements discussed in § IV.E.

Finally, the Court has sometimes stated that "generalized grievances" are precluded by prudential standing requirements. However, other cases have distinguished between "generalized grievances," which are not injuries for Article III purposes, and "widely shared" injuries, which satisfy Article III's standing requirement, but which perhaps should be left to the political process to rectify. Whenever Congress has created a cause of action that allowed persons suffering generalized grievances to sue, the Court has always held that the limitation was constitutional rather than prudential.

E. Statutory Standing

The general statutory standing requirement for review of agency action under the APA is codified in § 702, which provides that "[a] person suffering legal wrong because of agency action, or adversely affected or aggrieved by agency action within the meaning of a relevant statute, is entitled to judicial review thereof." Although this language significantly broadened pre-APA availability of review to challenge agency action, it does not confer standing to the limits of what is constitutionally possible. In addition to showing that she has suffered a constitutionally cognizable injury caused by the agency's action, the plaintiff relying upon § 702 must show that her injury is "arguably within the zone of interests to be protected or regulated by the statute . . . in question."

Individual regulatory statutes may contain their own statutory standing provisions. Statutory language authorizing challenge by "any person aggrieved" has traditionally been interpreted to confer standing to the full extent of Article III, without regard to such prudential limitations as the zone-of-interests requirement. Citizen-suit provisions (e.g., those conferring standing on "any person" without further requirements) are usually given the same interpretation. Other kinds of statutory standing provisions are typically construed to incorporate the zone-of-interests test and other prudential requirements absent evidence of a different legislative intent.

PART SIX
GOVERNMENT MANAGEMENT OF THE ADMINISTRATIVE PROCESS

I. SCOPE

This section concerns procedures relating to the management of administrative functions across federal agencies, particularly requirements for agencies to submit proposed actions for advance review and opportunities for executive and congressional supervision or correction of agency decisionmaking.

II. CONGRESSIONAL MANAGEMENT OF AGENCY ACTION

The Constitution prohibits members or houses of Congress, or Congress itself, from being, appointing, or removing officers of the United States, or from vetoing an agency action other than through the enactment of legislation. Therefore, Congress has no power of direct supervision or management over agencies even though its power to define and limit an agency's authority is virtually plenary within the bounds of the Constitution.

Nevertheless, Congress has the recognized constitutional authority to oversee agency action for a number of purposes, especially for determining whether new legislation is necessary or appropriate. Congress's ultimate control over the agency's budget and its organic statute means that congressional views will have influence with the agency. Also, inherent in the legislative power is a power of inquiry, including the power to subpoena witnesses and documents (subject to applicable privileges, including an executive privilege of uncertain scope) and to enforce compliance therewith through the contempt power. Congressional investigation and public hearings can lead to public scrutiny and political pressure on the agency.

Attempts by members or committees of Congress to influence the outcome of an agency proceeding are subject to the APA's constraints on ex parte communications and other restrictions that apply to such attempts by private persons. Beyond those requirements, however, congressional attempts to influence agency proceedings are largely unregulated. Use of the congressional hearing power to try to influence the outcome of a pending formal adjudication has been held a violation of due process, although hearings to explore policy issues that might be involved in an adjudication can be permissible and appropriate if properly managed. Outside the context of formal or other on-the-record proceedings, a court is not likely to set aside an agency decision because of alleged congressional influence unless the evidence shows that the pressure brought to bear caused the agency action to be affected by factors that are not relevant under the governing statute.

Under the Congressional Review Act, 5 U.S.C. §§ 801–808, a rule cannot take effect if Congress passes a joint resolution disapproving the rule. The act exempts rules relating to agency management or personnel or agency organization, procedure, or practice, as well as rules of particular applicability. Before a rule can take effect, the promulgating agency must submit a copy of the rule and a concise general statement relating thereto to both houses of Congress and the comptroller general. A joint resolution of disapproval must be introduced within sixty days of such submission and is considered according to expedited procedures set out in the act. A *major* rule *cannot* take effect for sixty days after it has been submitted to Congress, a delay designed to ensure Congress has time to disapprove the rule. Major rules include any rule (other than one promulgated under the Telecommunications Act of 1996 and its amendments) that the administrator of the Office of Management and Budget's Office of Information and Regulatory Affairs (OIRA) finds will result in an annual effect on the economy of $100 million or more; a major increase in costs or prices; or significant adverse effects on competition, employment, investment, productivity, or the ability of U.S.–based enterprises to compete with foreign enterprises.

III. PRESIDENTIAL MANAGEMENT OF AGENCY ACTION

A. President's Constitutional Authority

Two provisions of Article II of the Constitution are conceived to be the primary sources of the president's authority to manage agency action. The first, known as the Vesting Clause, states that the "executive power" shall be vested in the president. U.S. Const., Art. II, Sec. 1, cl. 1. The second, known as the "Take Care Clause," states that the president "shall take care that the laws be faithfully executed." U.S. Const., Art. II, Sec. 3. In addition, the president may "require the opinion, in writing, of the principal officer in each of the executive departments, upon any subject relating to the duties of their respective offices." U.S. Const., Art. II, Sec. 2, cl. 1. These provisions furnish authority to the president to supervise, consult with, and obtain information from executive officers in the performance of their statutory duties. For these purposes, an executive department includes cabinet departments, independent executive agencies, and independent regulatory commissions.

However, most statutes place rulemaking and adjudicatory authority in the agency head or the agency itself, not in the president. The extent to which the president can order agency officials to take actions within the officials' delegated authority is uncertain.

In practice, the president's exercise of his supervisory power has largely correlated with his ability on the one hand to appoint, with the advice and consent of the Senate, principal officers, U.S. Const., Art. II, Sec. 2, cl. 2, and on the other hand to remove agency officials who ignore his direction. While the Constitution may be read to preclude any statutory limitation on the president's appointment power, it is not uncommon for a statute creating an agency to place some limits on whom the president may appoint to head the agency. No cases have addressed the constitutionality of such limits, but presidents since Ronald Reagan have issued signing statements to the effect that some such limitations are an unconstitutional restriction on the president's appointment powers.

The Constitution, other than in the impeachment clause, does not address who may remove executive officers or on what basis, but impeachment is by no means the only permissible route to removal of executive officers. Where statutes do not address removal of particular officers, it is presumed that the president may remove them at will, except perhaps when their sole function is the adjudication of administrative cases. Thus, under these circumstances, the president may remove an official simply for failure to follow supervision.

A number of statutes provide that an officer may be removed only for cause. Exactly what kind of conduct can constitute "cause" is unclear, but in practice removals on this basis are rare, and the Court has never directly addressed the issue. However, in a case involving the ability of Congress to remove the comptroller general for "inefficiency," "neglect of duty," and "malfeasance," it characterized these terms as very broad and said they could be interpreted to include "any number of actual or perceived transgressions of the legislative will."

The validity of "for-cause" removal provisions is not well defined by case law. Even with respect to purely executive officers, such a provision may be valid if it does not impede the president's ability to perform his constitutional duties. This does not necessarily mean, however, that Congress could constrain the president's ability to remove a principal officer, such as the secretary of state, whose job involves execution of authorities granted by the Constitution to the president. Moreover, in some circumstances, "dual for-cause" provisions (whereby a principal officer can be removed only for cause and an inferior officer can be removed only for cause by that principal officer) unconstitutionally constrain the president's ability to oversee the executive branch.

B. Regulatory Review

Although the specifics have varied with each administration, all presidents since Richard Nixon have issued executive orders that require executive agencies, but not independent regulatory commissions, to perform certain analyses and submit proposed and final rules to an office in the Executive Office of the President for its review before publication. Since President Reagan's E.O. 12,291 (1981), responsibility for such review has been lodged with OIRA. The procedural requirements of such review are set out above in Part Two, § IV.

The relevant executive orders have also included provisions concerning regulatory planning, including the semiannual publication of a Unified Regulatory Agenda, identifying and describing all regulations each agency has under development or review. Under the most recent of these, President Clinton's E.O. 12,866, agencies must prepare an annual Regulatory Plan, submitted to OIRA and included in the Unified Regulatory Agenda, describing and justifying the most important significant regulatory actions that the agency reasonably expects to issue in proposed or final form in that fiscal year or thereafter. Under E.O. 12,866, but not under its predecessors, these planning requirements extend to independent regulatory commissions as well as executive agencies.

Current executive orders, which are by definition subject to rescission or revision by successor administrations, also require or encourage the pursuit of specific substantive policies by requiring agencies to (a) prepare a cost-benefit analysis for significant regulatory actions; (b) pursue the most cost-effective regulatory alternative; (c) consider the impacts of proposed regulations on certain specified interests, such as federalism, the environmental health and safety of children, Indian tribal governments, and takings of private property; and (d) undertake periodic review of existing rules.

Most executive orders governing agency rulemaking provide, as they must under the Constitution, that their provisions apply only "to the extent permitted by law." A violation of their requirements does not affect the validity of the rule or provide a basis for judicial review. Enforcement of the provisions of the oversight orders is left to the political process.

IV. STATUTORY REQUIREMENTS

A. Paperwork Reduction Act

The Paperwork Reduction Act of 1980, which covers essentially all agencies (including independent regulatory commissions and the Executive Office of the President) except the Government Accountability Office (GAO) and the Federal Election Commission, applies to agency "collection of information." This term includes an agency's (1) collecting facts or information from ten or more persons, (2) requiring ten or more persons to disclose facts or opinions to the public or third parties, (3) requiring ten or more persons to maintain records, (4) collecting information from federal agencies or employees for statistical purposes. It does not include the collection of information as part of criminal investigations, civil or administrative proceedings to which the government is a party, or intelligence activities.

Before an agency may engage in the collection of information, it must

(1) undertake an internal review to evaluate the need for the information, describe the information to be collected, create a plan for its collection, and estimate the burden on private parties that the collection will impose;
(2) publicly announce its reasons for collecting the information, the way in which the information will be used, the burden its collection will impose, whether responses are voluntary or mandatory, and the fact that in the absence of a valid control number a person is not bound to respond to any collection requirement;
(3) submit the proposal for public notice and comment;
(4) submit the proposal and an accompanying justification to OIRA, which then seeks public comment on the agency's submission for thirty days.

If OIRA takes no action within sixty days, the proposed collection of information is deemed approved. In the case of a collection of information that is not part of or required by a rule that goes through notice and comment, OIRA may disapprove the collection if it determines that it is "unnecessary for any reason." In the case of a collection of information that is part of or required by a rule that goes through notice and comment, OIRA must submit comments as part of that proceeding and may disapprove the collection of information only if the agency's response to OIRA's comments was unreasonable. An independent regulatory commission may override an OIRA disapproval by majority vote. The Paperwork Reduction Act states that OIRA's approval of (or failure to act on) a proposed collection of information is not subject to judicial review, but it is silent about judicial review of disapprovals. Presumably, persons adversely affected by a disapproval can obtain judicial review under the APA, subject to standard requirements for judicial review, and there is some authority permitting review.

When OIRA approves a collection of information, it assigns a control number to the collection. No one is subject to any penalty for failing to comply with an agency's collection of information requirement that does not display a valid control number. The absence of a valid control number, however, is no defense to a penalty for filing false information or for failing to file information required to be filed by statute.

B. Government Performance and Results Act

The Government Performance and Results Act of 1993, as amended by the GPRA Modernization Act of 2010, requires agencies to prepare a strategic plan and a performance plan annually, and to post these plans on the agency's website and notify the president and Congress of their availability.

The strategic plan must include a mission statement, a general statement of goals, a description of how those goals are to be achieved, a description of obstacles to their achievement, and a description of how the agency's performance goals contribute to its strategic goals, among other statements. The performance plan must establish performance goals, express those goals in objective, quantifiable, and measurable form (unless the director of OMB determines it is not feasible to do so), describe how these goals contribute to the agency's strategic plan and the federal government's performance goals, identify how these goals are to be achieved, provide a basis for measuring its performance, and identify low-priority activities, among other statements.

The agency head must also make available updates on performance, comparing actual performance achievements with the agency's performance goals, not less than 150 days after the end of the fiscal year, and more frequently if it can do so at a reasonable level of administrative burden. These updates must provide a detailed review and assessment of the agency's successes and failures in achieving its performance goals. OMB must make an annual determination of whether the agency met its performance goals, and report on unmet goals to the head of the agency, the House Committee on Oversight and Governmental Reform, and the GAO. If the agency's activities have not met its performance goals as determined by OMB for one fiscal year, the agency must designate a senior official to oversee its performance improvement and must submit a performance improvement plan to OMB. If OMB determines the agency's activities have not met its performance goals for two consecutive years, the agency head must submit to Congress a description of the actions the administration will take to improve performance, and describe any additional funding the agency will obligate to achieve the goal. If OMB determines the agency has not met its performance goals for three consecutive fiscal years, OMB shall submit recommendations to Congress on actions to improve the agency's performance, including reauthorization proposals, statutory changes, and planned executive actions.

The director of OMB must coordinate with agencies to improve the performance of the federal government and to establish priority goals, and every two years, or as otherwise determined by the director of OMB, the head of each agency shall identify a set of priority goals.

C. Regulatory Flexibility Act

The Regulatory Flexibility Act of 1980, 5 U.S.C. §§ 601–612, requires agencies to consider the special needs and concerns of small entities in the regulatory process. Small entities include small businesses as defined in the Small Business Act, 15 U.S.C. §§ 631, et seq.; not-for-profit organizations that are not dominant in their field; and governmental jurisdictions with a population of less than 50,000.

1. *Unified Agenda*

In October and April of each year, each agency must publish a "regulatory flexibility agenda" in the *Federal Register* that identifies and describes all rules under consideration that are likely to have a significant economic impact on a substantial number of small entities. The agenda must be submitted to the chief counsel for advocacy of the Small Business Administration (SBA) for comment.

2. *Regulatory Flexibility Analysis*

When proposing a regulation subject to notice-and-comment requirements, whether under the APA or any other law, an agency must make available for public comment an initial regulatory flexibility analysis (IRFA), unless the agency head certifies that the proposed rule will not have a significant economic impact on a substantial number of small entities. Courts have interpreted the significant economic impact as being limited to the direct cost effects of having to comply with a regulation and not including the indirect economic effects on small entities that may result from a regulation. The IRFA must be submitted to the chief counsel for advocacy of the SBA, and either a copy of the IRFA or a summary must be published in the *Federal Register*. An IRFA must contain a description of the reasons why the agency is considering the rule, a statement of the objectives of and legal basis for the rule, a description of and (where feasible) an estimate of the number of smal entities to which the rule will apply, a description of any reporting or record-keeping requirements contained in the rule, an identification of other federal rules that may duplicate or overlap with the rule, and a description of significant alternatives to the rule that would accomplish the stated objectives while minimizing economic effects on small entities. The Consumer Financial Protection Bureau must also include a discussion of those alternatives, a description of any increase in the cost of credit for small entities resulting from the proposed rule, a description of alternatives to the proposed rule that accomplish the stated objections of applicable statutes and minimize any increase in the cost of credit for small entities, and advice for small entities regarding impacts of the proposed rule on the cost of credit.

In the case of rules issued by the Environmental Protection Agency, the Consumer Financial Protection Bureau, or the Occupational Safety and Health Administration, the agency must, prior to publication of the IRFA, notify the chief counsel for advocacy of the potential impacts of the proposed rule on small entities, so that he may identify representatives of the likely affected small entities for their advice and recommendations about the potential impacts. Unless this requirement is waived by the chief counsel for advocacy, these agencies must then convene a review panel consisting of employees from the agency, OIRA, and the chief counsel's office to review the proposed regulation, any other material developed in connection with the proposed rule, and the comments of the small-entity representatives. Within sixty days, the review panel must publicly report on the comments and its findings on the issues discussed in the IRFA. Other agencies *may* in their discretion also utilize this procedure if they wish.

Unless the agency head certifies that the final rule will not have a significant economic impact on a substantial number of small entities, it must be published with a final regulatory flexibility analysis (FRFA). The FRFA must contain a statement of the need for and objectives of the rule; a statement of and response to significant issues raised by the comments received (including in particular those of the chief counsel for advocacy of the SBA); a description of the small entities to which the rule will apply and an estimate of their number; a description of any reporting or record-keeping requirements; a description of the steps the agency has taken to minimize the economic impact on small entities, including a statement of the reasons for adopting the alternative selected and for not adopting other alternatives, and, in the case of the Consumer Financial Protection Bureau, a description of steps the agency has taken to minimize any additional cost of credit for small entities. If a rule is a response to an emergency, the head of an agency may delay the completion of the FRFA until not later than 180 days after the publication of the final rule. If the FRFA is not published within 180 days, the rule automatically lapses and has no effect.

Neither the chief counsel nor a Regulatory Review Panel has authority to veto or reject an agency proposal or regulatory flexibility analysis. The chief counsel is required to report annually to the president and to relevant congressional committees on agency compliance with the act and is authorized to appear as amicus curiae in any action seeking judicial review of a rule.

3. *Periodic Review of Rules*

The Regulatory Flexibility Act also requires agencies to engage in a ten-year review cycle of their regulations that have a significant economic effect on a substantial number of small entities. Each year agencies are to publish in the *Federal Register* the list of such rules that are to be reviewed in the following twelve months.

4. *Judicial Review*

A small entity adversely affected or aggrieved by final agency action may obtain judicial review under the APA of an agency's compliance with the requirements applicable to FRFAs, the validity of any certification that a rule will not have a significant economic effect on a substantial number of small entities, and an agency's compliance with the requirement for periodic review of its rules. The act establishes a maximum statute of limitations for such actions at one year from the date of the final agency action. The act allows a court, in addition to or in lieu of its other remedial powers under the APA, to defer the enforcement of a rule against small entities.

D. Attorney General Supervision of Litigation

By statute, the Department of Justice authorizes and handles most litigation involving agencies, including both enforcement actions that an agency wishes to bring and challenges to agency action under the APA. Even where an agency does have independent litigating authority, the attorney general and the solicitor general, with rare exceptions, have the exclusive authority to pursue and conduct litigation in the Supreme Court on behalf of the agency. By controlling the agency's litigation, the Department of Justice is able to affect the manner in which agencies perform their statutory duties.

TABLE OF CASES

INDEX

D

E

H

I

J

K

L

M

N

O

P

Q

R

S

T

U

V

W